W9-AFS-299

The Wire, Deadwood, Homicide, and NYPD Blue

The Wire, Deadwood, Homicide, and NYPD Blue

Violence is Power

Jason P. Vest

 PRAEGER

AN IMPRINT OF ABC-CLIO, LLC
Santa Barbara, California • Denver, Colorado • Oxford, England

Copyright 2011 by Jason P. Vest

All rights reserved. No part of this publication may be reproduced, stored in a retrieval system, or transmitted, in any form or by any means, electronic, mechanical, photocopying, recording, or otherwise, except for the inclusion of brief quotations in a review, without prior permission in writing from the publisher.

Library of Congress Cataloging-in-Publication Data

Vest, Jason P., 1972–
  The wire, Deadwood, Homicide, and NYPD blue : violence is power / Jason P. Vest.
    p. cm.
  Includes bibliographical references and index.
  ISBN 978-0-313-37819-5 (alk. paper) — ISBN 978-0-313-37820-1 (ebook)
  1. Violence on television—United States. 2. Detective and mystery television programs—United States. 3. Television broadcasting—Social aspects—United States. 4. Milch, David, 1945– —Criticism and interpretation. 5. Simon, David, 1960– —Criticism and interpretation. I. Title.
  PN1992.8.V55V47 2010
  791.45'6552—dc22   2010031835

ISBN: 978-0-313-37819-5
EISBN: 978-0-313-37820-1

15 14 13 12 11   1 2 3 4 5

This book is also available on the World Wide Web as an eBook.
Visit www.abc-clio.com for details.

Praeger
An Imprint of ABC-CLIO, LLC

ABC-CLIO, LLC
130 Cremona Drive, P.O. Box 1911
Santa Barbara, California 93116-1911

This book is printed on acid-free paper ∞

Manufactured in the United States of America

For my best friend, Patricia Thomas,
For a marvelous writer, David Mills (1961–2010),
and
For my father, Merlin Vest (1933–1981)

Contents

Acknowledgments

This book exists due to the enthusiasm and insight of my editor, Daniel Harmon. His expertise and friendship have been invaluable.

This study quotes significant sources about David Milch's and David Simon's television work. All excerpts from *The Corner: A Year in the Life of an Inner-City Neighborhood* by David Simon and Edward Burns—copyright 1997 by David Simon and Edward Burns—are used with permission of Broadway Books, a division of Random House, Inc. All excerpts from David Simon's *Homicide: A Year on the Killing Streets*—copyright 1991 by David Simon—are reprinted with permission of Houghton Mifflin Harcourt Publishing Company (all rights reserved).

Special thanks go to the University of Guam's College of Liberal Arts and Social Sciences (CLASS), which awarded a grant that allowed me to purchase research materials crucial to this book's success. CLASS's Academic Affairs Committee, Dean Mary Spencer, Dean James Sellmann, and Acting Associate Dean Troy McVey have supported this project since its inception. Dean McVey's tireless efforts to secure all grant materials are greatly appreciated.

Kimberly Miller's copyediting expertise improved every page of this book. I commend her attention to detail, language, and syntax. The team at Apex CoVantage kept this book's publication on schedule, for which I am grateful.

My colleagues, as always, have provided encouragement and advice during this book's composition. Dr. Christopher Schreiner and Dr. Andrea Sant Hartig of the University of Guam's Division of English and Applied Linguistics have been especially helpful during a busy academic year.

My family and friends have provided peerless encouragement, humor, and inspiration.

Thank you all.

Usage Norms

This book analyzes six significant American television series or miniseries: *Hill Street Blues, NYPD Blue, Homicide: Life on the Street, The Corner, Deadwood,* and *The Wire.* It follows a standard designation system to note an individual episode's place within its parent program's overall chronology. The first appearance of all episode titles includes a parenthetical notation such as (1.1) or (2.4) that documents the season and installment number. "Hill Street Station" (1.1), therefore, indicates that it is the first episode of *Hill Street Blues*'s first season. "Bop Gun" (2.4) indicates that it is the fourth episode of *Homicide: Life on the Street*'s second season.

These citations follow the episode order established by each program's official DVD releases, which reproduce either the series's original broadcast order or the episodes' original production order. *Homicide: Life on the Street*'s DVD sets, however, follow the preferred viewing order of executive producers Barry Levinson and Tom Fontana, so all parenthetical citations for *Homicide* reflect Levinson and Fontana's preferences rather than the program's broadcast or production order.

Introduction: Prime-Time Realism: David Milch, David Simon, and Television Drama

Todd Gitlin, in the first line of the introduction to the 2000 edition of his book *Inside Prime Time*, claims, "At century's turn, writing about television tends to betray one of two tendencies: the sentimental and the breathless."[1] Gitlin disdains rhapsodic scholarly and popular commentaries that present television either "as an artifact of antiquity, quaint as childhood itself, redolent with the bygone virtues of a sappy but innocent old world" or "as the mother of still greater, faster-moving, more plenteous and convenient media forms"[2] because television, in Gitlin's estimation, does not value innovation, depth, or complexity as much as formula, shallowness, and simplicity. Gitlin's book remains a significant exposé about how American network television works: how its executives decide which programs to develop, fund, and air; how its broadcast-standards departments enforce officially sanctioned codes of morality, ethics, and values; and how its producers, writers, and other creative personnel generate the comedies and dramas that fill network television's evening schedules.

Gitlin offers withering criticisms of (and ceaseless skepticism about) American television programming in his meticulously researched book, declaring that "in analysis, as in technology, there is no way around television, there are only ways through it."[3] This statement usefully summarizes *Inside Prime Time*'s complex attitude toward its subject. Gitlin synthesizes fascination, despair, hope, and weariness to produce the jaded cynicism of a man who, having seen it all before, cannot deny television's cultural impact. Television, in Gitlin's telling, produces so much easy, pat, and silly "mind candy"[4] (for indifferent viewers who desire nothing more than escapism, entertainment, and distraction) that higher aspirations toward the complicated intellectual, emotional, social, and political nuances of art do not apply to this medium, which is more concerned with crass commercialism than careful explorations of the human condition.

Inside Prime Time, originally published in 1983, makes no mention of David Milch or David Simon, the subjects of this study, because neither man had begun writing television dramas when Gitlin prepared his book's first edition. By the time Gitlin composed his introduction to *Inside Prime Time's* 2000 edition, however, Milch—an executive producer of NBC's groundbreaking police drama *Hill Street Blues* (1981–1987) and cocreator of ABC's redoubtable cop show *NYPD Blue* (1993–2005)—had been writing and producing television dramas for 17 years, while David Simon—author of the nonfiction books *Homicide: A Year on the Killing Streets* (1991) and *The Corner: A Year in the Life of an Inner-City Neighborhood* (1997)—had written for *NYPD Blue* and had worked as a writer-producer for *Homicide: Life on the Street* (1993–1999), NBC's critically acclaimed adaptation of his first book. Simon, in addition, was preparing *The Corner,* HBO's six-hour miniseries adaptation of his second book, for broadcast during April and May 2000. Although *Inside Prime Time's* final chapter is a long, detailed, and remarkable analysis of *Hill Street Blues,* Gitlin never mentions Milch, who began writing for this series during its third season (1982–1983) and who authored the Emmy Award–winning teleplay for *Hill Street's* third-season premiere, "Trial by Fury."

Gitlin's suspicious approach to prime-time television has a long history, encompassing not only Federal Communications Commission (FCC) Chairman Newton N. Minow's famous 1961 proclamation—frequently taken out of context—that television is a "vast wasteland"[5] but also the objections of parents, politicians, clergy members, children's-rights advocates, and social critics who argue that television poses intellectual, emotional, and physical dangers to its audience members. These complaints have become so pervasive that, as the 21st century's second decade dawns, this study need not rehearse them in detail. Television, according to its harshest critics, promotes sexual indecency, moral depravity, ethical bankruptcy, mindless violence, political apathy, intellectual laziness, lowbrow entertainment, and physical obesity. The medium has been blamed for exacerbating (when not causing) American social ills since the first network broadcasts of the 1940s, while the artistic reputation of its programming is so low that television writers, actors, producers, and executives emerge from this bruising discourse as cultural pornographers interested in little more than quick cash, soft-core titillation, and venal cupidity.

Minow's comment has become shorthand for the fashionable contempt that even people who watch many hours of television routinely express about the medium's power, influence, and popularity. Minow spends comparatively little time highlighting the wasteland theme in his address, titled "Television and the Public Interest" (originally delivered as a speech to the National Association of Broadcasters on May 9, 1961, shortly after Minow's confirmation as President John F. Kennedy's first FCC chairman), going so far as to praise the integrity of programs such as *The Twilight Zone* (1959–1964) and *CBS Reports* (1959–1971). Minow's concerns about television's rampant commercialism, reputation for formulaic programming, obsession with ratings, and lowest-common-denominator approach, however, have influenced so many later commentators (including Gitlin) that his analysis seems unassailable to casual observers, media watchdogs, and uncritical scholars.

Gitlin's and Minow's skepticism about television has an even earlier, rarely mentioned antecedent: Theodor W. Adorno and Max Horkheimer's influential 1944 essay "The Culture Industry: Enlightenment as Mass Deception," first published in their book *Dialectic of Enlightenment* (*Dialektik der Aufklärung*). This bracing indictment of mass media—including radio, cinema, and magazines—argues that popular culture resembles a factory minting homogenized products whose wide distribution and easy familiarity manipulate large consumer audiences into unwitting passivity, lethargy, and disinterest. Adorno and Horkheimer coin the term *culture industry* to reflect their belief that mass media are such important, profitable, and pernicious facets of corporate capitalism that they erase distinctions between high and low culture to become opiates for the masses. Adorno and Horkheimer claim that culture-industry texts force their own pace, ideology, and formula on audience members, who have no time to think about any single work's larger themes or influences, thereby diminishing the artistic experience that the text purports to offer. Adorno and Horkheimer, in one unforgiving passage, identify movies as the greatest perpetrator of mass media's cultural crimes:

> Real life is becoming indistinguishable from the movies. The sound film, far surpassing the theater of illusion, leaves no room for imagination or reflection on the part of the audience, who is

unable to respond within the structure of the film, yet deviate [*sic*] from its precise detail without losing the thread of the story; hence the film forces its victims to equate it directly with reality. The stunting of the mass-media consumer's powers of imagination and spontaneity does not have to be traced back to any psychological mechanisms; he must ascribe the loss of those attributes to the objective nature of the products themselves, especially the most characteristic of them, the sound film. They are so designed that quickness, powers of observation, and experience are undeniably needed to apprehend them at all; yet sustained thought is out of the question if the spectator is not to miss the rush of facts. Even though the effort required for his response is semi-automatic, no scope is left for the imagination.[6]

Adorno and Horkheimer, by claiming that cinema creates perfect narrative illusions that viewers mistake for reality, charge the culture industry with impeding imagination, reflection, critical thought, and complex reasoning. Spontaneity recedes while more facile qualities (quick apprehension, rapid observation) replace stately reflection to weaken the viewer's mind. Cinema enforces a relentless tempo that deprives its audience of opportunities to pause, to consider, and to revisit a film's fictional events. Keeping pace with a movie's plot restrains the spectator's capacity to appreciate multiple details, reducing each audience member to a seemingly tardy child always in danger of falling behind the film's basic story.

Even more remarkable is how this passage predicts significant objections to network television's unending flow of images, sounds, and stories, particularly its ability to submerge its audience into vivid fictional worlds that obscure the viewer's life. Adorno and Horkheimer object not only to mass media's seductive capacities but also to the escapist tendencies inherent in its texts. On-screen entertainment strips its audience of activity and agency, offering rapid-fire images that prevent the viewer from contemplating their visual, narrative, and symbolic richness. Substituting the term *television* for *sound film* in the preceding passage ("The Culture Industry" mentions television, a recently developed mass medium in 1944, only twice) underscores how Adorno and Horkheimer's analysis of cinema has influenced, shaped, and dominated the misgivings about network television's aesthetic, political, and moral deficiencies that Gitlin's *Inside Prime Time,* Jerry Mander's *Four Arguments for the Elimination of Television,* and countless other books chronicle.

Arguments against television so commonly reflect Adorno and Horkheimer's analysis that their contours are familiar to anyone who has watched the medium for even a short time. Responding to the charges advanced by these frequently polemical texts would require more space than any single book contains, although keeping their doubts in mind is crucial for any serious work of television scholarship, especially a study that considers the television writing of David Milch and David Simon to be an artistically valuable contribution to American culture. Milch's and Simon's television dramas provocatively address the social, political, and economic inequalities that typify late 20th- and early 21st-century American life by examining the nation's political, racial, sexual, and class anxieties with the sociological precision of great literature. Both men, in short, are cultural critics of the first order.

These claims, unbelievable as they may seem to Adorno, Horkheimer, and Gitlin, locate this study within three related academic fields—cultural studies, media studies, and television studies—that consider television drama to be a legitimate object of scholarly research. Television studies has become an enormous (and evergrowing) field that, at its best, critically investigates television's possibilities, pleasures, and perils (and, at its worst, naively celebrates television's democratization of popular art as a force that improves its viewers' lives by offering cutting-edge drama, comedy, news, sports, music, and knowledge). The present study need not repeat, reinforce, or revise the learned analyses that the best scholarly examinations of television provide. John Fiske's *Television Culture;* Amanda D. Lotz's *The Television Will Be Revolutionized;* Janet McCabe and Kim Akass's *Quality TV: Contemporary American Television and Beyond;* Jason Mittell's *Genre and Television: From Cop Shows to Cartoons in American Culture;* Lynn Spiegel and Jan Olsson's *Television after TV: Essays on a Medium in Transition;* Leah R. Vande Berg, Lawrence A. Wenner, and Bruce E. Gronbeck's *Critical Approaches to Television;* and Raymond Williams's *Television: Technology and Cultural Form* are only seven of the best books that explore television's aesthetic, commercial, historical, and theoretical parameters, while monographs devoted to one or more specific television programs (including the present study) proliferate by the month. Academic journals, articles, reviews, and commentaries about television appear so frequently that even media scholars cannot keep pace with them. The authority and authenticity that cultural studies, media studies, and television studies enjoy in the 21st-century American academy, along with each field's many professional publications, permit the interested reader to research how television may, can, and should be taken seriously, even if much television programming cannot. This study does not theorize television's scholarly legitimacy, artistic possibilities, or commercial aspects but instead explores how David Milch and David Simon create small-screen dramas whose social realism challenges the bourgeois assumptions, bigotries, and mores that Adorno, Horkheimer, and Gitlin (among others) believe television imposes on its audience.

This project, therefore, attempts to avoid the breathless sentimentality that *Inside Prime Time* decries even while arguing that Milch and Simon are significant American writers. The newfound respect that television drama has received since *Hill Street Blues*'s 1981 premiere makes this argument easier, but not simple, despite the increasing esteem given to prime-time drama by popular-press authors and critics. Vincent Canby, indeed, coins the term *megamovie* to describe television series that achieve levels of character intimacy, narrative complexity, thematic depth, and social relevance rarely found in narrative cinema. Canby's 1999 essay "From the Humble Mini-Series Comes the Magnificent Megamovie" praises David Chase's *The Sopranos* (1999–2007) as a mesmerizing, provocative, and masterful example of televisual storytelling that has "a lot to do with the temper of American life, especially with the hypocrisies that go unrecognized."[7] Programs like *The Sopranos*, "packed with characters and events of Dickensian dimension and color, their time and place observed with satiric exactitude" and possessed of "the kind of cohesive dramatic arc that defines a work as complete unto itself,"[8] surpass their cinematic counterparts in realistic effect. Canby identifies two fundamental elements that affect a megamovie's aesthetic accomplishment: observational precision and social realism. *The Sopranos* is good not simply because it offers a fresh approach to the Mafia-kingpin story but because it "possesses a tragic conscience" that helps the program's first season become "a stunning original about a most particular slice of American life, a panoramic picture that is, by turns, wise, brutal, funny and hair-raising, and of significance to the society just beyond its immediate view."[9] Chase's series, for Canby, fulfills the potential "touted by friends who like to stir things up when they call such television dramas 'the literature of our time.'"[10] Canby's invocations of tragedy, panorama, social significance, and Charles Dickens raise television drama of *The Sopranos*'s quality to the level of literary art. His essay is not naively breathless but instead capably illustrates how accomplished good television can be.

Charles McGrath preceded Canby's optimistic appraisal of television drama by four years when, in his essay "The Triumph of the Prime-Time Novel," he claims that "TV is actually enjoying a sort of golden age—it has become a medium you can consistently rely on not just for distraction but for enlightenment."[11] McGrath argues that the prime-time dramatic series *Chicago Hope* (1994–2000), *ER* (1994–2009), *Homicide: Life on the Street* (1993–1999), *Law & Order* (1990–2010), *NYPD Blue* (1993–2005), and *Picket Fences* (1992–1996) are notable examples of "one of the few remaining art forms to continue the tradition of classic American realism, the realism of Dreiser and Hopper: the painstaking, almost literal examination of middle- and working-class lives in the conviction that truth resides less in ideas than in details closely observed. More than many novels, TV tells us how we live today."[12] These words, written by the then-editor of the *New York Times Book Review*, are heresy to people invested in Adorno and Horkheimer's culture-industry perspective that mass media, by broadcasting standardized programming that both promotes and obscures the inequities of industrial capitalism, have little (if any) artistic potential. McGrath announces significant themes (repeated in Canby's article) to assert that America's best prime-time drama does not merely aspire to realistic appearances but extends the literary tradition of American social realism. McGrath, by identifying television drama as a legitimate literary form, reverses the culture-industry argument to declare American prime-time drama relevant, serious, and valuable art.

The path from Adorno and Horkheimer's scornful stance to McGrath's and Canby's respectful positions involves so many writers, commentators, editorialists, pundits, and scholars that these endless analyses of television threaten to overwhelm even the medium's most vigorous defenders. This study does not tackle all of television (no book could), does not claim that all television is remarkable, and does not deny television's place as a prominent American art form but rather seeks to understand how David Milch's and David Simon's most significant television ventures—*Hill Street Blues, NYPD Blue, Homicide: Life on the Street, The Corner, Deadwood* (2004–2006), and *The Wire* (2002–2008)—achieve laudable narrative, visual, thematic, and political sophistication.

One curious aspect of television scholarship is that academic and popular-press writers habitually compare television to other media forms—most commonly cinema, stage drama, and the novel—to describe television's effects. One explanation for this impulse is that such judgments are natural because these earlier art forms inspired television's narrative and visual development, yet the act of routinely comparing television to its antecedents implies that television, rather than standing as an independent, sufficient, and autonomous medium, relies on other forms of expression to justify its aesthetic existence. Television, it seems, cannot be good on its own but must associate itself with more canonical art, particularly literature, to become truly refined. This elitist hierarchy, no matter how theoretically suspect, influences the present study because Milch and Simon both repeat its broadest principles when discussing their television writing, especially the two programs that this study argues are masterpieces: *Deadwood* and *The Wire*. Milch, in his 2006 book *Deadwood: Stories of the Black Hills,* writes that *Deadwood*'s large cast of characters does not intimidate him because "the serial form of the nineteenth-century novel is close to what I'm doing. The writers who are alive to me, whom I consider my contemporaries, are writers who lived in another time—Dickens and Tolstoy and Dostoevsky and Twain."[13] Simon, in his introduction to Rafael Alvarez's 2004 book *"The Wire": Truth Be Told,* refers to *The Wire* as a "visual novel" while criticizing network television cop shows for failing to capture the realities of American police work.[14] Milch (who taught literature at Yale University before moving to Hollywood) and Simon (who hired novelists Dennis Lehane, George P. Pelecanos, and Richard Price to write scripts for *The Wire*) elide each series's televisual precursors by connecting *Deadwood* and *The Wire* with more respectable literary forerunners. Milch and Simon, by hesitating to confess *Deadwood*'s and *The Wire*'s debts to the television Western and the cop show, also betray discomfort with the medium's inartistic reputation. Both men, for complicated reasons of their own, contrast their television work with previous televisual texts to adopt Adorno and Horkheimer's skepticism about the medium's aesthetic sophistication.

Milch and Simon, therefore, aim to create more lasting, meaningful, and literary television than the mind candy criticized by Gitlin. Neither man intended to become a television writer, which helps explain why Milch and Simon take singular approaches to small-screen drama. Milch was born on March 23, 1945, in Buffalo, New York, to Elmer and Molly Milch. Molly for a time headed the Buffalo Board of Education, while Elmer worked as a gastrointestinal surgeon. Elmer, who became the principal influence in Milch's life, was, according to Mark Singer's long *New Yorker* profile, titled "The Misfit," "multiply addicted—to alcohol, horses, and painkillers (a consequence of a near-fatal car accident two years before David was born)."[15] Milch connects his father's addictions to his (Milch's) own problems with heroin, alcohol, and gambling in *True Blue*, the 1995 book that recounts *NYPD Blue*'s development and first three seasons. Milch writes that Elmer's accident came during the man's World War II military service, when a transport truck collided with Elmer's jeep. "He was crushed from the midsection down," Milch says, recognizing in one of *True Blue*'s key passages that Elmer compensated for his pain by resorting to drugs.[16] After more than 10 years of heroin addiction, Milch checked himself into a rehabilitation unit where the facility psychiatrist said that Milch could not kick his heroin habit until he undertook an emotional recovery. "Later, after we'd talked a little while," Milch writes, "I found myself crying, saying I was afraid if I got involved with this I was going to lose my love for my father."[17]

These anecdotes, along with Milch's confessions that several uncles were involved in Buffalo's rackets, help explain his intense intelligence, his difficult early life, and his fondness for crime stories that create difficult, moody, and mercurial protagonists. Milch, an avid student, enrolled in Yale University, where he became a devoted follower of Robert Penn Warren, the literary scholar, novelist, and poet most famous for writing *All the King's Men*. Milch excelled at Yale despite his personal life's complications, which Singer describes in detail:

> A superior student—he graduated summa cum laude and won the prize given for the highest achievement in English—he was an unlikely member of the jock fraternity (Delta Kappa Epsilon; George W. Bush, president), which provided a venue for his main extracurricular activity: drinking. Jeffrey Lewis, a novelist, screenwriter, and television writer who worked with Milch for five years on *Hill Street Blues*, and who was his Yale roommate for three years, told me that one of the first things he understood about him was that he harbored "complicated and huge feelings about his father."[18]

Milch so desired to become a successful novelist that he once brought a finished chapter of a work in progress, the "narrative of four days in the life of a family in Buffalo whose teenage son has died in a car accident," to Penn Warren's home during the man's evening dinner and "asked him to read it on the spot."[19] Penn Warren not only obliged, praising the chapter's themes and dialogue, but also eventually arranged a teaching fellowship at the University of Iowa's prestigious Writers' Workshop. Milch's reputation for brilliance and arrogance took hold at Iowa, alienating fellow writers Richard Yates and Kurt Vonnegut but establishing Milch as an important new voice in American literature. Milch returned to Yale to teach fiction and poetry seminars while helping literary scholars Penn Warren, R.W.B. Lewis, and Cleanth Brooks compile their two-volume 1973 textbook anthology *American Literature: The Makers and the Making.* Milch, in addition, so capably assisted Lewis with *The Jameses,* Lewis's classic family history of William, Henry, and Alice James, that that book's acknowledgments page expresses "a very large and special debt of gratitude" to Milch, who worked in Yale's Calhoun College, "where Lewis was the master."[20]

In 1982, Milch married Rita Stern, "a documentary filmmaker and painter who had been an undergraduate while he was teaching,"[21] then accepted Jeffrey Lewis's invitation to join the writing staff of *Hill Street Blues,* the television series profiled by this study's first chapter. Milch moved to Hollywood, where his addictions continued, but his professional relationship with Steven Bochco, *Hill Street*'s cocreator and an influential producer of American prime-time drama, strengthened. Milch's first-ever teleplay, "Trial by Fury," not only opened *Hill Street*'s third season but also won him the Emmy Award, the Writers Guild of America Award, and the Humanitas Prize for television writing. Milch cocreated *NYPD Blue,* the television series profiled by this study's second chapter, in 1991, working closely with Bochco until departing this program, at the conclusion of its seventh season, in 2000. Milch also consulted on *Murder One,* the innovative legal serial that Bochco created with Charles H. Eglee and Channing Gibson in 1995. During this period, he continued abusing various drugs (particularly Vicodin and alcohol), entered rehab to end these addictions (he told Singer that he began getting clean on January 1, 1999, and "has stayed clean since"[22]), and survived a serious heart condition that impressed on him the need to embrace healthier living.

Milch's other television work includes cocreating and producing three short-lived series: *Beverly Hills Buntz* (1987–1988), a misbegotten *Hill Street* spinoff featuring Dennis Franz's gruff detective Norman Buntz working as a private investigator in Beverly Hills, California; *Capital News* (1990), a program about Washington, D.C., newspaper reporters that starred Lloyd Bridges; and *Brooklyn South* (1997–1998), a series about the lives of New York City's uniformed police officers that cast *Hill Street* actor James B. Sikking in a prominent role. Milch proposed a Western series to NBC in 2001; the network declined when Milch refused to make a pilot film without a 13-episode commitment,[23] leading Milch to pitch a drama series about beat cops in ancient Rome to HBO. When HBO executives Chris Albrecht and Carolyn Strauss told Milch that the network was already developing a similar series, simply titled *Rome* (2005–2007), Milch began two years of research into "the history of the West in general and Deadwood [the notorious Black Hills mining camp] specifically, gold mining, Indian wars, whorehouse and casino protocols, public-health records, politics in the Black Hills, criminality and extralegal justice, the Gilded Age, the bank panic of 1873, and biographies of historical figures"[24] to prepare the pilot script of *Deadwood,* the series profiled by this study's fifth chapter. HBO's suggestion that Milch locate the themes he wanted to examine in the Roman series elsewhere proved fruitful, for *Deadwood,* Milch's most compelling contribution to American popular art, embraces social realism more comprehensively than *Hill Street Blues* or *NYPD Blue.*

David Simon followed a different route to writing and producing television than Milch, but, like Milch, Simon's unusual background equipped him to create innovative small-screen drama. Simon was born in 1960 in Silver Spring, Maryland, to Bernard and Dorothy Simon. Bernard, according to Margaret Talbot's long *New Yorker* profile "Stealing Life," "was the public-relations director and the chief speechwriter for B'nai B'rith, and … Dorothy … was a homemaker who went back to college in her fifties and became a counsellor for runaway teens in McLean, Virginia."[25] Simon attended the University of Maryland (at the same time as his mother), writing and editing the college's newspaper, the *Diamondback;* there, he met David Mills, the future *Washington Post* reporter who collaborated with Simon on their first television script, "Bop Gun" for *Homicide;* on all six episodes of HBO's *The Corner;* and on two episodes of Simon and Eric Overmyer's HBO series *Treme.* Simon's profound belief in journalism, stoked by nightly dinner conversations about politics and by Bob Woodward's and Carl Bernstein's *Washington Post* articles about Watergate, fed his dreams of becoming a reporter. "I thought journalism was, 'You write, you expose, you change the terrain,'" Simon told *Seattle Times* writer Cynthia Rose in a 1999 profile, an attitude that went with him when, in his senior year of college, Simon became the *Baltimore Sun*'s College Park stringer.[26] "He wrote so many stories that a shop steward complained he was violating the union contract," Talbot reveals in "Stealing Life."[27]

The *Sun* hired Simon as a full-time reporter when he graduated from the University of Maryland, assigning him to the crime (or police) beat in 1984. Simon, according to Rebecca Corbett, his *Sun* editor, began to see "the cop beat as a whole window onto the sociology of the city, a way of examining the failings of the government, a way to think about policy, especially drug policy, and a way of telling stories."[28] This recollection precisely describes Simon's television writing in *Homicide* (the program profiled by this study's third chapter), *The Corner* (the program profiled by this study's fourth chapter), and, especially, *The Wire* (the program profiled by this study's sixth chapter). His interest in the interlocking features of urban life led Simon, in 1988, to secure permission from Baltimore Police Department commissioner Edward J. Tilghman to shadow the Homicide Unit detective squad commanded by Lieutenant Gary D'Addario for an entire year (while on leave from the *Sun*).

This sojourn provided the material for Simon's 1991 book-length exposé *Homicide: A Year on the Killing Streets*, which required three years of work to complete. Film director Barry Levinson optioned the book in 1991 as the source for Levinson's first television series, hiring Tom Fontana, the longtime writer-producer of *St. Elsewhere* (1982–1988), to supervise the writing staff of *Homicide: Life on the Street*, which premiered on NBC on January 31, 1993, after Super Bowl XXVII. Simon, according to his own account, refused producer Gail Mutrux's offer to write *Homicide*'s pilot episode because, while he was happy to receive money from Levinson's option and was hoping that the television program would increase his book's sales, he did not trust himself to write a decent teleplay: "Like an idiot, I said, 'You know, no, get somebody who knows what they're doing because I'll mess it up and there'll be no TV show.'"[29] Fontana, however, invited Simon to contribute to *Homicide*, leading Simon to write "Bop Gun" with Mills. Their script won the 1995 Writers Guild of America Award for Episodic Drama, an achievement that Simon, as a first-time television writer, shares with Milch.

Simon continued working at the *Sun* until 1993, when he took another year-long leave of absence to immerse himself in Baltimore's Franklin Square neighborhood (and its drug corners) to research his second book, *The Corner: A Year in the Life of an Inner-City Neighborhood*. He observed this area's goings-on with Edward Burns, a former

Baltimore Police Department detective whom Simon had interviewed while covering the *Sun*'s police beat and who would become Simon's principal collaborator on *The Wire* (Burns's detective career inspired many of *The Wire*'s cases and incidents). Returning to the *Sun* once again, Simon was dismayed that the paper's corporate owner, the Times Mirror Company, had begun offering buyouts to the *Sun*'s newsroom employees in an effort to cut costs. Simon bitterly accepted the *Sun*'s second buyout in 1995, at which time, after Simon declined an offer to join *NYPD Blue*'s writing staff,[30] Fontana hired him as a full-time *Homicide* writer. Simon's departure from the *Sun* remains controversial because he has criticized John Carroll and William Marimow—the *Philadelphia Inquirer* veterans hired by the Times Mirror Company as (respectively) the *Sun*'s editor and managing editor to run the paper while downsizing its newsroom staff—ever since (going so far as to fictionalize both men as the *Sun*'s executive editor James C. Whiting III, played by Sam Freed, and managing editor Thomas Klebanow, played by David Costabile, in *The Wire*'s fifth season). *A Year in the Life of an Inner-City Neighborhood*, coauthored with Burns, was published in 1997, the same year that Simon became a full producer on *Homicide*, first receiving on-screen credit for this role in "Blood Ties (Part 1)," the program's sixth-season premiere.

Simon stayed with *Homicide* until it concluded in 1999, learning about all aspects of writing and producing television from Fontana and Levinson. This work was so illuminating that Simon, in his introduction to Alvarez's book *Truth Be Told*, writes that "as a day job, it was a great one. And I found that the artifice of film and the camaraderie of set were enough to offset my exile from the *Sun*'s city desk, where I had long imagined myself growing old and surly, bumming cigarettes from younger reporters in exchange for back-in-the-day stories about what it was like to work with [H. L.] Mencken and [William] Manchester."[31] Fontana arranged a meeting between Simon and HBO executive Anne Thomopoulos so that Simon could pitch *The Corner* as a cable miniseries.[32] Writing and producing this six-hour adaptation of his second book consumed most of Simon's time until it premiered on April 16, 2000. *The Corner* won the 2000 Emmy Awards for Outstanding Miniseries and Outstanding Writing for a Miniseries or Movie, as well as the 2000 George Foster Peabody Award for a television miniseries. Simon, who had continued working as a freelance journalist and writer since leaving the *Sun*, then spent more than one year convincing HBO to film *The Wire*'s first season, writing the program's bible and first three episodes to demonstrate its narrative scope to Chris Albrecht and Carolyn Strauss, who were skeptical about HBO producing a police drama focused on protracted wiretap and surveillance investigations. Simon, however, eventually persuaded Albrecht and Strauss that *The Wire* would be an innovative, never-before-seen approach to the cop show, allowing the pilot episode, "The Target," to premiere on June 2, 2002. *The Wire,* this study argues, remains Simon's most lasting contribution to television drama, becoming, over its five seasons, one of the finest examples of American popular art ever created.

Milch and Simon, therefore, are figures worthy of extended attention and analysis. Their television work portrays America as an imperfect, tense, and fractious society beset by political, economic, and racial anxieties. *Hill Street Blues, NYPD Blue, Homicide: Life on the Street, The Corner, Deadwood,* and *The Wire* resonate so powerfully because, as Vincent Canby and Charles McGrath argue, these programs embrace, encompass, and extend the American literary tradition of social realism. This study will mention social realism so frequently that the term deserves precise definition. *Social realism,* for the purposes of the present argument, refers to the artistic tradition of portraying contemporary society (meaning American society at the time of a television program's production) as faithfully as possible by attending to the multifaceted details of daily life. Social realism concerns itself with all socioeconomic classes, although it strives to depict lower-class, working-class, and middle-class characters as they deal with the complexities, ambivalences, and nuances of quotidian existence. Social-realist texts engage an extended view of their chosen culture—in this case, 19th-, late 20th-, and early 21st-century America—to cut across all social strata in hopes of examining the interlocking economic, political, bureaucratic, religious, racial, gender, sexual, and artistic elements that make American life a sometimes bewildering struggle for its citizens to navigate while surviving their nation's nascent capitalism (in the case of *Deadwood*) or its postindustrial economy (in the cases of *Hill Street Blues, NYPD Blue, Homicide, The Corner,* and *The Wire*). Social realism offers an unglamorous, sober, and somber view of its events, characters, and themes by eschewing abstract symbolism in favor of concrete imagery to present life as less perfect, optimistic, and charitable than other literary modes depict it as.

The most commonly cited tradition of social realism in regards to Milch's and Simon's television work is the Victorian novel, with Charles Dickens the most frequently mentioned literary ancestor of

Milch's and Simon's artistic vision. Milch confesses *Deadwood*'s debt to Dickens in his book *Deadwood: Stories of the Black Hills,* while in a 2009 episode of *Bill Moyers Journal* Simon told Moyers that, while he was working at the *Baltimore Sun,* his editor—presumably Carroll or Marimow, although Simon never gives a name—perverted the word *Dickensian* into a prize-winning strategy by asking Simon to write stories about teenage drug dealers:

> I started to realize "Dickensian" was a shorthand for "I don't really actually care about the underlying economic dynamic that is creating this nightmare. I don't want to examine that. I just want some sweet stories about some kids who are poor and are being hurt. I could win a prize in that. Be Dickensian." And I thought it was sort of an affront to Dickens almost. I mean, if Dickens heard it, I think he would have gotten mad.[33]

Simon's sense that Dickens's fiction explores the urban panorama of Victorian London to diagnose the underlying economic forces that create poverty, corruption, debtor's prisons, and child labor concisely defines Simon's view of how social realism should function. This outlook coheres with novelist, journalist, and critic Tom Wolfe's definition of social realism, offered in Wolfe's controversial 1989 essay "Stalking the Billion-Footed Beast: A Literary Manifesto for the New Social Novel," as "a novel *of the city,* in the sense that Balzac and Zola had written novels *of Paris* and Dickens and Thackeray had written novels *of London,* with the city always in the foreground, exerting its relentless pressure on the souls of its inhabitants."[34] The soul-crushing tendencies of American life and the significance of city living inflect Milch's and Simon's television work (even *Deadwood*), while Wolfe sets social realism in the context of notable British and French novelists, which, when added to Milch's invocation of Russian novelists Leo Tolstoy and Fyodor Dostoyevsky and American novelist Mark Twain, and to Charles McGrath's invocation of American novelist Theodore Dreiser and American painter Edward Hopper, demonstrates just how thematically, culturally, and geographically rich the social-realist tradition is.

Social realism, then, attempts to represent American economics, politics, aesthetics, sex, religion, crime, and commerce as people actually experience them. Fiction, however, liberates the social-realist writer from rigorously reproducing the facts of daily life (as journalism requires) to permit the novelist, short-story writer, and television dramatist to imagine situations and characters that may be realistic but are not real in the sense that they actually exist (even if they spring from real people and events or, in the case of historical fiction such as *Deadwood,* mingle fictional and actual events to create a strong sense of reality). Since no brand of realism is immune from charges of not fully reproducing the world as it truly is, Milch's and Simon's television dramas may create a compelling impression of realism, but their respective programs mingle other literary modes—particularly melodrama—within social-realist narratives. Milch and Simon, indeed, weave domestic, workplace, and political melodrama into their television work in an effort "to uncover some ostensible truth about a social ill and to explain its existence and consequences to the audience," as Amanda Ann Klein argues in "'The Dickensian Aspect': Melodrama, Viewer Engagement, and the Socially Conscious Text," her fine essay about *The Wire.*[35]

This study, therefore, argues that Milch and Simon are important television dramatists because their best work—the six programs profiled in these pages—demonstrates its commitment to social realism even if it cannot be entirely realistic. Both men also locate their television writing within recognizable genres, including the crime drama (*Hill Street Blues, NYPD Blue, Homicide, The Corner, The Wire*) and the Western (*Deadwood*). This study discusses the conventions of genre fiction in relation to specific episodes, events, and characters of the six series it analyzes rather than theorizing the differences among genres. Jason Mittell's excellent *Genre and Television: From Cop Shows to Cartoons in American Culture* so admirably performs the latter task that this study adopts as a defining principle of its argument Mittell's most powerful statement about genre: "The members of any given category do not create, define, or constitute the category itself. Categories link a number of discreet elements together under a label for cultural convenience. While the members constituting a category might all possess some inherent trait binding them into a category…there is nothing intrinsic about the category itself."[36] This proviso particularly applies to Milch's and Simon's crime drama, a generic classification that critical viewers can further divide into the cop show and the drug-corner drama. *Hill Street Blues, NYPD Blue,* and *Homicide* offer different approaches to the cop show, *The Corner* is a superlative example of the drug-corner drama, and *The Wire* blends both types into its detailed urban vista. *Deadwood,* in similar fashion, is an atypical Western television series that owes many narrative debts to the Western films and television programs that preceded it (despite Milch's claims to the contrary). This study proposes that Milch and Simon react against the conventions and perceived constraints of genre fiction to create fascinating hybrid examples of the genres (and subgenres) that their television programs recall.

Milch and Simon, therefore, are mature fiction writers, cultural critics, and social realists who, by making television their medium of choice, force critical viewers to revise traditional suspicions about television's low aesthetic standards even while avoiding the breathless endorsements that Gitlin condemns. This study, by offering sustained analyses of *Hill Street Blues, NYPD Blue, Homicide: Life on the Street, The Corner, Deadwood,* and *The Wire,* hopes to elucidate how Milch and Simon reflect important perspectives about American life, politics, economics, and democracy in their intricate television narratives. These heady themes should not imply that Milch's and Simon's small-screen dramas are pretentious, portentous, or unwatchable. All six programs, indeed, are immensely entertaining even when presenting difficult subject matter for their audiences' consideration. This study, however, challenges the claim advanced by Terry Teachout's "The Myth of 'Classic' TV" and Mark Steyn's "The Maestro of Jiggle TV" that American television drama is too ephemeral to be artistically valuable. Steyn's article, published as an obituary for television producer Aaron Spelling in the *Atlantic Monthly,* begins by recalling Teachout's essay to claim that "before *The Sopranos* there were *Twin Peaks* and *Northern Exposure* and *Hill Street Blues*—and when was the last time you heard anyone say a word about them?"[37] Steyn invokes Teachout's dictum that, since television dramas must be watched serially, viewers can experience these programs as comprehensive aesthetic experiences only during their original broadcast incarnations, meaning that television series, once they end, acquire few new viewers and that no one can see them over a long-enough period to judge whether they will stand the test of time (which, for Teachout, is the primary characteristic of a classic work of art).[38] Steyn rejects "classic" television in favor of Spelling's famously shallow entertainments—the type of vacuous mind candy that Gitlin deplores—because "the 'better' television got at its art, the more transient it became. I doubt *The Sopranos* will be an exception to this rule. Ninety percent of all the people who'll ever be into it are already into it. That's not true of *Lucia di Lammermoor* or 'My Funny Valentine.'"[39]

Steyn's argument, written in the arch tone necessary to memorialize Spelling's diverting-but-awful television programs, cannot be taken seriously because its assertions are so spectacularly wrong. *Hill Street Blues*, for instance, had become an object of extensive scholarly and popular attention by the time that Teachout first published his essay in a 2001 edition of the Sunday *New York Times*, as the numerous academic articles and books analyzing the program's visual, narrative, and stylistic innovations attest. Writers and producers of television crime dramas, to take another example, so frequently cited *Hill Street Blues* as the standard by which they measured their efforts that Steyn and Teachout were simply ignoring the program's pronounced influence. The existence of cable channels that broadcast cancelled television shows (including Nick at Nite and TVLand), the success of DVD box sets that allow viewers to watch cancelled television series whenever they wish, and the development of streaming-video Web sites (such as Hulu.com and ShareTV.org) that permit users to watch episodes of long-finished television programs argue against Teachout's belief about such programs' impermanence (a point Teachout himself admits in the 2007 article "Still Repenting" posted to his blog[40]). Steyn's faith that Gaetano Donizetti's opera *Lucia di Lammermoor* and Richard Rodgers and Lorenz Hart's "My Funny Valentine" will continue to draw avid listeners may be touching, but this prediction is misguided since no precise measurement of either musical piece's popularity is readily available.

Good television, despite Steyn's assertions, is worth discussing around lunch counters, dinner tables, and water coolers. Exceptional television is worth careful attention, analysis, and preservation. This study argues that Milch and Simon have created exceptional television during their authorial careers. The achievements of *Hill Street Blues, NYPD Blue, Homicide: Life on the Street, The Corner, Deadwood,* and *The Wire*—along with their imperfections—make them fascinating, troubling, and compelling examples of American popular art. Milch and Simon prefer to nourish the viewer's mind rather than offering forgettable distractions that disappear as soon as their final images fade to black. The six programs profiled here make claims on their audiences' intellect, emotions, and patience, while counteracting the arguments that Adorno, Horkheimer, and Gitlin make against television's narrative intricacy, richness, and nuance. Milch and Simon consequently emerge as writers, thinkers, and critics who embrace social realism to tell stories that disturb their viewers' sense of America's utopian promise. Understanding Milch's and Simon's success at expanding television drama's scope, skill, and complexity, therefore, becomes the subject and the challenge of this book.

1

Peaks and Valleys: David Milch and *Hill Street Blues*

Hill Street Blues (1981–1987) not only initiated David Milch's television-writing career but also heralded an intriguing, if politically ambiguous, sophistication in American television drama. Milch joined the series, created by Steven Bochco and Michael Kozoll, during its third season (1982–1983) after Jeffrey Lewis (a *Hill Street* staff writer and Milch's Yale University college roommate) convinced Milch to leave his Yale teaching post to pursue more lucrative prospects in Hollywood. This decision proved wise, since Milch received sole on-screen credit for authoring *Hill Street*'s third-season premiere, "Trial by Fury" (3.1). This episode won Milch the 1983 Writers Guild Award, the 1983 Emmy Award for Outstanding Writing in a Drama Series, and the 1983 Humanitas Prize. These honors were unprecedented for a first-time American television author and staff writer, particularly considering that the four other nominees for that year's drama-writing Emmy were all *Hill Street* scripts.[1] The Humanitas Prize, which is bestowed, according to Milch's 1995 book *True Blue*, "by the Catholic Church," also netted Milch a $15,000 honorarium.[2]

"Trial by Fury" emblematizes Milch's narrative dexterity, insight, and myopia.[3] The episode chronicles how the police detectives and patrol officers of the program's eponymous Hill Street Station investigate two crimes: the brutal rape, mutilation, and murder of Rosa Lombardy—a Caucasian Roman Catholic nun known as Sister Anna Carmela—and the shooting death of a Hispanic shop owner named Eladio Rodriguez. Captain Frank Furillo (Daniel J. Travanti) responds to public anger about Sister Anna's violent death—she was, according to Detective Henry Goldblume (Joe Spano), "raped, beaten with fists and blunt instruments, mutilated. They carved crosses on her torso and thighs with a knife. Shock and severe hemorrhaging. Multiple skull fractures"—by allocating most of his district's police resources to capturing her killers. The Rodriguez investigation receives scant attention, provoking the shop owner's wife (Silvana Gallardo) eventually—and futilely—to beg Furillo to solve the crime committed against her husband.

"Trial by Fury," as its title implies, examines how the threat of mob violence upsets all claims that police departments dispassionately pursue justice for criminal victims regardless of race, ethnicity, and profession. Milch's teleplay honestly acknowledges the discomfiting truth that a white nun's murder receives preferential treatment because American communities—even inner-city communities—consider her more important than a Latino small-business owner. Milch's dramatic pacing ensures that Furillo receives so much external pressure—from media scrutiny, bureaucratic interference, and community anger—that the captain has little choice but to pursue Sister Anna's murder with nearly religious fervor. Milch also complicates Furillo's response by demonstrating the captain's personal horror and spiritual revulsion at the magnitude of the nun's injuries. Furillo not only leaves St. Mary's Church (the local Hill Street parish where Sister Anna's body is discovered) before becoming sick at the sight of her wounds (of which she later dies) but also, in the episode's final scene, enters another parish church to take confession. This act, significantly, is *Hill Street*'s first explicit acknowledgment that Furillo is Catholic.[4]

Milch's social concerns in "Trial by Fury," as faithful viewers of *Hill Street Blues* recognized during the episode's September 30, 1982, broadcast, fit perfectly into the dramatic format that Bochco, Kozoll, Lewis, and the program's other writers had developed during its first two seasons. "Trial by Fury," like nearly all *Hill Street* episodes before and after it, unfolds over the course of a single day, beginning with the precinct's morning roll call—supervised by the loquacious Sergeant Phil Esterhaus (Michael Conrad), whose gentle admonition to the assembled patrol officers and detectives, "Let's be careful out there," provides the series's most enduring tagline—before moving through numerous stories that examine the personal lives of the precinct's cops more than they track the workings of any single case. *Hill Street Blues,* in other words, is not a police procedural like earlier cop dramas *Dragnet* (1951–1959) and *Naked City* (1958–1963). Bochco and Kozoll's series dramatizes the emotional attrition that inner-city police officers face while also indulging in comedy, satire, and vaudevillian absurdity to create a portrait of urban policing unlike anything previously seen on American television.

Milch's season-opening teleplay does not ignore the lighter elements that, by its third year, *Hill Street Blues* had nearly patented. Patrol officers Bobby Hill (Michael Warren) and Andy Renko (Charles Haid) discover at the scene of a domestic dispute that Rudy, who is both the extramarital lover of Rena (Gloria LeRoy) and the best friend of Rena's husband, Carl (Allan Lurie), has his head stuck between Carl's bathtub and toilet. Carl threatens to kill his former friend, but Hill and Renko try to extricate Rudy by physically pulling on the man's body. They must smash the toilet to pieces when Rudy yells that he is suffocating, ending a ludicrous series of events that interrupts the somber story lines of Sister Anna and Eladio Rodriguez at key moments to alter the episode's pace, tone, and mood.

"Trial by Fury" also depicts the legal, ethical, and moral compromises that Furillo makes in order to punish Sister Anna's killers, Gerald Chapman (Maurice Sneed) and Celestine Grey (Juney Smith). After Hill and Renko arrest both men for selling stolen religious iconography to a local pawnbroker, Furillo realizes that the statements Chapman and Grey have made with their defense attorneys present will not convict them. Furillo recommends to Assistant District Attorney (ADA) Irwin Bernstein (George Wyner) that Chapman and Grey be charged with stolen property, then released on bail, to take advantage of the 200 irate community members who gather outside the Hill Street station house to protest Sister Anna's murder. Many of these people pack the courtroom during Chapman and Grey's arraignment, with a few protesters threatening to give the suspects the justice they deserve if the court does not. Bernstein tells Furillo that this strategy has signed each man's death warrant, but Furillo wishes to use Chapman and Grey's fear of mob violence to pressure them into confessing to Sister Anna's murder (a confession being the only certain method of convicting the men, since physical evidence does not prove their guilt beyond a reasonable doubt).

This decision alters the ethical behavior that Furillo manifests in *Hill Street*'s prior 35 episodes. The captain, indeed, has previously lectured the officers under his command about behaving responsibly if they wish to gain the community's trust, improve conditions for their inner-city neighborhood, and, especially, preserve the integrity of a complex series of treaties that Furillo has negotiated among the neighborhood's many criminal street gangs. In *Hill Street*'s second episode, "Presidential

Fever" (1.2), for instance, Furillo angrily confronts several officers in the station house's locker room who are assembling bats and other weapons to chase down the Hispanic men who roughed up two fellow officers and stole their guns.[5] Patrol Officer Harris (Mark Metcalf), one of the Hill Street precinct's many beat cops, had insulted these men by insisting that they prove ownership of many items, including a television set, at what was obviously the site of friends helping one of their own move out of an apartment building. Harris's racist behavior provoked his victims to justifiable anger, but his fellow officers want revenge. Furillo defuses the situation by equating his cops with the Ku Klux Klan: "What we're supposed to be here is the one thing people can trust. If you go out there like a bunch of night riders, what the hell are you but just another vicious street gang?" Furillo's message is clear: Police officers must act more responsibly than the criminals they oppose by refusing to endorse the worst stereotypes that urban police departments traditionally hold about minority citizens who resist police harassment.

An even clearer example occurs earlier in "Presidential Fever," when Furillo, while conducting a summit with the leaders of six criminal gangs to convince them to allow the president of the United States to take a walking tour of their territories, pressures each man to agree to this proposal by saying that, during Furillo's two-year tenure at Hill Street, "no dirty busts, no railroading, [and] no backroom games" have occurred. Furillo, by ending abusive police arrest-and-interrogation practices, has earned just enough credibility to convince the gang leaders to accept his requests. Throughout *Hill Street*'s first two seasons, Furillo declines to follow what he considers immoral orders from higher-ranking police officers, even the chief of police, thereby jeopardizing his chances for promotion.[6]

Furillo, in "Trial by Fury," demonstrates far fewer concerns with civil liberties, the rights of the accused, and police conduct. He so wishes to convict Chapman and Grey for their crimes against Sister Anna that he suggests an unethical, potentially illegal, and seemingly racist tactic against the two African American suspects (ADA Bernstein's designation of the community members who fill the courtroom as a "lynch mob," in this regard, is telling). Furillo's tactics infuriate Public Defender Joyce Davenport (Veronica Hamel), Grey's legal counsel, who, as the captain's longtime girlfriend (and eventual wife), challenges him more directly than any other character. Davenport vigorously protests Furillo's and Bernstein's court tactics to Judge Maurice

Schiller (Allan Rich), calling the decision to release Chapman and Grey a transparent attempt by the police and the district attorney's office to coerce murder confessions from the suspects, then branding the entire proceeding "a neat little exercise in legalist vigilantism."

Davenport does not stop here. Later that night, after Chapman agrees to testify against Grey in exchange for relocation to a federal maximum-security prison, Davenport tells Furillo, who calls Sister Anna's murder the type of crime that must be quickly solved before it rips apart the city, that he has contravened the law's spirit to gain a conviction. "I went by the book," Furillo says. "I pushed a little hard at the bindings." Davenport accepts none of this reasoning: "That's a crock of the well-known article, Furillo." She reserves her most lacerating words for Furillo's claim that she (and, implicitly, the public) can trust his instincts because Chapman and Grey did, indeed, murder Sister Anna. Davenport's retort, nicely played by Hamel, cuts to the issue's core: "But I don't want to trust everybody's instincts. I want there to be rules, and I want them obeyed, especially by people who wear badges and guns. You perverted the law tonight."

"Trial by Fury," therefore, provocatively explores the inequities of the American criminal-justice system. Milch's tight plotting, expert pacing, and evocative dialogue ensure a gripping premiere episode for *Hill Street*'s third season. The resulting ambiguities suggest that Milch infuses "Trial by Fury" with a jaded adult approach to the topic of policing that extends, even as it obeys, the dramatic rules established during *Hill Street Blues*'s first two seasons. Furillo has never before manipulated suspects in the way he pressures Chapman and Grey; Davenport has never before challenged Furillo so directly in court or accused him of perverting the law. "Trial by Fury" so thoroughly intermingles professional and private lives that the viewer realizes how much the daily workings of the criminal-justice system affect the program's protagonists. Furillo, who functions as a wise father figure to the officers in his charge, pushes the boundaries (or the bindings, in Milch's bookish metaphor) of ethical policing to achieve his version of justice. Davenport's passionate disagreement, however, prevents *Hill Street*'s audience from blindly accepting Furillo's self-serving rationalizations. "Trial by Fury" concludes even more ambivalently than the program's previous episodes, with Furillo's late-night confession recognizing that his actions, even if they solve a Catholic nun's murder, require forgiveness. In addition, Eladio Rodriguez's murder remains unsolved.

Milch, in "Trial by Fury," justifies Robert Penn Warren's faith in his ability to construct powerful, emotional, and thoughtful narratives (even if Penn Warren never wrote for television). Bochco is succinct in his praise of "Trial by Fury," calling it "arguably the best episode we ever made."[7] Although Milch would remain with *Hill Street Blues* for the remainder of its seven-season run, not only becoming executive producer in the program's final years but also writing (or providing stories for) at least 31 more episodes, "Trial by Fury" remains his most compelling contribution to Bochco and Kozoll's program. The episode's serious themes, moral ambiguities, and social conscience—like *Hill Street Blues* itself—remain compelling even 30 years after its initial broadcast. "Trial by Fury" also assembles the narrative concerns that characterize Milch's authorial career: the civilized and uncivilized behaviors of American life, injustice, violence, racism, religion, and redemption.

The episode, however, is not an undisputed triumph of socially honorable storytelling. *Hill Street* admirers, cast members, and crew personnel repeatedly discuss—in press interviews, DVD commentaries, and behind-the-scenes documentaries—how the series changed American television drama (particularly cop shows) forever. They laud its adult complexity, novelistic density, and true-to-life characters (novelist Joyce Carol Oates, in a 1985 interview quoted in Robert J. Thompson's book *Television's Second Golden Age,* says that *Hill Street Blues* is "one of the few current television programs that is as intellectually and emotionally provocative as a good book"[8]). They praise its honest assessment of urban policing and inner-city life during the 1980s. They marvel at the extent of Bochco and Kozoll's vision, which transferred to all the writers—including Milch—who fleshed out the world that Bochco and Kozoll created in *Hill Street*'s first season.

These accolades, although containing truths that recognize *Hill Street Blues*'s achievements as a work of television drama (and art), also overstate its impact. *Hill Street*'s large ensemble cast, while innovative for a continuing prime-time dramatic series, was (and remains) a regular feature of daytime serials and soap operas. Although *Dragnet* fetishized police officers who nobly fight crime for society's betterment, *Naked City* approached law-and-order storytelling with commendable sophistication. Trenchant social realism not only appeared in *Naked City* but also characterized Robert Alan Aurthur and David Susskind's 1963–1964 television series *East Side/West Side* (starring George C. Scott), which, set in a private social-work agency named the Community Welfare Service, dramatized problems of poverty, racism, sexism, and injustice in ways that few television programs before it had.

These examples do not diminish *Hill Street*'s accomplishments, but they caution critical viewers against accepting hagiographic praise. Grant Tinker, who lured Bochco and Kozoll to create the show for MTM Enterprises before becoming chairman of NBC Television, notes in Richard Zoglin's article about the series finale, "It Ain't Over Till It's Over" (7.22), that *Hill Street Blues* "proved that you could do something artistically worthwhile and commercially viable at the same time, something both good and popular."[9] Tom Shales, reviewing the script of "It Ain't Over Till It's Over"—cowritten by Milch, Lewis, and John Romano—for the *Washington Post,* zealously defends the program's reputation: "We usually think of a masterpiece as something that hangs from a wall or rests between covers or occupies a couple of hours on a stage or a screen, not something that unfolds over the course of 146 installments. But put them all together, and masterpiece is just about what you've got. The fate of *Hill Street Blues* is sealed. . . . Connoisseurs of television will never forget it."[10]

Milch, in Zoglin's article, takes a more temperate view, saying that *Hill Street* ended not only because of falling ratings but also due to creative aridity: "There was no financial reason to go on, and aesthetically nothing left to prove."[11] The same admiring yet clear-eyed perspective encourages a critical assessment of "Trial by Fury." The episode, like its parent series, has drawbacks that color its view of urban injustice, crime, punishment, and race. Larry Landrum thoughtfully responds to the series itself (as well as to its third-season premiere) in his fine article "Instrumental Texts and Stereotyping in *Hill Street Blues:* The Police Procedural on Television," noting that "within its institutional perspective the procedural predetermines a set of ideological values which are often exploitative of people depicted as representative of the external world."[12] Although *Hill Street Blues* is not a procedural cop drama like *Dragnet, Naked City,* or *Law & Order* (1990–2010) because most episodes do not slavishly follow the workings of one or more cases to the exclusion of personal concerns, Milch introduces elements of the procedural into "Trial by Fury" by tracking how Furillo drives the Sister Anna case to its conclusion. Rodriguez's murder may be initially assigned to detectives J. D. LaRue (Kiel Martin) and Neal Washington (Taurean Blacque), but they quickly transfer themselves to the Sister Anna investigation when they realize that the Rodriguez crime scene has been contaminated, that the case has little chance of being solved, and that, as LaRue callously (but accurately) says, "Now let's face it, on the homicide hit parade, this ain't exactly Number Ten with a bullet. Now we can stay here and waste time and play games, or we can move onto something more promising."

Milch's teleplay acknowledges that homicide detectives look for glory by investigating high-profile cases. When Washington indignantly protests LaRue's belief that Rodriguez's death is insignificant by saying, "Well, you tell her [Mrs. Rodriguez] that, huh?" LaRue replies, "You think I like it any better than you?" These sentiments do not stop the detectives from investigating Chapman and Grey when they learn that the suspects have recently sold religious items from Sister Anna's church to a pawnbroker or from never returning to the Rodriguez case. "Trial by Fury," therefore, operates more as a procedural than previous episodes, although it is not a perfect example of this fictional genre.

Landrum's analysis, however, notes that the police procedural emphasizes institutional hierarchies that define people outside the cop's immediate world (which, for *Hill Street Blues,* means the world outside the Hill Street station house and, in "Trial by Fury," outside the courthouse) as alien interlopers: "The procedural makes no claim on real questions of authority but portrays the public as an anti-structural crowd, as victims and victimizers, and as childlike in its unreasoned impulsiveness and emotionalism, while corruption from within is treated as aberration."[13] *Hill Street Blues* makes claims on real questions of authority, particularly Furillo's willingness to bend or break the law in "Trial by Fury," but Landrum recognizes that the mob that protests Sister Anna's murder is an undifferentiated crowd whose anger Furillo utilizes to pressure Chapman and Grey into confessing (even if the captain deplores mob violence early in the investigation by telling his lieutenant, Ray Calletano [René Enriquez], to contact all the community's religious leaders because "this crime is gonna make them ugly and we'll need all the help we can get keeping the hysteria at a manageable level").

Landrum employs a journalistic metaphor to describe *Hill Street's* narrative structure, commenting that the series, like the daily newspaper's filler items, includes stories whose bizarre motives or weapons create an "imagery of violence [that] constitutes a world characterized by indeterminacy, where violence erupts without warning and often with small cause, where coincidence suggests the hidden hand of fate."[14] Unanticipated violence is perhaps Milch's master theme in "Trial by Fury," for, apart from Sister Anna's unprovoked murder and Furillo's uncharacteristic attack on legal procedure, a man shoots bullets into the Hill Street station house trying to kill Chapman and Grey as they are transferred to the precinct's lockup pending their arraignment. The shooter may justify his violence by believing that Chapman and Grey will receive a rougher (meaning purer) form of justice from his weapon than from the criminal-court system, but both suspects, despite Furillo's and the mob's certainty about their guilt, remain innocent until proven guilty.

Landrum compares this inside-the-station-house assassination attempt to newspaper filler, while Sister Anna's murder resembles a front-page story: "*Hill Street Blues* is tightly structured around several such incidents and a central headline story.... The incidents are, in essence, filler items, but they constitute all of the world outside the precinct station and justify the crisis atmosphere of the station house."[15] Milch inherited this narrative structure from the previous 35 *Hill Street* episodes, but he massages it to enhance the story's procedural elements while challenging and changing Furillo's characterization. Whether Furillo's newfound willingness to break procedure, along with his newly revealed Catholicism, means an expanded, deepened, and mature character or a retreat to what Davenport identifies as "the oldest excuse in the world: the end justifies the means,"[16] Milch does not evade the implication that the captain—*Hill Street Blues*'s primary figure of paternal authority, wisdom, and respect—has become morally tarnished. As Furillo enters confession at the conclusion of "Trial by Fury," the camera briefly shows a mechanical cleaner washing the district's streets to presage Furillo's ritualized statement, "Bless me, Father, for I have sinned," indicating that cleansing the city is both a physical and metaphysical act.

Landrum, while recognizing the undeniable power of "Trial by Fury," feels that the episode's quick pace masks "the stereotyping resulting from the success of the narrative strategies. The Black youths are ready and willing to grovel and inform on one another; the Jewish District Attorney is shown to be easily compromised by the captain; and the mob, a straw affair that conjures up images of torches and pikes, is a plot device to bring the captain to a personal moral dilemma."[17] Landrum's ethnic, religious, and racial stereotypes extend even further in "Trial by Fury" when we recall that ADA Bernstein rapidly acquiesces to Furillo's legal strategy to extort confessions from Chapman and Grey; when we remember that Furillo believes Sister Anna's murder will make the city's faithful "ugly" and prone to hysteria; and when we consider that Chapman and Grey, the African American suspects whose guilt Furillo never doubts, have, in Landrum's words, "no clear motives"[18] for their senseless attack on Sister Anna. Milch, from this perspective, is not the brilliant author of his reputation so much as a talented television writer who perpetuates unconscious bigotries.

"Trial by Fury," to be certain, plays with stereotypes more carefully than Landrum's analysis admits. ADA Bernstein's Jewish faith, for instance, does not explain his willingness to follow Furillo's legal strategy as much as Bernstein's desire to win the case and punish Sister Anna's murderers does. Bernstein, well played by Wyner, appears in more than 30 *Hill Street* episodes during its final six seasons (having established himself as an honorable, if harried, prosecutor in two second-season episodes that precede "Trial by Fury"). He is a deeper character than the Jewish attorneys who populate *NYPD Blue*'s first dozen episodes. Those lawyers are so transparently selfish, aggrandizing, and unsavory that Milch, in his DVD commentary for *NYPD Blue*'s fourth episode, "True Confessions" (1.4), reveals that, early in *Blue*'s first season, he received a letter from an unnamed man claiming that only a self-hating Jew could write the series because all its Jewish lawyers were creeps (meaning that only a Jewish author would create such anti-Semitic characters). "I'm thinking to myself," Milch says in a garrulous, amusing, and confessional tone, "'well, what a presumptuous asshole,' and then I realized he was right."[19]

Bernstein, in "Trial by Fury," unlike the Jewish attorneys that Milch would create 10 years later, possesses none of these traits but rather cautions Furillo that the captain's actions may get Chapman and Grey killed. Bernstein, however, agrees that Sister Anna's attackers must be punished. He does not accept Furillo's legal strategy out of fear or weakness; instead, Bernstein's sense of justice and desire to win compel him to acquiesce to Furillo's unsavory alternative. Bernstein's Jewish background, significantly, plays no explicit role in his decision to prosecute the killers of a Catholic nun, so, while Landrum's belief (that Bernstein's ethnic and religious affiliation reproduces long-held bigotries about Jewish men) is a reasonable concern, his suggestion that Bernstein capitulates to Furillo's plan because Jewish attorneys are spineless ignores the episode's subtext, as well as the history that Furillo and *Hill Street*'s viewers have with Bernstein's character.

Landrum's dismissal of the mob as a poor dramatic device whose sole narrative function is to generate Furillo's moral crisis seems shortsighted as well, because this crowd's unruly behavior drives every incident of the final act of "Trial by Fury," affecting Furillo's, Bernstein's, and Davenport's working relationships while raising Furillo's professional stature in the eyes of the people under his command. Calletano tells Furillo that "the men are proud of what you did today" in a tone that expresses approval, although Furillo, who has just heard from Goldblume that the Rodriguez case will likely never be cleared, is not pleased by Calletano's news. The next scene is also the episode's final moment, in which Furillo seeks absolution for his sins. The captain's ethical crisis, therefore, becomes the nexus of the pessimistic assessment in "Trial by Fury" of the institutional failures that lead Furillo to regrettable decisions, that cause Chapman to betray his friend Grey, and that leave Mrs. Rodriguez with a dead husband whose murder goes unsolved. "Trial by Fury" demonstrates that the criminal-justice system's institutional failures are also personal failures because human beings create, maintain, and staff its institutions. The mob exposes these drawbacks more clearly than any other element of the episode's narrative, so, far from being the deus ex machina that Landrum implies, the mob (and the public anger that it embodies) forces all parties to make choices that they otherwise might not. Furillo's moral crisis, in addition, is no throwaway device that Milch includes in "Trial by Fury" for the sake of false character development. Furillo's decisions follow him into future episodes, reminding the captain that justice—as Davenport notes in this episode, throughout *Hill Street Blues*'s third season, and the remainder of the series—is rarely blind.

Landrum's article, however, incisively argues that Chapman and Grey are little more than stereotypical minority (specifically African American) characters. Their lack of motive for Sister Anna's assault and murder is the episode's most troubling aspect, implying that the suspects are little more than out-of-control animals who rape and mutilate the nun for pleasure. This senseless violence, Landrum writes, confirms *Hill Street*'s depiction of a beleaguered inner-city police precinct whose employees become surrogate family members while enduring, even as they attempt to ameliorate, the frequently inhumane conditions of what LaRue, in the pilot episode, calls "a war zone."[20] This melodramatic description becomes frighteningly real as *Hill Street Blues* unfolds during its first two seasons. The number of hostage takings, shootings, stabbings, kidnappings, and other violent encounters makes crime seem like the major factor in the lives of all Hill Street residents. This notion not only reproduces reactionary accounts of ghetto life that have haunted the American imagination since the late 18th century but also endorses the otherwise-laughable ideas of Lieutenant Howard Hunter (James B. Sikking), commander of the precinct's SWAT-like Emergency Action Team and resident representative of Reagan-style conservatism. Hunter's buffoonish political pronouncements and casual racism (couched in terms of eugenics, with Hunter stating that "the brown types," "the colored types," "the Latin types," or other minority "types" are degenerates who threaten the peace of America's social order and the health of America's body politic) may be comically played, but *Hill Street Blues*'s premise—of good, if imperfect, cops staving off crime, poverty, and violence in a bad neighborhood—acknowledges how Hunter's attitudes, although misguided, ring true in their concerns and content.

Hunter also melds the criminal and religious themes of "Trial by Fury" when he suggests that Furillo should allow the mob to string up Chapman and Grey even though Hunter knows that, for a police officer, such an idea is "blasphemy." This suggestion inadvertently inspires Furillo's decision to use the threat, rather than the reality, of mob violence to secure justice for Sister Anna. Hunter expresses no interest in understanding Chapman's and Grey's lives or in discovering the reasons for their assault on Sister Anna. He wants only vengeance, with all the secular and spiritual implications that such blasphemy implies. Hunter reduces Chapman and Grey to crude stereotypes, believing they are worthy of the gallows and the unhinged mob, not the presumption of innocence that the law guarantees them.

Chapman and Grey's thoughtless behavior, therefore, is never questioned, doubted, or investigated by any of *Hill Street Blues*'s principal characters. Davenport, who in previous episodes rails against the terrible living conditions that ensnare Hill Street's residents in uncertain and dangerous lives, neither wonders why Chapman and Grey commit such heinous crimes against Sister Anna nor attempts to ascertain their motives. The guiding assumption seems to be that both men—poor, black, and unlikable—may be savages because their unrestrained behavior is too animalistic to warrant psychological or sociological explanation. No one, particularly Furillo, utters racist epithets against the men, but the implication that Chapman and Grey remorselessly kill a white nun in a burst of frenzied violence reproduces, without challenging, the racial stereotypes that Furillo himself discounts in the program's previous two seasons.

Milch's teleplay, therefore, is neither as groundbreaking nor as reve-latory as its many awards suggest. "Trial by Fury" is an excellent epi-sode of a provocative television series. As Landrum says, "*Hill Street Blues* is not, to be sure, conceived as an intentionally racist or fascist production; it is well-written and performed, and production values are among the highest in the industry,"[21] but the program ignores—as much as it illuminates—the institutional, systemic, and social causes of the downtrodden district that its characters police. The limited scope of Milch's 55-page teleplay and the broadcast episode's 49 minutes, 11 seconds of screen time may prevent a full sociological probe of urban blight, violence, and injustice from emerging, but these explanations cannot counteract Landrum's assertion that *Hill Street*'s institutional setting, perpetual crises, and put-upon characters lose "any sense that to be more than the contemplation of intensely personal problems or reactions to immediate threats of chaos, life must incorporate connec-tion with a larger sense of humanity."[22] *Hill Street*'s viewer, Landrum concludes, "may be expected to understand that the [program's] small moments of empathy and pathos are supposed to represent such larger connections, but what we too often see is an imperfectly rendered hier-archy of institutional authority."[23]

Hill Street Blues, however, renders the imperfections of institu-tional authority more faithfully than any previous police drama. "Trial by Fury" evokes urban injustice, economic malaise, and so-ciological stereotypes more truthfully than some previous *Hill Street* episodes—to say nothing of 1960s and 1970s cop dramas such as *Ha-waii Five-O* (1968–1980), *The Streets of San Francisco* (1972–1977), *Kojak* (1973–1978), and, especially, *Starsky and Hutch* (1975–1979)—by dem-onstrating how Furillo becomes tainted by life in a ghetto society that destroys easy faith in the ideals of democracy, republicanism, and au-tonomy. Milch's teleplay becomes a fascinating, troubling, and politi-cally ambivalent text that refuses simplistic answers to the ambitious questions it raises. "Trial by Fury" is far from perfect (as Milch's later work on *NYPD Blue* and *Deadwood* illustrates) despite the episode's many accolades. Although his script is not as sociologically precise, racially nuanced, and politically complex as *NYPD Blue*'s and *Dead-wood*'s best episodes, "Trial by Fury" nonetheless outlines the param-eters of Milch's dense, demanding, and dramatic television writing.

Three additional factors influence this assessment of Milch's narra-tive authority. The first involves the committee (or communal) writ-ing process that most television programs follow. The second includes Milch's personal problems and well-known addictions during his tenure on *Hill Street Blues.* The third encompasses the ideological, political, and dramatic biases that *Hill Street Blues,* by focusing on the lives of inner-city police officers rather than inner-city civilians, forces on its writers.

Determining how responsible Milch is for the script of "Trial by Fury" remains an uncertain proposition. Milch joined a talented writing staff that, by the third season's conclusion, not only included Steven Boch-co, Karen Hall, Jeffrey Lewis, Michael Wagner, and Anthony Yerkovich but also accepted story ideas and teleplays from writers such as Joseph Gunn, Philip Lambest, and a pre–*Twin Peaks* Mark Frost. Three or more writers coauthored most of the third season's scripts, with only Hall's "Officer of the Year" (3.5), Milch's "Stan the Man" (3.6), Robert Earll's "Little Boil Blue" (3.7), and Frost's "Requiem for a Hairbag" (3.8) being credited to a single writer. According to the DVD commentary track recorded by second-season story editors Lewis and Robert Crais[24] for "Freedom's Last Stand" (2.11), *Hill Street Blues*'s writing chores were shouldered by the entire writing staff, with Bochco assigning most teleplay acts to different staff writers (cocreator Kozoll, who resigned his day-to-day production responsibilities after the first season concluded, continued to meet with Bochco and the writing staff to discuss Season Two's characters, plotlines, and story arcs). "This was a gang-written show,"[25] Crais says, revealing that Bochco and the writers would outline (or "break") stories in great detail. Once Bochco had A, B, and C stories (industry terms for the different plotlines that compose most episodic-television scripts) with almost every beat (or moment of action) covered, Bochco would dole out these story elements to different staff members, who would independently write acts 1, 2, 3, and 4 based on the story outline they had collectively generated. After a draft of the script was complete, two people—presumably Bochco and Kozoll in the first year, although, in later seasons, Bochco, Lewis, and, once he became executive producer, Milch—would stitch these disparate acts together, smoothing their edges to produce a finished teleplay.

Bochco and his writers must have quickly initiated Milch, who had just arrived in Hollywood from Yale, into this communal writing process. Milch likely generated the basic plot elements and character arcs of "Trial by Fury," then revised these ideas with the writing staff's help. Whether Milch wrote an entire draft of "Trial by Fury," participated in the gang-writing procedure that Crais outlines, or revised the teleplay according to Bochco's expectations is less important than the fact that

Milch received sole credit for *Hill Street*'s third-season premiere. The writing staff and producers of television series frequently agree on who receives on-screen credit for each episode, although the Writer's Guild of America determines final credits through an official arbitration process. No interviews, documentaries, or available sources suggest that any disagreement developed over Milch's credit for "Trial by Fury," while Bochco's high regard for this episode indicates that Milch is largely responsible for its script.

The contributions, suggestions, and criticisms of his fellow writers undoubtedly refined Milch's ideas about the story that "Trial by Fury" tells. The fact that *Hill Street Blues*'s cast, crew, and director Gregory Hoblit became key players in interpreting Milch's script also suggests that Milch is the episode's primary (but not sole) writer. Such collective authorship characterizes collaborative artistic ventures like television, film, and stage drama, but Milch, in this formulation, fathers "Trial by Fury" even if he remains one of many parents.

Milch's colorful behavior and personal problems also pose challenges to his narrative authority, or at least to his reputation as a careful television writer concerned with legal, social, and racial justice. Bochco, in Mark Singer's "The Misfit" (Singer's masterful 2005 profile of Milch in the *New Yorker*), says that, when Milch first moved to Los Angeles, "he was a madman. He had this little office and he managed to turn it into this place that looked like a bomb had gone off."[26] Bochco soon realized the extent of Milch's gambling addiction, which, even if it enhanced Milch's mystique as a "vibrant, earthy, and often derisively funny"[27] Yale literature teacher, might have interfered with his *Hill Street* writing duties. Bochco walked into Milch's office one day "and the drawer was open and there was a ton of cash inside. I said, 'How much is that?' He said, 'I won some money in Vegas.' It turns out he was commuting to work from Vegas. He'd catch a 6 A.M. flight to Burbank and at the end of the day he'd catch a flight back to Vegas and he'd be up all night gambling."[28]

Milch's unorthodox habits and addictions (at Yale, he was an alcoholic and a heroin abuser[29]) did not, however, upset his productivity. Milch received credit for writing all or part of 13 *Hill Street* episodes during the third season, a statistic that does not count the 19 additional episodes for which Milch received either story or teleplay credit during *Hill Street Blues*'s final four seasons (or the episodes whose stories he helped outline, revise, or supervise—without credit—as he ascended to executive producer). Milch's compulsions, in an irony not lost on him in later years, may well have enhanced his ability to create vulnerable, downtrodden, and realistic characters who suffer the indignities, depredations, and follies of life in an unnamed, economically depressed American city. Bochco—who, rather than firing Milch, entrusted *Hill Street Blues* to him and Lewis when MTM Enterprises (*Hill Street*'s production company) fired Bochco in 1985—not only created *NYPD Blue* with Milch in 1991 or 1992 but also believes that Milch's self-destructive behavior enhanced his storytelling gifts: "David had more miles on him the day I met him than I'll probably have the day I die. He'll wrestle with his demons forever, but I've never known anyone else who has learned to put his demons at his service in quite the way he has. I think that's his real genius. And David is a genius in the literal definition of that word. He is truly unique, truly original."[30]

Such high praise may be justified when considering Milch's full body of work, but the troubling stereotypes that Landrum recognizes in "Trial by Fury" (and that apply to other *Hill Street* episodes written or cowritten by Milch) demonstrate that Milch's perspective, at least during the *Hill Street* years, was not as wide, as deep, or as sophisticated as Bochco implies. The exigencies of writing a weekly, hour-long television drama—compounded by Milch's "madman" tendencies—also suggest that he had neither the time nor the energy to consider (or reconsider) the occasionally blinkered, partial, and restricted view of inner-city life that his contributions to *Hill Street Blues* endorse.

This last judgment, however, is not fully damning, for *Hill Street*'s premise of police officers fighting inner-city crime constrains the ideological, political, and sociological possibilities that its writers could explore. Presenting the program from the perspective of law-enforcement personnel creates a fascinating view of urban blight, crime, and injustice, but *Hill Street*'s refusal to accord the Hill Street precinct's civilian residents the same narrative significance as its cops results in a conservative drama that promotes order over justice, as well as authority over liberty, rather than striving to understand the social, institutional, and systemic causes of the many problems faced by inner-city citizens. *Hill Street Blues* indulges what Christopher P. Wilson calls the "cop shop" narrative, a genre that features "urban portraiture decisively mediated through the lens of police power."[31] Wilson cites novelists Joseph Wambaugh and Ed McBain as prototypical cop-shop authors whose fiction, along with "the police melodramas so common to television" (Wilson does not mention *Hill Street Blues* by name, but the series certainly fits this description), works within "the field of urban 'police populism.' That is, these works represent policing as the labor of a dedicated, hard-bitten knight of the city, an everyday, man-in-shirtsleeves servant of the mostly white working class, solving crimes not through eccentric genius but by shoe leather, hard work, and often tedious procedure."[32]

Hill Street Blues does not present its police officers as knights or even as pure-at-heart public servants, but its working-class setting, middle-class principal characters, and workaday themes fit Wilson's analysis. Furillo, Calletano, and Esterhaus embody the frustrations of good men trapped inside a heartless bureaucracy who perform their jobs well, protect the people under their command, and endure their thankless roles as disillusioned functionaries who embrace wry humor. The beat cops, particularly Renko, protest the dire conditions and unappreciative residents they meet every day, while some detectives— particularly LaRue—experience the downward spiral of alcoholism, drug abuse, violence, and career setbacks that police fiction (whether in print or on television) favors. *Hill Street* consequently participates in a tradition that Wilson ascribes to true-crime stories, a tradition that Pierre Bourdieu terms "the larger 'field of power' in urban politics— specifically, with what cultural studies has denominated the 'authoritarian populism' or 'popular conservatism' emergent in the 1980s."[33] While *Hill Street*'s episodes sometimes challenge, and even satirize, populist conservatism's most restrictive tenets (Hunter's absurd musings are the program's most common vehicle for such satire), they also accept conservatism's view of urban regress as the result of poor decisions by autonomous individuals (meaning that criminals always freely choose their fate), not the symptoms of social, economic, and political inequality. Wilson's analysis may focus on true-crime books (including David Simon's *Homicide: A Year on the Killing Streets*), but it comfortably applies to *Hill Street Blues*, whose episodes "exhibit a long-recognized double-edged potential in populist ideology, applications that are progressive and reactionary, liberal and authoritarian all at once."[34]

Milch's *Hill Street* writing, especially "Trial by Fury," fulfills these parameters so well that his teleplay, like Wambaugh's and McBain's novels, becomes a prototypical cop-shop text. Milch did not create *Hill Street*'s cop-shop conventions, while the people who did (Bochco, Kozoll, and the first two seasons' writers) were clearly influenced by the crime fiction and cop dramas that they had read, watched, or created.[35] Milch, by introducing more elements of the police procedural into his inaugural *Hill Street* script, manages to enhance the ambivalent populism that the program had previously developed.

Religion, race, ethnicity, and class all combine to depict the Hill Street precinct as an island of authority (although not of calm, as the many fights, shootings, and suicides that occur inside the station house attest) in an otherwise-chaotic environment, with the racially mixed police force attempting to keep order in a neighborhood that may once have been prosperous but that has declined economically as its demographic complexion has darkened. Despite Davenport's protestations about Furillo's unseemly legal maneuvering in "Trial by Fury," neither this episode nor its parent series deeply explores the reasons that urban America experienced the many changes that, by 1982, had resulted in stark dichotomies between inner cities and suburban communities. Milch would not fully engage such sociological analysis until *Deadwood* (2004–2006), with Simon's *The Corner* (2000) and *The Wire* (2002–2008) doing better jobs. Even Bochco's later series *Murder One* (1995–1997) and *Raising the Bar* (2008–2009), by focusing on the work of defense attorneys rather than police officers or prosecutors, articulate the social, systemic, and institutional causes of urban crime more forcefully than does *Hill Street Blues,* whatever its reputation or popularity. The depiction of inner-city police experience in "Trial by Fury" resembles Wilson's true-crime cop-shop texts by coming "to represent, at once, a borderland post not only of professional fields, but of ethnicities and divisive racial attitudes. Indeed, this is a crucial subtext to the general cover story of professional disillusionment, which turns out to hinge upon the politics of white resistance—on entertaining the plight, as it were, after white flight."[36] A more fitting epitaph for Bochco and Kozoll's program is difficult to imagine.

This conclusion should not imply that *Hill Street Blues,* "Trial by Fury," or Milch's other episodes are consciously reactionary productions that dismantle liberal pieties about inner-city crime, violence, and injustice to advocate a conservative political agenda. No text—whether a novel, academic treatise, newspaper story, or television series—can fully account for the nuances of urban life, the challenges of inner-city living, or the causes of social decline. Milch's dramatic instincts, even 30 years after the initial broadcast of "Trial by Fury," remain fresh, compelling, and powerful. His script inspires *Hill Street's* talented cast to give terrific performances (Travanti, for instance, expertly plays Furillo's moral dilemma and contradictory emotions), while Milch obeys one of his primary narrative rules—"You've got to

go out the same door you came in when you're writing a story"[37]—
by beginning and ending "Trial by Fury" with religious themes. This
episode, like *Hill Street* itself, becomes a politically ambiguous narrative that evades easy classification. Unlike *NYPD Blue* and *Deadwood*,
over which he exercised creative control from each program's first
moments, Milch came to *Hill Street Blues* after its setting, characters,
and themes had already been established. *Hill Street Blues*, however,
nurtured Milch's authorial gifts by providing a crucible for them to
expand, develop, and deepen. By the time Milch partners with Bochco
on *NYPD Blue*, his writing talents have visibly matured. This development leads the critical viewer to another inescapable conclusion,
namely, that neither Milch's growth nor American television drama's
narrative sophistication would have been possible without *Hill Street
Blues*.

2

Blue, Black, and White: David Milch's *NYPD Blue*

NYPD Blue (1993–2005) advanced David Milch's career as a television writer, producer, and creator; brought him even greater wealth than the $12 million he had earned during his final three seasons on *Hill Street Blues*;[1] and marked in the minds of many observers a watershed moment for televised American crime drama. Mark Singer, for instance, calls *NYPD Blue* "a reinvention of vérité storytelling and better than any police drama that has come along since" in "The Misfit," his long 2005 *New Yorker* profile of Milch.[2] Singer is not alone in this judgment, although his lofty proclamation about *NYPD Blue*'s peerless reputation unjustifiably promotes this program (created by Milch and Steven Bochco) above other excellent contemporaneous cop shows, particularly Paul Attanasio's *Homicide: Life on the Street* (1993–1999), a series that not only adapted David Simon's 1991 book *Homicide: A Year on the Killing Streets* for television but also premiered eight months before *NYPD Blue*.[3] Singer's opinion also ignores two later police dramas that radically revise the parameters and possibilities of prime-time cop shows, parameters that *NYPD Blue* confirms as much as it contests: Shawn Ryan's *The Shield* (2002–2008) and David Simon's *The Wire* (2002–2008).

This final comment does not reduce *NYPD Blue* to a conventional police drama that "evinces disdain for the common good of our society,"[4] as Richard Clark Sterne writes in a fascinating, blistering, and persuasive article about *NYPD Blue*'s approach to social realism, but this judgment suggests how Milch's authorial influence over *NYPD Blue* extends the narrative talent, vision, and shortsightedness that characterize his work on *Hill Street Blues*.[5] *NYPD Blue*, however, remains a prototypical cop show due to its profound influence on televised American crime drama. The quality of its production, particularly Dennis Franz's remarkable 12-season performance as the show's antiheroic protagonist, Detective Andy Sipowicz, is so high that the viewer can easily accept *NYPD Blue's* portrait of urban crime and punishment as unvarnished realism. This response testifies to Milch's gifts as a television dramatist, producer, and creator but also elides the politically reactionary stance that *NYPD Blue* occasionally purveys, particularly when dealing with race, racism, and bigotry.

NYPD Blue, therefore, poses a problem for Singer's evaluation of Milch's authorial career as an upward trajectory of narrative, social, and political nimbleness. The program confines itself even more closely to what Sterne identifies as the perspective of "decent, dogged, local police" and what Christopher P. Wilson, in his article "True and True(r) Crime: Cop Shops and Crime Scenes in the 1980s," calls the "cop-shop" story than does *Hill Street Blues.*[6] This worldview, in turn, prevents *NYPD Blue* from examining the institutional, social, and political reasons that the fictional 15th Precinct's Lower East Side neighborhood has fallen into economic disrepair.

Hill Street Blues's early seasons, on this score, offer a better portrait of urban life than *NYPD Blue* does by giving the audience a more comprehensive sense of the Hill Street precinct's immediate surroundings. "Trial by Fury," Milch's initial contribution to *Hill Street,* also complicates (even as it extends) the cop-drama genre's conventional depiction of inner-city neighborhoods as cesspools of crime, violence, and despair inhabited by minority residents whom the police distrust, misjudge, and dislike. "Trial by Fury," like *Hill Street Blues,* may endorse some of the racial, socioeconomic, and gender stereotypes that typify earlier cop shows, but the episode, through Joyce Davenport's passionate objections to Frank Furillo's unethical behavior, allows the audience to question the cop's-eye viewpoint that *Hill Street* promulgates.

NYPD Blue, therefore, may seem to reduce Milch's reputation as a social realist even while presenting the uncomfortable realities of inner-city police work. Sterne attributes the program's perspective on policing to Bill Clark, a veteran New York City detective whom Milch extensively consulted while preparing the first season's scripts.[7] Clark served as the program's first-season technical advisor, showing the actors and directors proper police procedures, and then, in the second season, became consulting producer. Clark's greater responsibilities included helping Milch and *NYPD Blue's* staff writers develop story lines that, Milch reveals in *True Blue* (his 1995 book about *NYPD Blue's* first three seasons), were based either on Clark's cases or on cases with which Clark was familiar.[8] Clark's counsel became invaluable, for, although Milch had finished *NYPD Blue*'s first two scripts—establishing the relationships among Sipowicz, Detective John Kelly (David Caruso), and the 15th Precinct's other characters—before meeting Clark, he states, "I'd painted them in broad strokes; I needed a better sense of the world's specific rhythms and textures. And here was Bill, with his hard-minded details and almost defiant pride in his job."[9]

Milch's concern for those rhythms and textures is laudable, recalling his repeated statements in press interviews, DVD commentaries, and behind-the-scenes documentaries about wanting *NYPD Blue* to capture the lives of New York City police detectives as faithfully as possible. Clark, who became one of *NYPD Blue*'s executive producers after Milch's seventh-season departure (in 2000), may have at first been wary about involving himself with Bochco and Milch's new television show, but, as *True Blue* makes clear, Clark was key to the program's success. Milch, writing about his reaction to dining with Clark at midtown Manhattan's P. J. Clarke's restaurant, expresses how fortunate he feels to have met the detective.[10] He also reveals how emphatic Bochco was about hiring Clark after eating lunch with the detective in Los Angeles: Bochco, according to *True Blue*, tells Milch (out of Clark's earshot), "Do not let this guy out of your sight."[11]

NYPD Blue's vaunted realism, in this account, results from Bochco's, Milch's, and Clark's desire to accurately dramatize the details of urban detective work. Their success accounts for much of *NYPD Blue*'s impact and influence. Milch's ability to write realistic police environments, procedures, and characters creates a gritty series whose grim atmosphere and imperfect characters expose the emotional angst that inner-city police detectives experience. Milch fearlessly makes the alcoholic, sexist, and racist Sipowicz *NYPD Blue*'s central character to depict how police work magnifies the bigotries, neuroses, and doubts that middle-aged, working-class white men bring to their law-enforcement jobs. This choice permits Milch and his writers to explore social, racial, and economic injustices from the viewpoint of a character whose initially blinkered perspective broadens as the series progresses. Even the program's first season, while presenting Kelly and Sipowicz as partners, friends, and equals, finds Sipowicz's flaws so intriguing that it regularly unveils them for the viewer to see, consider, and reject.

Milch quickly realized how powerful Sipowicz's character was, allowing Milch to follow what *True Blue* describes as "the writer's process of synthesizing aspects of his own nature and of personalities he's observed into a credible character."[12] Sipowicz emerges as a deeply flawed man who, with the help of coworkers, family, and friends, tries to face down his assumptions, addictions, and prejudices. This process—which can justifiably be called the redemption of Sipowicz—becomes *NYPD Blue's* grand theme, chronicling an everyman police detective's emotional and intellectual evolution amid the sometimes savage inequities of the urban environment that forms him. Milch achieves what he hopes is an honorable goal with Sipowicz by writing, in *True Blue*, that he hopes to "show [Sipowicz] in what another writer called his 'obstinate finality'—that is, in full human complication: to do him justice."[13]

This statement not only illustrates how careful, capable, and daring a television dramatist Milch can be but also indicates the difficulties that television's narrative constrictions impose on authors as sensitive and intelligent as Milch. His tenure at *Hill Street Blues,* particularly his time as executive producer, taught him that television authorship, unlike novel writing, does not end when an episode's script is finished. The vicissitudes of weekly production preclude teleplays from achieving the completeness that novels, short-story anthologies, and poetry books attain before appearing in print, forcing teleplays to change throughout an episode's production as directors, actors, and crew members recommend alterations to the script.[14] The accelerated pace of television shoots (especially compared to feature films) mandates that teleplay revisions happen quickly, even extemporaneously, to keep an episode's production on track. This rushed process forces television writers to collaborate with other creative personnel to develop an interpretation acceptable to all (or most) parties so that each episode meets its initial broadcast date.

Milch understands the obstacles that television drama poses for authors concerned with social justice, commentary, and realism. *True Blue's* 10th chapter deals with what Milch considers the most vexing problem by relating how Robert Penn Warren's university courses taught him that the secret subject of all worthwhile stories is "what we learn or fail to learn over time. It's a particular challenge to structure stories in television drama to illuminate rather than distort this theme."[15] The abbreviated running time of each *NYPD Blue* episode (43 to 46 minutes excluding opening and closing credits), as well as the cop-show convention of solving at least one case every week, requires Milch and *NYPD Blue's* writing staff to compress the procedural details of criminal investigations into a shorter span than real-life cases require. Milch states during his DVD commentary on the first-season episode "True Confessions" (1.4) that "we can't really be true to the dimension of time," causing *NYPD Blue* to meld what Milch calls three differently paced stories into every episode: "modular" (or self-contained) plots that resolve themselves during a single episode, "character arcs" that require two or three episodes to resolve, and "real big character arcs" that take entire seasons to develop.[16]

Since *Hill Street Blues,* as well as most soap operas, includes all three narrative forms, neither Milch nor *NYPD Blue* can lay claim to inventing them. *NYPD Blue,* however, presents so many different plotlines (many of which intersect during the course of an episode, a season, or the program's entire run) at such quick tempo that viewers can sometimes lose track. Sterne refers to *NYPD Blue*'s tendency to rush through scenes as "a convention that seems increasingly to have been adhered to in both movie and television dramas since the late 1960s: the velocity of speech (and of action) must be so great that the audience, instead of 'following' it, is immersed in it."[17] This velocity both supplements and retards *NYPD Blue*'s realistic approach to urban policing by placing the program's viewer in a world that looks, sounds, and feels authentic; that dramatizes how confusing, dismal, and depressing detective work can be; and that mirrors *Hill Street Blues*'s narrative concerns with injustice, racism, and poverty.

NYPD Blue, however, does not reproduce its fictional world's complexity as well as Milch and the program's most passionate fans claim. Sterne, while admiring *NYPD Blue*'s narrative ambition, handsome production, and excellent acting, persuasively analyzes its "constricted realism," meaning "its failure to face up to police brutality as an issue, its narrow view of what constitutes crime, its virtual ignoring of what must be the variegated nature of the community in which the 15th Precinct is situated."[18] Sterne's final charge is the most significant for, as he argues, "the show doesn't extend to the community in which the 15th Precinct is situated the generous understanding of flaws and problems with which it treats the detectives themselves."[19] This judgment recalls Larry Landrum's claim in "Instrumental Texts and Stereotyping in *Hill Street Blues:* The Police Procedural on Television" that *Hill Street* treats the community outside the Hill Street Station's walls as undifferentiated citizens whose lives receive little narrative attention, interest, or exploration.[20] Sterne, as if updating Landrum's argument for *NYPD Blue,* implies that, by concentrating on the experiences of the 15th Precinct's detective squad, *NYPD Blue* glosses over the social inequities that observers like Singer praise it for exploring (declaring *NYPD Blue* an example of vérité storytelling, for instance, indicates just how realistic Singer believes the program to be).

One response to Sterne's charge is that the narrative conventions of television cop shows (to say nothing of police procedurals in all media) compel their writers to make police officers their central concern. *NYPD Blue* not only narrows its attention to Lieutenant Arthur Fancy's (James McDaniel) detective squad (distinguishing itself from *Hill Street Blues,* which depicts the lives of plainclothes and uniformed officers in roughly equal measure) but also takes Sipowicz as its viewpoint character. Bochco and Milch, by choosing this narrative focus, ensure that *NYPD Blue* presents a white homicide detective's jaded law-enforcement perspective on crime, punishment, injustice, and poverty. To do otherwise would compromise *NYPD Blue*'s premise while abrogating the authenticity of the world that Bochco, Milch, the writing staff, and the production crew so painstakingly create.

The detective's perspective (particularly Sipowicz's perspective) does not reduce *NYPD Blue* to a simplistic rendering of the social issues that the program dramatizes. As George C. Thomas III and Richard A. Leo note in "Interrogating Guilty Suspects: Why Sipowicz Never Has to Admit He Is Wrong," "*NYPD Blue* is a powerful drama, teeming with moral judgments and moral ambiguities."[21] Many ambivalences arise from Sipowicz's struggle to become a better man. This character changes as *NYPD Blue* unfolds: Sipowicz—rather than remaining the racist and misogynistic "dinosaur" that Detective Martina Escobar (Wanda De Jesus) calls him in "Girl Talk" (3.16)[22]—begins to appreciate the origins of his bigotry rather than blundering forward without rethinking his regressive gender, ethnic, and racial attitudes. Sipowicz, however, is the primary narrative lens through which *NYPD Blue* views urban American society, meaning that his biases drive the program's approach to race, gender, poverty, and inequality more than the enlightened perspective of the other principal characters.

Race and racism, among all the themes that *NYPD Blue* regularly examines (including alcoholism, drug abuse, incest, domestic violence, homophobia, misogyny, injustice, and brutality), frequently interject themselves into the program's story lines. The explosive power of *NYPD Blue*'s racial confrontations—especially Sipowicz's prejudicial treatment of African Americans—transforms race into a narrative prism that separates American society's many bigotries into identifiable plot points that regularly confirm, but sometimes challenge, what Sterne defines as the program's "'conservative' slice-of-life realism," a perspective that "distorts social reality as badly as 'liberal' evasions of truth once did"[23] (these "liberal" evasions referring to the supposed preponderance of fictional crimes committed by Caucasian men—rather than women and minorities—in 1960s and 1970s American adventure television).

Milch's attitudes toward racism form an important aspect of this discussion, for *NYPD Blue* is not an ideologically pure program that advocates a resolutely conservative, liberal, authoritarian, anarchic, totalitarian, or utopian agenda. Focusing on the lives of police officers makes Bochco and Milch's series conservative insofar as its major characters defend the principles of law and order over social justice, but the fact that *NYPD Blue's* principal characters are agents of the state does not preclude them from dismissing, ignoring, or circumventing the law-enforcement tendency to divide the world into the simplistic dichotomy of good citizens versus bad criminals. This binary view may typify American police dramas (as well as actual police departments), but *NYPD Blue*, while endorsing this perspective in many episodes, counteracts it in others. Since race and racism underlie so many of Sipowicz's relationships to the community he polices, concentrating on *NYPD Blue's* racial ambiguities exposes how the series transcends rigid ideological boundaries even if it finally reflects Milch's respect for Clark's brand of police work. *NYPD Blue* does not interrogate the institutional, social, economic, and political causes of racism, poverty, and injustice as well as *Homicide: Life on the Street, The Corner, Deadwood,* or *The Wire* does, but its outlook is less repressive than Sterne contends. Milch's comments about writing authentic African American characters, when juxtaposed with key episodes that Milch wrote himself or those installments whose writing he supervised, demonstrate just how complicated, contradictory, and complex *NYPD Blue's* depiction of American racism is.

Sipowicz's most fractious professional relationship involves his immediate superior, Lieutenant Arthur Fancy, who repeatedly clashes with Sipowicz over the detective's racially insensitive remarks. Sipowicz, for his part, believes that Fancy, an African American, dislikes middle-aged white detectives who do not espouse politically correct beliefs about the working-class and poor minority residents that populate the 15th Precinct. Fancy's concerns about Sipowicz's job performance, however, do not initially involve race. The first scene of the

series pilot (1.1), written by Milch, shows a drunken Sipowicz testifying against mobster Alfonse Giardella (Robert Costanzo), only to
have Giardella's defense attorney, James Sinclair (Daniel Benzali), destroy Sipowicz's credibility during cross-examination by successfully
arguing that Sipowicz hammered nails into the rear tires of Giardella's
vehicle before planting several cartons of untaxed cigarettes in the
disabled car's trunk.[24] When the judge releases Giardella, an enraged
Sipowicz follows the mobster out of the courtroom, threatening to
"burn [him] down" before insulting Assistant District Attorney Sylvia
Costas (Sharon Lawrence), who is also Sipowicz's future wife, by telling her that she "prosecuted the crap out of that one" and by asking,
"You sayin' I queered that guy's tire?" Costas is not intimidated by the
detective's fearsome demeanor, replying, "I'd say *res ipsa locuitor* if I
thought you knew what it meant." Sipowicz, in an image that became
famous even before *NYPD Blue*'s September 21, 1993, premiere, grabs
his groin while screaming, "Hey, *ipsa* this, you pissy little bitch!" Sipowicz, in this scene, is an equal-opportunity offender, raging against
an Italian defendant and a Caucasian prosecutor with no regard for
the truth, his own reputation, or social decorum. Detective Kelly can
only observe his partner's behavior with exasperated amusement. The
pilot episode's teaser, indeed, ends as Kelly weakly smiles an apology
to Costas.

Fancy, after hearing about this breakdown, tells Kelly to change
partners yet expresses admiration for the detective Sipowicz once
was. When Kelly fibs about Sipowicz's location, Fancy corrects him:
"We both know where Andy is right now, and it's not running an
errand. He's on a bar stool at Patrick's getting loaded." Kelly defends Sipowicz, causing Fancy to pass harsh (but accurate) judgment:
"Andy was a great cop. Now he's a drunk that won't help himself."
Fancy recognizes that, no matter how bigoted Sipowicz may be, the
detective has honorably served the New York Police Department by
excelling at his job. Sipowicz, however, demonstrates no appreciation
of Fancy's calm and rational fairness when confronting the lieutenant two episodes later, in the Milch-written "Brown Appetit" (1.3).[25]
Fancy refuses to return Sipowicz, who is still recovering from gunshot
wounds sustained in the pilot episode, to active investigative duty
after Sipowicz visits Giardella's upscale hotel room, argues with him
(Giardella, having agreed to testify against his former Mafia associates, is under the protection of federal marshals), and throws a plant
at his head. Sipowicz, angered by Fancy's decision, yells about his

light workload to the entire squad. Fancy responds to this challenge to his authority by telling Sipowicz that the detective can speak his mind, without fear of reprisal from a higher-ranking officer, once the day's shift is finished.

This conversation is *NYPD Blue*'s first sustained depiction of Sipowicz's prejudice, demonstrating not only how deeply his racist feelings run but also how honestly the series dramatizes the workplace tensions that racial disharmony can produce.

FANCY. I've got my personal opinions about you. I think you're an asshole—

SIPOWICZ. I think you're an asshole.

FANCY. But that hasn't affected how I've treated you on the job.

SIPOWICZ. You really believe that?

FANCY. Yeah, I really believe it.

SIPOWICZ (*snorts*). You guys make me laugh.

FANCY. Now what guys would you be referring to?

SIPOWICZ. Black bosses.

FANCY. Well, that didn't take long.

SIPOWICZ. I thought I was supposed to feel free to express my opinions.

FANCY. Well, for you, I guess that means being a bigot.

SIPOWICZ. Hey, I'm not up nights thinkin' about the two of us out for ribs, but all I was sayin' is you guys live inside the books. You act like machines, you know? You don't like somebody, you go after 'em like Robohumps.

FANCY. Well, you think we might play it close to the vest because we know people are watching for us to mess up?

SIPOWICZ. Oh, makes you nervous, doesn't it, huh? Somebody always looking over your shoulders, waiting for you to make a mistake? . . .

FANCY. The truth is, I've cut you slack because you *were* a good cop and you *were* a good teacher.

SIPOWICZ. I could be that again. I could be that again if you would just get your damn foot off my neck.

Sipowicz, who claims to have raised "that kid" (Kelly), then asks Fancy, "You like this, huh? Seeing people embarrass themselves?" Fancy, studying Sipowicz's distressed features, tells him, "You're not embarrassing yourself. Not now."

This confrontation—masterfully performed by McDaniel and Franz—includes vividly charged racial imagery. Sipowicz invokes numerous stereotypes, including black men who eat ribs and black supervisors who robotically enforce bureaucratic rules no matter how absurd these regulations seem. The most startling image, of Fancy keeping his foot on Sipowicz's neck, literalizes the white fear that African Americans who gain positions of power, authority, and influence will vigorously oppress Caucasian men. Fancy, in this formulation, reverses the traditional power relationships between white and black Americans by becoming "the man" who keeps Sipowicz down. The fact that Sipowicz's irrational behavior causes his own problems does not occur to him, yet Fancy correctly notes that he (Fancy) has been more patient with Sipowicz than the detective deserves. Fancy's dialogue also invokes a significant challenge in the professional lives of African Americans: the fact that—due to the racist associations of black people with incompetence, indolence, and stupidity—African Americans must work harder and perform better than their white counterparts simply to be judged as equal.

Fancy gives no ground to Sipowicz's bigotry but credits the man's sincerity for wanting to reclaim his status as an effective cop and valued mentor. Fancy returns Sipowicz to active duty the next morning, illustrating how fair a squad commander he is, but this choice raises a troubling issue about Fancy's authority. Does the lieutenant's empathy with Sipowicz's emotional distress, no matter how admirable, undermine Fancy's avowed commitment to justice? Keeping a detective whom Kenneth Meeks, in his essay "Racism and Reality in *NYPD Blue*," accurately describes as "anti-immigrant, anti-poor and anti-African American"[26] on the force allows Sipowicz (no matter how good he is at his job) to mistreat, harass, and verbally abuse the minority residents whom he encounters. This policy seems counterproductive since Sipowicz's racial insensitivities can (and do) disrupt, as much as they assist, official investigations.

NYPD Blue, according to cocreator Bochco, does not evade these unfortunate facts. The program, Bochco claims, allows Milch "to exorcise some of his demons or, certainly, to turn a light on in the room where they reside. None of this was done from a distance. He took on addiction, alcoholism, racism—things that are just so fundamental to our nature and things that are dangerous in society he found a way to explore cold-bloodedly."[27] This cold-bloodedness, like Clark's hard-minded details, causes Milch to favor Sipowicz even when the detective's racism is contemptible. Milch, in writing "Brown Appetit," acknowledges Sipowicz's toxic racial beliefs, even giving Fancy the upper hand in the just-quoted scene, but still allows Sipowicz to escape the consequences that should follow any police officer (of any race or ethnicity) who behaves as abominably as Sipowicz. Milch and *NYPD Blue*, in Bochco's formulation, illustrate a regrettable truth about the American criminal-justice system: that prejudiced law-enforcement officers stay in their jobs unless extraordinary circumstances force their removal. As the acquittals of white officers involved in the Rodney King and Amadou Diallo cases prove, evidence of police racism can be not only contested by defense attorneys but also ignored by juries when allegations of racist behavior prove accurate. Overlooking this reality, according to Bochco's argument, would diminish *NYPD Blue*'s credibility even if, as Meeks writes, the police department depicted in *NYPD Blue* "captures a lot of the frustration and social problems (e.g., race relations, community mistrust, racial profiling, etc.) that New Yorkers of color have to deal with everyday. It's a sanitized version of real life, but still compelling enough to capture my attention."[28]

Fancy's refusal to fire Sipowicz (or at least sanction him) may speak to institutional constraints that prevent Fancy from doing so, whether these restrictions involve Civil Service hearings, civilian lawsuits, or both. The tenor of his argument with Sipowicz in "Brown Appetit," however, conveys compassion for Sipowicz's suffering more than fear of bureaucratic entanglements. Fancy is no pushover, but his decision to return Sipowicz to duty sanitizes the man's unacceptable conduct to suggest that Fancy's professionalism privileges Sipowicz's career over the community's need for justice.

To Milch's credit, Sipowicz's racism becomes an ongoing theme that *NYPD Blue* explores in sometimes commendable detail. The detective's rib comment, for instance, inspires the first season's two finest scenes, both in the episode "Oscar, Meyer, Weiner" (1.10).[29] Sipowicz, investigating the home invasion and massacre of the wealthy (and white) Sloane family, discovers that the only surviving daughter, Rebecca (Renée O'Connor), is a Bennington College student who once dated a black man named Lewis Futrel (Clifton Powell). Futrel, an architecture student at Hunter College, resents police questioning, causing a confrontation that surprises and angers Sipowicz.

FUTREL. Oh, I get it. I may not be a criminal, but you get enough niggers together and some of them must be.

SIPOWICZ. Mr. Futrel, Rebecca said one of the reasons she broke up with you was you hung with kind of a rough crowd.

FUTREL (*raising his voice*). So I go to the criminal niggers, say, "Guess what? I'm bonin' this rich white girl. Let me tell you where she lives, where her mama hides her jewelry." That the scenario you're envisioning, Detective Sipowicz?

SIPOWICZ. Mr. Futrel, have I been disrespectful to you?

FUTREL. *This* is disrespectful. Me being here is disrespectful.

SIPOWICZ (*raising his voice*). Hey, pal, you know I'm trying to find some assholes before they murder another innocent family. It so happens these particular assholes happen to be black. Now how do you want me to go about this, huh? Maybe I should start each question with, uh, you know, "I'm sorry for the injustices the white man has inflicted upon your race, but can you provide me any information?" Or "I'm sorry your people are downtrodden for three hundred years, but did you discuss the layout of the Sloane house with any of your friends?"

FUTREL. Yeah, do it like that.

SIPOWICZ. Yeah? Okay, all right. You know, I know that great African American George Washington Carver discovered the peanut, but can you provide names and addresses of these friends?

FUTREL. You know, you're a racist scumbag.

SIPOWICZ. Ouch.

Franz and Powell perform this scene expertly, but Futrel's rage seems unprovoked not only to Sipowicz but also to *NYPD Blue*'s regular viewers (who, by this point in the series, have seen enough interrogations that uncooperative witnesses strike them as unhelpful, unsophisticated, and unappealing). Futrel's reaction, indeed, illustrates the "angry black man" stereotype that Sipowicz's mocking references to injustice, segregation, and George Washington Carver implicitly deride. Although Sipowicz, the interrogator, should remain calm in the face of Futrel's anger, he instead exacerbates a tense situation. Sipowicz, beyond losing his temper, voices an idea common in late 20th-century racist formulations of the American experience, namely, white exhaustion with all discussions of race. Reminders about white complicity in the political, economic, and social oppression of minority populations becomes a burden that white people, according to Sipowicz's view, should no longer need to carry. Historical guilt about slavery and segregation, according to this argument, becomes an unproductive emotion that unfairly tags all Caucasians as racists.

Sipowicz, by dismissing Futrel's legitimate concerns about racial profiling, evokes these strong yet misguided feelings. The scene presents Sipowicz as the aggrieved party, as the honest investigator following leads (early in their discussion, Sipowicz tells Futrel that Futrel is a model citizen), even though Sipowicz's personal history of bigotry complicates the situation more profoundly than director Bradley Silberling claims in his DVD commentary for "Oscar, Meyer, Weiner." Silberling says, without further elaboration, that the episode creates a case where the racist Sipowicz is correct.[30] This conclusion is simply untrue. Futrel's friends prove to be innocent when Detective Kelly secures a confession from the Sloane family's Caucasian maid, Renee (Betsy Aidem), a drug addict in need of money, that she gave information about the home's layout to her drug dealer, who in turn sold it to the (African American) thieves.

Futrel, when he learns the truth, returns to the squad room to challenge Sipowicz. This scene also depicts Futrel as an irrationally angry black man who again raises his voice, invokes the term *nigger* ("I want to hear you say that me and my friends are not suspects, which Detective Andrew Sipowicz might find it hard to believe, since he thinks we're all a bunch of low-life niggers!"), and calls Sipowicz an "ignorant cracker bigot." Fancy intercedes, telling Futrel to leave, only to experience the man's ire: "They lettin' you work in the Big House now, boy? What door you come in?" Futrel, channeling Malcolm X, suggests that Fancy is a "house negro," or a black man who makes himself subservient to his white masters. This insult marks Futrel as a black-pride advocate, which, in the racial economy of a series centering on Sipowicz, also codes Futrel as an extremist. Powell's textured performance suggests the anger of a man who has experienced years of discrimination at the hands of unjust police officers, but no greater insight into his life appears, leaving "Oscar, Meyer, Weiner" to portray Futrel as a threatening, loud, and enraged black man who provokes justifiable disdain in Sipowicz.

Milch addresses this problematic representation of Futrel's personality in *True Blue*'s 15th chapter by recounting "the shitstorm created by a talk I'd given to some aspiring writers" organized by the founders of the Humanitas Prize.[31] Milch, during this lecture, speculates that many television programs place black characters in supporting, authority-figure roles because these shows desire the appearance of liberalism without portraying "in scope or depth minority characters with whom their writers were less comfortable or had less familiarity" before admitting that he, as a Caucasian, approached the portrayal of Fancy's character with "less sense of imaginative authority" than for *NYPD Blue*'s other characters.[32] This statement leads some members of Milch's audience to ask combative questions, including whether or not Milch enjoys writing racist characters like Sipowicz. Milch, in what reads like a confession to unconscious bigotry, replies that one of "writing's pleasures was giving yourself whole-souled in imagination to a different being, parts of whom you might have drawn from yourself."[33]

Milch's disquisition honestly confronts the problems that white authors face when writing authentic black characters for American television. His response enacts Bochco's supposition that *NYPD Blue* helps Milch examine, explore, and exorcise personal demons (in this case, racial prejudice). The pleasure that Milch takes in giving himself "whole-souled" to different characters also implies that he not only better understands his own racial biases by writing Sipowicz's bigotries into "Oscar, Meyer, Weiner" but also better comprehends the inequitable treatment of African Americans by writing Fancy's and Futrel's contrasting reactions. Commendable as these efforts are, Milch ignores the fact that Futrel, an interloper in the 15th Precinct's professional (if dysfunctional) family, appears unreasonable although the investigation's results prove his anger to be legitimate. *NYPD Blue*, rather than acknowledging this truth, adopts the cop-shop perspective that uncooperative witnesses are untrustworthy, unhappy, and unpleasant people who interfere with the smooth functioning of daily police work.

Milch, in his Humanitas lecture, titled "The Challenges and Pitfalls of Portraying Human Values in Entertainment Writing," tells the audience that, although he had enjoyed Sipowicz's attitude in the "Oscar, Meyer, Weiner" interrogation scene, "I'd equally enjoyed writing the part of Futrel,"[34] but failed to mention the pleasure he took in writing Futrel's responses to Sipowicz's racism due to the accusatory questions he had been asked. This notion further supports Milch's struggle to understand the lives of people unlike him by writing about their complexities and contradictions, but Futrel's character, no matter how enjoyable his creation was for Milch, remains little more than Sipowicz's racial foil. He receives none of the generous understanding that *NYPD Blue*, as Sterne notes, extends to its detectives.

Had "Oscar, Meyer, Weiner" concluded with Futrel and Sipowicz's second argument, the episode would demonstrate a reactionary political attitude toward black people, Lieutenant Fancy, and American racism. Milch, however, writes in *True Blue* that he felt uneasy after finishing the script's first draft.[35] Milch then composed a scene that demonstrates how insightful a television dramatist he can be. Fancy invites Sipowicz to dinner once Futrel leaves the squad room, taking the detective to Sherman's Bar-B-Q, a black-owned and -operated rib restaurant where Sipowicz, while eating, appears uncomfortable as he watches the establishment's black employees and patrons. His ensuing dialogue with Fancy becomes a remarkable exploration of race, power, police tactics, and social injustice, with Sipowicz defending his part in the Sloane investigation as procedurally sound because his witness statements implicated four black men. Fancy agrees, telling Sipowicz that he handled the case properly, and then asks why Sipowicz is not enjoying his meal.

SIPOWICZ.   Hey, Lieutenant, let me know when you get done busting my balls.
FANCY.   Is it the atmosphere, Andy?
SIPOWICZ.   Oh, that's possible. Something about me being the only white guy here.
FANCY.   Now why is that a problem? Is it because you feel this isn't your place, and maybe some of these people think so too? Maybe a few of 'em just don't like you?
SIPOWICZ.   Look, what's your point, Lieutenant?
FANCY.   You're being served, aren't you, Andy? They cooked those ribs for you. Maybe they wanted to spit in your plate (*Sipowicz's eyes widen*), but they didn't. They served your white ass just like they would anybody else who came in here. Even though some of 'em hate your guts. So why would you feel uncomfortable? You got your meal. What difference does it make what they're thinking? That they don't like you? Hey, that's just an opinion. Why should that bother you? They're still doing their jobs. (*Sipowicz says nothing.*) Now what if they had badges and guns?

This scene alters the power dynamic between Fancy and Sipowicz, for, despite Fancy's greater rank, "Oscar, Meyer, Weiner," like its parent series, awards narrative primacy to Sipowicz. Fancy's concluding monologue not only challenges but also reverses Sipowicz's unstated prejudices by, for a short time, placing him (and the viewer) in the subaltern position that African Americans (even those in positions of authority such as Fancy) occupy every day of their lives.

Director Silberling correctly evaluates this final scene as "a beautiful piece of writing with athletic performances" that forces the audience to reconsider Sipowicz's behavior.[36] Fancy's lucid monologue exposes the detective's response to Futrel as an example of unthinking ignorance and as one of the subtlest forms of racism that any person can indulge. Fancy's dialogue, delivered by McDaniel with restrained passion, allows the viewer to understand (and even empathize with) Futrel's rage at being questioned by a white detective who represents a police force famous for its dismissive treatment of African Americans. "Oscar, Meyer, Weiner" ends with a speechless Sipowicz considering Fancy's words as the lieutenant treats him to the meal. Fancy sketches the anxiety that African Americans feel around police officers with remarkably concise power, illustrating what Martin Luther King Jr., in his "Letter from Birmingham City Jail," calls the feeling of "living constantly at tiptoe stance never quite knowing what to expect next, and plagued with inner fears and outer resentments"[37] to demonstrate just how oppressive the police seem (and are) to minority populations. Fancy's speech, indeed, ironizes his judgment that Sipowicz handled the Sloane investigation properly, while the lieutenant's calm demeanor effectively counters Futrel's testy attitude to legitimize Futrel's feelings. This scene demonstrates how *NYPD Blue*'s best work punctures its conventional, us-versus-them, cop-shop perspective to probe the intricate social forces that keep racial tension, anger, and misunderstanding alive.

Milch, however, accepts no plaudits for the precision of this episode's social commentary, attributing the final scene's necessity to authorial integrity, recognizing that, if "Oscar, Meyer, Weiner" concluded with Futrel's second confrontation with Sipowicz, not only would it "take its final emotional stamp from Sipowicz's sensibility; it would also have portrayed Fancy as this sensibility's willing executioner. That wasn't true to *Fancy's* nature."[38] Milch, in other words, has few moral reservations about Sipowicz's racism (which, indeed, is true to the detective's character) but instead believes that concluding the story without the rib-joint conversation would fail to present "some act on Fancy's part that clarified his deeper feelings about what had transpired between Sipowicz and Futrel."[39] Writing the concluding scene causes Milch to begin "to feel Fancy come alive in my imagination."[40] The episode's conclusion, therefore, develops not from "its more morally elevated perspective...but from my sense of craft."[41]

Milch, by favoring craft over morality, not only implies that he resisted political correctness in fashioning Fancy and Sipowicz's final conversation in "Oscar, Meyer, Weiner" but also indicates lingering discomfort with the ugly realities of American racism, especially police racism. Yet the scene itself incisively demolishes the basis of Sipowicz's bigotry to illuminate how Milch's television writing is more sociologically sophisticated than his expository analysis. This pattern recurs throughout *True Blue* and *NYPD Blue*, for Milch's keen dramatic instincts occasionally dismantle the cop-show conventions that *NYPD Blue* obeys. Achieving a more capacious appreciation of Fancy's and Futrel's lives by writing the script for "Oscar, Meyer, Weiner" also justifies Milch's faith in television writing's significance. *True Blue's* 15th chapter ends with Milch telling the Humanitas lecture's audience that "[enlarging] our spirits through pursuit of our craft [is] one of the blessings of our profession."[42]

This enlarged spirit, however, does not lead Milch or *NYPD Blue* to erroneously conclude that bigots change their views easily or all at once. Sipowicz, rather than renouncing his racist ways as a result of Fancy's chat, continues the *NYPD Blue* tradition of "white (in most instances) detectives verbally and sometimes physically assaulting African-Americans or Hispanics in custody," images that, Sterne writes, are "bound to be vivid in the mind of anyone who has watched" the series.[43] Sipowicz mostly keeps quiet about his prejudices, at least in official discussions with Fancy, although stray comments about African Americans, Latinos, other ethnic groups, women, and homosexuals arise, mostly played for comic effect as other characters, particularly Sipowicz's partners—Bobby Simoné (Jimmy Smits), Danny Sorenson (Rick Schroeder), and John Clark (Mark-Paul Gosselaar)—shake their heads in amused acceptance of Sipowicz's foibles.

Sipowicz's racism rebounds in two fascinating episodes involving the community activist Kwasi Olushola (Tom Wright): "The Backboard Jungle" (3.10) and "Where's 'Swaldo?" (4.4). "The Backboard Jungle" finds the 15th Precinct investigating multiple shootings at a community basketball game organized by Olushola as a tribute to a young black man who died in police custody.[44] Fancy, prior to the episode's events, agrees to keep officers and detectives away from the game, but rival gang members begin firing at one another, killing two bystanders and wounding seven more. Sipowicz cannot hide his disdain for Fancy's decision, suggesting that the shooting started because "somebody missed a layup" and that the event was bound to result in violence because gang members freely mingled with onlookers.

Sipowicz and Simone go to a local hospital to question Olushola, interrupting the man's interview with *Village View* reporter Dave Bloom (Adam Goldberg). Olushola angrily yells about New York Police Department racism, telling Sipowicz, "I don't have to go anywhere with you. You dealin' with that one nigger in a thousand who knows what you can and cannot do." Sipowicz responds by saying, "I'm dealing with the nigger whose big mouth is responsible for this massacre." Simone tells Sipowicz to shut up, but when Olushola lays hands on Sipowicz, Simone arrests the activist for assaulting a police officer. While helping Simone herd Olushola into an elevator, Sipowicz refuses to answer Bloom's question about whether or not he (Sipowicz) frequently uses racial epithets.

The altercation, however, does not end here. Olushola continues to speak his mind.

OLUSHOLA.   Black people shootin' each other. Me in handcuffs. This day just keeps gettin' better and better for you.
SIPOWICZ.   I'm doin' my job, Kwasi. Plus, you know a white girl was shot, too. Her only mistake was bein' in a car on Houston Street when your low-life homeys decide to act their color.
OLUSHOLA.   You racist son of a bitch. I knew you were a stonecold racist the minute I laid eyes on you.
SIPOWICZ.   You're gonna make me bust out cryin' you keep calling me that.

Olushola's provocation in the first exchange does not justify Sipowicz's response, even though Sipowicz later claims that he was simply throwing the term *nigger* back at Olushola. Detectives, rather than escalating such confrontations, should minimize their tensions. Olushola also uses the word *nigger* mockingly, as a way of ridiculing what he perceives as the police department's prejudicial treatment of African Americans, but Sipowicz, angered by Olushola's defiant attitude, uses the word insultingly, to rebuke Olushola's political convictions. Sipowicz's later statement—about Olushola's low-life homeys acting their color—is perhaps the detective's most naked display of bigotry, stereotyping African Americans as thuggish, violent, and contemptible criminals. Simone is left speechless, a reaction that emphasizes his startled and angered expression.

Fancy removes Sipowicz from the case when Olushola tells him about the detective's behavior, but not before securing Olushola's assistance in helping find the shooters. Sipowicz takes the news poorly, but Simone (a man of French-Portuguese descent) refuses to let the matter drop.

> SIMONE.   Well, I guess Fancy's just actin' his color. What you said in that elevator, about those low-life homeys decidin' to act black?
>
> SIPOWICZ.   So you got a problem with me, too?
>
> SIMONE.   Partner, I was not comfortable with those words. I am not comfortable with the thoughts behind it. I just want you to understand that.
>
> SIPOWICZ.   So this Kwasi can break my balls. When I decide to give a little back, I'm the asshole.
>
> SIMONE.   Givin' it back? Was that all it was?
>
> SIPOWICZ.   Do me a favor, all right. Finish your sermon another time.

This short scene further illustrates the racial tensions that affect the squad's ability to work as a cohesive unit, although all problems emanate from Sipowicz. His attitude disrupts the investigation, which Fancy points out when Sipowicz confronts the lieutenant before going home.

This exchange parallels the final scene in "Oscar, Meyer, Weiner," with Fancy once again trying to show Sipowicz how unfair and unproductive his bigotry is. Sipowicz admits to having said the word *nigger* and to having "thought it plenty," but he says that he never used it "on the job till your hump pal put us on that road." Fancy claims not to be concerned about racial epithets as much as how Sipowicz's behavior interferes with the investigation, which, through Simone's efforts, concludes with the shooters in custody. Fancy also tells Sipowicz that he (Fancy) has spent part of his day "tryin' to save your sorry ass." When Sipowicz grunts, not believing Fancy, their conversation explores the hostile territory of institutional racism.

> FANCY.   I'm not gonna take you out, Andy. I move you out, my white bosses, they send me a little message. They send me

another one just like you, but maybe that one can't do the job like you can.

SIPOWICZ.   Geez, thanks a lot, boss.

FANCY.   If you go, it'll be somebody like Kwasi or like that reporter. I've been dealin' with white cops like you ever since the academy. I can manage you with my eyes closed. Now maybe you can't handle a black man bein' your boss.

SIPOWICZ.   I can handle it. I've been covering you three-and-a-half years except when you get so tied up in your brother-brother crap you won't let us work the streets. That's when you get yourself in trouble.

Fancy, who earlier in "The Backboard Jungle" takes the blame for the courtside shooting at the request of his superior, Inspector Aiello (Andy Romano), knows that his white supervisors may well punish him if he fires Sipowicz. Fancy also notes the racism that he has faced since his earliest days on the force, exposing the institutional bigotry that constrains his own power. These frustrations, however, do not prevent Fancy from recognizing, even under such difficult circumstances, Sipowicz's professional competence. Sipowicz, however, remains self-centered, even narcissistic, by claiming to have protected Fancy except for those moments when the lieutenant's racial allegiance to his own people interferes with good police work.

Sipowicz's opinion, however, overlooks the historically tense relationship between the New York City Police Department and African Americans (as well as other minority populations).[45] He presumes that "working the streets" is a racially, ethnically, and ethically neutral prospect, not a pursuit influenced by the ideas, preconceptions, and prejudices of the officers conducting investigations. These biases create enough mutual mistrust between the police and minority communities that establishing the facts of a case as overwrought as the basketball shooting is difficult, if not impossible. Sipowicz, the white detective, also assumes that he knows the streets, police work, and the truth about a case better than Fancy, thereby ignoring the history of discrimination that Fancy has faced inside the department. Sipowicz's perspective is frighteningly true to life insofar as bigoted white cops do not necessarily see themselves as bigots but rather as people enduring the political, social, and economic upheavals that destroy communities by upsetting the previous (and largely mythical) social order of a fair, democratic, and just society that, this viewpoint suggests, is plagued by criminals who parasitically destroy the values of law, order, and respect for authority (not people whom systemic bigotries constrain and oppress). Sipowicz dismisses the harsh experiences that Fancy and Olushola have endured as "brother-brother crap" but protests when he feels that Fancy dismisses his (Sipowicz's) grievances as a white detective whose lieutenant may harbor racial grudges against him. Sipowicz's inability to see the paradox of this position speaks to his narrow-minded perspective as much as to his explicit racism. *NYPD Blue,* by dramatizing Sipowicz's deepseated prejudices, clarifies how tragically absurd they are.

Sipowicz also dislikes Olushola because, like Futrel in "Oscar, Meyer, Weiner," Olushola aggressively asserts himself, refusing to bow to the detective's authority. Olushola's black pride (symbolized by his colorful African *kofia*) and combative attitude, however, code him as a bitter, forceful, and angry black man who resents the police on sight, while the episode criticizes institutional racism only elliptically, when Fancy briefly mentions his academy days and his white bosses. This depiction privileges Sipowicz over Olushola even though Fancy and Simone both rebuke Sipowicz for his beliefs, behavior, and obstinacy. Even Sipowicz's pregnant wife, Assistant District Attorney Costas, tells him in the episode's final scene not to teach their unborn son to think in racist terms, to which the clearly miffed Sipowicz mumbles, "Yeah, all right." The episode exposes Sipowicz's numerous bigotries in exacting detail (Franz gives a performance of amazing ferocity) but refuses to indict the legal system, the police department, or the divided society that allows his racial animosities to develop. Sipowicz, as always, requires redemption; the criminal-justice system does not.

This theme continues in "Where's 'Swaldo?" when Olushola is discovered shot dead in the driver's seat of a car (with another dead man in the back seat).[46] The investigation, during which Sipowicz expresses more disdain for Olushola's beliefs and actions, leads Simone and Sipowicz to question Olushola's young daughter, Hanna Torrence (Jurnee Smollett), an innocent girl who believes her father to be a good man who helped others. Sipowicz and Simone discover that Olushola was, in fact, assisting his brother-in-law Jerome (Anthony Lee), a building superintendent, when Jerome discovered drugs in his building's basement. Jerome turned the drugs in to his local police station, but the drug dealer—named Prince—threatened to harm Jerome if he did not compensate the dealer for the money that he had lost. Olushola was killed in a drive-by shooting while attempting to get Prince to leave Jerome in peace.

This information bears out Olushola's humanitarian nature, forcing Sipowicz to rethink his negative attitude toward the man. When Hanna and her mother, Mrs. Torrence (Suzzanne Douglas), come to the squad room to discover what happened to Olushola, Sipowicz expresses admiration for Olushola and sympathy for his loss. Mrs. Torrence, however, berates Sipowicz for calling Olushola a nigger, telling the startled detective that "people who hated him alive don't get to say nice things now." When Sipowicz apologizes to Hanna for using "that word" to describe her father, the girl shakes his hand.

These events so rattle Sipowicz that, in the episode's remarkable final scene, he unveils to Simone, in the squad's restroom/locker room, the basis of his antiblack racism. Sipowicz, asking, "Did you hear her tell that little girl to hate me?" reveals that he joined the police department immediately after returning from military service in the Vietnam War, then became an undercover informant infiltrating the Young Patriots, which Sipowicz describes as "like the woman's auxiliary for the Black Panthers." The language he chooses to describe this experience, however, provokes an angry response from Simone. Sipowicz, by his own account, became an errand boy for the Panthers, supporting their political views and even agreeing to help them rob a bank. Sipowicz, however, so disliked this work that he would "drink myself stupid so as not to run my head into the wall thinking how much I hate what I'm doin'." Sipowicz's contempt for his undercover work culminates when he says that he did not sit in rice paddies or endure the terrors of combat so that he could return to America to "hear my country get pissed on by a bunch of spades!"

Simone, at this point, forcefully tells Sipowicz not to use such language, but Sipowicz claims that he is only trying to explain his situation. Simone gives no ground to this rationalization.

> SIMONE.   And I'm telling you that when you use that kind of language I can't get to what you're saying. You don't have to call 'em spades to tell what happened.
> SIPOWICZ.   Spades is how I feel!
> SIMONE.   You call that little girl a spade?
> SIPOWICZ.   She's not who I was talking about.
> SIMONE.   Well, that's who I see when you're talking. You follow my problem?

Simone, who nearly walks out the door during this exchange, gives his partner permission to continue. Sipowicz, having already confessed to harboring profound self-hatred due to his service in Vietnam, now links this hatred to a difficult childhood.

SIPOWICZ. I dreamt of being a cop. Now a cop sees me on the street he spits—he spits on the ground. And I know he's supposed to 'cause, 'cause I'm kissing bastards' asses want to blow up the bank that my mother pays our house loans at. And I'm telling these bastards how brave and great I think they are. How I love it when my dad—he, he finally saved enough after he's in the service to move us from the Quonsets and we're finally in a decent neighborhood until they move in and I gotta fight to keep my lunch money and the project turns into a sty and he gets his eye put out by one of 'em drunk with a hammer who don't want his gas meter read! To have her tell that little girl to hate me—(*sighs*) I try to do my job. Put your own feelings aside unless they show you they're wrong and that sweet little girl is told to hate me.

SIMONE. But what is she supposed to do, Andy? She supposed to feel sorry for you? She's supposed to think it's okay you call her father a nigger because you had bad times growing up?

SIPOWICZ. I had bad times from them people my whole life.

SIMONE. Hey, my dad got his ass kicked at shape-ups by white longshoreman for being dark skinned. I don't hate *them people* and I don't hate you.

SIPOWICZ. But I'm supposed to care what happened to her people three hundred years ago.

SIMONE. There you go.

SIPOWICZ. At least she shook my hand.

SIMONE. Yeah.

SIPOWICZ. I don't think she hated me that much.

Franz and Smits are extraordinary in this long scene, with Sipowicz's bile, rage, and poisonous words forcing Simone to respond. Franz projects anger, disbelief, and self-loathing, while Smits remains quiet until Sipowicz's racial epithets provoke his irate response. Smits's expression, particularly as the scene concludes, mixes disgust, indignation, exasperation, and sorrow to illustrate Simone's conflicted emotions while listening to Sipowicz's rant.

The scene's taut, tense, and terrific dialogue characterizes Milch's writing (he coauthors this episode with Stephen Gaghan and Michael R. Perry), but the most illuminating element of "Where's 'Swaldo?" is the complex, contradictory, and compelling personal history that Sipowicz sketches. His rough childhood, when combined with the traumas of fighting in Vietnam and the difficulties of undercover police work, produces a ruinous, noxious, and unforgiving racism. Sipowicz voices specious charges against black Americans that dramatize the racist ideology of "white flight," the social phenomenon that not only followed the 1954 *Brown v. Board of Education* Supreme Court school-desegregation ruling but also accompanied the migration of African Americans into previously all-white enclaves of major American cities. This ideology holds that the dirty habits, violent tendencies, and low-class living standards of black Americans destroy previously stable neighborhoods, make life harder for white children (as if living in segregated America was easy for black children), and promote cultural, economic, and political miscegenation. Simone punctures Sipowicz's narcissism—an emotional blindness that reduces all racial slights to personal insults and that recognizes white Americans as inherently superior—by referring to his (Simone's) father's biography. Simone does not hate Caucasians in general or Sipowicz in specific, refusing to generalize his father's poor treatment by white men to an entire ethnic or racial group. The episode concludes ambivalently, with Sipowicz distressed by the possibility that Hanna may one day learn to hate him.

Sipowicz endorses many fallacies in this scene, beginning with the misperception that Mrs. Torrence instructs Hanna to hate him. Meeks, in "Racism and Reality in *NYPD Blue,*" claims that "racial prejudice still kept Hannah's [*sic*] mother from accepting Sipowicz's attempt at making things right," demonstrating "just how stupid racial prejudices are, and how they interfere with human compassion,"[47] but this response takes Sipowicz's statements at face value. Mrs. Torrence does not explicitly or implicitly instruct Hanna to hate Sipowicz, but rather passionately illustrates how his racism evokes dislike, distrust, and distress in the African American people whom he offends. Sipowicz holds Hanna apart from "them people" because of her young age, but Torrence wishes to expose, not hide, the racial malice that diminishes Olushola's person due to his skin color. Hanna's forgiving nature, in an ironic twist, promises partial redemption for Sipowicz, but, as his later interaction with Simone proves, this redemption remains fractious, incomplete, and unresolved.

"Where's 'Swaldo?" further interrogates Sipowicz's ongoing battle with bigotry but leaves the matter here, at a personal (rather than professional) level. The episode showcases Franz's and Smits's consummate acting talents along with Milch's ability to unflinchingly face the emotional attrition that racism costs a white homicide detective. "Where's 'Swaldo?" and, before it, "The Backboard Jungle" offer far more nuance about race, racism, and police bigotry than *Hill Street Blues*'s "Trial by Fury," but this accomplishment, however fascinating as a character study of individual white racism, avoids dealing with the institutional prejudice that allows such bigotry to flourish.

This analysis should not imply that Milch's work on *NYPD Blue* is racist, only that his allegiance to deepening Sipowicz's character ignores the broader social, economic, political, and structural causes of racism that Attanasio's *Homicide: Life on the Street*, Simon's *The Wire*, and Milch's *Deadwood* boldly examine. Such dramatic oversights lead Sterne to declare that "only people who are presumed to be criminals, or are witnesses to crimes, or informants about criminals, go to or get dragged to police stations. What this means is that the boundaries of the police show genre must be trampled if a 'realistic' series is to be other than a succession of narratives in which…the forces of law and order seek and grill and bash perps."[48]

Sterne's assessment of the police drama, while untrue in relation to *The Wire*, applies to many *NYPD Blue* episodes. His analysis, however, overlooks the manner in which Sipowicz's redemption frequently symbolizes the institution for which he works. Sterne also assumes that Milch's approach to racism, bigotry, police brutality, and social injustice is monolithic. In fact, Milch's hiring practices, personal feelings, and writing habits manifest more variation than Sterne suggests when he claims that Amnesty International's 1996 report *Police Brutality and Excessive Force in the New York City Police Department*—a document that rightly criticizes the widespread brutality (frequently linked to racism) that Amnesty's investigation revealed in New York's police force—"should make us want in television police shows—because they'll obviously continue to be popular—something more deeply true to reality than the kind of 'realism' of which David Milch is so proud."[49]

Sterne covets such realism while noting that *NYPD Blue* rarely lives up to this standard. Milch, however, allows different voices and attitudes to comment on *NYPD Blue*'s depiction of race. One of Milch's shrewdest decisions involved hiring David Mills, who worked as a staff writer during *NYPD Blue*'s second, third, and fourth seasons.

Mills wrote "The Backboard Jungle," among other episodes; authored a few excellent *Homicide: Life on the Street* scripts; and collaborated with Simon in writing HBO's six-hour 2000 miniseries *The Corner,* a splendid, realistic, and powerful adaptation of Simon and Edward Burns's 1997 book *The Corner: A Year in the Life of an Inner-City Neighborhood.* Mills also wrote two episodes of Simon's *The Wire* and two episodes of Simon and Eric Overmyer's excellent HBO New Orleans drama *Treme* (2010–present) before his untimely death on March 30, 2010. Mills came to Milch's attention in the controversial aftermath of Milch's 1994 Humanitas lecture. When asked why so few African Americans write television drama, Milch, according to his *True Blue* account, suggested that black American writers have difficulty succeeding in a mass medium like television:

> When they wrote out of the complexities of their own experience in full scope and detail, the result might be powerful and compelling as art but not commercially successful (*"I* love it, but the audience doesn't tune in"); yet, because their imaginations and interests had been so forged in the crucible of their racial experience, when, in order to avoid the imputation of parochialism, they tried to write what they thought the *white* audience wanted to hear, their writing might lose emotional thrust and drive.[50]

This analysis probes the restrictions placed on black American writers by white expectations, including Milch's. His declaration that racial experience so influences the imagination of African American writers that they can write authentically only about events, characters, themes, and issues concerned with black life—while true insofar as all writers' lives, memories, and backgrounds affect their fiction—implies that African American authors cannot fully participate in the opportunities to enlarge their spirits that Milch thinks are a blessing of the writing profession. Black writers, in this conceptualization, remain confined to "the crucible of their racial experience," unlike Milch, who, earlier in *True Blue,* suggests that writing Fancy's role in "Oscar, Meyer, Weiner" allows him to understand black life better than he previously did. Milch's subtext indicates that black authors, at least in a mass medium whose audience is predominantly white, cannot achieve this worthy aspiration.

Milch's comments struggle to articulate the double consciousness that, as W.E.B. Du Bois's *The Souls of Black Folk* claims, afflicts African

Americans. Du Bois writes, "It is a peculiar sensation, this double-consciousness, this sense of always looking at one's self through the eyes of others, of measuring one's soul by the tape of a world that looks on in amused contempt and pity. One ever feels his two-ness,—an American, a Negro; two souls, two thoughts, two unreconciled strivings; two warring ideals in one dark body."[51] Whereas Du Bois recognizes that this dual consciousness causes every black American to long "to attain self-conscious manhood, to merge his double self into a better and true self [that] wishes neither of the older selves to be lost,"[52] Milch—despite his good-faith effort to explain the low number of African American television writers—suggests that black television authors cannot achieve an integrated self because the American television audience will not allow them to write African American characters whose lives encompass, but do not always involve, issues of bigotry and racism.

Milch, in his Humanitas lecture, then comments that, years before, he taught a seminar to introduce minority writers to the television-writing process.[53] A few white students audited this course, but, of the four participants who found success as television writers, none were African American. Milch notes, "This was meant as analysis, not endorsement" because he told the seminar's participants that black writers who choose to write for television "should expect to be frustrated by the market's resistance to their work; to be prepared as well for self-doubt and self-division."[54] Milch blames the ensuing controversy on negative press coverage, although his analysis (helpful as it may superficially seem) reinforces the double consciousness that Du Bois (and presumably Milch, who held the seminar to assist minority writers) wishes to eliminate by telling black writers to expect a type of self-division that white writers do not experience.

True Blue then reveals that Mills sent a letter to Milch after the Humanitas lecture that "congratulated me on guaranteeing the future employment of 'so many mediocre white motherfuckers.'"[55] When Milch realized that Mills had submitted a speculation script to *NYPD Blue,* he read the teleplay, liked it, and hired the African American Mills to bring a new voice to the show's previously all-white writing staff. Milch, indeed, praises his lecture's problematic remarks about race (because they brought Mills to his attention) by remembering Penn Warren's adage that "life is never tidy. If I hadn't stuck my foot in my mouth, I'd never have read David's work."[56] Milch's pleasure in hiring Mills, no matter how praiseworthy, suggests that Milch is proud of giving a talented black writer the chance to work for television rather than understanding how decades of discriminatory hiring practices have prevented minority authors from entering or rising within the entertainment industry. Milch, like Sipowicz, seems incapable of facing the structural barriers that keep minority workers from succeeding as much as their white counterparts, ascribing the constricted opportunities faced by African American television writers to the vagaries of white-audience prejudice rather than acknowledging the significant influence that a producer as powerful as he is has on the industry. Several letters to Milch from black writers make this point by expressing concern that his opinions may become "prescriptive justification for the hiring practices of other shows."[57]

These writers' dismay—including Mills's—is justifiable considering Hollywood's long history of discrimination against African American artists. Michael Warren, the actor who played Officer Bobby Hill for seven seasons on *Hill Street Blues,* laments that program's problems with giving his character a meaningful romantic relationship. Tom Shales's 1983 profile of Warren's (and acting partner Charles Haid's) contributions to *Hill Street* quotes Warren as saying, "Maybe they don't know how to write a serious relationship for a black couple. There are no black writers on the show. They say they were unable to find any."[58]

Hill Street's paucity of black writers may be one reason that Milch taught the seminar for minority authors that *True Blue* mentions, but the inability of Milch (and *Hill Street*'s other producers) to locate minority writers for the program speaks to the industry's myopia as much as to the lack of talented black authors. Warren's skepticism ("They *say* they were unable to find any") suggests that Milch and his fellow producers may not have searched for qualified black writers as intensively as they should have. Bringing Mills aboard *NYPD Blue*'s writing staff addresses a similar problem by allowing a black author to write about racism (particularly Sipowicz's racism). Milch, no matter what limitations may affect his own perspective, permits authors of different racial backgrounds to interrogate, explore, and dramatize bigotry on *NYPD Blue,* although these writers, like Milch himself, rarely examine racism's structural causes.

An exception that proves this rule is Mills's excellent "Taillight's Last Gleaming" (4.15).[59] The episode's opening sequence finds Fancy and his wife, Lillian (Tamara Tunie), stopped by two white patrol officers while driving home from dinner. Fancy's car has a broken taillight, but one officer, Szymanski (Christopher Stanley), forces both Fancy and Lillian, at gunpoint, to exit their vehicle, place their hands on its roof, and be searched, despite Fancy's protest that he is a police lieutenant. Szymanski, once Fancy establishes his identity, dismisses an obvious case of racial profiling as on-the-job safety consciousness. The next day, Fancy holds a meeting with Szymanski that Szymanski claims is nothing more than Fancy turning an innocuous traffic stop into "a black-and-white thing." Fancy then asks his own direct superior, Captain Clifford Bass (Larry Joshua), to transfer Szymanski from Queens to a precinct where the officer will have more contact with African Americans. Bass agrees, sending Szymanski to the Bedford-Stuyvesant precinct, but later tells Fancy that he has mismanaged the entire situation.

FANCY. Why is that?

BASS. The both of us know the job has an Ethical Awareness Course for this kind of cop in this kind of situation.

FANCY. The sensitivity class isn't going to do it for this guy.

BASS. Arthur, if Szymanski's like you say he is, don't like black people much to begin with, plus resentful now, from his point of view, a black boss loused his life up. Is that the kind of cop you want walking around a neighborhood don't need any extra problems?

FANCY. So you're concerned I'd be lowering the quality of life in Bed-Stuy?

BASS. I'm just pointin' out what I know you know already. As bosses, our decisions have consequences outside the rooms we make 'em in.

FANCY. If you want to discuss the quality of policing in black neighborhoods, we can take that up at length, but what's going on here is what always goes on with a black man on this job who asks for an accommodation. It's assumed he's got a hidden agenda.

BASS. Look, I came here asking for you to look at using your juice to hurt this guy and remind you that people neither you nor I know are liable to pay the tab. Pretending it's about you being black so you don't have to face what it is you're doing, that's on you.

FANCY. Okay. Okay. Transfer him to this precinct.

BASS. Transfer him here?

FANCY. Yeah, that way I can deal every day with the consequences of the decisions we made here.

BASS (*considers*). I think over time, knowing the kind of man
  you are at heart, might turn out good for Szymanski. Might be
  good for you, too.
FANCY. I think we've looked enough into my heart and soul,
  Captain.

Fancy identifies the institutional bigotries that affect his life within
the department's bureaucracy, as well as the lives of black residents
who must deal with racially insensitive officers, to argue that transferring Szymanski from Queens will improve the safety of the minority
residents that Szymanski will encounter. Fancy refuses Bass's contention that sensitivity courses will improve Szymanski's disposition or
that Fancy's character is at issue. Bass's attempt to turn the problem
back onto Fancy meets with intelligent analysis, racial insight, and
emotional impatience, as the lieutenant's final line of dialogue indicates (McDaniel's fine performance projects integrity, disbelief, and
pride rather than arrogance). The scene's subtext also suggests that
Fancy wishes to reform Szymanski not because Szymanski's racial
slight drives Fancy to seek vengeance but because Fancy recognizes
Szymanski as a younger version of the bigoted Sipowicz.
    "Taillight's Last Gleaming" more forthrightly dramatizes the institu-
tional law-enforcement prejudices facing African Americans, whether
civilians or police officers, than is typical for *NYPD Blue.* The Szymanski story line continues into future episodes, particularly "Bad Rap"
(4.19), written by Thad Mumford, when Internal Affairs investigates
charges that Szymanski stole $600 from drug dealer Clyde Bell (Badja
Djola) while arresting him. Szymanski claims that Fancy orchestrated
this bogus charge, but Fancy, suspecting Szymanski's innocence,
presses Bell to recant his statement implicating the patrol officer. Szymanski's African American partner, Officer Jones (Justin Lord), did not
witness the incident in question and tells Fancy that Szymanski has accused him (Jones) of participating in a racist plot to frame Szymanski.
Fancy pleads with the recalcitrant Szymanski to tell Internal Affairs
that he is innocent of the crime, leading Szymanski to admit that Fancy
was not wrong to believe that racial animus played a role in the traffic stop that begins "Taillight's Last Gleaming." Szymanski and Fancy
remain wary of one another even after the former's admission, but the
mutual distrust between them lessens.
    NYPD Blue, in these episodes, examines workplace racism more
carefully than previous outings, but this development does not signal

an overall trend for the series. Milch permits alternative voices, attitudes, and perspectives to deepen *NYPD Blue*'s approach to racism, but the program rarely goes further than dramatizing individual—as opposed to institutional, political, and social—responses to racial disharmony. Milch, however, maintains realism by not allowing racial hatreds to easily evaporate, as Fancy discovers in "Raging Bulls" (6.8), when Internal Affairs accuses Szymanski of improperly shooting an undercover black detective.[60] The investigation causes Sipowicz to vocally defend Szymanski, who, when off-duty, gets shot in the shoulder while attempting to stop robbery suspects who run down a city street to escape an undercover African American cop. Szymanski mistakenly shoots the cop five times, believing this officer to be a perpetrator. Sipowicz, while yelling at Fancy in the lieutenant's office, points his thumb in Fancy's face in what clearly resembles Sipowicz giving Fancy "the finger." This act of extraordinary disrespect causes Fancy to follow Sipowicz into the squad's locker room, where both men exchange physical blows—beating one another bloody—before Sipowicz's new partner, Danny Sorenson, stops them.

This explosive confrontation teaches Fancy and Sipowicz that they can only tolerate one another, not repair the racial rifts that divide them. Sipowicz, however, presumes that Fancy pursues a racial vendetta against Szymanski when, in fact, the lieutenant once again helps exonerate the man. Szymanski also reveals that, three years before, black assailants had mugged him and his wife, threatening to cut off his trigger finger. Szymanski admits an uncomfortable truth that speaks to *NYPD Blue*'s willingness to present powerful narratives about racism: "Was I looking back at those three black kids? Maybe I was. And maybe that's what got that black plainclothesman shot five times." Meeks finds this confession ominously true to life, as well as an example of the program's ability to mimic the difficult realities of urban policing.

Fancy, as previously noted, saves Sipowicz's career more than once, especially in "Closing Time" (3.21), when Sipowicz, while grieving the murder of his son Andy Sipowicz Jr. (Michael DeLuise), drunkenly confronts three black men who then severely beat Sipowicz before stealing his gun. Fancy bargains with one of these men, Knowledge Islam (Aklam), to retrieve Sipowicz's service revolver, then agrees that Sipowicz may stay on the force. Fancy also recommends Sipowicz for promotion to first-grade detective (the highest honor a detective can receive) in "My Wild Irish Nose" (4.10). Fancy therefore treats

Sipowicz far more fairly than Sipowicz deserves, leading the viewer to question why Fancy would keep such a problematic detective, even one as skilled as Sipowicz, on the job.

The dramatic exigencies of keeping Sipowicz's character viable for *NYPD Blue* provide the best answer, diluting the realism that Milch celebrates in *True Blue,* press interviews, and other public venues. Meeks, in "Racism and Reality in *NYPD Blue,*" initially criticizes Milch's decision to make the racist Sipowicz *NYPD Blue's* protagonist: "It bothers me that he's a member of the NYPD, even in a fictional universe. It's extremely offensive that Hollywood has made a hero out of someone who is a racist by nature."[61] Meeks believes this narrative choice to be an unfortunate image for black viewers to watch because "a racist NYPD is a problem many New Yorkers of color have had to deal with in real life.... We don't need to see it reinforced and materialized in our living rooms. Imagine the message this sends to our community: the people hired to protect us, it turns out, really don't like us."[62] The fact that New York City's minority residents have experienced police racism argues in favor of *NYPD Blue's* social realism, leading Meeks to grudgingly admire Sipowicz for growing into a more tolerant person. Not all the program's principal characters are racists, but Sipowicz's narrative primacy permits Milch and his writers to dramatize multiple bigotries, none of which is more controversial than racism. Meeks, however, becomes sanguine about the program's realistic approach, stating that "the way officers and detectives are portrayed on the show is exactly how I see them operate, especially toward African Americans and other minorities, in real life. They are condescending, rude and downright hostile to people of color in most cases."[63]

NYPD Blue, for Meeks, offers a troubling portrait of urban law enforcement that concedes the difficult decisions confronting inner-city detectives. He concludes his essay by noting that Sipowicz's racial redemption encourages him (Meeks) to hope "that racist people watching the show can redeem themselves, too. Some people will never change. But some will. And that should give us all hope."[64] Meeks's optimistic assessment, however, too easily elides the social, political, and economic forces that promote and preserve racism (even in a television series that dramatizes pernicious bigotry). *NYPD Blue* provides a remarkable portrait of one man's journey from confirmed racism to tenuous tolerance, but, as Sterne notes, this singular focus deprives the program of narrative possibilities about the sociological causes of racism that *Homicide: Life on the Street, The Corner, The Wire,* and *Deadwood* more consistently, more confidently, and more compellingly realize. *NYPD Blue*'s isolated moments of social and institutional criticism offer excellent narrative texture to its ongoing story lines, but such moments are not frequent enough to pronounce the series a triumph of social realism. *NYPD Blue*'s fascination with Sipowicz, its willingness to explore the hostile aspects of his personality, and Franz's superlative acting instead transform the program into a triumph of deep, sophisticated, and detailed character development.

NYPD Blue, therefore, emerges as an intricate, contradictory, and ambiguous portrait of American racism. Milch's personal comments reveal ambivalences about this theme that help explain the program's fascinating (if troubling) approach to this topic. His attempt in *True Blue* to explain the limitations facing African American television writers, for instance, showcases not only an honest effort to analyze an important issue facing the television industry but also a shortsighted reaction that dismisses the institutional obstructions to minority advancement that historically characterize Hollywood (and, more broadly, the United States of America). The writings of artists and scholars as diverse as James Baldwin, Daniel Bernardi, Taylor Branch, Steven Alan Carr, Larry Ceplair, Ashley W. Doane, W.E.B. Du Bois, Gerald Early, Ralph Ellison, Adam Fairclough, John Hope Franklin, Henry Louis Gates Jr., Allison Graham, Henry Hampton, Nathan Hare, bell hooks, Zora Neale Hurston, Vincent F. Rocchio, Sasha Torres, and Cornel West document the stark oppression that excludes minority American artists, whether writers or performers, from mainstream success.[65] Milch ignores this work in favor of personal stories that mostly avoid the larger historical, structural, and political questions raised by his analysis (a pattern that *NYPD Blue* repeats).

Milch's interview with James L. Longworth Jr. in *TV Creators: Conversations with America's Top Producers of Television Drama* emblematizes his blindness about this issue. Asked by Longworth about the National Association for the Advancement of Colored People (NAACP)'s threatened boycott of the 1999–2000 American television season "because out of twenty-six new shows...there are no lead black characters on TV," Milch says he feels no responsibility to create programs with black lead characters because it is not his job as a dramatist to think in these terms, "which is not to say that I don't portray a heterogeneous society in my work—I do. A significant proportion of those characters are minorities."[66] Milch, however, claims that indulging such concerns is racially problematic: "But for me, it's putting the cart before the horse in an unhealthy and racist way to make a decision based on race. I mean, decisions based on race are racist, and I'm not going to do it. And I'm not going to be blackmailed by some guy who's looking to raise the enrollment of the NAACP by getting a high-profile issue. That issue is nonsense. It's just pure nonsense."[67]

Milch here commits the same error that Fancy accuses the New York City Police Department of making in "Taillight's Last Gleaming": presuming that the NAACP threatens a boycott to pursue the hidden agenda of enhancing enrollment rather than to raise legitimate concerns about the portrayal of African American characters on television. Milch also fails to recognize the contradiction at the center of his analysis, for, if decisions based on race are fundamentally racist (including decisions to create television dramas around African American protagonists), then Milch's refusal to do so (which he characterizes as a sensible reaction to unwanted political pressure) is also racist insofar as he chooses to create dramas that revolve around white protagonists. Milch assumes that television dramas starring Caucasian characters are a natural state of affairs, reproducing the bigotry that defines white people as the model against which all other minorities are judged, when, in fact, television dramatists, like network executives, make conscious decisions about what appears on-screen.

This analysis should not imply that Milch is deliberately racist, although it demonstrates that unthinking prejudices affect his worldview, at least in regards to writing and casting television. *NYPD Blue*'s excellent, contentious, and compelling episodes about race, when juxtaposed with Milch's comments, prove that he manifests great understanding, but also great ignorance, about matters of institutional bigotry. *NYPD Blue* advances a constricted realism (to adopt Sterne's term) that candidly and passionately tackles racism but rarely offers narrative depth about this issue. Highlighting Sipowicz's viewpoint over those of all other characters ensures a politically reactionary stance that endorses the police's us-versus-them mentality rather than bursting this cop-show convention to demonstrate wider compassion for (and understanding of) the minority residents that inhabit the 15th Precinct.

Sterne finds fault with the entire genre of police dramas when addressing their putative realism, claiming that questions about the nature of truth and the biases that affect a detective's judgment are not "in the realm of the cop show, but of classic drama. And classic drama is among the many fine things that don't survive on commercial television."[68] Sterne also states that "what's unfortunate about *NYPD Blue* is that so many talented people are confined within the borders of a purported fidelity to fact that actually tends to distort reality" by implying that "'crime' is definable in terms of what the police drama presents as crime [and] by helping to perpetuate—again with the excuse of 'realism'—stereotypes about African-Americans and Hispanics among an audience largely unaware of the history and social reality of people unlike themselves."[69] Sterne here identifies *NYPD Blue* as a politically conservative program that squelches authentic portraits of minority characters, particularly minority characters who are not police officers. Episodes such as "Oscar, Meyer, Weiner," "The Backboard Jungle," "Taillight's Last Gleaming," "Bad Rap," and "Raging Bulls" show that Milch permits other writers to explore racism at least as well, if not better, than Milch himself, making *NYPD Blue* less reactionary than Sterne contends but certainly less progressive than *Homicide: Life on the Street, The Corner, Deadwood,* or *The Wire.*

NYPD Blue, however, includes one episode, "Hollie and the Blowfish" (3.17), written by *The Wire* creator David Simon (based on a story by Simon and Bill Clark), that predicts significant elements of *The Wire.* This story finds Simone reconnecting with a former confidential informant named Ferdinand Hollie (Giancarlo Esposito), a criminal who not only sticks up drug dealers but also provides crucial information in a major drug case against kingpin Marvin Freeland that Simone and Sipowicz help investigate. Hollie, an HIV-positive gay man, presages one of *The Wire*'s richest characters, Omar Little (Michael K. Williams), while the episode itself sees both detectives, including the initially wary Sipowicz, become loyal to Hollie for his courage and his assistance, just as *The Wire*'s Detective Jimmy McNulty (Dominic West) comes to respect Little. The episode, beyond demonstrating the connections and contrasts between Milch's and Simon's television writing, depicts how thoughtless an institution the police department can be: The officer leading a narcotics task force devoted to arresting Freeland, Sergeant Ray Kahlins (Daniel von Bargen), reveals Hollie's identity to one of Freeland's associates, resulting in a revenge killing that claims Hollie's life. Simone beats Kahlins for imperiling Hollie's life, urging the sergeant to bring departmental charges against him (Simone) because that action will expose Kahlins's poor police work.

"Hollie and the Blowfish" depicts the community outside the 15th Precinct, as well as Hollie, more genuinely than many other *NYPD Blue* episodes. Simon's sensitive treatment of Hollie's character, particularly the man's homosexuality, allows Esposito, in only a few short scenes, to create a complicated human being. The episode offers eloquent testimony to the police drama's capacity to realistically portray injustice, sexuality, and drug violence, as well as proving that *NYPD Blue*, in its finest moments, exceeds *Hill Street Blues*'s gritty portrayal of inner-city policing to achieve a sociological accuracy that Sterne thinks American television rarely conveys.

Milch's work on *NYPD Blue*, in its finest moments, achieves equal authenticity. The program's constricted police worldview may limit its social realism, while its famously groundbreaking use of sexuality and profanity pales in comparison to its dark, depressing, and distorted portrait of urban law enforcement. *NYPD Blue*, however, chronicles Clark's version of policing as much as Milch's (or Bochco's), a fact that Milch recognizes in *True Blue* by mentioning how irritated Clark becomes when *NYPD Blue* violates police procedure. After Clark quits the New York City Police Department late in 1994, relocates to Los Angeles, and begins working on the show full time, Milch realizes how passionately Clark cares about getting the details right: "In fact, since Bill moved here, I've learned to budget a portion of time each day to disentangling him from disputes at varying levels of heatedness on the subject of what is and isn't good law enforcement."[70] Clark himself believes that his strong insistence on accuracy enhances *NYPD Blue*'s account of detective work, as he asserts in a 1995 *New York Times* interview with Andy Meisler: "I'm working on a show where realism is the name of the game, and everything we do is to try to stay as realistic as possible."[71]

Such realism, however, limits itself—with notable exceptions—to the cop-shop perspective so common in police dramas, while Clark's advice about proper procedure sometimes downplays civil liberties. *True Blue* includes an illuminating passage that quotes Clark, as he recounts a homicide case involving two Dominican drug dealers who shoot a Haitian man, saying that both suspects go free "'cause of the horseshit rules of evidence."[72] Clark propounds the police perspective that due-process protections limit a detective's ability to arrest criminals, protect victims, and secure justice, saying that he will not endanger witnesses by forcing them to testify in court without first extracting a confession from the suspect: "Then after I've got his statement, let the guilty prick have all the rights he wants."[73] This viewpoint, seemingly contemptuous of civil liberties, resonates with Sipowicz's worldview in *NYPD Blue*, lending credence to the notion that Milch combines elements of his father Elmer's, his friend Clark's, and his own personality to create Sipowicz's character.[74] Clark's statement also presumes that he has privileged access to truth when investigating cases; he thereby contends that veteran detectives can quickly determine who is honest, who is evasive, who is innocent, and who is guilty.

This fallacious reasoning, so common to fictional police detectives (and, as numerous studies conducted by Amnesty International, Human Rights Watch, the United Nations, and the New York Police Department attest, real-life detectives), typifies *NYPD Blue*'s portrait of inner-city law enforcement. The program's realism, therefore, should not be mistaken for reality no matter how often Milch, Clark, and Bochco make this claim. The series, instead, nicely relays a working-class detective's view of the world that conveniently matches Clark's outlook.

NYPD Blue, even so, remains an important, intriguing, and influential police drama that, like *Hill Street Blues* before it, exhibits Milch's talents as a writer, creator, and producer. The program's quirky plots, exceptional acting, comedic undertones, and smart dialogue produce a cop show not to be missed but also a program not to be trusted as a rigorously faithful account of police work. Milch's firm control of *NYPD Blue*'s writing staff during the program's first seven seasons makes it one of the most compelling prime-time dramas ever broadcast on American television, even if it obeys cop-show conventions more often than it flouts them. *NYPD Blue* is an excellent program but one that reflects the feelings, thoughts, and biases of its major creator, David Milch.

NYPD Blue may avoid the institutional, social, and political criticism that Simon's work on *Homicide: Life on the Street*, *The Corner*, and *The Wire* regularly engages, but this truth cannot diminish *NYPD Blue*'s influence or impact on televised American crime drama. Simon's television writing, when not nurtured by Milch, develops in response to Milch's work. Without *Hill Street Blues* and *NYPD Blue*, Simon (along with many other producers) would have less freedom to explore the narrative territory that Milch so thoroughly charts. *NYPD Blue*'s significance, as a result, cannot be overstated. The program's adult (if imperfect) treatment of serious social themes (including racism, poverty, injustice, sexuality, and personal redemption) and its unflinching portrayal of Sipowicz's multifaceted character prepare Milch to create, write, and produce a program that, while not a cop drama, shares many similarities with *NYPD Blue*. That series, as chapter 5 of this study argues, is Milch's masterpiece: *Deadwood*.

3

Red Balls: David Simon and
Homicide: Life on the Street

Homicide: Life on the Street (1993–1999) not only adapted David Simon's 1991 book *Homicide: A Year on the Killing Streets* into a critically acclaimed television series but also inaugurated Simon's television-writing career. Although each episode credits Paul Attanasio as the program's creator, executive producers Barry Levinson and Tom Fontana developed *Homicide: Life on the Street* (hereafter known simply as *Homicide*) from Simon's book when film director Levinson optioned the rights to *Homicide: A Year on the Killing Streets* (hereafter referred to as *A Year on the Killing Streets*) soon after its 1991 publication. Levinson—best known for directing the feature films *Diner* (1982), *The Natural* (1984), *Good Morning, Vietnam* (1987), and *Rain Man* (1988)—came to believe that the book's rich details about the fractious professional lives of Baltimore homicide detectives deserved the narrative attention that an ongoing series—with its multiple episodes, continuing story lines, and complex characters—could offer. Confining Simon's 650-page book (originally pitched to Levinson as a movie) to a film's two-hour running time would have, in Levinson's mind, eviscerated *A Year on the Killing Streets*'s factual complexity, narrative density, and sociological precision.[1]

Levinson quickly hired Fontana, the veteran writer-producer of *St. Elsewhere* (1982–1988), to adapt Simon's mammoth book into a workable dramatic program, supervise *Homicide*'s writing staff, and ensure that the series avoided cop-drama clichés. Levinson also offered Attanasio, the screenwriter who had adapted Michael Crichton's 1993 novel *Disclosure* into Levinson's 1994 film of the same title, the opportunity to write *Homicide*'s pilot episode after Attanasio finished the screenplay for Robert Redford's 1994 film *Quiz Show*.[2] Attanasio, however, did not function as a producer, staff writer, or consultant for the series, penning only one additional *Homicide* episode, "See No Evil" (2.1), during the program's seven-season run. Critical observers, in light of these facts, more properly consider Levinson and Fontana to be *Homicide*'s originators. Fontana's input became so crucial to *Homicide*'s success that writer-producers James Yoshimura and Eric Overmyer, in their DVD commentary for "The Documentary" (5.11), explicitly credit Fontana as the program's creator.[3]

This tangled genesis, however familiar to American television, did not initially include Simon, who worked as a crime (or police-beat) reporter for the *Baltimore Sun* newspaper from 1982 until 1995. During his tenure at the *Sun,* Simon took two year-long leaves of absence to research and write his massively detailed accounts of urban Baltimore: 1991's *Homicide: A Year on the Killing Streets* and 1997's *The Corner: A Year in the Life of an Inner-City Neighborhood* (this final book was cowritten with Edward Burns, who would become Simon's writing and producing partner for HBO's 2008 miniseries adaptation of Evan Wright's *Generation Kill* and, most crucially, for *The Wire*). Simon sold the rights to *A Year on the Killing Streets* but did not involve himself in creating, running, or supervising the program's early seasons, even though he and David Mills cowrote the teleplay (based on a story by Fontana) for "Bop Gun" (2.4). That episode was broadcast by NBC, *Homicide*'s parent network, as the premiere of its abbreviated, four-episode second season to capitalize on guest star Robin Williams's presence. (Levinson, in a pattern that would recur throughout *Homicide*'s network life, enticed cinematic actors such as Williams—whom Levinson had directed to a breakout performance in *Good Morning, Vietnam*—and film directors such as Barbara Kopple, Gary Fleder, and Kathryn Bigelow to work for the program.)

Simon's minimal involvement, however, belies his importance to *Homicide*'s television incarnation. Fontana, for one, sees *A Year on the Killing Streets* as decisively influential during his audio commentary for the show's first episode, "Gone for Goode" (1.1). While discussing *Homicide*'s origin with Levinson, Fontana says, "I think by the end of the six years [of the program's production] we had pretty much sucked every comma and question mark out of [David Simon's] book."[4] So many characters, plotlines, and criminal cases from *A Year on the Killing Streets* make their way into *Homicide* that Fontana's cheerful hyperbole underscores how much the process of bringing *Homicide* to television differed from David Milch's process in creating *NYPD Blue*.

Adapting Simon's book required the fidelity to a journalistic source that Milch attempted, but could not approximate, by basing so much of *NYPD Blue*'s early narrative material on Bill Clark's detective career. This judgment does not diminish Milch's research in preparing *NYPD Blue*'s portrayal of urban police, but it emphasizes how faithfully Fontana and his writers attempted to preserve the integrity of Simon's work.

Homicide: Life on the Street premiered eight months before *NYPD Blue*, although Milch and Steven Bochco began working on that program in late 1991 or early 1992 (at roughly the same time that Levinson and Fontana began working on their series).[5] *Homicide*, however, never matched *NYPD Blue*'s ratings success, mainstream popularity, or press coverage. The usual explanation for this disparity—propounded by Simon, Levinson, Fontana, Yoshimura, Overmyer, other *Homicide* production personnel, fans, and critics (such as John Leonard)—is that *Homicide* offers a more realistic, variegated, and accurate view of detective work than *NYPD Blue*, a depiction that generally eschews car chases, gunplay, nudity, and profanity. *Homicide*, in other words, challenges its viewers' expectations of cop shows even more than does *NYPD Blue* (or another contemporary drama cited for its realistic approach to the criminal-justice system, Dick Wolf's *Law & Order*) to attain a level of social realism not seen in other police dramas (even *Hill Street Blues*).

Homicide, to be certain, is one of the best cop shows ever broadcast on American television. Only Simon's *The Wire* surpasses the breadth, depth, and intricacy of *Homicide*'s depiction of a major American city's urban life, while *Homicide*'s portrait of the complicated lives of African American characters is unmatched in the history of American network television. The series nicely captures *A Year on the Killing Streets*'s complex tone—journalistic, analytical, reflective, cynical, sardonic, and unsentimental—even as it diverges from Simon's book by allowing its fictional detectives to indulge more abstruse musings about life, crime, religion, and love than their real-life counterparts.

Simon, whose involvement with the program began in earnest in its fourth season (he did not receive screen credit as story editor until the fifth season and did not become a full-fledged producer until the sixth season), potently analyzes *Homicide*'s literary aspirations by stating, in "Homicide: Life in Season 4," the behind-the-scenes documentary included in the program's Season 4 DVD set, that, when he began writing for *Homicide*,

I had to put aside in my mind the characters that I saw when I was in the Homicide Unit. There were very few characters that were reflective of the real detectives I knew, which is not to say they were not completely vibrant and worthy of the drama that was written about them. They were interesting to me because I'd watched them just, consumed them like any other viewer. But they had no real connection to me, in my head, to the book characters, who were very real and a lot less philosophical.[6]

This assessment both credits and criticizes *Homicide's* dramatization of police lives by acknowledging the program's vivid characters while underscoring its narrative departures from the street-level reality that *A Year on the Killing Streets* so painstakingly documents. Simon distinguishes real-life detectives' disinterest in questions of morality, ethics, and justice from their fictional avatars' concern with these issues. Simon advances a seemingly sophisticated appraisal of the different parameters of journalism and television by recognizing how the show's characters philosophize about their work and their lives more explicitly than the actual detectives that Simon's book chronicles.

This perspective, however, ignores the expert pacing, nuanced characters, and precise details that *A Year on the Killing Streets* includes. The book masterfully integrates these techniques into its sociological evaluation of the problems besetting late 20th-century Baltimore to erode the boundaries between neutral reportage and literary license that Simon insists set his book apart from its television counterpart. *A Year on the Killing Streets,* indeed, includes continuous third-person commentary that analyzes the nature of police work alongside the economic disillusionment, political lethargy, racial animus, and cultural dislocations that define Baltimore's civic life during the late 1980s and early 1990s. Fontana and *Homicide's* writers, since their program rarely employs voiceover narration to advance an episode's plot, allow their characters to verbalize ideas, concepts, and opinions that *A Year on the Killing Streets* presents more objectively, or at least as the work of a single, unnamed, third-person narrator (who seemingly reflects Simon's perspective).

Simon, in the same behind-the-scenes interview, elaborates how *Homicide's* detectives diverge from the men and women whom he observed during his year-long sojourn with the Baltimore Police Department's Homicide Unit:

There was not a lot of great debate about religion or good or evil. The nature of good and evil was determined based on "I have enough to charge or I don't have enough to charge" or "he's an asshole or he's not an asshole." That struck me as the difference in the show, between the show and the book is that, uh, the show really was like trying to tackle some great moral questions through the use of character, and real life often isn't like that.[7]

This assessment invokes an implicit dichotomy between *A Year on the Killing Streets*'s putative realism and *Homicide*'s moral drama. Ethical concerns arising from murder cases, in Simon's telling, do not plague actual detectives. Real-life homicide cops—or "murder police," in Baltimore parlance—focus on a case's essential details rather than becoming emotionally, spiritually, or intellectually invested in a heinous act whose motives, Simon implies, they try not to ponder. Such philosophizing amounts to reckless folly for people whose task is closing murder cases, not comforting the family members of homicide victims, even if determining who committed the crime, arresting the perpetrator(s), and relinquishing the suspect(s) to the criminal-court system helps these family members manage their grief. The emotionally draining experience of probing murder, in other words, requires homicide detectives to reduce their field of vision to a case's details. This reaction is a psychological defense against the sadness, anxiety, and depression that contemplating the tragedy of murder might induce.

Homicide detectives' impulse to judge their job performance by tracking which cases result in arrests rather than indictments or convictions typifies *A Year on the Killing Streets*'s depiction of late 20th-century urban American policing as a bureaucratic morass that sporadically, if ever, seeks justice as its goal. Two notable passages speak to the heartless statistical ballet that Baltimore's homicide detectives must dance to please their superior officers. The first excerpt alternates sacred diction with profane imagery to make this point: "It is the unrepentant worship of statistics that forms the true orthodoxy of any modern police department. Captains become majors who become colonels who become deputies when the numbers stay sweet; the command staff backs up on itself like a bad stretch of sewer pipe when they don't."[8] Homicide detectives may refuse to debate the merits of individual murders, but Simon's account stresses how pursuing higher clearance rates subordinates all talk of good and evil to the utilitarian demands of bureaucratic authority, which co-opts religious language to demand that police officers venerate a new master: cold, hard numbers that permit no sentiment other than success.

The second passage remorselessly punctures the hope—sustained, if not created, by the hundreds of television cop shows broadcast by American networks since the 1940s—that homicide detectives wish to do right by murder victims: "Consider the fact that a case is regarded to be cleared whether it arrives at the grand jury or not. As long as someone is locked up—whether for a week or a month or a lifetime—that murder is down."[9] This single sentence demolishes the image of virtuous detectives crusading for justice, while the following lines underscore the officious mentality that creates this heartless system: "If the charges are dropped at the arraignment for lack of evidence, if the grand jury refuses to indict, if the prosecutor decides to dismiss the case or place it on the inactive, or stet, docket, that murder is nonetheless carried on the books as a solved crime. Detectives have a tag line for such paper clearances: Stet 'em and forget 'em."[10] Closing homicide cases is, *A Year on the Killing Streets* repeatedly argues, less a matter of righteous indignation than a procedurally driven, paperwork-laden, and administratively burdensome occupation that, like so many careers in postindustrial America, diminishes authentic human feeling to the point that all decisions seem soulless.

This jaded vision characterizes Simon's nonfiction work, television writing, and political outlook. *Homicide* effectively captures this perspective, particularly in the single-minded determination of its most original and bracing character, Detective Frank Pembleton (Andre Braugher), to close cases regardless of the victim's identity, the perpetrator's motivations, and the police hierarchy's interference. Pembleton's partner, Detective Tim Bayliss (Kyle Secor), does not share Pembleton's cold-blooded fascination with the facts of murder but instead becomes emotionally involved in cases—particularly the murders of young children—that prompt him to wonder about "the why," meaning the reason(s) that one human being murders another.[11] *Homicide*'s inaugural episode, along with much of its first season, follows Bayliss's initiation into the seemingly uncaring world of homicide detectives, who jettison empathy to prevent the emotional damage that afflicts several principal characters—including Bayliss, Detective Steve Crosetti (Jon Polito), Detective Beau Felton (Daniel Baldwin), and Detective Mike Kellerman (Reed Diamond)—throughout the program's seven seasons. Felton's deteriorating marriage is one of the third season's major plotlines, while Crosetti commits suicide in "Crosetti" (3.4).

Kellerman nearly shoots himself in the head in "Have a Conscience" (5.13), avoiding this fate only because his partner, Detective Meldrick Lewis (Clark Johnson), talks him out of it. Bayliss never goes this far, but the death of Adena Watson, a young African American girl whose murder is Bayliss's first case as primary investigator, haunts him for *Homicide*'s entire broadcast run. Bayliss, in *Homicide*'s strongest rebuke to the cop-drama convention of closing major cases by the end of an episode, a season, or the series itself, never solves Watson's murder.

These narrative developments parallel *A Year on the Killing Streets* better than Simon recognizes, while Levinson and Fontana's commitment to civil liberties ensures that *Homicide* offers a more progressive portrayal of urban policing than *NYPD Blue*. Only the early seasons of *Hill Street Blues* match *Homicide*'s realistic depiction of urban life, although *Hill Street*, by setting its police station in a harsh (even animalistic) ghetto neighborhood, indulges stereotypes about the diminished, damaged, and violent lives of its district's minority population. *Homicide*, thanks to Fontana's insistence on avoiding cop-drama formulas, breaks these conventions more frequently than it obeys them, mixing elements of the traditional police procedural, the observant social comedy, and the classic drama (which Richard Clark Sterne, in his essay about *NYPD Blue* in *Prime Time Law*, believes commercial television feebly reproduces[12]) into a unique series whose terrific writing, documentary camera work, and superlative acting enhance its social realism.

This final statement should not imply that *Homicide* is, in fact, an objective or neutral account of homicide detection. By sympathizing with its cop characters, even while presenting them unsentimentally, *Homicide* fails to dramatize the lives of criminals, suspects, and residents with the same careful attention that it accords the police (only Simon's *The Wire* achieves this goal). The series, however, offers a more vibrant portrait of its urban community than any previous (or contemporary) network police drama, permitting *Homicide* to stand apart from the generic tradition in which it participates. Fontana acknowledges this complicated lineage during an interview with James L. Longworth Jr. in *TV Creators: Conversations with America's Top Producers of Television Drama*, revealing that Levinson originally approached *St. Elsewhere* producers John Tinker and John Masius to adapt *A Year on the Killing Streets* into a television series. When they departed the project, Tinker and Masius recommended that Levinson contact Fontana. "I went out and met with Barry," Fontana tells Longworth, "and when the whole idea of a cop show was presented to me, I was like, 'Well, there's never going to be a better cop show than *Hill Street Blues*, there's no other way to do it better.'"[13] This assessment, however, did not deter Levinson, who outlined a different vision for his first television program: "'I want to do a cop show without car chases and without gun battles. I want to do *Homicide* as a thinking man's unit.' And so, the minute [Levinson] said that, I [Fontana] said, 'That's impossible. I have to be part of this!'"[14]

Fontana's enthusiasm led to him to hire writers, particularly Chicago-born playwright James Yoshimura, who would upset the conventions of television crime drama, resist network pressure to make *Homicide* a more predictable program, and honor the spirit of Simon's book. Fontana's general success in this venture allows *Homicide* to fulfill Levinson's aspiration for the series by becoming a thinking person's police show even while indulging elements of traditional cop dramas, whether infrequent shootouts, car chases (that sometimes end with detectives crashing their squad cars into other vehicles), and on-screen violence. Placating NBC's desire to improve the show's ratings occasionally forced *Homicide*'s writers to honor the network's demands for more romance, more violence, and more closed cases, but these compromises demonstrate that *Homicide* differs from typical cop shows by stressing authenticity in tone, mood, atmosphere, pace, and procedure. The series generally avoids rushing from scene to scene, while the long conversations and interrogations that typify *Homicide*'s structure allow its principal characters to achieve fully rounded lives of their own.

Fontana, however, refuses to demean *Homicide*'s major competitor, *NYPD Blue*, in an effort to improve his own program's stature. He tells Longworth, "My opinion is that David Milch and Jimmy Yoshimura are probably the two most talented people writing television today, or, at least, episodic television" (this interview was conducted before *Homicide*'s 1999 cancellation, although Longworth's book was not published until 2000).[15] Fontana's invocation of *Hill Street Blues*'s quality and Milch's talent may demonstrate his awareness of *Homicide*'s antecedents and contemporaries, but his respect for Yoshimura counters charges that *Homicide* cannot escape the shadow of its more popular rival. "My whole attitude toward Yosh is when he comes to me with an idea that he is excited about, I would be an idiot to stand in his way,"[16] Fontana comments, implicitly declaring that *Homicide* is just as good as *NYPD Blue*.

Little rivalry exists in Fontana's mind between his and Milch's series, however, due to *Homicide*'s singular style. Not every author can master it, making *Homicide* a challenging, but not impossible, program to write: "In my mind, not every writer can write everything. There are a lot of incredible writers who could not write an episode of *Homicide*, and that doesn't mean they're not good writers. That just means that they're not right for this particular show."[17] Such generosity of spirit explains how Simon became an intelligent television dramatist, for Fontana closely mentored Simon's transition from journalist, book author, and social critic to small-screen writer. Simon, in "Homicide: Life in Season 4," confesses that he declined producer Gail Mutrux's offer to write the first episode because he knew nothing about television writing: "There was a moment where Gail called me up and said, 'Would you like to try your hand at writing the pilot?' and, uh, like an idiot, I said, 'You know, no, get somebody who knows what they're doing because I'll mess it up and there'll be no TV show.'"[18]

Simon, once he left the *Baltimore Sun*, came aboard *Homicide*'s writing staff, where Fontana instructed him in the challenges, pitfalls, and pleasures of producing television. Simon thanks Fontana for this tutelage in "Inside *Homicide*: An Interview with David Simon and James Yoshimura" (a short documentary included in *Homicide*'s *Complete Season 5* DVD set) by explaining Fontana's attitude toward writing television: "Tom made a promise to me, which was, uh, he said, 'I don't pay as much as some producers and I don't give titles easily—I won't make you a producer until you're really producing—but I'll teach you how to do this, I'll teach you everything I can possibly teach you about not just writing for television, but protecting the writing,' which is what producing is in a sense."[19] Simon recognizes that Fontana's concern for preserving the integrity of every writer's story distinguishes television from cinema: "The writer has no authority to protect his story, his telling of the story, in features. It's, it's a director- and star-based medium, but in television, the writer rules."[20]

Simon, as chapter 6 of this study argues, takes this final dictum to heart when creating, producing, and writing *The Wire*, but, despite Simon's status as author of *A Year on the Killing Streets*, his first television job required him to work as one member of *Homicide*'s busy writing staff under Fontana's supervision. This arrangement benefited Simon by allowing him to learn the rigors of producing a weekly series, to recognize the limitations that the major American networks impose on prime-time drama, to negotiate the resulting narrative constrictions, and to appreciate the unique possibilities that fiction affords socially conscious authors when constructing incisive, relevant, and realistic stories about crime, race, class, and politics. "Homicide: Life in Season 4" reveals that Fontana dubbed Simon "Nonfiction Boy" because Simon initially approached writing *Homicide* with a journalist's eye for accuracy. His talent for lucid detail explains how *A Year on the Killing Streets*'s exacting portrait of urban police work enriched *Homicide*'s early seasons by providing Fontana and his writers with exhaustive material that they could fashion into inventive, unconventional, and quirky crime drama. Simon, once he joined the writing staff, "was always the guy at the meeting that went, 'Well, it really wouldn't work that way,'"[21] but this perspective misunderstands the power of television drama. *Homicide,* by emphasizing, altering, and enhancing Simon's account of real-life murder police, sketches a more viscerally intimate portrait of fictional events than *A Year on the Killing Streets* does with its journalistic (and supposedly detached) tone. *Homicide*'s signature visual style of handheld footage, jump cutting, and quick montage may approximate the vérité storytelling of documentary films, while *A Year on the Killing Streets*'s fulsome details may create a comprehensively realized world, but *Homicide*'s lively characters, compelling stories, and handsome production values ensure that its audience relates to its imaginary portrait of Baltimore more immediately, more incisively, and more intensely than to the book's factual accounts of urban crime.

Fontana, because he understood these differences, ably honed Simon's dramatic instincts while taking advantage of Simon's vast knowledge of police culture to meld fact with fiction, generate *Homicide*'s distinctive style, and teach Simon how powerful a medium television can be. Simon, in the "Inside *Homicide:* An Interview with David Simon and James Yoshimura" documentary, praises Fontana's willingness to consider his (Simon's) desire for accuracy: "Tom, to his credit, he would listen and...sometimes he would say, 'Okay, well, let's do it the way it really would be' and, other times, he would say, 'No, this is better storytelling. You know, let's do the make-believe here because this makes a better episode.' And the purposes were different, you know. It wasn't journalism. It was episodic drama." This formulation's invocation of "make believe" concedes that television drama's fictional imperatives—rather than always promulgating tired, hackneyed, and formulaic stories—can, at their best, submerge viewers in an invented environment that offers stunning appraisals of everyday life. *Homicide,* in other words, may not be journalism, but its documentary tone permits Fontana, Simon, and the program's other writers to fashion a cop show that is also an absorbing, if imperfect, work of social realism.

The dichotomy between journalistic accuracy and televisual imagination suggested by Simon's comments is in at least one significant respect, false. Simon implies that his book's account of one year (1988) in the life of the Baltimore Homicide Unit reports the events he observed more clinically than *Homicide*'s fictional narrative. But as Christopher P. Wilson notes in "True and True(r) Crime: Cop Shops and Crime Scenes in the 1980s," his masterful analysis of three popular true-crime books published in the early 1990s (Simon's *A Year on the Killing Streets*, Mitch Gelman's 1992 *Crime Scene: On the Streets with a Rookie Police Reporter*, and Robert Blau's 1993 *The Cop Shop: True Crime on the Streets of Chicago*), this presumption elides the social, political, economic, and ideological biases that influence how *A Year on the Killing Streets* represents late 20th-century urban policing. Simon's book may construct a dispassionate, even neutral, façade, but this impression cannot long withstand critical analysis. Wilson identifies *A Year on the Killing Streets* as an exemplary "'liberal-realist' initiation narrative," or a story of "baptism into an urban, street-smart wisdom" that, despite its liberal credentials, participates in the "'authoritarian populism' or 'popular conservatism' emergent in the 1980s."[22] Simon's cop-shop narrative, like Gelman's and Blau's books, proclaims its neutrality while replaying a "dramatic 1980s clash of posts and dispositions: the encounter of young liberal reporters, in the twilight years of Reagan-Bush America, with the supposed pathology of our inner cities."[23]

Wilson perceptively argues that true-crime (or cop-shop) books such as *A Year on the Killing Streets* advance a specific view of American crime, namely, a hard-boiled perspective that "might well be described as working in the field of urban 'police populism.'"[24] These books represent police power as necessary to preserving social order; claim sympathy for impoverished citizens who live in crime-infested areas, but rarely deal with the institutional, structural, and social reasons that poverty and crime exist; and see criminals as social deviants who fail to follow civilized rules, not as complex human beings trapped in an unjust system. They offer "a terribly unrepresentative look at American violence" because, as a "murder-based genre," the true-crime narrative "overemphasizes female victims, older victims, and—intriguingly—white offenders and white victims" and reproduce Vance Thompson's compelling insight that "the police reporter's daily lesson is 'the fall of man.'"[25] The true-crime book's tendency to regard police work as a notable (even noble) effort to preserve order, in other words, compromises true crime's much-celebrated courage in facing urban America's bitter realities. Critical readers, therefore, should notice how *A Year on the Killing Streets* adopts law enforcement's Manichean view of its task as defending civilization from the chaos originating in faceless, forbidding, and frustrating American cities that threaten to spin out of control at any moment.

Simon's mammoth book, to its many admirers, is a masterpiece of field research, vigilant observation, and critical analysis that confronts uncomfortable truths about race, class, politics, and crime in late 20th-century urban America. Wilson's article, however, reminds Simon's audience that *A Year on the Killing Streets* is not the objective account that the author's comments about the differences between book and television claim. This judgment can neither diminish Simon's superlative writing in *A Year on the Killing Streets* nor dismiss its extensive study of American policing because the book's literary fineness is as impressive as its vivid reportage. Simon, simply stated, is a compelling author whose control of language, theme, symbol, and pace gives *A Year on the Killing Streets* a novelistic quality that predicts his attentive, elegant, and darkly humorous television writing.

Perhaps the best example of how the book fuses journalism, social conscience, literary prose, and police populism is the section that recounts the discovery of the corpse of Latonya Kim Wallace, an 11-year-old African American girl dumped in a Baltimore alleyway after being molested, strangled, and disemboweled:

> It is the illusion of tears and nothing more, the rainwater that collects in small beads and runs to the hollows of her face. The dark brown eyes are fixed wide, staring across wet pavement; jet black braids of hair surround the deep brown skin, high cheekbones and a pert, upturned nose. The lips are parted and curled in a slight, vague frown. She is beautiful, even now....
>
> Among the detectives and patrol officers crowded over the body of Latonya Kim Wallace there is no easy banter, no coarse exchange of cop humor or time-worn indifference. Jay Landsman offers only clinical, declarative statements as he moves through the scene. Tom Pellegrini stands mute in the light rain, sketching the surroundings on a damp notebook page. Behind them,

against the rear wall of a rowhouse, leans one of the first Central District officers to arrive at the scene, one hand on his gun belt, the other absently holding his radio mike.

"Cold," he says, almost to himself.

From the moment of discovery, Latonya Wallace is never regarded as anything less than a true victim, innocent as few of those murdered in this city ever are. A child, a fifth-grader, has been used and discarded, a monstrous sacrifice to an unmistakable evil.[26]

This passage emblematizes Simon's authorial talent by offering lucid sensory details that re-create Wallace's murder scene yet emphasize its emotional aridity by underscoring the near silence that overtakes the assembled officers and detectives. Simon reverses his reader's expectations by noting how the detectives refuse the gallows humor that characterizes every previous crime scene that *A Year on the Killing Streets* records. The passage's richness of detail contrasts with its starkness of feeling to prepare the reader for the final paragraph's moralizing conclusion. Mentioning monstrosity, sacrifice, and evil reveals the suppressed horror that the officers and narrator feel but do not verbally express. Identifying Wallace as a "true victim" purer than most murdered people, whom the killer has treated as garbage, transforms the girl into an angelic symbol while juxtaposing good and evil so effectively that Pellegrini, the primary investigator, must now avenge Wallace's death if he wishes to right this hideous wrong. The police, as the excerpt concludes, no longer serve as simple investigators but rather as populist defenders of the city's vulnerable children and as metaphysical defenders of innocence itself.

This passage also substantiates Wilson's point that *A Year on the Killing Streets* cannot reproduce true journalism's impartiality. Simon synthesizes clinical observation with moral passion to represent the homicide detective, in true cop-shop fashion, as "a dedicated, hard-bitten knight of the city"[27] who seeks truth, pursues justice, and bears witness for defenseless victims. Depicting homicide detectives in this fashion positions Simon's book as an exemplary cop-shop narrative that exhibits "a long-recognized double-edged potential in populist ideology...that [is] progressive and reactionary, liberal and authoritarian all at once."[28] Such contrary motives lead Simon to merge dispassionate observation, righteous indignation, and conscientious police work into a powerful vignette that dismantles all claims to objectivity. The Wallace murder—fictionalized in *Homicide* as the never-closed Adena Watson case—is the book's primary example of a red-ball investigation, or, as Simon baldly defines this term, "murders that matter."[29] Although homicide detectives may disclaim caring about motive or morality, their practiced world-weariness extends only so far. The emotional attrition of working as murder police, therefore, requires detachment, dark humor, and defensive cynicism. The homicide detective, according to Simon's book, "gives what he can afford to give and no more" by "carefully measur[ing] out the required amount of energy and emotion" before he "closes the file and moves on to the next call."[30] For the best investigators, however, this dispassion never becomes psychological numbness.

This sympathetic portrait of homicide detectives proves that *A Year on the Killing Streets,* far from offering a neutral account of their grim work, weaves symbols, themes, and tropes about justice, morality, and religion throughout its narrative, bringing it closer to *Homicide's* imaginary portrait of Baltimore than Simon may care to admit. The television series, indeed, reproduces the book's tone better than Simon recognizes, so much so that most episodes disrupt the documentary approach that Levinson creates in "Gone for Goode" with flashbacks, surreal images, musical montages, and repeated scenes. *Homicide* develops into a faithful adaptation of *A Year on the Killing Streets* that, by employing stylized visual, aural, and storytelling strategies to modulate the program's sharp dialogue, naturalistic performances, and realistic settings, combines imaginative extrapolation with memorable imagery into an artistic work that reflects, even as it transcends, reality. Simon, in fact, masters these narrative techniques during his tenure at *Homicide* thanks to Fontana's guidance. Simon's participation in writing five noteworthy *Homicide* episodes best illustrates his flair for melding fact, fantasy, and fiction into compelling episodic drama while predicting the excellent television that he creates once *Homicide* ceases production. Examining "Bop Gun" (2.4), "Bad Medicine" (5.4), parts 2 and 3 of "Blood Ties" (6.2 and 6.3), and "Sideshow (Part 2)" (7.15) in the light of Fontana's Emmy-winning script for "Three Men and Adena" (1.6) demonstrates the storytelling gifts that permit Simon to craft *The Corner's* unflinching depiction of inner-city drug addiction and *The Wire's* unparalleled portrait of urban decline.

"Three Men and Adena" may be *Homicide's* best-known and best-reviewed episode.[31] The story takes place almost entirely in "The Box," the Homicide Unit's stark, functional, and unattractive interrogation room. Detectives Bayliss and Pembleton interrogate Risley Tucker (Moses Gunn), Bayliss's prime suspect in Adena Watson's murder, for 12 hours to elicit a confession. Tucker, an "Arabber" who sells fruits and vegetables from a horse-drawn cart that roams Baltimore's many neighborhoods (a nomadic existence that marks Tucker as untrustworthy in the eyes of many residents, including Adena's mother), has been interrogated on two previous occasions, making this third attempt the final time that Bayliss and Pembleton can legally question the man. "Three Men and Adena" adapts a relatively short passage from *A Year on the Killing Streets* into a remarkable hour of television that is, as John Leonard notes in Theodore Bogosian's excellent documentary *Anatomy of a "Homicide: Life on the Street,"* a masterpiece of writing, setting, and acting that exceeds "Ariel Dorfman's *Death and the Maiden* and a number of Don DeLillo novels about what happens to men in small rooms."[32] Simon's book recounts how detectives Tom Pellegrini and Harry Edgerton question a suspect called "The Fish Man, as he has long been known in the neighborhood," a "fifty-one-year-old living alone in a second-floor apartment across the street from his [fish] store" and a "grizzled, time-worn piece of work [who] was quite friendly with Latonya [Kim Wallace]—a little too friendly, as far as the child's family was concerned."[33]

"Three Men and Adena" transforms the Fish Man into Arabber Risley Tucker to dramatize the fissures of race, class, age, and gender that crime drama frequently portrays but rarely interrogates as maturely as Fontana's script does. The episode allows Tucker, after enduring alternately respectful, scornful, friendly, and angry questioning by Bayliss and Pembleton, to reverse the interrogation's dynamic by articulating the emotional baggage that defines both detectives. Tucker calls Pembleton a member of the "Five Hundreds," or a successful and professional black man who condescends to working-class colored folk such as Tucker, before accusing Pembleton of hating himself for chasing "the white dream" rather than authentically connecting with his racial roots. Tucker also verbally attacks Bayliss by comparing him to the white plantation owners who raped slaves, claiming that Bayliss not only carries a darkness inside himself that terrifies the detective but also fears being perceived as an amateur by his colleagues. Tucker, in a long monologue, then mournfully tells both detectives how he (Tucker) talked with Adena as often as possible, how he noticed the small details of her behavior, and how he came to adore her. Tucker weeps, finally confessing that, to the profound shame of a man in his sixties, "the one great love of my life was an 11-year-old girl." Tucker, however, never admits to killing Adena. The episode concludes with Pembleton certain that Tucker murdered Adena, Bayliss unsure about this possibility, and Tucker watching the squad room's television before being set free.

Fontana's rich, provocative, and perceptive script questions the possibility that homicide detectives can conclusively determine the truth during any investigation. As Sterne argues when comparing "Three Men and Adena" to *NYPD Blue*'s more conventional interrogation scenes, the episode "evokes with an insight rare in television fiction mutual tensions and distrust" between African Americans and police departments "that can militate against the establishment of 'the facts' in a police interrogation."[34] Tucker's ability to recognize the inner doubts, fears, and inadequacies that afflict Pembleton and Bayliss reflects a street vendor's talent for observing people, while Tucker's success at undermining the self-assured demeanor of even so confident a character as Pembleton illustrates how uncertain a venture investigating homicide cases is.

Although Pellegrini's and Edgerton's questioning of the Fish Man does not see the lonely, middle-aged store owner take control of the interrogation in the same way that Tucker does in "Three Men and Adena," Fontana's episode illuminates two important truths about police work that *A Year on the Killing Streets* also emphasizes. The first lesson may surprise viewers accustomed to the cop-drama convention of crack detectives pursuing every possible lead en route to solving each week's case: "Even with the murders themselves, much of what clears a case amounts to pure chance."[35] The second lesson involves the "detective's Holy Trinity, which states that three things solve crimes: Physical evidence. Witnesses. Confessions."[36] Fontana's script incisively dramatizes each element by depicting a long interrogation in which Bayliss and Pembleton offer so much physical evidence against Tucker that the viewer initially takes this information to be overwhelming. The moment when Pembleton rips a map of the neighborhood where Adena's body was discovered off the wall to reveal grisly photos of her mutilated corpse is especially effective. Tucker, however, is neither as shocked nor as saddened as Bayliss hopes, thereby diminishing Bayliss's attempt to force him to recognize just how horrific Adena's death is. Tucker never confesses to murder but, by revealing his shameful love for the young girl, demonstrates why, according to *A Year on the Killing Streets*, "the detective's trinity ignores motivation, which matters little to most investigations. The best work of Dashiell Hammett and Agatha Christie"—to say nothing of police dramas such as *Hill Street Blues, NYPD Blue,* and *Law & Order*—"argues that to track a murderer, the motive must first be established; in Baltimore, if not on the Orient Express, a known motive can be interesting, even helpful, yet it is often beside the point."[37]

"Three Men and Adena" exposes Tucker's reason for consenting to a third interrogation as his twisted need to purge the pedophiliac feelings he holds for Adena. This unexpectedly tragic motive fails to secure a confession that justifies Bayliss's frenzied work on the case, Pembleton's belief in Tucker's guilt, or the viewer's expectation that the episode will see justice done by tricking Tucker into admitting his complicity in butchering a child. "Three Men and Adena," thanks to Fontana's firm control of all dramatic elements, even invalidates the *Year on the Killing Streets* passage that summarily dismisses the significance of determining a killer's motive: "Fuck the why, a detective will tell you; find out the how, and nine times out of ten it'll give you the who."[38] Bayliss and Pembleton know how the girl was murdered, but this information cannot tell them who committed the crime despite their best suspicions. Bayliss's misgivings about Tucker's culpability mark the episode's final statement about the ambiguity of establishing guilt and innocence. "Three Men and Adena" smartly upends the expectations of its genre and its source material to undermine the efficacy of the investigative methods that Simon's authoritative book recounts.

This accomplishment illustrates the capacity of skillful television drama to challenge its viewer's preconceptions. Fontana's script, beyond inspiring Braugher, Secor, and Gunn to deliver extraordinary performances, also sets a pattern for *Homicide*'s writers (including Simon) to follow. Simon's best scripts for the program capture police work's frequently disappointing realities while indulging the artistic liberties, strategies, and techniques unique to episodic drama. His first episode, "Bop Gun" (2.4), written in collaboration with David Mills and based on a story by Fontana, displays *Homicide*'s penchant for musical montage, crosscutting, and realistic portrayals of homicide detectives' indifference to the crimes they investigate.[39] Iowa tourist Catherine Ellison is murdered as three young men rob her, her husband Robert (Robin Williams), and her two children, Abby (Julia Devin) and Matt (Jake Gyllenhaal), at gunpoint. Catherine refuses to relinquish a golden locket, then receives a fatal gunshot that sets the story's emotional dynamic into motion.

The episode's teaser (the sequence that precedes the opening credits) is a terrific montage that intercuts images of the Ellisons enjoying a walking tour of Baltimore's sights (including Camden Yards) while consulting a guidebook; of three young men—Vaughn Perkins (Lloyd Goodman), Marvin (Antonio D. Charity), and Tweety (Vincent Miller)—playing basketball in an alleyway until Marvin brandishes a .45 pistol; and of detectives Beau Felton (Daniel Baldwin) and Kay Howard (Melissa Leo) going about their daily routine while Seal's song "Killer" plays over the soundtrack. When Perkins, Marvin, and Tweety see the Ellisons walking down a street, still looking for tourist spots, the men, clearly intending to rob the family, move toward them. "Bop Gun" follows Robert Ellison as he gives Felton and Howard information about the crime, makes arrangements for his wife's remains to be transported to Iowa, comforts his children, and expresses shame at being too afraid to intervene during the robbery. Felton, Howard, Bayliss, and Lewis eventually arrest, interrogate, and charge Tweety, Marvin, and Perkins, but even Perkins's conviction does not compensate for Ellison's loss.

The episode's signature scene comes when Ellison overhears Felton, Howard, and Detective John Munch (Richard Belzer) joking about how Ellison described the gun that shot Catherine as "big and metal." When Felton enthusiastically remarks, "I am telling you, I am going to rack up the overtime on this one" (the case has become an instant red ball because it involves a tourist's death), Ellison demands that Felton be removed from the investigation. Lieutenant Al Giardello (Yaphet Kotto), *Homicide*'s shift commander and Felton's superior officer, explains his detective's cold attitude to Ellison: "A few weeks ago, he was working on a father of four shot in East Baltimore. After that, a domestic stabbing and, after that, a drug shooting in a project where an innocent bystander was killed. And next week, it will be somebody else. He's not going to feel what you feel. None of us are." Ellison comments that Giardello is not as insensitive as Felton, causing the lieutenant to say, "Mr. Ellison, I can still remember the first murder I ever handled. . . . I can't remember my fiftieth or my fortieth. None of us can. But the only difference between Felton and the rest of us is that he doesn't have the patience to hide that fact. You need him to solve your murder, not to grieve."

This unsentimental dialogue reflects *A Year on the Killing Streets*'s casual attitude toward homicide. Simon, in the documentary *Anatomy of a "Homicide: Life on the Street,"* stresses the scene's authenticity by noting that Felton's overtime comment is "a conversation that would happen. It would happen in any homicide unit anywhere in America, and when I saw it actually being acted out, I got a real kick in the pants because I thought, 'Wherever they are, homicide cops are watching this and they're cracking up 'cause they know how true it is.'" Williams's, Baldwin's, and Kotto's excellent performances enhance the moment's realism, while Ellison's grief—he later cries while clutching his wife's nightgown—adds an emotional poignancy that counteracts Felton's unfeeling attitude. The fact that Ellison's children, lying in bed in the next room, hear him weep transforms "Bop Gun" into a touching, resonant, and accurate portrait of human anguish. Simon and Mills do not downplay the family's sadness but allow Felton's insensitivity to cast the Ellisons' heartache in even greater relief.

"Bop Gun" employs visual and aural techniques to generate narrative effects that *A Year on the Killing Streets* cannot replicate. The teaser resembles a music video, but juxtaposing the disparate behavior of the unsuspecting Ellisons, the initially jovial yet larcenous basketball players, and the murder police foreshadows how these people's lives will violently intersect while underscoring how tenuous human life, freedom, and safety are. The episode repeats this opening sequence's parallel editing during Marvin's and Tweety's dual interrogations. While Felton and Lewis question Marvin in the Box, Howard and Detective Stan Bolander (Ned Beatty) grill Tweety in the Box's observation room as Public Enemy's "Get Off My Back" provides the scene's dialogue. Rather than resorting to the longer, more deliberate interrogations that characterize *Homicide* and *A Year on the Killing Streets,* this short montage adroitly intercuts Marvin's and Tweety's interviews to demonstrate how homicide detectives play suspects against one another, upset each man's intellectual equilibrium, and exhaust each arrestee's emotional endurance. The sequence's brevity distorts the actual time that such interrogations require but emphasizes their inherent unpleasantness. An agitated Tweety eventually offers information, yet Marvin remains stoic, telling Felton and Lewis only that he will survive prison before mentioning that Perkins was provoked by Catherine Ellison's refusal to hand over her locket. This statement culminates a frenetic scene whose jump cuts reflect the intensity that Tweety and Marvin experience while under interrogation.

"Bop Gun" also deals with issues of race and justice. Giardello asks Howard, a detective with a perfect case-clearance rate, to look into the Ellison investigation because its implications trouble him. When

Giardello doubts that his superiors would demand results if the victim were a black Baltimore woman rather than a white female tourist, the episode briefly (but effectively) acknowledges the regrettable truth that American society privileges homicide victims based on their racial and socioeconomic background. Giardello's statements lead Howard to observe Perkins's interrogation, in which Perkins seems genuinely remorseful, even asking to write a letter of apology to Robert Ellison. Based on this behavior, Howard wonders whether Perkins truly shot Catherine Ellison or whether he is confessing to the crime to protect Marvin from prosecution. Simon and Mills, in a further example of *Homicide*'s penchant for telling ambiguous crime stories, do not resolve Howard's doubts. When Howard visits Perkins in prison, he, having converted to Islam, claims the Ellison shooting as his own. Howard, although she agrees with Felton when he says that she should never have distrusted Perkins's guilt, seems uncertain about this prospect. Leo's carefully modulated acting throughout "Bop Gun," particularly in Howard's final scene with Perkins, stresses the ambivalence that haunts police detectives when determining guilt and innocence. Simon's contributions to this episode give it an authentic sense of procedure, atmosphere, and tone that exposes the emotional, intellectual, and legal complexities confronting homicide detectives during murder investigations.

"Bad Medicine," by contrast, features a more self-consciously literary style.[40] Simon's script for this episode, based on a story by Fontana and Julie Martin, sees Meldrick Lewis team with Terri Stivers (Toni Lewis), a narcotics detective investigating several deaths that result from people snorting, shooting, or smoking impure heroin. The victims, in a small but important detail, belong to all gender, racial, and socioeconomic groups, reflecting the tragic reality of Baltimore's drug abuse, while Simon bases this story line on several actual Baltimore deaths caused by ingesting heroin laced with scopolamine.[41]

Lewis and Stivers connect this bad heroin to Luther Mahoney (Erik Todd Dellums), a man they suspect of being one of the city's most prominent drug moguls. Mahoney, first encountered by Lewis and Mike Kellerman in "The Damage Done" (4.19), works as a community activist and philanthropist to cover his illegal activities. Mahoney becomes a recurring nemesis for the Homicide Unit throughout Season Five, but "Bad Medicine" showcases his charm, intelligence, and unflappability. Dellums plays the role with cultured menace, particularly when Lewis and Stivers interrogate Mahoney about the killings of two low-level drug dealers named Bo-Jack Reed and Carlton Phipps. The detectives suspect that Mahoney has ordered these slayings, so Stivers invites him to the squad room for a chat. Mahoney arrives in an expensive sports-utility vehicle wearing upscale clothing, only to find himself handcuffed to the Box's table. Mahoney, however, willingly participates in the interrogation, condescending to Lewis and Stivers by playing along with them in a scene that captures Simon's talent for good dialogue. Lewis begins by saying that a witness has identified Mahoney as the man behind the murders.

MAHONEY.   Are you suggesting a motive?
LEWIS.   Well, we have, uh say, your theoretical drug slinger and, you know, he's marketing a viable product, proper purity, proper cut, until some no-name, know-nothing, old-school, just-out-of-Jessup knucklehead starts messing around with his home chemistry set and he starts killing off the customers quick.
STIVERS.   As opposed to killing them slow.
LEWIS.   Even if this drug slinger—this theoretical drug slinger—was, was a reasonable man, I mean, your guy might be compelled to act.
MAHONEY.   You know, your case makes sense. I like it.
LEWIS.   I like it, too.
MAHONEY.   Except I don't sling bags and I didn't kill Bo-Jack Reed.
STIVERS.   Then who did?
MAHONEY.   A guy named Carlton Phipps.
LEWIS.   No, he's dead, too.
MAHONEY.   You know, I heard that.
LEWIS (*sighs*).   See, our problem is that we don't have any way of connecting Carlton Phipps with the murder of Bo-Jack Reed. (*Mahoney raises his hand and shrugs.*) Well see, I worked that case. I talked to Carlton's people. You know what they told me? They said that he was despondent, that he may even have taken his own life.
MAHONEY.   He killed himself? He shot himself in the back of the head? Who are you fooling? He was murdered. Bo-Jack's people came back on him. I mean, he had the gun that killed Bo-Jack right on the table—(*Mahoney stops, realizing he's given away too much.*)

LEWIS (*laughs*). Let me ask you this: How you know where Carlton caught that bullet? And let me ask you this: How in the hell you know what was on the table in front of the man?
MAHONEY. Well, the word was all over about what happened to Carlton.
LEWIS (*laughs as he and Stivers move to exit*). Oh, Luther, Luther, Luther, you just fell for the oldest trick we got, baby.
MAHONEY. I want a lawyer.
LEWIS. I bet you do.

This interrogation initially parallels "Three Men and Adena" when Mahoney, like Risley Tucker, reverses the usual dynamic by quietly taking control of the questioning. Mahoney compliments Lewis's theory, denies involvement in the crime, and offers crucial information. Lewis's ploy, however, becomes clear when his effusive discussion of the investigation's problems prompts Mahoney to provide details about the crime scene never released to the public. Lewis lies to Mahoney, who realizes too late that he has inadvertently implicated himself in Phipps's murder. Mahoney, however, does not become flustered, angry, or truculent (as so many suspects before him have when tricked into revealing their complicity in violent crimes). Mahoney says that news of Phipps's death was common knowledge, then requests legal representation to protect his interests. The scene is an exemplary verbal sparring match that ranks among *Homicide*'s best interrogations, with Dellums and Johnson delivering effective performances.

Mahoney's calm response is justified, as Lewis and Stivers discover when they talk to Assistant State's Attorney (ASA) Ed Danvers (Zeljko Ivanek), who tells them that, since the door to Phipps's house was unlocked before his corpse was discovered, anyone in the neighborhood could have learned the details that Lewis has withheld from press reports. Mahoney is set free the next morning, ruefully smiling as he steps into his chauffeured vehicle. This pattern repeats during much of Season Five, with the Homicide Squad suspecting Mahoney of drug-related murders for which no conclusive evidence exists. The squad's inability to jail Mahoney reflects the difficulty of securing drug convictions, but the character himself seems preternaturally calm during almost every appearance. This fact leads Simon, in the "Inside *Homicide*" documentary, to declare, "to me, honestly, the character was always a little arch, again not resembling the drug traffickers that I knew in Baltimore in any sense." Simon then identifies Mahoney as a

Shakespearean villain whose sophisticated persona avoids stereotypical portrayals of the thuggish drug dealer, although Simon might also
have compared Mahoney to the master villains that populate the mystery fiction of Arthur Conan Doyle, Agatha Christie, Dashiell Hammett,
and Patricia Highsmith. The apparent naturalism of "Bad Medicine"
reveals itself as a literary construct that privileges Mahoney, making
him more refined than the drug dealers whom Simon and Burns profile in *The Corner* (both the book and the miniseries) and whom *The
Wire* authentically depicts. "Bad Medicine," however, demonstrates
that the literary strategy of giving protagonists worthy adversaries offers *Homicide* a classical storytelling integrity that the series normally
evades when striving for realistic accounts of urban police work. The
episode allows Simon to extend his dramatic range by fashioning one
of *Homicide*'s most memorable, intriguing, and complicated characters,
even if Mahoney is larger than life.

Simon's work on parts 2 and 3 of "Blood Ties," however, combines
his skillful characterization, fluid dialogue, and political savvy into episodes of rare power. These final two segments of the three-part story
line that opens *Homicide*'s sixth season (based on stories by Fontana,
Martin, and Yoshimura) trace the racial, socioeconomic, and political
ramifications of the murder of Malia Brierre, a domestic servant employed by wealthy philanthropist Felix Wilson (James Earl Jones Jr.),
one of Baltimore's most respected citizens. Wilson, known as Fabu-
lous Felix, has earned his fortune by mass-producing cookies, dough-
nuts, cupcakes, and other confections (the character is loosely based
on Wallace Amos, founder of the Famous Amos cookie brand[42]). Brierre's corpse is discovered in the men's room of the Belvedere Hotel
during a black-tie gala that honors Wilson's charitable contributions
to Baltimore's African American community. Giardello, an old friend
of Wilson's wife, Regina (Lynne Thigpen), attends the event, only to
see Pembleton, the primary investigator, interrupt the proceedings to
begin questioning attendees. Neither Pembleton nor Giardello considers the Wilsons or their children, Hal (Jeffrey Wright) and Thea (Ellen
Bethea), to be suspects, instead professing respect for Wilson's generosity to Baltimore's civic life.

"Blood Ties (Part 2)" examines the racial divisions among the Homicide Unit's squad.[43] Simon's script acknowledges its principal characters' tangled racial feelings in three powerful scenes that illustrate
how *Homicide,* in Thomas A. Mascaro's words, "depict[s] not 'The
Black Man' but a wide range of blackness among the population of

black men. As with real-life racial interactions, *Homicide* [is] complex" by portraying "African American men who [have] the freedom to sculpt their own identities while negotiating with whites and each other as they [enforce] the law."[44] Pembleton, *Homicide*'s most dynamic and intelligent character, confronts three accusations from detectives Stuart Gharty (Peter Gerety) and Laura Ballard (Callie Thorne) that he protects Wilson from criminal scrutiny due to his (Pembleton's) racial allegiance with a powerful black man. During the first, Gharty and Ballard discuss the case while driving to the squad room after questioning Hal Wilson. Ballard—who has recently arrived in Baltimore from Seattle, Washington—says that her friends and family call Baltimore a tough town and a hard-core place, meaning that it is a black city. Ballard disagrees with how Pembleton investigates the case, thinking that the police should obtain hair and blood samples from Felix and Hal to determine their involvement with Brierre, who had sexual intercourse not long before her murder. Ballard then claims that Pembleton perceives suspecting the Wilsons of murder as evidence of racism, prompting Gharty to offer this blunt assessment of the Homicide Unit's racial politics.

> GHARTY.   Even if Pembleton wasn't the primary, say you caught the case. You think you could work this murder the way you want? Not a chance in hell. Giardello would still be in our faces, still maneuvering to protect Wilson and his family. All I'm saying is, you and I, we're just working the case, just taking in the facts, trying to identify suspects, uh, through simple common sense. Giardello and Pembleton, they are covering Wilson's ass because Wilson's ass is the same color as theirs.
> BALLARD.   Okay, hold up a second.
> GHARTY.   It is what it is. I'm not saying that Giardello is a bad lieutenant. I'm not saying that I think Pembelton is a lousy cop, but the racial stuff on this case is right there on the table. Nobody's talking about it, but it's there.

This discussion highlights the perception among white detectives that black men protect their own. Ballard's discomfort with Gharty's description of Giardello and Pembleton as racial "ass kissers" offers only temporary disagreement to Gharty's statement that he and Ballard employ common sense to investigate the case while Giardello and Pembleton pursue ulterior agendas. Gharty considers his position to be neutral, but concluding that his African American colleagues make decisions based solely on race endorses the unexamined bias that black men place their racial loyalties above all other concerns. Pembleton and Giardello's refusal to suspect Felix and Hal seems unusual until the viewer recalls that no physical evidence points to either man, even if determining Felix's and Hal's involvement with Brierre, as Ballard indicates, is a wise investigative decision that may substantiate each man's innocence. The circumstantial case that Gharty and Ballard construct against the Wilsons, however, is flimsy, as Pembleton and Giardello later note.

Gharty also ignores two key points. Giardello's close friendship with Regina Wilson motivates his defense of the Wilson family, while Pembleton defers to Felix more out of respect for the man's accomplishments than because of his race. Pembleton, who admires Wilson's initiative, intelligence, and compassion, praises Wilson's charitable work in all three "Blood Ties" episodes. Pembleton cannot ignore how Wilson has overcome the humble life of an East Baltimore project child to achieve financial prominence yet maintains close ties with the city's working-class and poor residents.

This admiration, however, contains a racial element that makes the episode's political stance more ambivalent. The event honoring Wilson's philanthropy acknowledges the man's support of African American causes, particularly education, to suggest that Pembleton cannot fully separate race from class. The scene immediately following Gharty and Ballard's conversation, however, finds Pembleton doing exactly that while conversing with Bayliss. Pembleton claims not to lean on race, telling Bayliss that "since my first day on patrol, I've worked this job as hard as it can be worked. I ask no quarter, I give no quarter. When people think of Frank Pembleton, they don't think in terms of black or white. On the street, in the Box, on the witness stand, I come to people as a cop, a detective." Pembleton emphasizes that the Wilsons' status as African Americans does not affect his investigative judgment, but Pembleton's need to articulate this caveat illustrates his sensitivity to accusations of racial bias. Pembleton also asserts his credentials as a cop above his status as a black American, demonstrating how nimbly Simon reflects the competing personae that Pembleton must integrate into his workplace identity as a dogged, determined, and gifted detective.

This reality underscores the double consciousness that Pembleton must negotiate as a police officer of African descent but that Bayliss,

Gharty, and Ballard do not. Pembleton's talent as an investigator never fully overcomes his racial identity, making the third scene that Simon includes in "Blood Ties (Part 2)" even more significant as a statement about preferential treatment. Giardello angrily tells Pembleton, Bayliss, Gharty, and Ballard that the *Baltimore Sun*'s crime reporter has learned important details about the case nearly as soon as the lieutenant has, leading Giardello to suspect that someone inside the department has leaked the information. Pembleton distrustfully glances at Ballard, provoking an argument that reveals the fundamental grievances that each detective holds. Ballard thinks that Felix and Hal's proximity to Brierre, when coupled with Brierre's beauty, makes them suspects, but this conclusion troubles Pembleton.

> PEMBLETON.   Because we all know that black men can't con-
> trol themselves when it comes to blue shoes and tight pants.
> BAYLISS.   Hey, Frank. Frank! No one is saying that.
> BALLARD.   What I'm saying is that these people—
> PEMBLETON.   These people?
> BALLARD.   Black, white, or blue, Pembleton.
> PEMBLETON.   So you can prove once again that you can take
> the nigger out of the ghetto but not the ghetto out of the nigger,
> is that it?
> BALLARD.   Are you joking? All I want is some straight
> answers.

Bayliss's response casts Pembleton's statement about sexually voracious black men as an oversensitive reaction to Ballard's point, but Pembleton does not relent. Referring to ghetto niggers intensifies the dispute, causing Ballard to suggest that Pembleton deliberately misreads her comment to infer racist implications that do not exist. Gharty then claims that the Wilsons' reputation will not suffer from police scrutiny because the family has half of City Hall, Giardello, and Pembleton in their pocket.

> PEMBLETON.   Excuse me, I'm in someone's pocket?
> GHARTY.   Hey, this is Baltimore. They're black, successful.
> That's the deal. End of story. This is your city, Pembleton. Your
> house. Your department. Your rules.
> PEMBLETON.   Oh, so it wasn't that way when the Italians ran
> it or when the Irish owned it? How many favors have been

called in in the name of the Knights of Columbus or St. Michael's Society, huh?

Pembleton refutes Gharty's statement about African Americans privileging themselves within the Baltimore Police Department by reminding Gharty that departmental favoritism has long depended on ethnicity. Pembleton also illustrates the subtle point that these racial and ethnic groups resemble one another more than they diverge by using bureaucratic power to benefit their own members. Pembleton, indeed, does not deny that race and ethnicity are factors in investigative or administrative decisions but instead places this lamentable truth in its broader historical context.

The scene's most explosive exchange, however, occurs when Gharty, upset by the special treatment that the Wilsons have received, tells Pembleton, "You're the errand boy here, not me."

PEMBLETON. I'm a boy now?
GHARTY. Oh, don't bait me, you son of a bitch! I didn't use the word that way! I didn't use the word that way!
PEMBLETON. Why don't you crawl up to one of those, uh, Hampden gin mills and buy a round for your Irish brothers on me and cry the blues about how your time has passed, okay?

This heated confrontation depicts how rigidly each man clings to his preconceptions. The term *errand boy* may not have specific racist connotations in the context in which Gharty employs it, but his enraged reaction when Pembleton bristles at having the word *boy* applied to him suggests that Gharty thoughtlessly employs a term that has historically infantilized, diminished, and demeaned black men. Pembleton, in turn, again insults Gharty's Irish background by accusing Gharty and his white brethren of bemoaning their reduced importance in the Baltimore Police Department's new hierarchy. Pembleton recognizes a tendency in ethnic white men to claim positions of authority, power, and influence by unfairly excluding racial minorities but then complain that those minorities—after years of struggle to achieve the authority that has been unjustly denied them—illegitimately usurp political power. The sense that history has abandoned white Americans (particularly white men) thereby justifies the prejudice that white men should control America's centers of power to prevent African Americans from wrongly excluding white people from the political, social, and economic institutions that have historically oppressed racial minorities.

Pembleton and Gharty's argument deftly criticizes institutional racism, ethnic grievances, and personal animus. Simon prevents any single character from possessing the moral high ground, resulting in a scene whose political ambivalence produces rich dramatic texture. The quarrel's rawness illustrates how honestly *Homicide* faces racial division and how capably Simon integrates socially realistic themes into his television writing. The situation becomes even more complex when Pembleton, enraged by his confrontation with Ballard, Bayliss, and Gharty, questions Felix to prove that the man had no reason to murder Brierre. Wilson, however, confesses to having consensual sexual intercourse with the young woman. Pembleton's palpable disappointment at this news forces him to realize that Ballard's concerns were justified. Wilson expresses shame at betraying his wife's loyalty but soon hires an attorney to protect his legal interests, leaving Pembleton to reevaluate his faith in Wilson's rectitude.

"Blood Ties (Part 2)" is Simon at his best. The episode, by shattering Felix's spotless public image, forces Pembleton and Giardello to question their own assumptions about a heroic civic figure whom they respect, yet the story does not certify Gharty's careless accusations of racial bias. The episode instead mines the ambiguities of American race relations to display the individual, institutional, and ideological compromises that the nation's contested racial history forces on its citizens. This mature theme extends to "Blood Ties (Part 3)" (cowritten by Simon and Anya Epstein, based on a story by Fontana, Martin, and Yoshimura), as Pembleton, with Bayliss's assistance, begins intensively investigating the Wilson family's peccadilloes.[45] Pembleton finds that Hal loved Brierre, going so far as to write passionate letters that he could not bring himself to deliver. Hal, during an off-the-record conversation with Felix and Pembleton, confesses to murdering Brierre after he—furious with his father for betraying his mother, for seducing the much younger Malia, and for stealing Hal's beloved—confronted Brierre at the Belvedere Hotel. Hal's misdirected anger led to homicide, but his confession exposes his tortured relationship with Felix.

HAL.   You can question me ad nauseum, Detective. I'm not
     gonna answer.
FELIX.   Yes you are.

HAL. What are you going to do? Send me to me room? Cut off my allowance? Take off your belt and give me a good ass-whipping?

FELIX. I never punished you like that.

HAL. Maybe you should have.

FELIX. I denied you nothing. You wanted a pony, I got you a pony, a motorcycle, a computer, education, trips to Europe, a new car every year.

HAL. You couldn't write a check big enough. You couldn't pay me enough to compensate for having spent my entire life listening to your up-from-the-projects, East Baltimore war stories. Your history. Your journey. You denied me nothing? You denied me everything.

FELIX. What? You wanted your own place, your own history? You should have taken it, demanded it!

HAL. Well, you take what you want, Dad.

FELIX. Answer the detective's question.

HAL. I'm a twenty-eight-year-old man. I don't need you to tell me what to do anymore.

FELIX. Well, you're twenty-eight years old? You're a grown man? Then act like a man instead of a pubescent child who stayed up late writing heartfelt letters to his puppy love and then didn't have the courage to give them to her.

HAL. What do you know about love? You and Malia, that had nothing to do with love. That was about an old man chasing his spent youth. Must have taken a lot of courage, huh Dad, to deceive my mother.

FELIX (*sighs*). Well, I'll claim that lie as my own. Which lies are yours, son?

This scene, marvelously acted by Jones and Wright, reveals the bitterness, inadequacy, and rage that Hal feels at being the son of a famous, powerful, and ambitious man whose achievements he will never surpass. Felix, for his part, not only criticizes his son's sense of entitlement (fostered, Felix admits, by his own largesse) but also emphasizes Hal's weakness. Their competing claims to manhood, when coupled with Felix's fatherly disappointment, lay bare the contradictory passions that wealth, entitlement, parental indulgence, and filial jealousy evoke within a prominent, tight-knit, and secretive family. The scene also illustrates Simon and Epstein's authorial shrewdness by constructing a civilian interrogation in which Pembleton plays no active role. The detective merely watches the conversation between Felix and Hal develop, allowing the household drama unfolding before him to provide the necessary information to close the Brierre case. Felix becomes Pembleton's unwitting stalking horse by sharply questioning Hal to get to the truth, which is uglier than Felix expected.

"Blood Ties (Part 3)" then obscures the investigation's thorny racial and class implications by having Felix refuse Hal's incarceration. The lack of direct evidence, along with Hal's inadmissible confession (Pembleton does not inform Hal of his Miranda rights before speaking with him), means that Hal cannot be arrested. When Pembleton returns to the Wilson estate, the family is preparing to move to San Diego, California. Pembleton says Hal cannot outrun Brierre's murder, but Felix replies, "I'm gonna do everything in my power to make sure that he does." Pembleton wonders whether Felix can live with this decision, provoking an honest response from the older man: "I don't know, but I'm sure as hell gonna try." Felix, in other words, uses the power that his privilege conveys to keep his son out of prison, speaking to Felix's sense that wealth exempts his family from punishment. Pembleton, who disagrees with Felix's behavior in shielding Hal from the legal consequences of his crime, can reflect only on his (Pembleton's) error in judgment. Pembleton later tells Ballard that she was correct about the Wilson case: "Your instincts were dead-on. Mine, for once, were not." The detectives do not discuss racism, suggesting that Pembleton—who, earlier in "Blood Ties (Part 3)," tells his wife Mary (Ami Brabson) that his personal feelings have affected the investigation—protects the Wilsons to preserve Felix's reputation rather than helping a fellow black man in a misguided attempt at racial comity. David P. Kalat's analysis of "Blood Ties (Part 3)" notes that Pembleton "is not the one-note supercop many fans would like him to be. Instead, he is a human being, with a complex set of motivations, one of which is vanity. Pembleton takes great pride in his instincts, and enjoys taking credit when his instincts close a case."[46] Pembleton's apology to Ballard acknowledges this truth, which dissipates the racial bias that Gharty and Ballard believe characterizes Pembleton's attitude. Kalat accurately summarizes the resulting complications: "Ultimately, Frank has so much respect for Felix Wilson that the detective allows his emotions to influence his instincts. This is not racist behavior on Frank's part, merely a very human error that all of us are prone to make."[47] Pembleton stumbles during the Wilson investigation, which illustrates Simon's talent not only for realistic characterization but also for portraying homicide detectives as fallible human beings rather than as flawless investigators.

Giardello confesses to similar failings when reminding Pembleton that the Wilson case will remain open until they accrue enough evidence to charge Hal with Brierre's murder: "For all the good the Wilsons did for this city, for the black community, well, to you and I, that means nothing now. I was blindsided by my personal involvement. I refused to see the truth of their guilt." Race plays a minimal role in Giardello's reaction. Loyalty to his friend Regina Wilson, rather than racial preference, dominates all other issues. "Blood Ties (Part 3)" shows the significant influence that emotion, friendship, and favoritism have on homicide investigations. The episode, like its predecessor, is a notable example of *Homicide*'s and Simon's penchant for social realism in that it allows Hal to get away with murder. Wealth, prominence, and privilege conspire to produce an ambivalent resolution that satisfies few characters or viewers.

If parts 2 and 3 of "Blood Ties" demonstrate Simon's aptitude for complex characters, "Sideshow (Part 2)" illustrates his control of intricate plots. "Sideshow (Part 2)," the concluding segment of *Homicide*'s third (and final) crossover story with Dick Wolf's *Law & Order,* may feature *Homicide*'s most elaborate story line.[48] The episode's numerous subplots force a narrative fluency that Simon skillfully interweaves with good character moments for ASA Ed Danvers, Detective Rene Sheppard (Michael Michele), and *Law & Order*'s Assistant District Attoryney (ADA) Jack McCoy (Sam Waterston). "Sideshow (Part 2)" continues the opening *Law & Order* segment's politically charged investigation into the death of Janine McBride, a federal employee whose murder draws the notice of Independent Counsel William Dell (George Hearn), a man charged with probing the financial misdeeds of Bill Clinton's presidential administration. (The episode originally aired on February 19, 1999, only seven days after Clinton was acquitted of impeachment resulting from Kenneth Starr's real-life investigation into Clinton's participation in the Vince Foster, Whitewater, and Monica Lewinsky scandals.) The episode's cynical portrait of political power's deleterious effect on the lives of civil servants predicts Simon's later work on *The Wire* while highlighting how narcissistic the legal system can be.

"Sideshow (Part 2)" poses a challenge for Simon in that he must continue numerous story lines begun in the first episode (written by

Law & Order producer René Balcer). Although both programs' writing staffs coordinated their efforts, Simon has the difficult task of constructing a satisfying resolution to the two-part episode's complex plot, which suggests a criminal conspiracy emanating from the White House. The true story of McBride's death, however, is just as sordid but far less sinister than Dell believes in his quest to bring down the president by unveiling how McBride's romantic encounters with two female federal employees spiral into jealousy, broken marriages, violence, and murder. "Sideshow (Part 2)" depicts a remarkably Byzantine police investigation that sees Munch and Sheppard partner with New York City detectives Lennie Briscoe (Jerry Orbach) and Reynaldo Curtis (Benjamin Bratt) to discover why McBride, a resident of Baltimore, is found dead in New York City. Danvers and McCoy work together to protect the investigation's integrity from interference by Dell's office, resulting in Danvers losing his appointment as a Maryland state judge when Dell, reacting to Danvers's insistence that an incarcerated witness be deposed before a Baltimore grand jury, exposes Danvers's teenage membership in the Durham Street Raiders, an all-white street gang that severely beat an African American man when Danvers was 14 years old. This revelation causes Giardello to call all black officers, detectives, and administrators of the Baltimore Homicide Unit—including Colonel George Barnfather (Clayton LeBouef)—into his office to recommend that they support Danvers. Everyone agrees, but when Barnfather tells Giardello that no amount of support can salvage Danvers's judicial nomination, Giardello simply responds, "He knows that."

This subplot is only one of many that plays against the background of cutthroat Beltway politics, bureaucratic infighting, and sexual intrigue. Simon also includes Sheppard's difficulties in recovering her reputation among her fellow detectives after she survives an assault by a drug suspect who savagely beats her with her own gun in "Shades of Gray" (7.10). Sheppard's former partner, Meldrick Lewis, now avoids her, believing that she is physically incapable of backing him on the street. Perhaps more surprising is the discussion that Ballard and Stivers have while exercising in the squad's gymnasium. Stivers lays part of the blame for Sheppard's injuries on the detective herself, saying that Sheppard should not have pulled her service weapon if she was not prepared to fire it. The tensions over this issue lead Sheppard to confront Stivers and to declare, in a drunken yet impassioned monologue at the Waterfront Bar (a pub co-owned by

Lewis), that people must not only trust one another but also judge one another based on the totality of each person's actions, not on one or two mistakes. Lewis tells Sheppard, "That's what I'd want for myself," but the scene concludes ambivalently when Sheppard decides to take a cab home. Sheppard's problems with the squad are not resolved, while no one pledges to partner with her on the next case. Simon parallels Sheppard's and Danvers's disgrace to underscore the unfair treatment they both face and to reflect the episode's larger theme of how mistrust in matters of sex, marriage, and politics unleashes forces that destroy relationships, careers, and lives.

"Sideshow (Part 2)," however, finally revolves around Independent Counsel Dell's egotism. Dell utilizes his nearly unfettered power to investigate the private lives of several characters, including McCoy and Danvers. McCoy, in "Sideshow (Part 1)," is arrested for refusing to answer questions in front of Dell's federal grand jury about his (McCoy's) sexual relationships with two female colleagues and about the identity of an anonymous witness whose name he refuses to disclose. McCoy, in "Sideshow (Part 2)," sympathizes with Danvers regarding his shoddy treatment by Dell, even answering, "Hell yes," when Danvers asks McCoy if pursuing the McBride investigation to the highest levels of the U.S. government frightens him. Dell prevents Baltimore's and New York's police departments from concluding the McBride investigation by transferring witnesses, suspects, and defendants into his custody, then offering these people deals that abrogate justice for McBride's family. Dell, in fact, grants immunity to Theodore Dawkins (Jimmy Ray Weeks), McBride's killer and a former Drug Enforcement Agency officer working as a private investigator for the president's chief of staff, in exchange for testimony that will damage the president's reputation. Although Danvers, McCoy, Munch, Sheppard, Briscoe, and Curtis determine that Dawkins acted alone in killing McBride, Dell does not care.

Danvers and McCoy confront Dell in a scene that illustrates Dell's inflated sense of importance.

DELL. There are larger issues at stake. This is more than a murder here.
DANVERS (*scoffs*). More than a murder?
DELL. Corruption at the highest level.
MCCOY. What proof do you have? Dawkins has no corroboration. All you've got is innuendo and allegation.

DANVERS. That's all he needs. He set it up so that this case
will never get to court. (*to Dell*) You don't want a jury trial, a
chance to determine who's guilty and who's not, because, let's
face it, the only case he can make in court stops with Theodore
Dawkins. But outside a courtroom, at a press conference or an
impeachment report to Congress, he can allege just about anything he wants.
MCCOY. And never have to prove a thing!
DELL. I remember when I was clerking at the Supreme Court,
a justice asked me why it was that, inside the Beltway, the
lawyering seemed so worthy and dignified, while outside the
Beltway, the same kind of labor came off as savage and bitter.
I told him I didn't know. He smiled and explained that the
lawyers outside the Beltway seemed so damn savage because
the stakes are so damn small. (*Moving to exit the room*) It's been
a pleasure, gentlemen.

Identifying McBride's murder as a small-stakes event demeans
Danvers's and McCoy's efforts to prosecute her killer while lionizing
Dell's own work, which Danvers identifies as petty political mudsling-
ing. Simon writes resonant dialogue that, in less than three minutes,
explores issues of injustice, political skullduggery, legal brinkmanship,
and vaulting ambition. Apart from giving Hearn, Ivanek, and Waterston the basis for superb performances, the scene also reveals the cynicism at the heart of all three branches of America's federal government.
"Sideshow (Part 2)" justifies its title by depicting Dell's investigation
as a distraction meant to glorify Dell's political vendetta against the
president, not as an attempt to find truth, obtain justice, and uphold
law. Although the episode may strike the viewer as a fictional defense
of Bill Clinton, "Sideshow (Part 2)" probes the criminal-justice system's
fault lines to conclude that this system is an uncaring, destructive, and
repressive bureaucracy that thrives on ego. This attitude, so typical of
Simon's writing, demonstrates how different a crime drama *Homicide*
is. Far from romanticizing police detectives and lawyers as defenders of justice, "Sideshow (Part 2)," like its parent series, depicts them
as struggling civil servants who cannot ennoble, improve, or reform
the institutions that employ them. The episode's final scene confirms
this analysis by having Munch, Briscoe, and Curtis exit the Waterfront
Bar, only to see the American flag flapping atop the Baltimore Police
Department's headquarters building. Munch sardonically salutes the

flag, says, "I'm too damn sober," and returns to the bar with Briscoe and Curtis in tow. Simon not only expresses the frustration, ennui, and disappointment that Dell's defeat of the detectives' investigation provokes but also concludes "Sideshow (Part 2)" more pessimistically than most other *Homicide* episodes.

This fact further establishes how Simon's contributions to *Homicide* help fictionalize the concerns, issues, and problems that *A Year on the Killing Streets* presents as nearly intractable. Neither the book nor the television series offers easy answers to the social challenges that crime, poverty, racism, and injustice pose to Americans living at the end of the 20th century. Simon's book may have inspired *Homicide: Life on the Street* to become one of the best, most thoughtful, and most progressive cop shows seen on American television, but this adaptation's success results as much from Fontana's keen dramatic instincts as from Simon's work. Simon, thanks to Fontana's (and Levinson's) mentorship, learns to transform his journalism into compelling, convincing, and socially realistic crime drama. This accolade, however, has limits. *Homicide*'s long network life does not depend on Simon's approval or dramatic gifts for its success, even if the series benefits from his involvement. Simon, however, immeasurably profits from his professional relationship with *Homicide*. The series launches his television-writing career; teaches him that television can powerfully dramatize his most pressing social, racial, and political concerns; and demonstrates how effective a fictional author he can be.

Homicide: Life on the Street, therefore, nurtures Simon's narrative talents. This series, by telling unconventional stories about murder, crime, and police work, continues the tradition inaugurated by *Hill Street Blues* and *NYPD Blue* but surpasses them in quirkiness, realism, and courage. Simon does not create, develop, or oversee *Homicide*, but his apprenticeship on this program educates him about all aspects of writing, producing, and sustaining worthwhile television drama. This training equips Simon to create *The Corner*, his incomparable HBO miniseries about Baltimore's drug culture, and *The Wire*, the superlative social drama that qualifies as Simon's masterpiece. This study will profile *The Corner* in chapter 4 and *The Wire* in chapter 6, but one truth about both programs is unassailable. Neither would be possible without *Homicide*'s example, making Fontana and Levinson's program a vital inspiration, influence, and development in Simon's television career.

4

Street Talk: David Simon's *The Corner*

The Corner (2000), HBO's six-part miniseries adaptation of David Simon and Edward Burns's 1997 book *The Corner: A Year in the Life of an Inner-City Neighborhood*, not only offered Simon the opportunity to oversee his first solo television production but also provided the chance to dramatize the forgotten lives of people surviving the drug trade of Baltimore, Maryland. Simon's concern for these individuals—significantly, all members of the African American underclass—is palpable in both the book (hereafter referred to as *A Year in the Life of an Inner-City Neighborhood*) and the miniseries (hereafter referred to as *The Corner*). Simon's desire to present the experience of the book's protagonists as authentically as possible produces six television episodes that are remarkable in their clarity, compassion, and pacing. *The Corner*, which won three Emmy Awards (including Outstanding Miniseries and Outstanding Writing for a Miniseries or Movie) and the George Foster Peabody Award, stands as a landmark contribution to televisual dramatizations of drug abuse by humanizing the difficult experiences of addict Gary McCullough (T. K. Carter); his addict ex-wife, Fran Boyd (Khandi Alexander); their son, DeAndre McCullough (Sean Nelson); DeAndre's girlfriend, Tyreeka Freamon (Toy Connor), who is the mother of his child; aging drug tout Curtis "Fat Curt" Davis (Clarke Peters); drug-addicted local artist George "Blue" Epps (Glenn Plummer); neighborhood activist Ella Thompson (Tyra Ferrell); and the Crenshaw Mafia Brothers (a youth gang comprised of several of DeAndre's male friends). The miniseries, like its literary source, also forms the basis for many characters, themes, and story lines that appear in *The Wire*.

    The Corner's stark portrayal of Baltimore's poverty-stricken Franklin Square neighborhood, particularly the open-air drug market at the

corner of Monroe and Fayette streets (known locally as "Fat Curt's
Corner"), so overwhelms the viewer that critics like *Slate*'s Jacob Weisberg find the miniseries too distressing to abide, particularly when
compared with *The Wire*. Stating that "*The Wire* feels startlingly lifelike,"
Weisberg observes that Simon's later program "is not in fact a naturalistic depiction of ghetto life. That kind of realism better describes... *The
Corner*," which, Weisberg claims, "is nearly unwatchable, because—
however true to life—the extended depiction of shrieking crack whores
and broken-down junkies 10 cents short of the price of a 'loosie' is too
much to take."[1] This assessment offers a common evaluation of Simon's
accomplishment in adapting *A Year in the Life of an Inner-City Neighborhood* for television (with considerable assistance from his creative partners: cowriter David Mills, director Charles S. Dutton, and producer
Robert F. Colesberry). *The Corner,* Weisberg implies, mirrors life so
closely that the audience feels the same existential claustrophobia that
its characters experience. The sense of being trapped in a nightmare
that may never end looms over the entire venture, rendering *The Corner*
a notable example of naturalistic television drama that acknowledges
the harsh realities of urban America's social decline.

Weisberg's analysis emphasizes the horrors of drug abuse that *The
Corner* aptly demonstrates but overlooks how the miniseries, through
the slow accretion of detail that develops in every episode, presents the
challenges of addiction as mundane elements of its characters' daily
lives. The quotidian nature of drug addiction defines the program's
narrative approach so comprehensively that the audience begins to see
Gary, Fran, DeAndre, Blue Epps, and Fat Curt as they see themselves:
downtrodden people enduring difficult circumstances who cannot, no
matter how much they struggle, resist what appears to be an inevitable
descent into oblivion. Even the characters who avoid addiction, such
as Tyreeka and Ella, find themselves living in a culture pervaded by
the rules, precepts, and codes that the drug trade creates, obeys, and
sustains. *The Corner,* by refusing to ignore the resulting despair, also
refuses to pander to its characters or its audience.

The miniseries, therefore, embodies the epigraph, from Franz Kafka,
that begins *A Year in the Life of an Inner-City Neighborhood:* "You can hold
back from the suffering of the world. You have free permission to do so
and it is in accordance with your nature. But perhaps this very holding
back is the one suffering you could have avoided."[2] This quotation sets
the tone for Simon and Burns's book to suggest that overlooking the
world's misfortunes perpetuates the suffering that ignorance seeks to

repudiate, thereby compounding problems that go unnoticed, unaddressed, and unsolved. *The Corner* even includes a visual corollary to Kafka's epigraph when Dutton, director of all six episodes, appears in a prologue to the first installment, "Gary's Blues." Dutton, looking straight into the camera, reveals that he was born and raised on the same Baltimore streets where *A Year in the Life of an Inner-City Neighborhood* takes place and where *The Corner* is set. Dutton comments that the drug market at Monroe and Fayette is only one of 100 such locales in Baltimore, to say nothing of the thousands that exist throughout America. Dutton's voice is measured, yet his sadness becomes evident when he observes that "the Corner" embodies an urban paradox by pulsing with life even while bringing death to many residents. Dutton then says that, in 1970, Maryland had five major penal institutions, but, 30 years later (in 2000), 28 such prisons exist, with more under construction. These depressing statistics lead Dutton to a melancholy conclusion: "This film is a true story of men, women, and children living in the midst of the drug trade. Their voices are too rarely heard."[3]

Dutton's final statement, along with the data he cites, alerts *The Corner*'s viewer that the miniseries avoids morally upright depictions of unfortunate yet resolute characters bravely enduring their impoverished circumstances. Melodrama gives way to social realism in a program of rare power, depth, and complexity that challenges its viewers' narrative expectations, political assumptions, and economic biases. Weisberg's opinion, therefore, is misguided because *The Corner* exposes its characters' vulnerabilities without degenerating into sentimental rubbish that teaches lessons, preaches homilies, and achieves closure. *The Corner*, by mixing fact with fiction, equals its source material's willingness to expose uncomfortable truths about 20th-century urban America that find little resolution.

This final aspect—*The Corner*'s refusal to solve the problems that it expertly dramatizes—accounts for reactions like Weisberg's admiring yet finally gloomy evaluation. Viewers who wish for happy endings, life-affirming denouements, and exciting climaxes will find Simon's miniseries disappointing, just as readers who expect *A Year in the Life of an Inner-City Neighborhood* to offer bright forecasts for its characters' futures must judge Simon and Burns's book a failure. *The Corner*, Weisberg suggests, presents such a pessimistic appraisal of the American drug war that the audience, unable to find solace in apparently insoluble problems, retreats from the program's ugly view of American

poverty. *The Corner's* bleak portrait of the drug trade, by verging on nihilism, lessens its dramatic effectiveness.

Such assessments, however, overlook *The Corner's* mordant wit,
splendid performances, and unconventional pace. Simon, Mills, and
Dutton, along with cinematographer Ivan Strasburg and the talented
cast, so thoroughly meld fantasy with reality that the audience can forget that *The Corner* adapts Simon and Burns's journalistic book into
a work of fiction. The authors' note in *A Year in the Life of an Inner-
City Neighborhood,* indeed, outlines how Simon and Burns chronicled
12 months in the lives of the Corner's residents: "Our methodology
was simple enough and is best described as stand-around-and-watch
journalism. We went to the neighborhood each day with notepads
and followed people around."[4] This plan proved more complicated
than Simon and Burns expected, as any reader of their intense account
soon realizes. The book's novelistic qualities—serious themes, three-
dimensional characters, authentic dialogue, and vivid settings—raise
questions about how two writers could transcribe such confidential
details about the people under observation without using audio or
video recorders. Even these devices would miss some facts, but Simon
and Burns's book includes entire conversations among three or more
individuals. *A Year in the Life of an Inner-City Neighborhood* also unveils
interior monologues in which Gary, Fran, DeAndre, and the other residents think about their lives without censoring their opinions.

Astute readers of Simon and Burns's long book, in other words,
might suspect that the authors, to keep the story moving, fictionalize certain elements by reconstructing entire passages from after-the-
fact conversations. Simon and Burns deny any fictionalizing intent by
describing their research-and-writing process as one of painstaking
reportage:

> The dialogue in the book was either witnessed by one or both
> of us, or, in a handful of instances, reconstructed from detailed
> interviews with those involved in the conversation. Similarly,
> when it is indicated that characters are thinking about some-
> thing, we have not simply interpolated their thoughts and feel-
> ings from their actions. More often than not, we were present at
> the events upon which the person is reflecting, and their thoughts
> were verbally expressed to us at the time of the incident or im-
> mediately after the fact. In other cases, interior monologues were
> constructed from repeated interviews.[5]

This passage helps explain *A Year in the Life of an Inner-City Neighborhood*'s sociological precision, laudable detail, and factual density. Simon and Burns indulge the journalist's privilege of reconstituting events, feelings, and conversations from retrospective discussions with the principal players. The authors, however, employ terms commonly associated with literary criticism by identifying the people whose lives they recount as *characters* and these individuals' inner thoughts as *interior monologues*. This tendency emphasizes the fact that journalism depends on narrative, so much so that reporters typically refer to their articles as *stories*. The need to maintain reader interest is particularly crucial in "a work of journalism"[6] as long as *A Year in the Life of an Inner-City Neighborhood* (540 pages). Simon and Burns, indeed, so skillfully create suspense, build character, and reveal surprises that their book reads like a gripping, lucid, and rich novel.

Simon and Burns, in other words, choose not to author an anthropological case study, which would bleach their book of all color, emotion, and humor. Simon followed much the same path in *Homicide: A Year on the Killing Streets*, making this earlier text an excellent candidate for fictional adaptation. *A Year in the Life of an Inner-City Neighborhood*'s literary qualities make it equally adaptable, which clarifies why Simon approached HBO to produce *The Corner* as a miniseries rather than as a documentary. Simon, in his long introduction to Rafael Alvarez's book *"The Wire": Truth Be Told*, details *The Corner*'s protracted genesis, identifying the success of Tom Fontana's *Oz*, the no-holds-barred prison drama that Fontana (Simon's scriptwriting mentor when he worked on *Homicide: Life on the Street*) produced for HBO from 1997 to 2003, as a decisive influence: "By the time *The Corner* was published, Tom was already locked down in Oswald Penitentiary, proving to HBO and the world in general that even the most discomfiting drama now had a place on American television. Perhaps, I thought to myself, there was room at HBO or some other premium channel for something as dark as life on an open-air drug corner."[7] This darkness may cause Weisberg to declare *The Corner* nearly unwatchable, but Simon's comments reveal his hope that HBO would tackle his unlikely project to complement *Oz*'s brutal-yet-honest approach by staging the drug trade as network television never had.

Simon then notes that Fontana and Barry Levinson, *Homicide*'s executive producers, did not "see *The Corner* as material for a continuing series" but that Fontana contacted HBO on Simon's behalf.[8] The premium channel's executives, however, were nervous about the potential racial insensitivities of allowing Simon to script the entire program:

> At the resulting meeting, it became clear that the cable channel was willing to take a shot, provided I could pair myself with a black writer.
>
> It didn't matter to me one way or the other—I knew I had those Fayette Street voices in my head—but the other white folk in the room were not about to let a lone pale scribbler produce a miniseries about black drug addicts and dealers.[9]

Simon suggested David Mills—the former *Washington Post* reporter who had collaborated with Simon on their first television script, *Homicide*'s "Bop Gun"—as his writing partner. Simon's nonchalant attitude about this development bespeaks his intellectual confidence in accurately depicting African American addicts and dealers whom network television programs (particularly crime dramas) dismiss as criminals, layabouts, or social parasites. Simon's faith in his knowledge of corner life brazenly posits that *A Year in the Life of an Inner-City Neighborhood*'s meticulous research imparts a true understanding of the challenges faced by Gary, Fran, DeAndre, and the book's other subjects. Simon's declaration claims an extraordinary privilege that transcends the detailed appreciation of lives, issues, and events that the best journalism makes available. Hearing the voices of corner residents in his head makes Simon a fellow traveler—that is, nearly an equal—with the people whom his book profiles.

This implication, by overstepping the professional boundaries that press reporters traditionally respect, surpasses the objectivity that journalism cherishes. Simon's formulation casts him as no mere expert commanding facts about the Corner's residents from a comfortable distance but as each person's interpreter, confidant, and comrade. This conclusion exceeds those moments when Simon and Burns, in the authors' note to *A Year in the Life of an Inner-City Neighborhood,* confess to breaching reportorial objectivity. They admit that "as a rule, we did not intervene in the swirl of events. But there were a few instances when we ignored the rule. We came to this project as reporters, but over time we found ourselves caring more about our subjects than we ever expected."[10] This disclosure does not trouble Simon and Burns because, even if their interference "helped or hurt someone more than he or she otherwise would have been helped or hurt" (thereby tainting their neutrality), "the limited support we provided had decidedly little effect."[11] Simon and Burns's rationale, indeed, suggests egotism of a different sort, which they immediately puncture: "Perhaps all our journalistic concerns about nonintervention are predicated on a touch of vanity. The corner culture and addiction are powerful forces—equal to or greater than all the legal barriers and social programming arrayed against them. On Fayette Street, the odds do not change because someone pops up with a notepad and the occasional kindess."[12]

These statements, even if advancing certain truths about addiction's unassailable control over its victims, fail to match Simon's arrogant attitude about faithfully portraying African American drug abusers in his HBO miniseries. Simon nonchalantly dismisses working with Mills ("It didn't matter to me one way or the other") before mocking himself as a "pale scribbler" whom HBO does not trust to do what Simon insinuates he can so capably achieve: depict the corner's residents more honestly than a black scriptwriter who has never experienced, studied, or scrutinized a drug neighborhood's paradoxical, perplexing, and pulsating life.

Simon's stance might strike the reader as peerless journalistic narcissism, even for the author (or coauthor) of so fine a book as *A Year in the Life of an Inner-City Neighborhood*. This judgment, however, diminishes when the reader recognizes that Simon's discussion of bringing *The Corner* to HBO describes a fiction writer's prerogatives, not a reporter's mindset. His analysis, therefore, underscores the capabilities, benefits, and license that fiction affords its practitioners. Simon's time as a writer and producer for *Homicide*, according to his introduction in *Truth Be Told*, liberated him from the strictures of journalism and the pain of departing the *Baltimore Sun*: "As a day job, it [working on *Homicide*] was a great one. And I found that the artifice of film and the camaraderie of set were enough to offset my exile from the *Sun*'s city desk."[13] Simon, thanks to his *Homicide* tenure and Fontana's tutelage, realizes that fiction enables socially conscious writers to achieve intimacies of person, place, and event that extensive (even exhaustive) reporting cannot equal. Since *A Year in the Life of an Inner-City Neighborhood*'s journalistic account employs narrative strategies reminiscent of fiction, transforming the book into a miniseries allows Simon and Mills to go beyond the book's facts to dramatize private moments in its characters' lives that a documentary might miss, overlook, or withhold.

The Corner, therefore, becomes a docudrama that merges objective facts, subjective opinions, and literary elements into a narrative that continuously subverts its own fictional enterprise. Director Dutton, apart from appearing in the prologue to "Gary's Blues," interviews the Corner's residents in short segments that begin and conclude each *Corner* episode. These vignettes find the off-screen Dutton speaking to his subject, who responds while looking into the lens. This visual setup suggests that Dutton holds the camera while questioning Gary, Fran, DeAndre, Tyreeka, Ella, and the other interviewees in classic direct-to-camera, talking-heads documentary style. The difference, however, is that Dutton converses with the actors playing the people profiled in *A Year in the Life of an Inner-City Neighborhood,* not the subjects themselves. This crucial change destabilizes the boundaries between fact and fiction, reality and fantasy, and objectivity and subjectivity to endorse a peculiar form of reflexivity that *The Corner* develops into its primary thematic style. The audience knows that actors perform roles in these wraparound segments, yet each scene's sober presentation enhances the realistic tone that Dutton's presence enforces. These bookends, in a pattern that characterizes the entire miniseries, simultaneously consolidate and shatter the fourth-wall effect on which cinema and television rely to unsettle comfortable relationships between *The Corner*'s viewers and the unconventional material presented to them.

Jonathan Boudreaux, in his review of *The Corner*'s DVD release, feels that this result attenuates the program's dramatic power: "While this [strategy] does help to remind us that what we are seeing is based on a true story, it often comes across as an acting exercise." The closing interviews, in Boudreaux's analysis, "often interrupt the flow of the series, muting the effect of the shows' final scenes."[14] This last comment overlooks how each episode's concluding dialogue, between Dutton and the actor playing a character based on a real person, complements the final scene to offer useful glosses on the preceding action. The ending segment of the third episode, "Fran's Blues," testifies to how powerful Dutton's interviews can be.[15] The episode itself sees Fran Boyd, who wishes to kick her heroin and cocaine habit, spend time trying to secure space in a local rehabilitation facility. Fran, after months of waiting, proudly informs her family, friends, and neighbors that she has been awarded a bed at the Baltimore Recovery Center (BRC) and then enlists her brother Scoogie (Clayton LeBouef)—an ex-addict who has been sober for six years—to drive her to BRC on the day of her intake. When Fran arrives with a trash bag full of clothes and supplies, Antoinette (Willette R. Thompson), BRC's director, tells Fran that she has the wrong date: The bed will be available one week later. Fran has mistaken Antoinette's request to come to BRC to finalize all intake procedures as confirmation that the treatment will begin that day. Fran, perplexed by this turn of events, cannot believe her unfortunate circumstances. She briefly points her penknife at Antoinette, then says that she (Fran) will suffer embarrassment if she returns to her Franklin Square neighborhood with news that she misunderstood so significant a detail as her therapy's start date. Khandi Alexander's performance poetically expresses Fran's anger, mystification, embarrassment, and disappointment to reveal how important recovery is to the character's dignity. The next scene finds Fran, having declined Scoogie's offer to wait outside BRC, trudging toward her home. She walks into the house, past her sister Bunchie (Maria Broom) and sons DeAndre (Sean Nelson) and DeRodd (Sylvester Lee Kirk), and then walks upstairs, passing a room where her brother Stevie Boyd (Cyrus Farmer) is preparing to shoot heroin into his arm. Fran moves away from the camera, enters her bedroom, and sits on the bed. The episode's narrative ends with a long shot—both in its duration and its distance from her body—of Fran, dejected by failure, sitting silent and still.

This forlorn image dissolves to Dutton's conversation with Officer Bob Brown (Brian O'Neill), the white police officer who persistently interrupts the Corner's daily commerce by hassling, cajoling, and arresting the men and boys who sling drugs. Simon and Burns's book describes Brown as "the predominant constabulary scourge of every doper in the Franklin Square neighborhood—fiends in this part of town invoke the name as something distinct from the rest of the Baltimore Police Department. Whenever he makes an entrance, lookouts actually shout 'Bob Brown,' rather than the generic 'Five-Oh' or 'Time Out.'"[16] In *The Corner*'s first three episodes Brown is shown patting down, body searching, and threatening DeAndre when Brown's "jump-out squad" patrols the neighborhood's streets. Brown, in these scenes, finds no drug paraphernalia on DeAndre but tells the boy that selling narcotics will eventually land him in prison. Dutton, in the concluding interview of "Fran's Blues," questions Brown about how the neighborhood has changed. The officer, played with no-nonsense brio by O'Neill, says, "The rot started in the projects: Lexington Terrace, Murphy Homes. Just kept creeping uphill." When Dutton cites statistics about the futility of fighting the drug war to Brown (the Baltimore Police Department annually arrests 18,000 to 19,000 people for drug offenses; only 700 get prison time; an estimated 50,000 addicts live in the city), their conversation encapsulates the ambiguities, possibilities, and discontents that attend corner life. Brown's tone softens when he comments that good people still live in the neighborhood.

> BROWN. I got ladies who let me in the back doors of their houses so I can use a window to watch a corner. I got people call me with information. Church people. Working people.
> DUTTON. What about the corner people?
> BROWN. Half of them I've seen come up as kids. Saw 'em on the stoops, on the playgrounds. Saw them go off to school. It hurts to watch, man.
> DUTTON. The corner boys don't like you much, but they say the younger police are way worse.
> BROWN. By the time these younger guys came on, this place had already been all shot to hell. They see these people and fig-ure they always were junkies. Makes them act hard, I guess.
> DUTTON. Let me ask you something, Officer Brown. Are we going to win this war on drugs?
> BROWN (*pauses, thinks, sighs*). No comment.

Brown then walks out of the frame, concluding "Fran's Blues" on a disheartening note. This segment summarizes the long passage in *A Year in the Life of an Inner-City Neighborhood*'s third chapter that recounts Brown's losing crusade to close the Corner's drug market (a passage that allows Simon and Burns to incisively analyze the economic and political forces that condemn Brown, the police, the residents, the ad-dicts, and the dealers to endless confrontations). It also compounds the social insecurity that Fran's inability to enter treatment represents.

Dutton's interview with Brown, far from muting the final scene's drama, enhances Fran's despondency by illustrating how uncertain, unstable, and provisional all victories in the drug war are. Brown's comments offer public testimony to Fran's private defeat, while Dut-ton's patient-yet-probing questions demonstrate the pointlessness of regarding widespread drug addiction as a war. Brown, the viewer sees, is not an enemy so much as a man trapped by his sense of duty to po-lice a neighborhood whose deterioration he mourns. *The Corner* com-presses the sadness, outrage, and ambivalence that *A Year in the Life of an Inner-City Neighborhood* takes 10 pages to express into 90 seconds of screen time that, when juxtaposed with Fran's setback, eloquently recognizes the arduous circumstances confronting every person who lives in, works in, or visits the Franklin Square neighborhood.

The wraparound segments, therefore, allow each *Corner* episode to dramatize *A Year in the Life of an Inner-City Neighborhood*'s fluid mixture of reportorial observation, narrative commentary, and sociological analysis. Dutton's questions, rather than pontificating about the evils of drug abuse, elicit honest responses from their subjects. These faux interviews (Dutton, the viewer may easily forget, speaks to actors playing roles, not the actual participants) avoid the political, cultural, and intellectual bromides that Simon and Burns witheringly deconstruct in *A Year in the Life of an Inner-City Neighborhood*, particularly when discussing the drug war's best-known slogan:

We have swallowed some disastrous pretensions, allowing ourselves a naive sincerity that, even now, assumes the battle can be restricted to heroin and cocaine, limited to a self-contained cadre of lawbreakers—the quaint term "drug pusher" comes to mind— when all along the conflict was ripe to become a war against the underclass itself. We've trusted in the moral high ground: Just say no.[17]

Dutton's interviews may not characterize First Lady Nancy Reagan's famous "Just Say No" antidrug public-service campaign as a morally, legally, and socially bankrupt program based on unsophisticated ideas about addiction's causes and solutions, but they expose this campaign's hollowness by dramatizing the untidy realities of corner life. *The Corner* conflates fact with fiction—the real Charles S. Dutton talks with performers playing roles who speak on behalf of their real-life counterparts—to reject the easy assumptions, prevalent stereotypes, and illogical expectations that have transformed the drug war, in Simon and Burns's words, into "an absurdist nightmare, a statistical charade with no other purpose than to placate a public that wants drug trafficking attacked and vanquished—but not, of course, at the price it would actually cost to accomplish such an incredible feat."[18] This cost, *A Year in the Life of an Inner-City Neighborhood* makes clear, would involve near genocide—the utter destruction of America's underclass—that only the most heartless citizens would advocate. *The Corner* need not state this opinion as baldly as *A Year in the Life of an Inner-City Neighborhood* does because Dutton's interviews quietly make this point.

These bookend scenes, by inserting *The Corner*'s African American director into the program's action, accomplish another goal: counteracting HBO's concern about white producers misrepresenting the experience of black Americans. Dutton's empathy not only extends *The Corner*'s compassionate portrayal of addicts, dealers, residents, and police officers but also demonstrates that the drug trade is an all-consuming endeavor that, far from casting heroes and villains, victimizes everyone who comes near it. The miniseries offers contradictions, paradoxes, ambiguities, and ambivalences that rebuke the crude portrayal of drug addiction on other programs, functioning as an effective response to the derision that even progressive cop dramas like *Homicide: Life on the Street* purvey.

The Corner balances *Homicide* in the same way that *A Year in the Life of an Inner-City Neighborhood* balances *A Year on the Killing Streets*. The miniseries pays respectful attention to the complicated, depressing, yet worthwhile lives of the Corner's residents, addicts, and dealers in the same way that *Homicide* reveals the turbulent, challenging, and unglamorous lives of police detectives. This approach, according to Hugh K. David, places *The Corner* in a narrative lineage that includes Uli Edel's 1989 film adaptation of Hubert Selby Jr.'s 1964 novel *Last Exit to Brooklyn*, Darren Aronofsky's 2000 film adaptation of Selby's 1978 novel *Requiem for a Dream*, and Mathieu Kassovitz's 1995 film *La Haine*. All four texts, David writes in his review of *The Corner*'s DVD release, are "raw, gritty, uncompromising, realistic, smartly directed, supremely well-acted, compulsively watchable, but harrowing and with little light at the end of the tunnel."[19] They acknowledge the human dignity that the people they portray maintain in the face of terrible circumstances, making all three films and Simon's miniseries noteworthy examples of realistic fiction that refuse to dismiss poor people as unworthy of notice, sympathy, and kindness.

David's analysis suggests another comparison between Selby's novels, *A Year in the Life of an Inner-City Neighborhood*, and their visual adaptations. Edel, Aronofsky, and Simon faced the challenge of compressing complicated books into short durations. Even *The Corner*'s six-hour running time is short compared to *A Year in the Life of an Inner-City Neighborhood*'s long page count, forcing Simon and Mills to select representative anecdotes from the book in their attempt to replicate its scope, complexity, and density. They choose to adopt reflexive narrative and visual strategies that, by including ordinary and extraordinary details of their characters' daily experience, allow the audience to imaginatively enter each principal character's life so that a more comprehensive sense of the person emerges.

One technique—the cast, in character, interacts with Dutton during each episode's opening and closing interviews—more directly challenges the boundary between fiction and reality than a subtle choice made by Simon and Dutton does: They hire many of the people profiled in *A Year in the Life of an Inner-City Neighborhood* to play small *Corner* roles. The real-life Fran Boyd, for instance, plays BRC's administrative assistant, known only as the Detox Clerk, thereby sharing scenes with Khandi Alexander, who plays Boyd's fictional avatar. One scene from "Fran's Blues" nicely dramatizes the gallows humor and small kindnesses that *A Year in the Life of an Inner-City Neighborhood*'s parallel passage evokes. Fran, realizing that she must wait one week to enter rehab, briefly points a penknife at Antoinette, then, embarrassed by this outburst, turns to leave the BRC. The Detox Clerk, having watched the entire conversation, gently comments, "If you'd brought a bigger knife, you probably would've got in." This moment breaks the scene's tension to acknowledge Fran's violent gesture as an empty threat that reveals how confused, alone, and unhappy she is. The sad compassion in the Detox Clerk's eyes reflects Boyd's real memories of living this scene, while the artifice of film allows Boyd to witness just how lost she was at this time in her life by participating in a dramatic re-creation of this tragicomic event. Boyd's casting, for the attentive viewer, merges fact and fiction to supplement *The Corner*'s realism while advertising the project's fictional nature. This reflexive realism obscures and enhances *The Corner*'s documentary tone, permitting Simon and Mills to condense extended passages of *A Year in the Life of an Inner-City Neighborhood* into short but effective scenes that cover similar emotional, thematic, and symbolic territory.

These cameo appearances condition *The Corner*'s viewer to question the program's portrait of urban decay even while accepting its reality. The real-life Tyreeka Freamon plays a convenience-store cashier in the fourth episode, "Dope Fiend Blues." George "Blue" Epps plays the homeless-shelter supervisor who outlines the shelter's house rules to the character Blue (Glenn Plummer) when he, hoping to renounce addiction, arrives at its doors in "Dope Fiend Blues," as well as the leader of a Narcotics Anonymous meeting that the characters Blue and Fran attend in the final episode, "Everyman's Blues." DeAndre McCullogh, ironically cast as Police Officer Hurricane in the final installment, arrests his fictional counterpart (played by Sean Nelson). Richard Carter, DeAndre's Crenshaw Mafia Brothers running buddy (whom everyone calls R.C. in *A Year in the Life of an Inner-City Neighborhood* and whom

Corey Parker Robinson plays in *The Corner*), plays the part of a crime scene officer in "Everyman's Blues," while Veronica Boice—the girl-friend of Gary McCullough, played by Tasha Smith in *The Corner—* appears as the One-Day Woman, who receives a keychain for being drug free at least 24 hours, in the final episode's opening scene. Simon and Dutton, by populating their miniseries with actual participants in the events that *The Corner* dramatizes, contribute to its authenticity in the same way that filming the Franklin Square neighborhood locales where the events actually occurred enhances *The Corner*'s realism. These cameos, however, cause thoughtful viewers to recognize how extensively the miniseries employs artifice to tell its stories, particularly when watching actors whom the viewer has seen in other films and television programs perform the major roles. As real as the proceedings seem, the careful viewer can never forget that *The Corner* is a work of fiction.

This artifice enables a faithful rendering of certain events, as Fran Boyd testifies in comments made during *The Corner*'s coda. This scene concludes "Everyman's Blues" (and the entire miniseries) by bringing Dutton back on camera to interview the real Fran Boyd, Blue Epps, Tyreeka Freamon, and DeAndre McCullough.[20] Dutton asks the participants an apparently simple question: "Like any story, what would be a happy ending for this one?" Boyd's response exposes how cathartic filming *The Corner* has been for her: "No turning back. After watching this...wow. After watching this and watching Khandi, who portrayed my character, wow. She really made me have the opportunity to see just how I used to live and just watching her has made me even stronger than what I was before the movie even started." The ability to draw strength from Alexander's textured performance, particularly her talent for exposing Fran's contradictory personality (humor, passion, integrity, and compassion exist alongside venality, crudeness, cupidity, and dishonesty), illustrates fiction's power to reflect hard, uncomfortable, and upsetting truths that a documentary film might not have captured as intensely as the miniseries does. Fran Boyd becomes both an object and a subject of *The Corner*'s narrative, allowing the viewer to understand Fran in six hours as well as the reader of *A Year in the Life of an Inner-City Neighborhood* does in 540 pages. This accomplishment is possible due to Alexander's terrific acting, as well as Simon's, Mills's, and Dutton's success in reproducing the natural rhythms, moods, and events of corner life as only the most observant fiction can.

The Corner, therefore, qualifies as a work of reflexive naturalism that disrupts its documentary tone by integrating Dutton's prologue, epilogue, and wraparound interviews; by casting the book's actual participants in minor roles; and by incorporating flashbacks into its narrative. These flashbacks depict the Franklin Square neighborhood during the 1950s, 1960s, 1970s, and early 1980s to demonstrate just how far the neighborhood has fallen into economic, social, and political disrepair. *A Year in the Life of an Inner-City Neighborhood* contains passages in which individual subjects recall earlier events to complement Simon and Burns's historical disquisitions about the socioeconomic, political, and historical forces that change the neighborhood into a drug haven, but *The Corner*'s flashbacks are even more effective by visually juxtaposing the past's tidier image with the present's stark reality. Dutton shoots the flashbacks in softer focus, with a slight sepia tint, to suggest that these memories are vaguely idealized portraits of the neighborhood's glory days. The clean streets, neatly manicured lawns, and well-tended houses of the 1950s contrast with the harsher light, trash-strewn alleyways, and graffiti-covered buildings of the 1990s to shock the viewer into recognizing how much the drug trade and the drug war have cost the neighborhood's residents. Images of younger, healthier, and vibrant incarnations of Gary, Fran, and Gary's parents (W.M. and Roberta McCullough) visualize Simon and Burn's description of the neighborhood's initial appeal to an African American family living through the Jim Crow era in one of the East Coast's most segregated cities:

> Black and white got along well enough—W.M. felt a camaraderie with all of his neighbors that seemed to him genuine. They worked hard; so did he. And when one family was in trouble, everyone else on the block was quick to pitch in. Newly integrated by the Supreme Court decisions, the schools around Franklin Square were still strong, still stable. The streets were clean, the corners clear.[21]

This portrait does not endorse the naively conservative viewpoint that America's past was better, brighter, and happier than its present—the camaraderie between white and black is far from perfect in an era just recovering from segregation, a time when, in Baltimore, "racial separation was the civic firmament"[22]—even if it notes that fear and suspicion have replaced neighborly concern.

The Corner's flashbacks give life to these historical snippets while showing just how much the Franklin Square neighborhood has changed. The viewer cannot ignore this decline because Dutton's precise direction and Vince Peranio's careful production design of the flashback sequences ensure that the audience viscerally experiences the differences between past and present.

Other flashbacks illustrate Gary's and Fran's early experimentation with drugs, their descent into addiction, their resulting job loss, and the economic dispossession that strips them of their home, their family, and their stability. These sequences occur more frequently in *The Corner* than in *A Year in the Life of an Inner-City Neighborhood* to accelerate the pace of decline, decay, and despair that each text illustrates. This narrative compression distinguishes *The Corner* from its source material to disturb the audience's sensibilities about the possibility of winning the drug war, an outcome that reproduces the book's pessimistic tone, mood, and attitude.

The Corner, however, is not a pitiless rendering of urban blight. Simon's commitment to social realism demands that the program dramatize its characters' flaws, strengths, setbacks, triumphs, indignities, and decency. *The Corner,* rather than blaming the drug trade's victims, shows how personal flaws and impersonal forces bring the characters to their seemingly dead-end lives. Gary McCullough is the prime representative of a good man whose promising future is destroyed by drug abuse. When Dutton, in the opening interview of "Gary's Blues," gets Gary to admit that he once held two jobs, ran his own real-estate development company, and drove a Mercedes-Benz car, Gary's sheepish reaction reveals how much he has lost to addiction. An embarrassed Gary then refuses to answer Dutton's question about why he fell into drugs. T. K. Carter's remarkable performance as Gary, in this interview and in all other scenes, demonstrates the man's fundamental decency even as he plans "capers," small crimes that yield enough money to buy heroin and cocaine. Carter is so good in the role that he embodies Simon and Burns's description of Gary in *A Year in the Life of an Inner-City Neighborhood:* "The sad and beautiful truth about Gary McCullough—a man born and raised in as brutal and unforgiving a ghetto as America ever managed to create—is that he can't bring himself to hurt anyone."[23] Carter shuffles and shambles along sidewalks and across streets to suggest that Gary is slightly off-balance, while his open face brightens when ideas and jokes occur to him. Several shots of Gary reading chemistry books, novels, and the Bible in his parents' basement allow Carter to remain still yet convey Gary's all-consuming passion for knowledge. The sight of Gary planning and executing scams not only illustrates how the drug trade wastes his considerable intelligence but also becomes *The Corner's* primary metaphor for how the drug war squanders human potential.

Three sequences involving Gary demonstrate *The Corner's* mature approach to its subject matter. The first, from "Gary's Blues," finds Gary working with Tony Boice (Ron Brice), his girlfriend Veronica's cousin, to rob a Fulton Avenue apartment of its electronics and appliances. As Gary and Tony use a dolly to wheel a refrigerator out the apartment's back door, they see a man who lives in a neighboring apartment (Stanley Boyd) watching them. The man offers to keep quiet if Gary and Tony "hook me up." The scene cuts to Gary and Tony rolling the refrigerator down the street, in broad daylight, toward a junkyard that will give them money for their stolen materials. Gary comments, "Mentality, man, mentality. I, I don't know." When Tony asks what Gary means, Gary says, "That was the man's neighbor," as if the outrage of one man selling out another should be obvious. A police cruiser passes but does not pause to investigate the sight of two men moving a refrigerator down the middle of a city street. This detail, also from *A Year in the Life of an Inner-City Neighborhood,* bespeaks law enforcement's disinterest in preventing crime because, with so much drug activity in Franklin Square, theft "is unseen by a police department that has neither the will nor the temperament to investigate property crimes."[24] This indifference, along with the local residents' ruthlessness, amazes Gary, but he is either unwilling or unable to recognize his contributions to the rot that surrounds him. The sequence captures addiction's selfishness, hypocrisy, and pettiness, while Carter's restrained performance enacts the book's observation that "Gary can't let it go, this idea that some moral thresholds still exist."[25] The fact that "Gary couldn't imagine ever being so trifling and low as to betray a next-door neighbor for the price of a blast"[26] indicates that, while his conscience might bother him, Gary fails to acknowledge his culpability in perpetuating the same trifling mentality that he criticizes.

The Corner, in this sequence, refuses the drug-addict-as-unwitting-victim trope that *Hill Street Blues, NYPD Blue,* and *Homicide* indulge to illustrate that Gary's problems are at least partly his own fault. The miniseries, however, refutes the drug-addict-as-unsympathetic-criminal trope that cop dramas more frequently portray to demonstrate Gary's inherent goodness even as he commits larceny. This ambivalent portrait matches *A Year in the Life of an Inner-City Neighborhood's* view that the drug trade mistreats everyone who participates in it, meaning that addicts may be responsible for themselves but that larger social forces circumscribe their actions, desires, and choices. Relieving Gary of all blame while assigning no blame to society misses this point, so *The Corner*, by dramatizing Gary's regret that a man's neighbor would sell him out (but not regretting his decision to rob another human being), reflects *A Year in the Life of an Inner-City Neighborhood's* cynical appraisal that "in the empty heart of our cities, the culture of drugs has created a wealth-generating structure so elemental and enduring that it can legitimately be called a social compact."[27] This compact, in one of *The Corner's* key ironies, separates people from one another in ways both small and large, becoming so fundamental to the neighborhood's inhabitants that they see it as natural. Gary's ethical qualms, in light of this development, are even more tragic in their blinkered compassion.

The second sequence, in "Everyman's Blues," finds Gary coming upon Tyreeka Freamon while on his way to work a caper with Veronica Boice in which he and Veronica will sell heroin gel caps full of baking soda to earn money for their own drug blast. Tyreeka, who gave birth to DeAndre McCullough's son, DeAnte, in "Corner Boy Blues" (the fifth, previous, and penultimate episode), invites Gary into Fran and DeAndre's apartment to see his grandson for the first time. Gary holds the infant, saying that he resembles DeAndre, causing Tyreeka to comment that she hopes the boy takes after her side of the family in certain ways. Gary acknowledges that DeAndre is a little rough but, when Tyreeka leaves the room, cradles the baby in his arms: "You know who I am? Do you? Yeah, you do. I'm your grandpa. You know what I am? Do you?" The final two questions disturb Gary, who appears embarrassed by his own status as a drug fiend. Leaving the apartment, Gary's disappointment comes to the fore: "I'm a drug addict. That's what I am. When you're growing up, you're thinking about what you might be, you never ever think to yourself that 'I'll be addicted to drugs.' You never ever think that." Veronica, who has waited for Gary, pronounces this talk "bullshit" before hustling him to their caper. These short scenes illuminate Gary's wounded pride, as well as the difficult future that all Franklin Square neighborhood children face. DeAnte, the sequence implies, has as much promise as Gary once did, but he may follow his father's and grandfather's path into joining the American underclass. The momentary embarrassment that

Gary feels after encountering his grandson dissipates when Gary and Veronica return to their drug-money scam. *The Corner* demonstrates in muted yet praiseworthy fashion the promise and peril that the neighborhood represents.

The Corner's most devastating scene involves Gary's death. "Everyman's Blues" concludes with an epilogue (preceding the coda that has already been discussed) in which Dutton's off-camera narration, accompanied by a montage of the actors playing each person, updates the audience about the lives of each major participant. "A year is an arbitrary measure of lives lived. This story goes on," Dutton says, revealing that some residents have escaped addiction while others still fight it. DeAndre McCullough continues to sell drugs, use heroin and cocaine, and struggle with "the temptations of the Corner," while Tyreeka Freamon "is now a part-time college student and full-time hospital employee." Liver disease has claimed Fat Curt's life, Ella Thompson has died from a heart attack, and George "Blue" Epps, having remained clean ever since checking himself into the homeless shelter, now works for a drug-treatment program. Fran Boyd, who lives in Baltimore County with her son DeRodd, "has been clean for more than four years and she is employed as a drug-outreach worker."

This victory, however, precedes Gary's sad fate. The scene switches to Gary sleeping in bed (in his parents' basement) as Curtis Mayfield and the Impressions's 1965 song "People Get Ready" comes from a nearby radio. This detail is important, for, as Simon and Burns reveal in *A Year in the Life of an Inner-City Neighborhood*, Mayfield "used to mean everything to Gary. Curtis, always speaking for sanity, warning that if there's hell below, we're all going to go."[28] Mayfield's music has formed the background of more than one scene involving Gary to create intertextual references to Mayfield's celebrated soundtrack for Gordon Parks Jr.'s 1972 film *Super Fly*, an album whose socially conscious lyrics criticize the drug trade and drug culture. Dutton's voiceover informs the viewer that Gary died of a heroin overdose in March 1996 and that, after the funeral, DeAndre spoke of his father's passing. The real DeAndre (not Sean Nelson, the actor who portrays DeAndre in *The Corner*) then says, in a voiceover, "I know this sounds wrong, but I'm almost glad for him. I feel like he was never going to get out of it, you know? He was never going to be what he was. I think he was sad from knowing that. I feel like he's at peace now."[29] As DeAndre finishes speaking, the final lyric of "People Get Ready" ("You just thank the Lord") is heard before the image fades to black.

Juxtaposing DeAndre's hope that his father has found peace with the song's invocation of gratitude and grace honors Gary's gentle disposition while confronting the tragedy of his loss. The scene leaves its viewer upset yet affirms Gary's life as valuable, worthwhile, and significant. This ambivalence expertly summarizes *The Corner*'s narrative project while honestly capturing *A Year in the Life of an Inner-City Neighborhood*'s sociological ambiguity.

The scene also alters reality to convey its point that drug addicts deserve the viewer's empathy. *A Year in the Life of an Inner-City Neighborhood* includes an epilogue that, like *The Corner*'s parallel scene, informs the reader how the book's subjects have fared since Simon and Burns finished their year-long observation of the Franklin Square neighborhood.[30] Gary, after several attempts at detox, shoots heroin with his brother June Bey in their parents' basement. "After nearly three months in which he had used only a handful of times," Simon and Burns write, "Gary's body couldn't handle the usual dose, and suddenly he fell from the bed to the floor."[31] Bey panicked, moving Gary from the basement to another home before calling an ambulance. The epilogue's clinical detachment contrasts with its mournful attitude by noting, "Gary was dead on arrival at Bon Secours [Hospital]."[32] *The Corner* omits these events to underscore Gary's tender personality and regrettable death. His peaceful, sleeping features not only enhance DeAndre's eulogy but also mirror Mayfield's song to dramatize Simon and Burns's reaction to Gary's passing: "Especially, we hold to the memory of Gary McCullough, a man of great heart and gentle spirit. His true friendship and his interest in this book helped sustain us."[33]

Gary's presence, as embodied by Carter, also sustains *The Corner*. The miniseries does not condemn its characters or its viewers to unremitting pessimism, as Weisberg's comments imply, but instead melds fact, fiction, documentary visuals, superb performances, journalistic observations, and literary themes to expose the mundane aspects of a drug addict's seemingly foreign existence. Simon, Mills, and Dutton do not lecture, sermonize, or moralize; rather, they dramatize the drug trade's complexities, contradictions, and complications. This accomplishment depends on reflexive narrative strategies (flashbacks, Dutton's wraparound interviews, the prologue, the epilogue) to adapt *A Year in the Life of an Inner-City Neighborhood*'s sober assessment of Baltimore's drug culture into compelling television. This success disproves Simon's initial suspicion, expressed in a 1999 interview with *Seattle Times* reporter Cynthia Rose, that scripting *The Corner* would be "completely impossible."[34] The program achieves authenticities of place, person, and event that demonstrate Simon's skill as a television writer, as well as the medium's capacity to create mature drama for discerning audiences. *The Corner,* therefore, is a crucial middle step between Simon's work on *Homicide: Life on the Street* and his creation of *The Wire* that deserves the high praise it has received.

5

American Savagery:
David Milch's *Deadwood*

Deadwood (2004–2006) is David Milch's highest achievement as a fiction writer, social realist, and television dramatist. This three-season HBO series, first pitched to the network as "St. Paul gets collared,"[1] explores, interrogates, and elaborates three significant themes: how law emerges from lawlessness, how order emerges from chaos, and how America's savage founding gives way to the idea, necessity, and reality of community. Milch, in the words of Mark Singer's profile "The Misfit," originally "wanted to write about the lives of city cops in ancient Rome during Nero's reign, before a system of justice had been codified."[2] Since HBO was developing the series *Rome* (2005–2007) for broadcast when Milch proposed *Deadwood* in 2002, Carolyn Strauss and Chris Albrecht, the network's top executives, asked Milch to locate the same themes elsewhere. Milch, who had proposed a Western series to NBC in 2001 that never materialized,[3] began researching life in the Old West, finally focusing on Deadwood, the notorious Black Hills mining camp that arose in 1876 after gold was discovered by an 1874 expedition commanded by George Armstrong Custer. Deadwood was located on Dakota Territory land originally deeded to the Sioux Indians. Milch, by setting his series in Deadwood, chooses a locale famous for its brazen, flagrant, and unrepentant illegality. The gold rush that brought Caucasian prospectors to sacred Native American territory recapitulated the nation's tradition of officially sanctioned thievery, making Deadwood a nexus of licentiousness, criminality, and vice.

Deadwood, therefore, falls in line with Milch's other major contributions to television drama—*Hill Street Blues* and *NYPD Blue*—despite its different genre. Singer calls *Deadwood* "an unlike-any-Western-you've-ever-seen Western" in "The Misfit,"[4] an assessment that seems

fitting for a television series that, on the surface, features few identifiable cowboy-and-Indian motifs, many unconventional violent
encounters, and meager trappings from traditional cinematic and television Westerns. *Deadwood* has provoked ample commentary about
how the program demolishes the conventional Western that graced
American television screens during the 1950s, 1960s, and early 1970s,
setting Milch's program apart from the simplistic, good-versus-evil
portrait of the American West that *Gunsmoke* (1955–1975), *Wagon Train*
(1957–1965), *The Rifleman* (1958–1963), *Bonanza* (1959–1973), and *The
Big Valley* (1965–1969) epitomize. *Deadwood's* graphic violence, sex,
and profanity, according to this argument, distinguish it from all previous television Westerns, even programs such as *The Wild Wild West*
(1965–1969) and *The Adventures of Brisco County, Jr.* (1993–1994) that
ridicule, parody, or satirize the genre.

Milch occasionally endorses this viewpoint in interviews, behind-
the-scenes documentaries, and panel discussions about *Deadwood*.
He believes that the traditional Western originated in Hollywood's
desire to sanitize American history by offering the nation a mythical,
noble, and purified past. In "The New Language of the Old West"
and "An Imaginative Reality," two behind-the-scenes documentaries
included in *Deadwood's* Season One DVD set, Milch tells Keith Carradine, the actor who plays Wild Bill Hickok in the program's first
five episodes, that the traditional Western reflects Hollywood's Hays
Production Code as much as authentic American history.[5] Milch's
March 5, 2005, interview with *Salon.com's* Heather Havrilesky expa-
tiates on his notion that the experience of immigrant Jews largely
generated the Hollywood Western:

> The idea of the western, I believe, as people conceive of it, is re-
> ally an artifact of the Hays Production Code of the '20s and '30s
> and it has really nothing to do with the West, and much to do
> with the influence of middle-European Jews who had come out
> to Hollywood to present to America a sanitized heroic idea of
> what America was. The first term of the Hays Code is that ob-
> scenity in word or fact or action is an offense against God and
> man[6] and will not be depicted. In the early '20s there were start-
> ing to be films that were kind of racy and these guys didn't want
> their hustle to be jeopardized.[7] So they formed this production
> board which essentially announced that, let us run the show and
> we will give you an America disinfected and pure.[8]

Commerce, in Milch's judgment, drove Hollywood's major movie studios to produce Westerns that reassured their audiences about America's glorious past. This decision, according to Milch, also counteracted the "real vein of anti-Semitism and misgiving"[9] that developed during the 1920s and 1930s, fostered by Charles Lindbergh's and Henry Ford's warnings against the social, economic, and political power of "the money lenders," a common euphemism for Jewish bankers, merchants, and entrepreneurs. "The dream factory was operated exclusively by immigrant Jews," Milch says. Samuel Goldwyn and Louis B. Mayer wanted to "stay sort of behind the scenes.... So, what these guys did was come up with a four-square American kind of vision with an unwritten guarantee: Let us run the show, and you will get 150 features a year which glorify innocence and the absence of conflict and so on."[10] Milch's sense that Hollywood Westerns are, in effect, parables of assimilation—stories that symbolically chronicle how immigrants become Americans by courageously confronting a wild frontier—clues the critical viewer into one of *Deadwood*'s profoundest ironies: Assimilation, civilization, and law, in Milch's series, are merely by-products of the ceaseless quest for profit, not noble ideals inherent to the American character.

Milch is even more forthright about his intentions in *Deadwood: Stories of the Black Hills*, the book that he published in 2006 during the program's third (and final) season (this book is hereafter referred to as *Stories of the Black Hills*). Confessing that he did not wish to write a contemporary drama after the events of September 11, 2001, Milch states that he settled on a story about Deadwood because "the camp came together in the mid-1870s, deep into the Industrial Revolution, and yet it was a reenactment of the story of the founding of America, and a reenactment, too, of the story of Original Sin. I suppose I accept [Nathaniel] Hawthorne's definition of Original Sin as the violation of the sanctity of another's heart."[11] Conflating the sacred and profane within historical fiction, per this analysis, allows Milch to dramatize the uncomfortable, unfortunate, and ugly realities of America's birth as a political, economic, and civic entity. Deadwood and *Deadwood* enact America's founding by indulging the basest forms of avarice, theft, brutality, and murder as necessary adjuncts to securing wealth, land, and political supremacy. Violating the sanctity of another's heart not only suggests trampling on an individual's rights but also evokes the historical crimes of land dispossession, human bondage, and cultural genocide that, despite politically conservative attempts to deny them, are significant aspects of American history. *Deadwood,* for Milch, emerges as a fictional attempt to come to terms with shameful historical truths that traditional Westerns overlook.

Not all critics, however, credit Milch's appraisal of the Hollywood Western as accurate or *Deadwood's* revisionist tendencies as groundbreaking. Lee Siegel, in his review of *Deadwood* in the *New Republic* (reprinted in Siegel's 2007 book *Not Remotely Controlled: Notes on Television*), calls statements about how *Deadwood* shatters the conventions of the traditional Hollywood Western "hysterical proclamations of cultural revolution" that ignore the genre's rich history.[12] "The tired old genre of the Western," Siegel writes, is a "hackneyed American invention, we are told, in which evil is purely evil and good purely good, the difference between them usually indicated by sneering, black-hatted villains and tight-lipped, white-hatted heroes."[13] Such characterizations, Siegel implies, simplify the Western's underappreciated complexity: "Except, that is, for Clint Eastwood's *Unforgiven* and Larry McMurtry's *Lonesome Dove,* made way back in 1992 and 1989, respectively, both of which, we are further told, also shattered the tired old genre of the Western."[14] Anthony Mann's and Sam Peckinpah's contributions to the genre, by motioning toward greater realism, seem revolutionary because, in Siegel's estimation, the Western idealizes the American past (here Siegel agrees with Milch). *Deadwood,* for Siegel, only appears to redefine Western conventions rather than breaking the genre's narrative strictures: "The seeming paradigm-bursting change introduced by *Deadwood,* however, is really no more than an extra-emphatic expression of a single element. Which in the case of *Deadwood,* and so many other so-called innovative shows, is the seamy, sordid side of life."[15]

Siegel's world-weary tone typifies his facile reviews, but he correctly notes that *Deadwood* participates in a revisionist tradition that deconstructs the Western's mythic nobility. Arthur Penn's *Little Big Man* (1970), Clint Eastwood's *High Plains Drifter* (1973), and Kevin Costner's *Open Range* (2003) are just three additional films that expose the violence, racism, sexism, and immorality of life in the Old West. *Deadwood,* therefore, may not stand alone in repudiating the traditional Western's reputation for simplistic morality, but it defies Siegel's misguided declaration that "take away the show's moderate (by current standards) sex and violence, and its immoderate cussing, and *Deadwood* is really a very enjoyable, good old-fashioned cowboy series whose characters are, in the end, no more discomfiting than characters in more conventional-seeming cowboy movies."[16] Siegel's seen-it-all-before attitude provokes critical myopia, for *Deadwood*'s approach to sex and violence is far from moderate, while Milch's program exceeds the old-fashioned cowboy series that Siegel invokes but refuses to name. Critical viewers cannot mistake *Deadwood* for *Gunsmoke, Wagon Train, Bonanza,* or *The Big Valley* or seriously place it in the same category of television drama as these earlier shows, because *Deadwood,* as Jason Jacobs notes, is a "filthy joy" to behold.[17]

Even so, Siegel usefully suggests that Milch's analysis of the Western's generic development overlooks many contrary examples, to say nothing of the extensive literary tradition that the Western enjoyed before migrating to cinema and television. Dime novels that chronicled the exploits of real-life Western celebrities like Wild Bill Hickok and fictional characters like Deadwood Dick were popular in 19th-century America, while novelists from Owen Wister and Zane Grey to Louis L'Amour and Larry McMurtry have enjoyed tremendous success writing Western fiction (with Wister's 1902 novel *The Virginian,* Grey's 1912 novel *Riders of the Purple Sage,* L'Amour's 1955 novel *Guns of the Timberlands,* and McMurtry's 1985 novel *Lonesome Dove* being consummate contributions). Milch admits to little initial familiarity with cinematic and television Westerns, telling Havrilesky, "It wasn't that I didn't like them; it's just I didn't watch them particularly. When I was growing up, it was not the heyday of the western."[18] Readers should doubt this final statement's veracity, since Milch, born in 1945, came of age in an era when each year averaged between 40 and 60 Western films, with more than 600 Westerns produced between 1950 and 1959.[19] So many Western series were part of network television during Milch's teenage years that he could avoid them only by not watching. Milch, one infers from these comments, preferred other cinematic and television genres to Westerns, while he omits references to Western novelists and short-story writers from his comments.

Milch, however, became an avid student of the genre during the two years he researched Old West history while preparing *Deadwood.* This extensive reading taught Milch that he need not react against the Western's established conventions because "I was mystified when I began to do the research. It seemed so obvious to me that the West I was encountering . . . had nothing to do with the westerns, which I was experiencing secondhand, which weren't even good on their own terms. But then going back and seeing the classical westerns, those, too, had nothing to do with the West I was studying."[20]

Milch thinks his early generic ignorance "turned out probably to be a good enough thing" because the traditional Western "had everything to do with what Hollywood was about at that time, and nothing to do with what the West was about."[21]

No matter how distant Milch feels from classical film and television Westerns, observers like Siegel and John Leonard note that his series nonetheless reproduces their broadest conventions. Leonard's *New York Magazine* review of *Deadwood* sees it as part of a long lineage: "From Homer and the Bible to John Ford, men are hanged, women raped, and children stolen by savages because of turf wars, sexual property rights, and different ideas on how to look good dying. Sometimes, too, a sheep is dipped. Not even *Deadwood* fiddles with this Western formula."[22] Milch's protestations to the contrary cannot change Siegel's and Leonard's opinion that *Deadwood* is more traditional, more conventional, and more usual than its creator, producers, or audience recognize.

Horace Newcomb's thoughts about *Deadwood* complicate attempts to determine the program's generic freshness even more than Siegel's assurances that Milch's program, despite its revisionist tendencies, evokes the traditional Western. "The structure of the conventional western," Newcomb writes, "is the movement from savagery to civilization....So-called revisionist westerns undercut this narrative by showing how truly difficult the process can be, how 'the winners' in this contest must often engage in corruption as deeply as those who lose."[23] Newcomb, however, concludes that his own analysis implies that *Deadwood* "is not a western at all, neither conventional nor revisionist. The ease with which Milch transferred his thematic exploration from one setting to another confirms this. It is the 'people' who interest him; it is improvisation in the absence of law."[24] Milch's desire to examine how law develops from lawlessness, for Newcomb, "is an abstract concept if ever there was one. But the abstraction is made concrete by context, by the social impulse. And that impulse is defined. It is the attempt," Newcomb says, quoting Milch's words in Singer's profile of him, "'to minimize the collateral damage of the taking of revenge.'"[25]

Deadwood, however, remains a revisionist Western (according to Newcomb's terms) no matter how much attention the series pays to its characters. Milch's program repeatedly dramatizes how civilization and savagery are not dichotomies but instead interpenetrate one another during the mining camp's evolution from illicit settlement to legal municipality. The impulse to restrain vengeance and vendettas underscores other notable Western novels, films, and television series—including *Lonesome Dove, Unforgiven,* and *Gunsmoke*—that, like *Deadwood,* engage social, political, and moral questions. Perhaps the single most important forerunner of Milch's series is Pete Dexter's masterful 1986 novel *Deadwood,* which combines obscene language, graphic sexuality, chilling violence, and mordant wit into a grim narrative leavened by gallows humor.[26] Milch does not credit (or even mention) Dexter's novel in interviews, documentaries, DVD commentaries, or *Stories of the Black Hills,* but Dexter's example unquestionably influences Milch's effort. The novel slowly reveals Charlie Utter—Wild Bill Hickok's loyal friend (the character played by Dayton Callie in Milch's series)—as its protagonist, while the section devoted to the Chinese prostitute Ci-an (known colloquially as the China Doll) includes details that Milch's *Deadwood* assigns to the character Mr. Wu (Keone Young) and to the area of town called Chink's Alley (even if the Chinese prostitutes in Milch's series are minor—even insignificant—characters).

Deadwood, therefore, is neither wholly original nor utterly conventional. Milch's Western series casts a jaundiced eye on the myth of the American frontier as European society's heroic confrontation with, struggle against, and triumph over the vast wilderness (and its indigenous peoples) to forge an exceptional, exemplary, and unitary American identity that transforms European refinement into an inveterate pragmatism that enshrines white society as America's most authentic population. The young nation discards its primitive impulses (by marginalizing the African slaves and Native Americans who symbolize undiluted savagery to the white frontiersmen venturing across the continent) to embrace a social compact that regulates human desire by outlawing deleterious behaviors like vengeance while licensing immoral actions, particularly bondage and land dispossession, that support Manifest Destiny's expansionist project.

Milch's series, therefore, ambivalently regards the frontier mythology that Frederick Jackson Turner lionizes in "The Significance of the Frontier in American History," his landmark address to the American Historical Association meeting held during Chicago's 1893 Columbian Exposition (an event that celebrated the 400th anniversary of Christopher Columbus's landing on the American continent). This piece, perhaps the most famous essay ever written about the American West, invokes metaphors of political germ theory and microbiological evolution to assert, "Our early history is the study of European germs developing in an American environment" before making its signature declaration: "The frontier is the line of most rapid and effective Americanization."[27] This statement endorses the notion of civilized Europeans subjugating nature to their economic and political will, but not before the frontier changes their cultured manners into more elemental behaviors. Turner recognizes the symbiotic relationship between Americans and their physical environment by noting, "The wilderness masters the colonist. . . . Little by little he transforms the wilderness, but the outcome is not the old Europe, not simply the development of Germanic germs, any more than the first phenomenon was a case of reversion to the Germanic mark. The fact is, that here is a new product that is American."[28] The United States's historical development, in other words, depends on flexibility, adaptability, and fluidity rather than fixed, stilted, and rigid identities. This American capacity for change produces unique cultural traits that Turner avidly chronicles. "That coarseness and strength combined with acuteness and inquisitiveness," Turner writes, "that practical inventive turn of mind, quick to find expedients; that masterful grasp of material things, lacking in the artistic but powerful to effect great ends; that restless, nervous energy; that dominant individualism, working for good and for evil"[29] not only define but also embody the American character.

Deadwood is less sanguine about the frontier's salutary effects on American identity, industry, and enterprise than Turner's triumphal celebration of rugged individualism. The series exposes the camp's energetic pursuit of gold, liquor, and sex as a barbaric façade that cannot fully sever America's connection to its European ancestors. A scene from the pilot episode, simply titled "Deadwood" (1.1) and written by Milch, illustrates the camp's complicated revision of those qualities that Turner defines as quintessentially American.[30] Prospector Whitney Ellsworth (Jim Beaver) delivers gold to Al Swearengen, proprietor of the Gem Saloon, Deadwood's largest and most profitable bordello. Swearengen, who in real life was born in Iowa, is played by English actor Ian McShane, and Ellsworth, after Swearengen calculates the gold's value as $170, launches into a profanity-laden monologue that incorporates many terms from Turner's essay:

ELLSWORTH.   Now, with that Limey damn accent of yours, are these rumors true that you're descended from the British nobility?
SWEARENGEN.   I'm descended from all them cocksuckers.

ELLSWORTH. Well, here's to you, Your Majesty. I'll tell you what: I may of fucked my life up flatter than hammered shit, but I stand here before you today beholden to no human cock-sucker. And working a paying fucking gold claim. And not the U.S. government saying I'm trespassing or the savage fucking Red Man himself or any of these limber-dick cock-suckers passing themselves off as prospectors had better try and stop me.
SWEARENGEN. They better not try it in here.
ELLSWORTH. Goddamit Swearengen, I don't trust you as far as I can throw you, but I enjoy the way you lie.

Ellsworth's sarcasm dismisses Swearengen's tenuous connection to British royalty before announcing his (Ellsworth's) independence from all civic and moral authority. Only gold and the commodities it can purchase matter to him (Ellsworth tells Swearengen to inform the Gem's card dealers and whores of his $170 credit before asking about Swearengen's accent), while no restraints can contain Ellsworth's declaration of total freedom from human, governmental, and historical obligation. His speech's casual contempt for federal authorities and implicit racism against Native Americans recall Turner's statement that the frontier is "the meeting point between savagery and civilization"[31] where nature must give way to culture but not before the wilderness diminishes the civilizing tendencies of European settlers (and their descendants) to generate the dominant individualism that Turner and Ellsworth (who functions in this scene as the fictional avatar of Turner's thesis) identify as exceptionally American.

Ellsworth, however, knows not to expect fair treatment from any-one, even the man who purchases his gold, in an illegal camp where no law exists. Milch's script for "Deadwood" includes a detail that the scene as edited obscures. After Swearengen tells Ellsworth that his gold weighs 8.5 ounces, the script reads, "The camera's CLOSER SCRUTINY reveals Swearengen's thumb adjusting the scale's bal-ance in his favor,"[32] but the episode's viewer does not see Swearen-gen cheating Ellsworth because the scene begins after Swearengen weighs the gold. Director Walter Hill and Milch may have found such visual confirmation unnecessary since Ellsworth's final line, jauntily delivered by Beaver, alerts the viewer to Swearengen's dishonesty. Beaver and McShane skillfully convey how both men recognize thiev-ery as a fact of life in Deadwood, with Ellsworth implicitly preferring

Swearengen's brand of larceny to the depredations of prospectors who might rob his claim to offset their own losses.

The sexual violence of Ellsworth's conversation with Swearengen, moreover, implies that Deadwood's prospectors and entrepreneurs need not sublimate the virility that Turner's "coarseness," "strength," and "restless, nervous energy" suggest is necessary to tame the frontier. The term *cocksucker,* first mentioned by Swearengen to repudiate his British ancestry, becomes, for Ellsworth, a way to distinguish his economic potency from the powerless, "limber-dick" prospectors who might steal his gold rather than pursuing their own busted claims. Swearengen, by stating that no one should try to cheat Ellsworth while he patronizes the Gem Saloon, feminizes these hypothetical thieves even more by insinuating that they occupy a place beneath the Gem's prostitutes who, rather than stealing from the camp's male residents, offer sexual services in exchange for money. This arrangement's suppression and exploitation of women's freedom mirrors the suppression and exploitation of Indian rights that permit Ellsworth to mine gold in the first place (the pilot episode occurs roughly two weeks after Custer's defeat at the Little Bighorn), eroticizing the American confrontation with the frontier as a rape of the land, its indigenous inhabitants, and their cultural heritage.

Ellsworth, as the scene's primary representative of this desire to master the natural, political, and historical forces in play, utters language whose crudity, obscenity, and vulgarity shocks even audiences that, by *Deadwood's* March 21, 2004, premiere, had become accustomed to the profanity that typifies HBO dramas like Tom Fontana's *Oz,* David Chase's *The Sopranos,* and David Simon's *The Wire.* Singer, in "The Misfit," aptly recognizes that "the language on *Deadwood* ranges from Elizabethan-like ornateness to profanity of a relentlessness that makes *The Sopranos* seem demure. Both extremes often coexist in a single speech."[33] The inverted rhythms of Ellsworth's monologue, particularly their tendency to place predicates before subjects, suggest an opulent quality that the speech's unyielding profanity counteracts. This vulgar discourse is the episode's (and, therefore, *Deadwood's*) first extended excursion into the spoken obscenity that not only characterizes the series but also provoked passionate controversy after the pilot episode's initial broadcast. Milch has claimed many times that *Deadwood's* profanity has firm historical roots, telling Carradine in the DVD documentary "The New Language of the Old West" that "it's very well documented that the obscenity of the West was striking, but the obscenity of mining camps was unbelievable." Ellsworth's comments embody this judgment, particularly their absurd imagery. How, for instance, does a person make such a mess of his life that it becomes "flatter than hammered shit"? The comparison here, like the notion of hammering manure, makes no logical sense but calls to mind, as Scott Eric Kaufman observes, blacksmith iconography: Pounding an anvil becomes a metaphor for a hard life ruined "through long effort, through the labor evoked by the mention and soundscape of hammering."[34]

Ellsworth, despite the gold he sells to Swearengen, confesses to wasting his life so badly that material wealth cannot undo the damage. Ellsworth's plan to spend his money drinking, gambling, and whoring also indicates his desire to embrace the romance of the frontier rather than accumulating wealth. The freedom from legal authority that the frontier offers, however, cannot compensate for the failure that Ellsworth feels he has become, leading the prospector to indict the federal government, the Indians, and the camp's other prospectors for their imagined crimes against the unfettered life that he tries to carve from Deadwood's unscrupulous environment. Ellsworth's anger, hidden under his cheerful demeanor, unleashes a torrent of profanity that hammers this point home while eliminating the possibility of fellowship with the surrounding community. Ellsworth trusts no one, not even Swearengen, to understand, sympathize with, or care about his predicament.

Milch, in *Stories of the Black Hills,* states that the people who traveled to gold-strike camps sought linguistic and political liberation because "there has to be a cleaning away—the purgation of meaning that profanity permits,"[35] meaning that obscene language paradoxically cleanses its speakers of their linguistic and political fetters. Ellsworth's monologue temporarily purges his disappointment, with its obscene language informing the viewer that this prospector—whose importance to *Deadwood*'s narrative increases until his murder in the third season by agents of mining mogul George Hearst (Gerald McRaney) in "The Catbird Seat" (3.11) provokes shock, sorrow, and rage in the camp's inhabitants—cannot reconcile his economic ambitions with the stark realities of surviving the frontier. Gold promises wealth, comfort, and serenity, but the unlikely possibility that Ellsworth will "strike it rich" forces him to realize just how hopeless his future is.

Ellsworth's profanity, then, reveals a theatrical personality continually staging its own identity. This impulse to re-create oneself when encountering unfamiliar places is a prototypical American trait that

Deadwood's florid dialogue expertly captures. Such dialogue, moreover, is literary language as much as authentic 19th-century speech, a point that Newcomb lucidly acknowledges:

> As presented by an outstanding cast, the language is most often described as Shakespearian [*sic*], and it is indeed important to note that the language is performed, not merely spoken. Subtle distinctions of diction and voice, vocabulary, and inflection serve to distinguish characters. Soliloquies and muttered musings offer insight into the psychology, the motivations and speculations, of individuals, but also into the relationships among them.[36]

Ellsworth and Swearengen, as Geoffrey Nunberg comments, would not have talked in real life as *Deadwood* makes them speak because the profanity used by 19th-century frontiersmen would have "had religious overtones rather than sexual or scatological ones,"[37] but their conversation permits Beaver and McShane to refashion the stock Western characters of weary prospector and sly saloonkeeper into specific personalities that the viewer cannot mistake for any other individual in *Deadwood's* massive cast. Milch's achievement in this regard will not surprise anyone who recalls the memorable speech patterns of *Hill Street Blues's* and *NYPD Blue's* characters or who knows that Robert Penn Warren once favorably compared Milch's dialogue to Ernest Hemingway's,[38] a faith justified by the linguistic richness that Ellsworth's outwardly crude yet deceptively poetic words manifest. Milch's shrewd casting also deserves praise, for only talented actors can bring alive *Deadwood's* elaborate dialogue without indulging arch or campy performances that call attention to themselves. The unexpected resonance of Ellsworth's speech—no viewer who hears it, despite Siegel's opinion, can look on *Deadwood* as a conventional Western— illustrates Milch's claim, made in *Stories of the Black Hills,* that "what follows [profanity] is a regeneration of meaning, so that words come to have a different meaning in a world that has been made new."[39]

Deadwood's eccentric language, sex, and violence make its narrative world seem unexplored. The series includes no clichéd street standoffs or barroom brawls, managing to refresh even hackneyed Western plot points. The first scene of the pilot episode, "Deadwood," for instance, finds Montana marshal Seth Bullock (Timothy Olyphant) protecting Clell Watson (James Parks), a man sentenced to hang at dawn, from a mob that wishes to kill Watson before sunrise. Bullock is infuriated by the repeated threats of Byron Sampson (the mob's leader, played by Christopher Darga) to storm the jail, injuring or even killing Bullock and his business partner Sol Star (John Hawkes) in an effort to reach Watson. Bullock intends to resign his position as marshal the next morning, after the hanging, so that he may travel to Deadwood and open a hardware business with Star, but Sampson's intransigence makes Bullock's plan impossible. This story line, of an Old West peace officer defending a condemned man's life before a town mob, is so familiar to regular viewers of Westerns that *Deadwood* initially strikes its audience as a run-of-the-mill entry in the genre. This situation abruptly changes, however, when Bullock, seething with anger, carries out Watson's sentence rather than fighting Sampson's gang. Bullock fashions a noose to the jail's front porch, telling Sampson that the execution will be carried out "under color of law." Bullock asks Watson what message the man wishes to give his sister (who intends to attend the execution), writes these words on a piece of paper, and then hangs Watson. The distance between the noose and the porch floor, however, is so short that Bullock tugs on Watson's struggling body until the man's neck breaks. Bullock then gives the paper to an onlooker who promises to deliver it to Watson's sister, boards the fully packed wagon that Star drives, brandishes his weapon at Sampson, and rides out of town.

This unexpected development transforms an apparently trite scene into a disquisition about law, order, violence, and responsibility. Bullock's determination to carry out Watson's execution by legal means bespeaks his belief that order is necessary to maintaining civil society by quelling the violence that Bullock himself perpetrates when angered. After arriving in Deadwood, for instance, Star and Bullock unload their wagon in the middle of the street, to the chagrin of a loudmouth driver who cannot pass until they finish. The fellow yells, "This the first wagon you ever fucking unloaded? Hold onto my horse. I'll show you how to do it," causing Bullock to tell the man to stay where he is. When the man asks, "And what if I don't?" a belligerent Bullock moves toward him, saying, "Stand there mouthing off and you'll find out." Bullock clearly intends to strike the man, but Star intervenes, offering the fellow a free chamber pot as an apology. Wild Bill Hickok and Charlie Utter pass by this confrontation, with Hickok noting Bullock's ferocity. Later, while Star and Bullock hawk their wares outside the tent that serves as their temporary storefront, another man (Gill Gayle) attempts to steal business by claiming that he just bought a 50-cent soap bar with a five-dollar prize inside its wrapping. Bullock walks toward the shill, telling him, "Front your game away from our tent." This combative attitude intimidates the man, who moves down the street.

These incidents, beyond demonstrating Bullock's temper, alert the viewer to his fundamental hatred of bullying, confidence games, and bad faith. Although Bullock settles in Deadwood to work as a merchant, not a lawman, he behaves so much like a peace officer that Hickok (a former Kansas marshal) instantly recognizes their similarity. A major story line in the pilot episode concerns Hickok and Bullock leading a search party for the Metzes, a family that has been massacred while returning in their wagon to Minnesota along the Spearfish Road. Ned Mason (Jamie McShane)—a road agent who works for Swearengen— reports that Indians have slaughtered the family, but Hickok and Bullock suspect that the nervous and twitching Mason perpetrated the crime with unknown accomplices (who then double-crossed Mason, forcing him to return to Deadwood). Hickok, Bullock, Mason, Star, Utter, and the owner of the *Deadwood Pioneer* newspaper, A. W. Merrick (Jeffrey Jones), ride to the site, finding that five-year-old Sofia Metz (Bree Seanna Wall), the only survivor, is barely alive. They take the girl to Dr. "Doc" Amos Cochran (Brad Dourif) in Deadwood, with Bullock and Hickok telling Mason to remain in town because Sofia, when she recovers, may implicate him in the murders. A truculent Mason pulls his weapon, but both Hickock and Bullock fire their guns first, shooting Mason in the eye. One of the pilot episode's best moments occurs when, as Mason lies dead on the ground, Hickok asks, "Was that you or me, Montana?" and Bullock replies, "My money'd be on you." Although Deadwood (a camp that abrogates federal statute by sitting on land awarded to the Sioux Indians by the 1868 Fort Laramie Treaty) has no formal laws, Hickok and Bullock preserve order by trying, con- victing, and executing Mason in the street. Their violence satisfies Bul- lock's need to secure justice by avenging the greater crime of killing an innocent family, then blaming it on Native Americans. Bullock restores order even though he left Montana to escape a marshal's life.

Bullock becomes an unusual Western character in these scenes. He acts outside legal authority but behaves like a conventional lawman. Milch, in *Stories of the Black Hills*, notes that the actual Seth Bullock was regularly beaten by his father, provoking a rage that made him despise the act of one human being bullying another. Bullock comes to believe that "the law is going to protect him [by] disinfect[ing] his own murderous rage,"[40] but Deadwood's lawless environment challenges

Bullock's assumptions. He discovers, in Milch's words, that "law and order are not the same....Our desire for order comes first, and law comes afterward."[41] Bullock must adapt to his new circumstances, discharging the sheriff's duties although no such office yet exists in Deadwood. Bullock's need to master his own anger drives him to pursue order, in private and public, just as *Deadwood*'s first season dramatizes how the camp begins ordering its civic affairs to become a functioning municipality so that residents may continue mining gold, selling goods, and accruing profit. Milch's program illustrates how law arises from order, creating new obligations and responsibilities for its characters. Violence, Bullock's pilot-episode trajectory illustrates, is as crucial to establishing the camp's legitimacy as regulating violence is necessary to sustaining its community.

This approach to screen mayhem converts the stock Western sheriff into a more thoughtful and brooding character whose taciturn nature belies his underlying passion. The resulting paradox creates fascinating drama. "Bullock's capacity for violence and his impulse to order are conjoined in the same personality," Milch writes in *Stories of the Black Hills*. "That's the making of the new American hero."[42] Noting that the real Bullock became one of Theodore Roosevelt's best friends, Milch argues that the future president helped develop the rhetoric of the West "in his book *The Winning of the West*. He (Roosevelt) based that rhetoric in some large part on Bullock's character, including his anger as well as his habitual silence."[43] Bullock's contradictory impulses, with order and disorder inhabiting the same body, reflect the historical conflicts (freedom and bondage, democracy and authoritarianism, compassion and vengeance, generosity and greed) that inhabited Deadwood, making the camp, for Milch's purposes, the perfect replica of America's civic genesis.

Language, as always in *Deadwood,* becomes central to depicting a town that develops a civilized veneer to cover the camp's personal, political, and historical savageries. The program's approach to frontier life is less a progression (or evolution) from barbarism to refinement than an admission that such progress shrouds in noble rhetoric the violence that forms Deadwood. Bullock and Swearengen, for instance, appear diametrically opposed in their linguistic talents. Bullock, in Milch's words, thinks that "language is a way that he bound up his rage" because Bullock is a "primitive" creature, not a lawman, who has "just emerged out of the primordial ooze, and he's slouching around, barely able to control his impulses to wreak savage violence on whoever crosses the street the wrong way."[44] Swearengen indulges long soliloquies and monologues whose verbal dexterity often·bemuses his listeners—especially henchmen like Dan Dority (W. Earl Brown), Johnny Burns (Sean Bridgers), and the educated Silas Adams (Titus Welliver)—as they hatch plans to rob, assault, or murder the people who thwart Swearengen's attempts to consolidate power in Deadwood. Bullock and Swearengen, however, both utter words that meld violence, politics, sexual aggression, and profanity into examples of wounded masculinity that, as David Scott Diffrient observes, exude "vigor, rage, intensity, and authority" despite their expressive inadequacies.[45]

The scene preceding Bullock and Swearengen's brutal fight in the second-season premiere, "A Lie Agreed Upon, Part I" (2.1), written by Milch, exemplifies this tendency.[46] Bullock, although married to his brother's widow, Martha (Anna Gunn), has pursued an affair with Alma Garret (Molly Parker). Alma is a New York–born woman who inherits a massive gold claim after Swearengen dispatches Dority to murder her husband, Brom Garret (Timothy Omundson), during the first-season episode "Reconnoitering the Rim" (1.3). She has also overcome an addiction to laudanum with the assistance of Swearengen's chief prostitute (and occasional mistress) Trixie (Paula Malcomson) and has agreed to become Sofia Metz's guardian. Swearengen, in "A Lie Agreed Upon, Part I," insults Bullock—who accepted an appointment as Deadwood's sheriff in the previous episode, the first-season finale "Sold Under Sin" (1.12)—after Bullock emerges from Alma's hotel following a tryst. Bullock glares at Swearengen, telling the saloonkeeper to remain at the Gem so that they can have words later in the day. Bullock, upon arriving in Swearengen's office, learns that Deadwood's political fortunes will change.

> SWEARENGEN.   We're getting ass-fucked, carved into counties, but not one fucking commissioner coming from the [Black] Hills.
> BULLOCK.   How do you have this information?
> SWEARENGEN.   From the governor himself in a pricey little personal note. They want to make us a trough for Yankton's snouts, and them hoopleheads out there [Deadwood's miners], they need buttressing against going over to those cocksuckers. Now, I can handle my areas, but there's dimensions and fucking angles I'm not expert at. You would be if you'd sheathe your prick long enough.

BULLOCK. Shut up.
SWEARENGEN. And resume being the upright pain in the
  balls that graced us all last summer.
BULLOCK. Shut up, you son of a bitch.
SWEARENGEN. Jesus Christ. Bullock, the world abounds in
  cunt of every kind, including hers. (*Bullock removes his badge
  and gun belt.*) Of course, if it'd steer you from something stu-
  pid, I, uh, could always profess another position.
BULLOCK. Will I find you've got a knife?
SWEARENGEN. I won't need no fucking knife.

Bullock and Swearengen then strike one another, beginning an altercation that sees them stumble onto Swearengen's second-story balcony,
tip over the balcony's railing, and land in the main thoroughfare's mud.
Both men are injured, but the duplicitous Swearengen pulls a knife to
stab Bullock, stopping only when he sees Bullock's wife, Martha, and
stepson, William (Josh Eriksson), staring at him through the window
of a newly arrived stagecoach that has transported them from Michi-
gan. "Welcome to fucking Deadwood," Swearengen yells at mother
and son before stumbling into the Gem Saloon. Bullock, who, despite
a nasty cut to his head, seems less hurt than Swearengen, goes to his
family rather than retrieving his badge and gun.

This altercation has many ramifications: It sets the stage for Bullock and Swearengen's eventual rapprochement, it forecasts the uneasy and tempestuous partnership they will form as Deadwood becomes a legally recognized part of the Dakota Territory, and, most
important, it threatens Swearengen's health. Swearengen, dismissing Dority and Adams after insulting Bullock early in the episode,
grimaces when he feels pain in his side or groin. He stands over his
chamber pot, futilely trying to urinate, when Bullock arrives to confront him for the insult. "Age impedes my stream, not fucking fear
of you," Swearengen says by way of greeting, informing the viewer
that his body has betrayed him. This detail is doubly important since
it anticipates not only Swearengen's messy and nasty fight with Bullock but also his subsequent debilitation by septic shock and kidney
stones, resolved only when Cochran, in "Requiem for a Gleet" (2.4),
inserts a metal probe known as a Van Buren's sound into Swearengen's urethra to allow him to pass the stones. This painful procedure
requires Dority, Trixie, and Burns to hold Swearengen down while he
screams and writhes in pain, much as he does while fighting Bullock.

The parallelism between physical violence, bodily ailment, and moral sickness is a deliberate Milchian equation that, Erin Hill recognizes, stresses how "the representation of ailments on *Deadwood*...tends to saddle its afflicted with bodily troubles that match or force to the surface the troubles of their souls."[47] Swearengen and Bullock perpetrate the physical violence against one another presaged by their verbal sparring during the first season (Swearengen, in the second episode, "Deep Water" [1.2], is upset that Bullock tries to negotiate a better deal for the lot—owned by Swearengen—on which Bullock and Star wish to build their hardware store; he tells Bullock, "Here's my counteroffer to your counteroffer: Go fuck yourself!"[48]). Swearengen and Bullock, in other words, vent their turbulent inner lives in a spectacle of public aggression.

Their conversation before the fight, however, fuses political corruption, rampant profanity, sexual crudity, open misogyny, and personal hostility into a scene of remarkable expressive power. This densely packed short dialogue, especially its references to numerous ongoing plotlines, exposes Milch's talent for economical prose even while respecting the characters' well-established personalities: Swearengen talks while Bullock glowers, seethes, and simmers. Swearengen's contempt for women drives this discussion forward, extending the man's discomfort with bodily fluids into the realm of sexuality. Bullock's coitus with Alma disturbs Swearengen not because it offends him (a hypocritical position for any brothel owner to hold), but because, to Swearengen's mind, such copulation distracts Bullock from his sworn duty to protect the camp, which includes defending the economic interests on which Swearengen parasitically preys. Swearengen's dialogue includes no fewer than seven allusions to genitalia, intercourse, fellatio, and anal sex, all within the political context of the Black Hills being divided into counties by a distant government that awards no representation to the camp's residents. This linguistic formulation juxtaposes anxieties about urological, excremental, and sexual impotence with fears of governmental, administrative, and bureaucratic marginalization. Swearengen's woman hatred ("cunt of every kind" is perhaps the most misogynistic declaration in *Deadwood*'s 36 episodes) reveals his fury that Yankton feminizes the camp by making it a passive spectator to its own fate. Swearengen, the pimp and whoremaster accustomed to enforcing his will over defenseless women, becomes one of their number in the Dakota Territory's ruthless political economy (a connection extended by Swearengen's first words to Dority upon recovering from the kidney-stone procedure: "Did you fuck me while I was out"[49]). The unfamiliar and distasteful sensation of being controlled, ignored, and degraded provokes rage in Swearengen, who targets Bullock's active sexuality as an improper response to the bureaucratic rape—the ass-fucking—that Deadwood, in Swearengen's opinion, has experienced.

Swearengen routinely invokes anal sex to describe unwelcome events that disempower their victims. When Cy Tolliver (Powers Boothe), freshly arrived in camp, prepares to open the competing Bella Union casino and brothel in "Reconnoitering the Rim," Swearengen combines latent homophobia with anti-Indian racism to describe Deadwood's viability as an ongoing commercial enterprise.[50]

TOLLIVER.   How long you been in camp, Al?
SWEARENGEN.   Well, this year, Cy, since March. I was here last year, too, but the fucking cavalry drove us out.
TOLLIVER.   Put all the whites out, didn't they?
SWEARENGEN.   Oh, deep fucking thinkers in Washington put forward that policy. This year, though, so many soldiers deserting to prospect, give up the ghost and let us all back in. And, of course, Custer sorted out the fucking Sioux for us, so now we're all as safe as at our mothers' tits.
TOLLIVER.   Did a job for our side, didn't he, Al?
SWEARENGEN.   How about that longhaired fucking blowhard, huh? I'll tell you this, son, you can mark my words: Crazy Horse went into Little Bighorn, bought his people one good long-term ass-fucking. (*Swearengen pumps his fist back and forth.*) You do not want to be a dirt-worshipping heathen from this fucking point forward.

Swearengen, rather than seeing Custer's famous defeat as a debacle, thinks it may benefit Deadwood because the federal government will pursue a revenge campaign against the Sioux, a perception proved true in "Sold Under Sin" when General George Crook (Peter Coyote) leads a detachment of soldiers into town for rest and provisions before seeking reprisals against all Native Americans living in the Dakota and Montana territories (even if they did not participate in the Battle of the Little Bighorn). Swearengen represents Native Americans as sexual inferiors who must endure a violation they cannot prevent, resist, or stop, thereby equating them with two other minority populations that

Swearengen loathes: women and homosexuals. Swearengen applauds the passivity that "ass-fucking" implies for the Sioux (McShane relishes the word by enthusiastically enunciating it) but derides the subservience that he (along with Deadwood's residents) must endure after Yankton's decision to partition the Black Hills into counties without consulting the local populace. Swearengen's comments in both "Sold Under Sin" and "A Lie Agreed Upon, Part I" suggest that Deadwood's political destiny is a form of sexual trauma that not only plays out on a municipal scale, but also demonstrates how the camp's (and region's) body politic can be abused and dismembered by the Dakota Territory's paternalistic government.

Milch and his writers draw *Deadwood's* master themes together in these sequences to meld sex, violence, profanity, and history into a dizzying fictional reproduction of the American frontier. Singer accurately writes in "The Misfit" that, during the 1980s and 1990s, Milch "had enormous success, critical and otherwise, writing for television, ... and *Deadwood* demonstrates that his narrative gifts have deepened,"[51] a judgment that the program's intelligent, ambivalent, and elliptical approach to the Western substantiates. *Deadwood,* despite its self-consciously literary dialogue, strikes the viewer as an authentic portrait of 19th-century American frontier society by depicting a fractured, incomplete, and quarrelsome community that constructs itself from base, vulgar, and unpleasant elements that defy the sunny rhetoric that Turner, Roosevelt, and other Western apologists promulgate. This unvarnished presentation is plausible precisely because it evokes a complex, lived-in West rather than the disinfected environment of the traditional Westerns to which Milch objects. *Deadwood,* indeed, challenges simplistic symbolic readings by including vivid details that reward multiple viewings. "The symbolic, the allegorical, is always generated out of the particular," Milch writes in *Stories of the Black Hills* to argue that surface meanings are incomplete: "I never thought of the name Swearengen as connected to his profane language, any more than I thought of Bullock as bull-headed...or anything of the sort. It is the life of this fiction, of the world of *Deadwood,* that generates these similarities. Symbols generate their meaning out of the closed system of a fiction."[52] The violence, profanity, sexuality, and historical backdrop that typify *Deadwood,* in other words, create realistic effects by inventing a fiction that resonates with lived experience. Viewers may not experience *Deadwood* as they do consensual or quotidian reality, but the program's autumnal tone not only counteracts Bullock's and

Swearengen's objectionable behavior but also reflects the mature style that Milch, his writers, his cast, and his production staff achieve.

Deadwood's attempt to chronicle the camp's day-to-day existence leads Milch to compare his series to literature of an earlier era. "The number of characters in *Deadwood* does not frighten me," he writes in *Stories of the Black Hills*. "The serial form of the nineteenth-century novel is close to what I'm doing. The writers who are alive to me, whom I consider my contemporaries, are writers who lived in another time—Dickens and Tolstoy and Dostoevsky and Twain."[53] This claim may seem pretentious for a man working in television, but it indicates Milch's narrative ambitions and accomplishments as he makes *Deadwood* a long, interconnected, and dense story. This novelistic approach, while not new (*Deadwood*'s 2004 premiere was preceded by daytime soap operas; *Murder One*, a series for which Milch served as creative consultant in its first season; *Oz*; *The Sopranos*; *24*; and *The Wire*, among other examples), forces the viewer to pay attention to detail, to accept a different (and more languid) narrative pace, to track numerous intersecting story lines, and to negotiate the program's literary effects. Joseph Millichap finds Robert Penn Warren's influence decisive in this final regard, stating that "like the best of Warren's works, Milch's finest creations, especially *Deadwood*, employ a distinctive, diverse, and mannered style to delineate a harshly naturalistic vision of the dark and divided depths within the American national character, an identity simultaneously and paradoxically both innocent and corrupted."[54] The literary influences that Millichap traces in "Robert Penn Warren, David Milch, and the Literary Contexts of *Deadwood*," the finest essay yet written about this theme, prove that Milch's demand for historical accuracy in settings, costumes, and music supplements his political, psychological, and moral vision for a program in which Deadwood represents America's genesis, development, and expansion. Milch, by pursuing this narrative project, resembles Dickens, Tolstoy, Dostoevsky, and Twain because all four novelists create wildly imaginative worlds that employ realism and naturalism to legitimize their fictional enterprise. *Deadwood* succeeds because Milch and his writers honor the literary legacy that these authors (along with Penn Warren) impart to produce a disturbing, resonant, and evocative television series.

Deadwood, as Singer notes, is a more mature work than even *NYPD Blue*. Despite their similar concerns (racism, sexism, law enforcement), both programs occupy distinct positions in Milch's development as a television dramatist. Their perspective on legality distinguishes them from one another, with *NYPD Blue* presenting law enforcement as a frequently disturbing, always difficult, yet finally noble effort to regulate human desire that, for Richard Clark Sterne and other observers, adopts an authoritarian stance. *Deadwood*, however, portrays law as a corollary to economic, civil, and political order that shares the same vulgar basis as the criminality it ostensibly polices. Continuities exist (Bullock's rigid outlook in *Deadwood*'s opening episodes, for instance, matches Andy Sipowicz's worldview in *NYPD Blue*'s early seasons), but Milch, in creating a lawless mining camp that predates *NYPD Blue*'s urban metropolis by one century, offers a more cynical appraisal of American commerce, politics, and jurisprudence. This paradoxical position—one would expect the police drama to be gloomier than the frontier Western—makes sense insofar as returning to the earlier era frees Milch from the 20th-century historical events, developments, and influences that *NYPD Blue* inherits, while working for HBO frees Milch from network television's censors.

This dramatic liberation gives weight to Newcomb's contention that "*Deadwood* is not a western because it tells its tale by digging out the root elements of the western. It neither revises those elements nor replays them. It exposes the western, the genre itself, as an attempt to provide 'endings' that can never be true."[55] *Deadwood*, for Newcomb, becomes an anti-Western in the same manner that Leslie Fielder, in *Love and Death in the American Novel*, sees Penn Warren's fiction about the American South's antebellum and postbellum societies as attempting "the risky game of presenting to our largest audience the anti-Western in the guise of the Western, the anti-historical romance in the guise of the form itself."[56] This generic indeterminacy—*Deadwood*, after all, revises numerous Western conventions, embracing them even as it hollows them out—generates the complications that the series unveils to an audience that may find the program's elliptical dialogue, unconventional pace, and odd characters mystifying. Viewers must return to individual *Deadwood* episodes to catch their nuances, details, and subtexts, a practice that HBO enabled during the program's broadcast life by airing a single episode many times in a given week on multiple channels and, later, by releasing entire-season DVD box sets (*Deadwood*'s complete-series collection even resembles a thick novel to extend Milch's invocation of 19th-century authors as his literary forefathers).

Milch follows a reverse progression, moving from crime drama to Western drama, when American television has traced the opposite path. The urban crime thriller, as David Simon notes in his introduction to Rafael Alvarez's *"The Wire"*: *Truth Be Told,* "long ago became a central American archetype, and the labyrinth of the inner city has largely replaced the spare, unforgiving landscape of the American West as the central stage for our morality plays."[57] The career of Elmore Leonard, to take one well-known example, emblematizes Simon's analysis. Leonard, one of America's most prolific authors, began writing Westerns during the 1950s but became an eminent crime novelist during the 1960s (he continues writing crime drama—sometimes heavily influenced by Western motifs—in the 21st century). Milch's career, however, goes against this trend to examine the origins of America's political, legal, and economic structures. *Deadwood,* in Ned Martel's memorable phrase, gets down in "the muck from which [law enforcement's] basic concepts and rituals began to evolve. The town's attempt to govern itself is corrupt, sporadic and bloody, as the main characters attempt—and often fail—to impose some stability on the society they are building."[58]

Deadwood, by making Swearengen and Bullock its protagonists, continues Milch's fascination with antiheroes. *NYPD Blue'*s Andy Sipowicz is the spiritual father of these characters, who frequently find themselves (despite their baser natures) demonstrating compassion, a trend that allows the camp to establish itself as a legitimate community rather than a lawless frontier town. The first motion toward Deadwood's eventual municipal identity occurs in "Plague" (1.6), when a smallpox outbreak forces the camp's "elite"—Swearengen, Star, Tolliver, Cochran, Merrick, bar owner Tom Nuttall (Leon Rippy), hotel owner E. B. Farnum (William Sanderson), and Reverend H. W. Smith (Ray McKinnon)—to convene a meeting to decide how to protect Deadwood's healthy residents while treating the disease's victims. Their decision to set up a "pest tent" at the camp's outskirts is far more charitable than Tolliver's choice in the previous episode, "The Trial of Jack McCall" (1.5), to leave his associate Andy Cramed (Zach Grenier), a gambler and con man infected with smallpox, to die in the woods outside Deadwood's perimeter. The meeting's participants also volunteer money to pay riders to purchase vaccine in Fort Kearny, Nebraska; Bismarck, Dakota; and Cheyenne, Wyoming, and, in the episode "Suffer the Little Children" (1.8), they distribute it free of charge to all residents. Swearengen organizes and runs this meeting, held in the Gem Saloon, but does not hold court in his usual fashion. He instead solicits opinions, makes suggestions for Merrick's article about the outbreak (advocating benign misinformation that downplays the crisis's severity), and accepts Reverend Smith's advice not to stigmatize the victims.

This embryonic government, in Hill's words, "contains an answer to what is perhaps the central question of *Deadwood*, which is whether or not residents can be trusted to handle their business themselves without being regulated by a larger power, or, put more simply, whether order is possible without law."[59] This admirable civic-mindedness, however, is undemocratic. The camp's inhabitants do not elect the town council; instead, Swearengen, in the absence of election codes, appoints them by asking (in truth, commanding) the members to participate. When, in "No Other Sons or Daughters" (1.9), word comes from Yankton that the federal government will sign a treaty with the Sioux Indians to annex the Black Hills to the Dakota Territory, Swearengen again assembles the town fathers—this time including both Bullock and Tolliver's right-hand man, Eddie Sawyer (Ricky Jay), but not the ailing Reverend Smith—to formalize their council.[60] Only rudimentary democracy ensues. Swearengen, when telling Star about the meeting, says that the council must create an informal municipal organization (rather than an official government, which would indicate that the camp rebels against federal authority) with "structure enough to persuade those territorial cocksuckers in Yankton that we're worthy enough to pay them their fucking bribes." He then tells the assembled group that this organization will help the miners, prospectors, and business owners keep title to their lands by becoming a legally recognized government whose "proper order of fucking business is to make titles and departments before the territorial cocksuckers send in their cousins to rob and steal from us." When Farnum, perfectly described by Singer as "an oleaginous toady [who] lives suspended between mortal fear of Swearengen and mercenary eagerness to do his bidding,"[61] asks to be mayor, Swearengen calls for objections and then, before Merrick can speak, pounds his hand on the table like a gavel to appoint—not elect—Farnum to this largely ceremonial position (no one doubts that Swearengen, who already acts as the meeting's de facto chief executive, will continue in this role). Farnum quickly proposes taxing the camp's residents to pay the Dakota Legislature's bribes, but Merrick nervously asks when elections will be held to replace the temporary council with permanent officials. After Farnum affirms that the council is ad hoc, the irritated Swearengen says, "Ad fucking hoc.... Can we just get on with the fucking meeting?"

Swearengen's and Merrick's opposing views illuminate *Deadwood's* complex, ambivalent, and cynical rendering of America's democratic origins. Swearengen, the pure pragmatist, finds government to be a necessary illusion that enables the camp's residents to lay legal claim to the land they already occupy and the profits they already earn. Merrick, the romantic journalist, desires representative democracy that upholds the virtues of freedom and liberty that he holds dear. This conflict encapsulates the problems that the camp faces throughout the second season, when Francis Wolcott (Garret Dillahunt), a geologist employed by George Hearst, arrives to buy gold claims that prospectors such as Ellsworth work. Wolcott immediately enlists Tolliver to begin spreading rumors that all such claims will be declared invalid by the territorial government (since they violate the Fort Laramie Treaty) but that their owners may sell their land to Hearst for a fair price. This ruse is a confidence scheme that allows Hearst to acquire valuable land at little cost and that will result in hefty profits after Deadwood becomes a legitimate municipality. This story line also becomes *Deadwood's* innovative spin on the conventional Western land-grab plot, being much more complex than the typical tale of a cattle baron running off innocent homesteaders. Hearst, the millionaire prospector who arrives in camp during the second-season finale, "Boy-the-Earth-Talks-To" (2.12), uses his wealth, influence, and power to rig the official elections that, much to Merrick's delight, Yankton demands Deadwood hold to establish a permanent legal government.[62] The third season sees all major characters, particularly Bullock and Swearengen, align themselves (at first quietly and then more openly) against Hearst's machinations. Deadwood's experiment with democracy, therefore, melds Swearengen's practical and Merrick's ethical viewpoints into an alternately hopeful and disappointing movement toward self-rule that cannot escape the depredations of Hearst's economic desire. His greed ensures that Deadwood, rather than ridding itself of the impure motivations that feed the camp's development, expands the social, political, economic, and moral compromises that give it life.

The Hearst story line most fully synthesizes *Deadwood's* major themes, particularly the connection between money, violence, profanity, and community. The third season dramatizes Milch's belief, stated in *Stories of the Black Hills,* that "before violence was anything else, it was simply a way of doing business."[63] The confrontation between Swearengen, Hearst, and Hearst's chief enforcer, Captain Turner (Allan Graf), in "I Am Not the Fine Man You Take Me For" (3.2) embodies *Deadwood's* sophisticated, if cynical, treatment of the relationship between wealth, power, and desire.[64] Hearst, through Wolcott, has purchased nearly every gold claim in the camp but has failed to acquire the rights to Alma Garret Ellsworth's massive strike (Alma, in "Boy-the-Earth-Talks-To," has married Whitney Ellsworth—who manages her claim so well that she becomes rich enough to underwrite the camp's first bank—to prevent the shame that news of her pregnancy by Bullock would entail). Hearst summons Swearengen to a meeting to discuss how to force Alma to sell, but Swearengen, knowing that such a decision could place the camp under Hearst's perpetual control, refuses.

HEARST.   I'll not name how you would benefit from the action I wish you to take, saying only instead it's my will, to which I will have you bend. (*Hearst indicates a shot glass of whiskey on the table.*) I suggest you drink that.
SWEARENGEN.   No. (*Behind Swearengen, Captain Turner produces a pistol.*)
HEARST.   I would incorporate into my holdings the claim now owned by Mrs. Ellsworth. I am told that you can help me bring this about. (*Turner pistol-whips Swearengen in the back of the head, knocking Swearengen to the floor. Turner then grabs Swearengen from behind and pins Swearengen's left hand on top of the table.*) Tell me how you will help. (*Hearst hefts a rock pick.*) This is a grip I'm used to.
SWEARENGEN (*fighting to stay conscious*).   Well, far as making your way into her, act averse to nasty language and partial to fruity tea. (*Hearst, angered by Swearengen's refusal, brings the rock pick down on Swearengen's left hand. Swearengen gasps and collapses.*)

Swearengen's vulnerability is notable, with Hearst speaking to him much as Swearengen speaks to his own underlings, employees, and prostitutes. Bending Swearengen to his will underscores not only Hearst's arrogance but also his symbolic sexual mastery of the camp's ruling elite, here represented by Swearengen, who becomes a victim of the physical violence that he (Swearengen) customarily perpetrates against others. Hearst's talk of incorporation indicates his unappeased (and perhaps unquenchable) appetite for "the color," or the gold that makes him wealthy enough to control Deadwood's municipal, economic, and political affairs. Hearst simply buys enough votes from residents of the Black Hills (including Deadwood) to ensure that people sympathetic to his interests gain positions of power.

Hearst's interference upsets the tenuous civic equilibrium that the camp achieves during *Deadwood*'s second season. Bullock, thanks to Hearst's rigging, loses the election as sheriff to Harry Manning (Brent Sexton), a bartender at Tom Nuttall's saloon who wishes to found the camp's first fire department, in the series finale, "Tell Him Something Pretty" (3.12). The camp's nascent democracy, therefore, begins as a corrupt enterprise that circumvents the will of the people, Swearengen's pragmatism, and Merrick's romanticism by preferring greed over community. The final episode, moreover, illustrates how Hearst's power is comprehensive when he purchases the services of Pinkerton Detective Agency workers to menace the local population by forming a private militia that enforces Hearst's will on the camp's populace. Two agents murder Whitney Ellsworth in "The Catbird Seat," prompting a distraught Trixie to shoot Hearst in the shoulder before this episode ends.[65] Farnum's comment about this event, with gallows humor marvelously delivered by William Sanderson, reflects the camp's (and, likely, the viewer's) perspective: "Hearst. Shot. The wound, alas, not mortal."

Hearst, despite his injuries, completes his quest to dominate the camp's affairs by purchasing Alma's gold strike after a Pinkerton agent, in "A Constant Throb" (3.10), shoots at her while she walks to the camp's bank. This threat convinces Alma to sell her claim because remaining in Deadwood and protecting Sofia Metz are more important than frustrating Hearst's plans. In "Tell Him Something Pretty," Bullock, as sheriff, and Star, as chief officer of Deadwood's bank, along with a Pinkerton agent named Newman, attend the meeting that sees Alma transfer her title to Hearst.[66] The scene's dialogue emphasizes Hearst's need to manipulate the transaction's every aspect, as well as Alma's and Bullock's refusal to capitulate to his petty demands.

HEARST. Mr. Newman, I ask you to ready payment to the officers of Mrs. Ellsworth's bank.

BULLOCK. We'll receive it where we can put it in her safe.

HEARST. May I hope, Madam, you do not subscribe to this insulting and juvenile precaution?

ALMA. I do not find the precaution juvenile, so many having been murdered with whom you've had dealings in this camp.

HEARST.   At least you acknowledge the insult.

ALMA.   I acknowledge the pretense to civility in a man so bru-
tally vicious as vapid and grotesque. (*Alma rises, followed by
Hearst.*)

HEARST.   Have the gold seen to her bank, Newman. Have its
purity assayed. Let her or her seconds choose the man. When
that tedium is completed, have the documents witnessed as
though we were all of us Jews and bring the business back to
me. Excuse my absence, Mr. Star, as I hope you forgive my
thoughtless aspersion on your race. You stand for local office,
but some contests being countywide, I await wires from other
camps. (*Hearst goes to the door. Alma passes him.*) You've changed
your scent.

BULLOCK (*to Star*).   Can't shut up. Every bully I ever met can't
shut his fucking mouth. Except when he's afraid.

HEARST.   You mistake for fear, Mr. Bullock, what is, in fact, pre-
occupation. I'm having a conversation you cannot hear.

Hearst's final line refers to his Indian name, Boy-the-Earth-Talks-To,
a designation that explains his uncanny talent for discovering gold,
silver, and other precious metals as the ability to hear (and to translate)
the earth's voice. Alma, however, highlights Hearst's venality, while
Bullock accurately describes the man as a bully whose menacing demeanor covers insecurity, anxiety, and apprehension. Hearst gets what
he wants materially, but not morally, when Alma castigates his stunted
character. Alma and Bullock rebuke Hearst's irritation by insisting on
following sensible procedures to secure her payment, thereby resist-
ing Hearst's control of the deal's linguistic and emotional elements.
Hearst's perfume comment, in this context, becomes the scene's most
juvenile moment, proving that the mining mogul's wealth does not
ensure wisdom, decency, or integrity.

A more potent example involves Hearst's demand that his assailant
be killed in "Tell Him Something Pretty," forcing Swearengen to murder
Jen (Jennifer Lutheran)—the Gem prostitute whom Burns fancies—in
Trixie's place when Burns proves unable to do so (Swearengen stabs
Jen in his office, off-camera). Hearst accepts Jen's corpse as Trixie's, not
realizing (or not caring about) the ruse that Swearengen perpetrates,
then leaves town to see to business and political interests in other
camps. "Tell Him Something Pretty" and *Deadwood* end with Swearengen scrubbing Jen's bloodstain from his office floor when Burns arrives

to ask if she suffered. "I was gentle as I was able," Swearengen says, "and that's the last we'll fucking speak of it, Johnny." Burns departs, leaving Swearengen, still scrubbing the floor, to mutter, "Wants me to tell him something pretty" as the screen fades to black.

This scene is a fitting conclusion for *Deadwood* (despite Milch's intention to produce one or two more seasons) because it so thoroughly muddies Swearengen's ethical, personal, and political choices that the viewer cannot fully condemn or excuse his actions. Swearengen resolves earlier in the episode to kill Hearst should the ruse fail, but he ensures that Jen resembles Trixie by dressing her cadaver in Trixie's clothes. He murders Jen to protect the camp from Hearst's wrath yet sacrifices an innocent woman to save Trixie's life. He regrets his decision, personally cleaning the blood he has spilled, yet offers only a mild apology to Burns for killing the woman that Burns loves. Swearengen's actions recapitulate the camp's morally ambivalent responses to external power, authority, and money to offer a skillful metaphor for *Deadwood*'s appeal—Jacobs's "filthy joy"—as a Western that depicts a complicated, compromised, and corrupt nation whose entrepreneurial energy, political pragmatism, coarse strength, and material mastery reveal the frontier as far less romantic, admirable, and simplistic than Turner and Roosevelt believe.

Deadwood's final scene also replays the gender and racial marginalization that the series interrogates. The camp's political and physical survival depends on white men viewing the body of a woman murdered to satisfy a wealthy bigot's vengeful masculinity. Hearst's sexism has been evident since his arrival in camp, with his disregard for every woman except his absent wife, Phoebe, and his personal cook, "Aunt" Lou Marchbanks (Cleo King), enhanced by a courtliness that, Alma notes, departs when he is challenged by any woman who opposes him. Hearst's racism is more complicated because his protestations about respecting and following the African American Aunt Lou's commands prove hollow when her son, Odell Marchbanks (Omar Gooding), arrives in Deadwood in "A Rich Find" (3.6) with news that a massive gold strike has been discovered in Liberia, the country founded by freed American slaves. Odell has traveled from there to seek Hearst's counsel. Odell intends to dupe Hearst but approaches the matter subtly when sitting at dinner with the man in "Unauthorized Cinnamon" (3.7).[67] Hearst insults Odell's slovenly approach to fleecing him, causing Odell to threaten to leave after saying that he expected Hearst to send a man to Liberia to confirm the find's legitimacy. Hearst relents, apologizing to Odell before lecturing him about gold's power.

> HEARST.   Before the color, no white man—no man of any hue— moved to civilize or improve a place like this had reason to make the effort. The color brought commerce here and such order as has been attained.
> ODELL.   Yes, sir.
> HEARST.   Do you want to help Liberia, Odell?
> ODELL.   I want to help myself. (*Hearst chuckles.*) If Liberia's where my chance is, that's all right with me.
> HEARST (*offers a cigar to Odell*).   Gold is your chance, Odell.
> ODELL (*takes cigar*).   Thank you, sir.
> HEARST.   Gold is every man's opportunity. Why do I make that argument? Because every defect in a man, and in others' way of taking him, our agreement that gold has value gives us power to rise above.
> ODELL.   Fond as you are of my mother, without that gold I showed you, I don't expect we'd be out here talking.
> HEARST.   That is correct. And for your effrontery at our meal a moment ago, I'd've seen you shot or hanged without a second thought. The value I gave the gold restrained me, you see, your utility in connection to it. And because of my gold, those at the other tables deferred to my restraint. Gold confers power. Power comes to any man who has the color.
> ODELL.   Even if he's black?
> HEARST.   That is our species' hope: that uniformly agreeing on its value, we organize to seek the color.

Hearst expresses more racial tolerance than he feels by giving the word *color* different connotations than *Deadwood*'s viewers (or Odell, in an earlier scene) expect. Rather than referring to "colored people," Hearst uses the term to connote gold, as well as gold's symbolic and material power because, for Hearst, gold creates commerce, civilization, and the hope of racial solidarity. Hearst, however, cannot hide his contempt for Odell sitting at his table or rising from it in anger. Mentioning Odell's effrontery becomes a metaphorical reference to the anger felt by Southern white Americans at the freeing of slaves at the Civil War's conclusion. Hearst's entire speech, occurring in 1877 or 1878 (at the end of the period known as Reconstruction), laments the

lost civilization that he suggests America has become. Hearst, however, retains his core belief that Odell, a black man, is not good enough
to sit at his table (only Odell's connection to gold makes him worthy). Hearst, the careful viewer notes, never allows Aunt Lou to dine
with him, either. She, indeed, is little more to Hearst than his "nigger
maid,"[68] whom Hearst quietly complains about, berates, and intimidates on more than one occasion.

Hearst, according to Milch, "was a Southern sympathizer and maintained a form of genial, condescending racism"[69] that Gerald McRaney's
performance of Hearst's gold speech well captures. Hearst's gentility,
however, cannot lessen the hatred that lies behind his words or his
anger at being challenged by Odell. Aunt Lou, who has begged Odell
to leave Hearst alone, worries for her son's safety, a well-founded concern when the viewer considers Odell's later, suspicious death while returning to New York City. Hearst, in "Amateur Night" (3.9), tells Aunt
Lou that Odell was robbed and killed near Rapid City, but Hearst's
menacing behavior in the previous episode, "Leviathan Smiles" (3.8),
reveals both his racism and his rage.[70] Aunt Lou asks Heart to send a
rider to deliver a garnet brooch that Odell accidentally leaves behind.

> HEARST. My imagination resists the approach in that however
> quickly he might catch Odell, until he did, the man would
> know he rode in the service of a colored person. I'd suggest,
> having packed the brooch carefully and securely, we ship it to
> New York, where my man Fitzpatrick can give it to your son
> when he arrives.
> AUNT LOU. All right.
> HEARST. Are you afraid that by his not receiving today the
> token of your love something untoward might befall Odell?
> Are you superstitious that way, Aunt Lou?

Hearst's concern that a white rider would object to serving a black
man expresses his own intolerance, while Hearst's final two questions,
delivered by McRaney with faint anger and bitterness, imply that Odell
is unprotected. Hearst seems genuinely pained when telling Aunt Lou
about Odell's death in "Amateur Night," but she will not let him hug
her in support, fleeing from Hearst to confirm that she believes that he
ordered Odell's murder.

Deadwood, therefore, does not employ the documented racism of its
setting merely to indulge racial epithets under the guise of historical

accuracy but rather illustrates how nonwhite characters face exclusion despite their intelligence and entrepreneurial spirit. Aunt Lou, for instance, is not the camp's only African American resident. Hostetler (Richard Gant), the owner of Deadwood's livery, makes a reasonable living until one of his horses escapes while being castrated in "Amalgamation and Capital" (2.9), running wildly through the streets before trampling William Bullock, who later dies of his injuries. Neither Seth nor Martha Bullock blames Hostetler for this tragedy, but Steve (Michael Harney), a white racist also injured by the horse, begins openly hating Hostetler during drunken ramblings at Tom Nuttall's saloon. Hostetler leaves camp to capture the horse, accompanied by Samuel Fields (Franklin Ajaye), a black man who calls himself "the Nigger General." When Hostetler returns in "Full Faith and Credit" (3.4) he finds that, in his absence, Steve has taken over the livery, caring for its horses and incompetently running its business. Bullock, in "A Two-Headed Beast" (3.5), then mediates the sale of Hostetler's livery to Steve, who balks at working for a black man. Steve, despite Bullock's warnings, continues to provoke Hostetler, calling him a baboon and a liar until Hostetler, saying, "I will not be called a fucking liar. I didn't live my life for that,"[71] walks into the next room. A shot rings out, and Bullock discovers the suicidal Hostetler dead in a chair.

Milch's approach to race and racism here is more mature than *NYPD Blue*'s sometimes reactionary stance. Hostetler endures Steve's explicitly racist comments (the viewer imagines that Hostetler, born before the Civil War, has experienced vicious verbal attacks all his life) but cannot tolerate having his honesty, integrity, and reputation questioned. Hostetler equates these qualities with his full humanity, so his death shakes Bullock in its passionate rejection of Steve's toxic racism. Hostetler's complex motivations for his suicide, however, illustrate Milch's commitment to creating authentic human beings who react in unexpected, ambiguous, and complicated ways. *Deadwood* is no mere cesspool of unrepentant racism but a place where minorities strive to better their lives only to find that the restrictions of American society are inescapable.

Deadwood, in a departure from conventional Westerns, dramatizes no extensive contact with Native Americans. Apart from Bullock's fight to the death with an unnamed Lakota Indian at the beginning of "Plague" (a contest provoked by Bullock's trespass on a sacred burial site) and the delivery, in "Here Was a Man," of a Native American's severed head by a Mexican rider wishing to claim the bounty on Indian scalps that Swearengen offers in the pilot episode, no Native Americans are ever seen in the program's 36 episodes. Talk of encounters, battles, and treaties with Indians is frequent, with several characters (particularly Swearengen) referring to Native Americans by such epithets as "savages" and "dirt-worshipping heathens." The pilot episode illustrates how Native Americans become all-purpose bogeymen for Deadwood's residents when they are easily blamed for the Metz family massacre, while General Crook's arrival in "Sold Under Sin" demonstrates the federal government's determination not only to punish the Sioux for defeating Custer's troops at the Battle of the Little Bighorn but also to take their land by whatever means necessary. Swearengen keeps the Indian head, which he address as "Chief" during occasional soliloquies in which he compares Deadwood's unstable political position to the Native American history of land dispossession. These moments may strike the viewer as odd, but they express Swearengen's sense that, despite his racism, he is more connected to the Indians than he initially admits.

Deadwood's lengthiest examination of race, racism, and assimilation comes in the form of Mr. Wu. This character, skillfully played by Keone Young throughout the program's three seasons, runs Chinatown (known colloquially as Chink's Alley), the area of Deadwood where Chinese immigrants work as launderers, meat packers, drug runners, and prostitutes. Wu refuses to learn English, but he provides Swearengen with meat, opium, and information about the camp's legitimate and criminal dealings. Wu's English vocabulary, at least in the first season, consists of three words: *Swedgin* (Wu's mangled version of Swearengen's name), *San Francisco,* and, most prevalently, *cocksucker* (normally yelled as "cocksucka!"). The relationship between these two men is one of *Deadwood's* most complicated and most enjoyable, for Swearengen's frequently irritated and always racist treatment of Wu (Swearengen, for instance, forces Wu to enter the Gem Saloon through its back door) cannot obscure Swearengen's affection and respect for Wu's business acumen. "In fact," Paul Wright and Hailin Zhou write in "Divining the 'Celestials': The Chinese Subculture of *Deadwood,*" their shrewd assessment of Wu's significance, "it is precisely Al and Wu's intertwined interests and often-murderous exchange of professional courtesies that fuel many of the show's central conflicts, as well as its brutal and blunt depiction of racial politics."[72] Wright and Zhou note that *Deadwood* offers an unvarnished portrayal of racism that is important to the program's narrative progression. Although minority people remain minor characters in *Deadwood,* they exceed the stereotypes that their white counterparts assign them. Swearengen and Hearst are just as savage in their professional dealings as they accuse Wu of being, while Wu's willingness to feed human corpses to his pigs is an apt metaphor for how the camp consumes its residents' ambitions, hopes, and lives.

Wu, as such, clings to pragmatism as much as Swearengen, Hearst, Bullock, and Ellsworth. Wu is American, Milch writes in *Stories of the Black Hills,* because "he makes do with what's in front of him. He takes things the way they are and doesn't pretend they're something else."[73] True as this statement may be, it underplays Wu's—and, by extension, *Deadwood's*—complicated relationship with Americanism. Wu adapts to, but does not fully accommodate, an American-as-European-descendant model of assimilation; instead, he preserves those aspects of his native culture that allow him to serve as leader of the camp's Chinese community while defying the racism that defines his life. In the episode "Mr. Wu" (1.10), for instance, Wu causes a minor uproar by entering the Gem's front door to complain to Swearengen that two white men have robbed and killed his (Wu's) opium courier, leading Swearengen to agree to kill one of these thieves in recompense.[74] Swearengen refuses Wu's demand that both robbers be murdered because killing two white men to avenge a single Chinese man's death is unacceptable to Swearengen. Later in the episode, Cy Tolliver tells Swearengen, "I don't deliver white men to chinks" when Swearengen consults him about which thief should be sacrificed.

Tolliver's statement expresses *Deadwood's* pervasive nativism. The program's racial economy is stark but not simplistic. Characters like Tolliver and Steve may hold uncomplicated beliefs about white supremacy, but Bullock, Swearengen, and Calamity Jane (Robin Weigert) (who befriends Samuel Fields, loudly declaring that she will drink with anyone, no matter who he is, in "Complications" [2.5]) are more tolerant in their outlook even if they do not crusade for civil rights. Bullock's treatment of Hostetler, Fields, Wu, and the camp's unnamed Chinese residents, indeed, is eminently fair, while Steve's visible racism toward Hostetler upsets the sheriff, as do all slights against Star's Jewish background. *Deadwood* portrays a continuum of racial attitudes rather than blind, unthinking bigotry from all white characters, dramatizing Milch's belief that it is "a mistake to think that white people have a corner on prejudice or parochialism."[75] *Deadwood's* many racial aspersions against nonwhite characters (particularly references to Native American, African American, and Chinese savagery), however, demonstrate that the camp's white residents are responsible for more racial animus than any other single group.

The program also illustrates how racism becomes a commercial strategy. Francis Wolcott, on Hearst's behalf, hires a polished, English-speaking Chinese man named Mr. Lee (Philip Moon) to become the camp's primary opium runner and Chinese-prostitute dealer in the second season's "Requiem for a Gleet." Lee treats his women so abominably (they live in squalid quarters with no health checkups, eventually expiring from overwork) that both Doc Cochran and Wu confront Lee, but to no avail.[76] The tension between Wu and Lee culminates in the second-season finale, "Boy-the-Earth-Talks-To," when Swearengen assigns Dority, Burns, and Adams to dispatch Lee's henchmen while Wu murders Lee. They do so by hiding their identities with Chinese masks and dress provided by Wu, who celebrates his rival's death by standing in the main thoroughfare and cutting off his queue, the distinctive hair braid that Wu wears as a sign of his Chinese identity. Looking up at Swearengen, Wu yells, "Wu! America!" to which Swearengen replies, "That'll hold you tight to her tit." This scene's staging, with Swearengen looking down on Wu as the latter man declares his allegiance to America, dramatizes the difficulties of assimilating into American culture: Minority characters must voluntarily suppress their native identities (or elements of those identities that mark them as foreign to the white populace) if they wish to participate fully in America's economy, government, and society. Wu's enthusiasm contrasts Swearengen's ironic recognition that Wu has sacrificed part of himself to join Deadwood's community, a theme that continues in the third-season episode "True Colors" (3.3) when Wu arrives on a stagecoach from San Francisco wearing a fancy Western suit rather than the traditional Chinese clothing he has previously displayed.

Wu, by transforming himself, becomes for Milch "the absolute pragmatist, and, simultaneously, the absolute outsider, which makes him of the essence of Deadwood."[77] Wu is one of *Deadwood*'s primary representatives of America's complex, contested, and controversial emergence as an economic powerhouse, a status that depends on civilization, savagery, entrepreneurialism, thievery, hard work, dishonesty, order, chaos, racism, tolerance, law, and crime to organize the nation's pursuit of its political interests. This paradoxical formulation of the American experience means that *Deadwood* refuses to tell its audience pretty lies about the nation's glorious past. Milch rewrites the traditional Western into a more intricate, challenging, and disturbing narrative than the genre's fans may expect, but his series makes the point, articulated by Milch in *Stories of the Black Hills,* that "none of us want [*sic*] to realize that we live in Deadwood, but all of us do. That is the point of the exercise. After first recoiling in horror, we come to love the place where we live, in all of its contradictions. To love not just America, but the world of which America is simply the most recent form of organization."[78]

Milch concludes *Stories of the Black Hills* with the hilarious statement, "I'd guess I'd paraphrase Jefferson, that with all its horrors, Deadwood is the last, best chance of all human cocksuckers."[79] This sentence's profanity, both literal and metaphorical, invokes one of the nation's Founding Fathers to emphasize the ambiguities that lie at the heart of American democracy. *Deadwood*'s dramatic sophistication, therefore, discomfits its audience to create a fascinating, memorable, and depressing vision of America whose authenticity develops from the program's unflinching acknowledgment that the nation's genesis was not easy, pure, or noble. This message resonates with 21st-century viewers by matching their sense that America, no matter how inspiring its rhetoric, rarely lives up to its reputation. Milch, by exposing the dark impulses central to the American dream, finds in the 19th century what David Simon's *The Wire* discovers in the 21st: hope, fear, promise, and peril in roughly equal measure. *Deadwood,* as a result, represents the summit of Milch's career as a fiction writer, social realist, and television dramatist. It is his undeniable masterpiece.

6

All the Pieces Matter: David Simon's *The Wire*

The Wire (2002–2008) is a stunning achievement for David Simon, for HBO, and for television drama. This series offers one of the most comprehensive, authentic, and detailed fictional portraits of an American city ever captured on film, testifying to Simon's talents as a writer, producer, and social realist. *The Wire*, by dramatizing the lives of residents across the social, cultural, economic, political, and criminal strata of Baltimore, Maryland, forms a fascinating counterpoint and bookend to David Milch's *Deadwood*. Whereas *Deadwood* depicts the origins of American political and economic dominance in 19th-century brutality, theft, racism, and entrepreneurship, *The Wire* reveals the exhaustion of American confidence in 21st-century bureaucracies that demean, diminish, and degrade the lives of average citizens. *Deadwood*'s characters struggle to construct a viable community from the basest forms of avarice, repression, and murder to secure a better future, while *The Wire*'s characters struggle to survive the decline of their community's economic, political, and democratic potency in an environment where hope seems ever more distant. Simon's program, therefore, refuses an optimistic, bright, and happy vision of American life to offer its audience a darker, more cynical, and more troubling view of the unrestrained capitalism that *Deadwood* depicts in its infancy. Both series, however, share an unrelenting skepticism about bureaucratic institutions that, to casual viewers, verges on civic nihilism.

The Wire, indeed, has ambitions beyond the status of mere entertainment that Simon's writing, DVD commentaries, behind-the-scenes documentaries, and press interviews dismiss as network television's fundamental goal. Simon, in his long introduction to Rafael Alvarez's *"The Wire": Truth Be Told* (the 2004 book that chronicles the program's genesis, development, background, and influences), states that while "the best crime shows—*Homicide* and *NYPD Blue,* or their predecessors *Dragnet* and *Police Story*—were essentially about good and evil," *The Wire's* creators "are bored with good and evil. We renounce the theme."[1] Differentiating his HBO series from the NBC cop show on which Simon first worked as a television writer and producer allows Simon to declare that he and *The Wire's* creative team "are not only trying to tell a good story or two. We are trying, in our own way, to pick a fight."[2] This fight not only opposes the crime dramas and cop shows that fill network television's programming landscape but also enacts Simon's belief that network television is indifferent to the forgotten people, places, and aspects of American life that have become, in the 21st century's postindustrial economy, superfluous. "*The Wire,*" Simon states in a supremely confident yet revealing passage of his introduction to Alvarez's book, "is most certainly not about what has been salvaged or exalted in America. It is, instead, about what we have left behind in our cities, and at what cost we have done so. It is, in its larger themes, a television show about politics and sociology and, at the risk of boring viewers with the very notion, macroeconomics. And frankly, it is an angry show."[3]

This anger forces *The Wire's* viewer into an occasionally awkward relationship with the program's narrative. Simon's argumentative intentions may lead viewers to believe that they will encounter the television equivalent of a mediocre thesis (or problem) play, in which radical politics unveils contemporary society's terrible conditions before proposing preachy, pretentious, and unpalatable solutions. *The Wire's* audience, in other words, may prefer crime dramas and cop shows to the dreary, depressing, and downtrodden program that Simon's comments seem to promise. Such drama risks becoming not only dull but also irrelevant in its zeal to promote social justice over the merits of well-told stories that capture the viewer's narrative, rather than political, interest.

That *The Wire* exposes the challenging, upsetting, and negative aspects of 21st-century urban American life without degenerating into maudlin sloganeering testifies to the storytelling talents of Simon and his production staff. *The Wire* becomes, during its five seasons, an elegy for "the other America," Simon's term for the working-class and underclass citizens whom he defines as "ex-steelworkers and ex-longshoremen; street dealers and street addicts, and an army of young men hired to chase the dealers and addicts; whores and johns and men to run the whores and coerce the johns—and all of them unnecessary and apart from a New Millennium economy that long ago declared them irrelevant."⁴ This concern for dramatizing the complicated lives of people trapped in the terrible economic, political, and bureaucratic nightmare that *The Wire* constructs for its characters demonstrates how Simon finds bourgeois attitudes, assumptions, and outlooks to be distasteful, if not contemptible.

The Wire's sympathy for individuals who try to preserve their dignity in systems that betray them places Simon's program in a tradition of protest fiction that seeks not only to reveal the connections among society's political, economic, educational, media, legal, and criminal elements but also to uncover the hollow rhetoric at the core of America's civic life. Simon notes that "*The Wire* and its stories are rooted in the logic and ethos of a second-tier city, of a forgotten rust-belt America," but does not suggest that this ethos transforms *The Wire*'s writers into social activists who walk the streets promoting urban-renewal projects: "It would be a fraud to claim that those of us spinning these stories are perfectly proletarian. We are professional writers and paid as such, and it is one thing to echo the voices of longshoremen and addicts, detectives and dealers, quite another to claim those voices as your own."⁵ This awareness dilutes the narcissism implied by what Margaret Talbot, in "Stealing Life" (her long *New Yorker* profile of Simon), refers to as Simon's formidable belief in *The Wire*, a faith that "leads him into some ostentatious comparisons that he sometimes laughs at himself for and sometimes does not."⁶ These comparisons typically cite Greek tragedy as *The Wire*'s most important forerunner, with Simon telling Talbot that his program "[rips] off the Greeks: Sophocles, Aeschylus, Euripides. Not funny boy—not Aristophanes. We've basically taken the idea of Greek tragedy and applied it to the modern city-state." Rather than portraying indifferent, venal, and selfish Olympian gods toying with "fated and doomed people," Simon says that *The Wire* depicts "postmodern institutions [as] the indifferent gods."⁷

Such assertions, when juxtaposed against Simon's biting criticisms of other crime dramas and cops shows, illustrate not only his unshakable confidence but also his blinkered view of the genres to which *The Wire* owes its dramatic existence. Arguing that *The Wire* is, in fact, "about The City," Simon begins *Truth Be Told*'s introduction by declaring, "Swear to God, it isn't a cop show. Really, it isn't. And though there be cops and gangsters aplenty, it isn't actually a crime show, though the spine of every season is certain to be a police investigation in Baltimore, Maryland."⁸ Separating *The Wire* from its generic roots, however, is as misguided as claiming that *Deadwood* is not a Western. Simon, like David Milch, seems so invested in pronouncing his series more sophisticated, capacious, and provocative than its generic forebears that he loses sight of the narrative conventions that define those earlier programs (conventions that *The Wire* reproduces even while revising them). Although critical viewers may partly ascribe this tendency to Simon's need to promote his program's singular qualities, Simon's repeated references to Greek tragedy, 19th-century novelists such as Charles Dickens, and contemporary crime novelists such as Dennis Lehane (*Mystic River*), George P. Pelecanos (*The Sweet Forever*), and Richard Price (*Clockers*)—all three of whom served as *Wire* scriptwriters—expose his prejudices against network-television drama as a valuable, relevant, and artistic medium.

Jane Gibb and Roger Sabin, in their fine essay "Who Loves Ya, David Simon? Notes toward Placing *The Wire*'s Depiction of African-Americans in the Context of American TV Crime Drama," challenge Simon's monolithic appraisal of crime shows and cop dramas (which are, in Simon's opinion, unrealistically tidy narratives that reaffirm their audiences' faith in truth and justice) by analyzing how *Kojak* (1973–1978), *Hill Street Blues* (1981–1987), *Miami Vice* (1984–1989), *NYPD Blue* (1993–2005), and *Homicide: Life on the Street* (1993–1999) are more important (and immediate) precursors to *The Wire* than *Oedipus Rex* or *Medea*. Gibb and Sabin, while admiring *The Wire*'s complex approach to racial identities and politics, nevertheless place the program within a definable tradition of televised American crime drama that Simon frequently denies. "Both Simon and Ed Burns"—the former Baltimore homicide detective and middle-school teacher who became Simon's producing-and-writing partner for *The Wire*—"have claimed they never wanted *The Wire* to be a cop show. You get the impression they want *The Wire* to be something else. They want it to be art."⁹ Gibb and Sabin, however, recognize the critical myopia of Simon's and Burns's devaluation of earlier cop dramas:

> The problem with this claim—good as *The Wire* may be—is that it takes a narrow view of what genre might be capable of. It may even imply a number of prejudices against TV (low culture, commercial, etc.) and crime drama more specifically (formularized, politically conservative, etc.), without taking into account how malleable and dynamic this forum can be. For, as we have seen,

it was never one, fixed entity: just as *Hill Street* was a long way from *Kojak*, so *The Wire* is a long way from *Hill Street*. And in ten, twenty years time, *The Wire* will look as creaky as those shows appear today.[10]

This analysis properly credits the generic conventions that form *The Wire*. Even if Simon thinks his program deconstructs network crime drama's most common narrative devices, *The Wire* still obeys many cop-show staples, including the buck-the-system mentality of Detective Jimmy McNulty (Dominic West), whom Elayne Rapping, in *Law and Justice as Seen on TV*, describes as "another rogue cop who doesn't let the policies or politics of the police department stop him from doing what he personally feels necessary to catch 'bad guys.'"[11] McNulty, careful observers might add, resembles many crime-fiction and cop-show characters from Ed McBain's 87th Precinct novels, Chester Himes's Harlem detective thrillers, *Naked City*, and *NYPD Blue*, making McNulty one in a long line of self-absorbed, alcoholic, and promiscuous police detectives who risk their careers to pursue criminals.

The Wire, in other words, does not diverge from earlier crime dramas as stridently as Simon claims, making his harsh criticism of other cop shows unreasonable. Simon, for instance, in a June 27, 2001, letter to HBO executives Chris Albrecht and Carolyn Strauss, recommends beginning production on *The Wire* so that HBO may confront what Simon perceives as network television's unrealistic approach to cop shows: "No one who sees HBO's take on the culture of crime and crime fighting can watch anything like *CSI*, or *NYPD Blue*, or *Law & Order* again without knowing that every punch was pulled on those shows."[12] This self-promoting analysis (the primary objective of Simon's memo, after all, is to convince Albrecht and Strauss to authorize filming of *The Wire*'s first season) is a particularly misbegotten evaluation of *NYPD Blue* and *Law & Order*, two programs whose approach to criminal justice is more mature than Simon allows. The only false note in Gibb and Sabin's analysis, indeed, is their belief that *Kojak* and *Hill Street Blues* look creaky 30 or 40 years after their initial broadcasts. *Kojak* tackles departmental corruption and institutional lassitude in several episodes, while *Hill Street Blues* retains its dramatic urgency, narrative sophistication, and visual power. *The Wire*, it seems, will age just as well as its predecessors because, despite Simon's excessive claims, his program remains a superlatively written, acted, and filmed television series.

The Wire, however, pioneers an explicit critique of postindustrial capitalism that powers each season's narrative disenchantment with institutional bureaucracy. Gibb and Sabin, for instance, state that "on a more sophisticated level, we can see that *The Wire's* claim to originality lies in its openly class-based politics,"[13] a point supported by Simon's contention, first made during his June 18, 2008, address to London, England's National Film Theatre and repeated during his July 15, 2008, interview with Lauren Laverne on BBC's *The Culture Show,* that *The Wire* is "a political tract masquerading as a cop show."[14] Such comments have spurred Marxist and neo-Marxist readings of *The Wire* that interrogate the program's deconstruction (if not destruction) of neoliberal capitalism (the economic philosophy that seeks to transfer fiscal, industrial, and commercial control from the public to the private sector, resulting in the dominant multinational capitalism that Fredric Jameson famously equates with postmodernity in his influential 1991 book *Postmodernism, or, the Cultural Logic of Late Capitalism*). Alberto Toscano and Jeff Kinkle's "Baltimore as World and Representation: Cognitive Mapping and Capitalism in *The Wire*" may be the finest exploration of *The Wire's* socioeconomic concerns and contradictions yet published. As Toscano and Kinkle note, "The lack of any proletarian revolutionary subject and the depiction of the working class that continues to exist after its supposed disappearance is the frame through which the series...approaches the dynamics of the world system."[15] Here, *system* refers to international means of production, trade, communication, and consumption that compose the infinitely complicated "free market" that economists, journalists, and pundits routinely define as globalization.

Simon, beyond commenting that *The Wire's* writers are not perfectly proletarian, agrees that members of America's working class and underclass no longer revolt against their diminished economic circumstances but instead find themselves compromised by the massive institutional bureaucracies that corporate capitalism creates. Simon's introduction to *"The Wire": Truth Be Told* minces no words on this subject, stating that *"The Wire* begins a story wedged between two competing American myths."[16] The first myth, that the most intelligent, talented, and visionary people can become wealthy "by virtue of basic free-market processes[,]...happens to be true." A countervailing myth, Simon continues, "serves as national ballast against the raw, unencumbered capitalism that asserts for individual achievement and the amassed fortune of the wise and the fortunate," namely, that average people who work diligently while fulfilling their civic responsibilities not only will find a place in American society but also "will not be betrayed." Simon, however, finds this promise incompatible with 21st-century urban America: "And in Baltimore, it is no longer possible to describe this as myth. It is no longer possible even to remain polite on the subject. It is, in a word, a lie."

This pessimistic (yet probing) analysis gives *The Wire* its reputation, burnished by Simon at every available opportunity, for confronting uncomfortable truths about American politics, economy, and culture. "Unencumbered capitalism," in Simon's memorable phrase, leaves behind factory workers, longshoremen, and other blue-collar employees who find few places in an information-and-services economy that no longer values their skills. "These are the excess Americans,"[17] Simon declares in a *Truth Be Told* passage that expresses his anger, dismay, and regret at the broken social compact that *The Wire* chronicles. His program not only dramatizes but also empathizes with those people who, excluded from American prosperity's overt trappings, struggle to remain relevant in a nation that regards them as unnecessary. The institutional bureaucracies that *The Wire* so witheringly portrays become symptoms of a systemic refusal to create equality of political, economic, and social opportunity for individuals whose lives go unacknowledged by their better-off peers.

This antibourgeois attitude transforms *The Wire* into a television crime drama that, in its inaugural season, creates a fractured, fractious, and unfair criminal-justice system that parallels inner-city Baltimore's drug trade. This conceit avoids the good-and-evil theme decried by Simon to embrace ambivalent cynicism about the tactical, philosophical, and ethical similarities between the Baltimore Police Department and the drug organization run by Avon Barksdale (Wood Harris) that McNulty begins tracking after observing Barksdale's nephew D'Angelo (Larry Gilliard Jr.) avoid a murder conviction in the pilot episode, "The Target" (1.1). A key witness in the case against D'Angelo, security guard Nakeisha Lyles (Ingrid Cornell), refuses to identify D'Angelo as the killer in a fatal project shooting while testifying in Judge Daniel Phelan's (Peter Gerety) courtroom. McNulty realizes that Barksdale's right-hand man, Russell "Stringer" Bell (Idris Elba), who sits in the courtroom's gallery during Lyles's testimony, has either pressured or paid the woman to perjure herself. McNulty, rather than decrying this development as a miscarriage of justice, informs Phelan while chatting in the judge's chambers that Bell and

Barksdale not only run West Baltimore's drug trade but also routinely outmaneuver the legal system. Phelan then contacts the police department's top officials to complain about the Barksdale organization, causing Deputy Commissioner for Operations Ervin H. Burrell (Frankie R. Faison), the department's second-in-command, to authorize a surveillance detail to which McNulty is assigned. McNulty, by speaking to Phelan, deliberately ignores the police department's chain-of-command rules just as Bell and Barksdale ignore the court's due-process protections to manipulate the situation for personal advantage. McNulty, Bell, and Barksdale, therefore, resist the institutional authorities that seek to limit their actions even though each man, within his specific role (as police detective or as drug kingpin), functions as an authority figure.

This paradoxical portrait underscores *The Wire*'s contribution to television crime and cop drama. Although programs in both styles destabilize the boundaries between crime and justice (including *Hill Street Blues, NYPD Blue,* and *Homicide*), *The Wire* so thoroughly blurs these lines that the viewer cannot comfortably classify characters as good or bad depending on their occupation. Bell, for instance, attends college business and management courses, reads Adam Smith's *The Wealth of Nations,* and, in the third season, conducts meetings of his drug lieutenants according to *Robert's Rules of Order*. McNulty's self-destructive tendencies mark him as a damaged soul who cares little for the problems that he creates for fellow officers, while his alcoholic philandering alienates his ex-wife, Elena (Callie Thorne); his occasional lover, Assistant State's Attorney Rhonda Pearlman (Deirdre Lovejoy); and Beatrice "Beadie" Russell (Amy Ryan), the Port Authority cop who becomes integral to the second season's story line about corruption in the local longshoreman's union and who enters what she believes is a monogamous relationship with McNulty in the third season. *The Wire,* as Simon's comments in *Truth Be Told* indicate, sees these individuals trapped within postindustrial bureaucratic institutions that seek to mollify, control, and punish their own workers, resulting in a morally tangled social system that can neither sustain nor fulfill those employees.

The Wire, therefore, unapologetically demolishes audience expectations about good triumphing over evil because these dichotomous concepts cannot accurately capture, describe, or explain 21st-century America, requiring Simon's program to become, in his words, a "visual novel"[18] that fulfills Tom Wolfe's formulation, propounded in an important (albeit controversial) essay, "Stalking the Billion-Footed

Beast: A Literary Manifesto for the New Social Novel," of "a novel *of the city*, in the sense that Balzac and Zola had written novels *of Paris* and Dickens and Thackeray had written novels *of London*, with the city always in the foreground, exerting its relentless pressure on the souls of its inhabitants."[19] *The Wire*'s openly class-based politics—variously characterized as liberal, liberalist, libertarian, socialist, social democratic, Communist, and anti-American by scholars, sociologists, and passionate visitors to HBO's official *Wire* Web site—mark, for Simon, a return to the type of large, detailed, and ambitious novel that Wolfe, in his essay and his book *The New Journalism*, asserts must be "based on reporting" so that its realism "would portray the individual in intimate and inextricable relation to the society around him."[20] Wolfe's approach to social realism agrees with Simon's attitude about what *The Wire* (and all relevant television drama) should be. Simon's success in imagining Baltimore as alive, vivid, and whole as he does in *The Wire* leads Mark Bowden, in "The Angriest Man in Television" (Bowden's *Atlantic Monthly* profile of Simon), to doubt that Wolfe "imagined that one of the best responses to this call [to revive social realism] would be a TV program, but the boxed sets blend nicely on a bookshelf with the great novels of American history."[21]

This statement's truth confronts any first-time *Wire* viewer. The initial scene of the pilot episode (and the program), for instance, exemplifies *The Wire*'s narrative approach to the intricate social, racial, and economic codes that, in their Baltimorean precision, signify important observations about 21st-century America. The episode's opening shot tracks blood trails on pavement as flashing blue-and-red police lights bathe the scene in familiar crime-drama colors.[22] The camera sees both a bullet and the corpse of a young African American man lying in the street before finding McNulty, who sits on the stoop of a boarded-up ghetto rowhouse next to the only witness, an unnamed African American man. Their dialogue emblematizes *The Wire*'s evocative storytelling, particularly when the witness says that the victim's name was Snot (short for Snotboogie).

MCNULTY.   He like the name?
WITNESS.   What?
MCNULTY.   Snotboogie. (*Witness says nothing.*) This kid, whose mama went to the trouble of christening him Omar Isaiah Betts? You know, he forgets his jacket, and so his nose starts running, and some asshole, instead of giving him a Kleenex, he calls him Snot.

WITNESS.   Huh.
MCNULTY.   So he's Snot forever. Doesn't seem fair.
WITNESS.   Life just be that way, I guess.
MCNULTY.   So, who shot Snot?

Snotboogie's name, for McNulty, reveals the casual unfairness of "the other America" that *The Wire,* from its opening moments, addresses. This initial exchange may remind viewers of *Homicide: Life on the Street's* passages of elliptical dialogue in which characters comment on seemingly unimportant details that acknowledge their environment's idiosyncrasies. The witness's comment that "life just be that way" indicates how nonchalant ghetto living can be about matters of identity, even in moments of great tragedy.

The witness, however, finds the manner of Snotboogie's death more objectionable than his unusual name.

WITNESS.   Motherfucker ain't have to put no cap in him, though.
MCNULTY.   Definitely not.
WITNESS.   He could've just whipped his ass like we always whip his ass.
MCNULTY.   I agree with you.
WITNESS.   He gonna kill Snot. Snot been doing the same shit since I don't know how long. (*McNulty says nothing.*) Kill a man over some bullshit. (*McNulty says nothing.*) I'm saying, every Friday night, we in the alley behind the cut-rate, we rolling bones, you know? I mean, all the boys from 'round the way. We roll till late.
MCNULTY.   Alley crap game, right?
WITNESS.   And like every time, Snot, he would fade a few shooters. Play it out until the pot's deep. Then he'd snatch and run.
MCNULTY.   What, every time?
WITNESS.   Couldn't help hisself.
MCNULTY.   Let me understand you. Every Friday night, you and your boys would shoot crap, right? (*Witness nods.*) And every Friday night, your pal Snotboogie, he'd wait till there was cash on the ground, then he would grab the money and run away? (*Witness nods.*) You let him do that?
WITNESS.   We catch him and beat his ass, but ain't nobody never go past that.

MCNULTY. I gotta ask you, if every time Snotboogie would grab the money and run away, why'd you even let him in the game?

WITNESS. What?

MCNULTY. If Snotboogie always stole the money, why'd you let him play?

WITNESS. Got to. This America, man.

This scene reproduces, nearly verbatim, a passage from Simon's book *Homicide: A Year on the Killing Streets* in which Baltimore Detective Terry McLarney tells "the parable of Snot Boogie" to Detective Dave Brown.[23] Identifying this anecdote as a parable hints at its symbolic power because Snotboogie's story becomes a perfect microcosm of the program's attitude toward law, justice, equality, and economic opportunity. The unfairness that McNulty notes about Snotboogie's—or Omar Betts's—name represents the larger inequity that leads the man, living in economically depressed West Baltimore, to steal compulsively from his friends, who tolerate his behavior because they understand that Snotboogie cannot control the impulse to snatch what lies before him. Seizing opportunity, in other circumstances, would be a praiseworthy accomplishment that helps Snotboogie get ahead, but, in this instance, it proves a fatal violation of the neighborhood's shadow economy. Street gambling, like drug dealing, may be risky, but loyalty to one's friends, the witness indicates, should overrule even the quest for profit.

Murdering Snotboogie, however, is an unnecessary response because an inevitable beating reclaims the money for a game of chance that serves as metaphor for both the uncertain lives of the men who play it and for the disenchantment that, according to Talbot, illustrates "how some dollar-store, off-brand version of American capitalism could trickle down, with melancholy effect, into the most forsaken corners of American society."[24] The scene allows *The Wire*'s viewer, rather than taking umbrage at Snotboogie's robbery, to understand that the man's behavior may be a rational response to the economic dislocation that he, his friends, and his neighborhood experience. The witness's final line expresses his sense that America is (or should be) a place of inclusion, even for a back-alley thief who creates opportunity where none exists. Snotboogie's willingness to take the beatings provoked by his thievery bespeaks a personal integrity that the witness mourns, explaining why Snotboogie's murder is "bullshit" rather than a predictable response to robbery. Snotboogie, the viewer recognizes, accepts responsibility for his actions by enduring weekly beatings that are sufficient punishment for his crime.

This perspective highlights McNulty's atypical presence in the scene. Rather than pursuing the confrontational questioning that viewers might expect from a television cop drama (particularly one created by the writer who inspired *Homicide: Life on the Street,* famous for its artfully intense interrogations), McNulty prompts the witness to talk by endorsing the man's feelings, asking simple questions, and, most important, remaining silent. The scene's visual composition encourages this reading: Longer shots frame McNulty and the witness as equal participants, while close-ups are evenly divided between them. McNulty and the witness, therefore, share a more equitable relationship than the conventional power dynamic (between dominant detective and passive information giver) that cop shows routinely indulge. Talbot writes that this approach demonstrates "how the police and the policed [can], at moments, share the same jaundiced view of the world,"[25] with McNulty and the witness resigning themselves to Snotboogie's unjust murder in a scene whose gallows humor mitigates its jaded outlook. Proclaiming the virtues of American inclusion, after all, means little when confronted by the fact of Snotboogie's death and the expression of surprised betrayal on the corpse's face, making the witness's final comment a eulogy for the diminished opportunities that urban America offers its excess citizens. Freedom in the 21st-century's inaugural decade, *The Wire*'s opening scene suggests, promises less than it once did, with "This America, man" ironically reversing the optimism implied by its patriotic rhetoric.

The pilot episode's first scene also underscores the tragic moralism that Blake D. Ethridge sees as *The Wire*'s primary narrative effect. The program's creator, Ethridge writes in "Baltimore on *The Wire*: The Tragic Moralism of David Simon," "is as much interested in accurately and caringly depicting the character and difficulties of his city as he is in projecting a criticism of the ideas and myths of America,"[26] leading *The Wire* to create characters (like Snotboogie's friend) who earnestly cling to American ideals of inclusion, equality, and fairness despite the social, political, and institutional betrayal of those ideals that the program dramatizes. Perhaps *The Wire*'s signature innovation is its refusal to privilege law enforcement's cop-shop perspective over the viewpoints of criminals, addicts, and average citizens. The series, indeed, hybridizes Simon's massive books *Homicide: A Year on the Killing Streets* and *The Corner: A Year in the Life of an Inner-City Neighborhood* (as well as their television adaptations) into a crime drama that avoids middle-class judgments about how law-enforcement personnel are ethically, morally, and civically superior to the people they police. This attitude dismisses the single standard of justice that typifies cop dramas to embrace, in Sophie Fuggle's words, "multiple and conflicting truths" that blur boundaries between right and wrong while undercutting "the division, so clearly maintained in other crime dramas, between those who break the law and those who maintain it."[27] This division evaporates in the pilot episode's opening scene to portray McNulty and the witness as fellow travelers in an urban pageant that prevents its participants from realizing the American dream.

Ethridge argues that the witness's "This America, man" line has deeper significance, for "Snot and his friend are part of the urban underclass shunned by and segregated from the rest of the country,"[28] but this observation does not go far enough. Simon's audio commentary for "The Target," however, recognizes how the parable of Snot-boogie is a "wonderful metaphor for what is going on in the American city, that those who are excluded from the legitimate economy make their own world. And we're trying to depict the world that they've created upon being excluded from the rest of America."[29] This comment recognizes the agency that excess Americans develop when they cannot participate in legitimate social institutions, occupations, and opportunities. *The Wire*, rather than offering a pitiless portrait of doomed people who passively accept their destinies, dramatizes how they survive an uncaring postindustrial economy that ignores their potential contributions. The series is less a Greek tragedy than a story of stifled dreams, broken promises, and bleak futures that nonetheless places faith in individual action (even if that action frequently seems futile).

This approach, as Amanda Ann Klein recognizes, places *The Wire* squarely in the tradition of American melodrama. Klein, in her insightful essay "'The Dickensian Aspect': Melodrama, Viewer Engagement, and the Socially Conscious Text," argues that melodrama, despite its checkered reputation, is a genre as valuable as tragedy because melodrama seeks "to uncover some ostensible truth about a social ill and to explain its existence and consequences to the audience."[30] Klein claims that *The Wire* is less tragic than David Simon believes, while its melodramatic aspects connect it with other crime dramas and cop shows that may be less accomplished and less ambitious but that do tackle issues of poverty, addiction, and abuse to illustrate their causes and effects.

The Wire's stately tempo, however, differentiates it from many other crime dramas and cop shows—particularly programs like *Law & Order, CSI: Crime Scene Investigation,* and *The Shield*—to evoke the narrative rhythms of long novels and stage drama. While these other contemporaneous series feature staccato pacing that cuts quickly among events (and that rarely includes scenes more than 2.5 minutes long), *The Wire* unveils scenes that, lasting 4 or more minutes, feature extended passages of dialogue or—in the case of Baltimore City Councilman (later Mayor) Thomas "Tommy" Carcetti's (Aidan Gillen) political speeches—of monologue that comment on the narrative's action even as they build character and advance plot. Carcetti's passionate address to Police Commissioner Burrell and Deputy Commissioner for Operations (later Commissioner) William Rawls (John Doman) at a subcommittee meeting during the third-season finale, "Mission Accomplished" (3.12), about that season's major story line—Western Police District Commander Major Howard "Bunny" Colvin's (Robert Wisdom) de facto decriminalization of illegal narcotics by establishing three "free zones" where drugs may be sold without police interference (a plan that causes his district's crime to plummet)—demonstrates *The Wire*'s talent for fusing multiple subtexts into scenes that move more slowly and more spontaneously than in other crime dramas.[31]

Carcetti's speech, unlike the articulate closing arguments that conclude most *Law & Order* episodes or the rapid-fire banter that typifies *The Shield*, is no mere response to a single issue (Colvin's controversial decision to suspend drug enforcement) or to a single plot development (Burrell and Rawls's attempt to salvage the police department's battered public image) but is instead an unbridled lament for, sociological analysis of, and lecture about his city's urban decline:

We can forgive Major Colvin who, out of his frustration and despair, found himself condoning something which can't possibly be condoned. We can do that much. But, gentlemen, what we can't forgive, what I can't forgive, ever, is how we—you, me, this administration [of Baltimore Mayor Clarence V. Royce], all of us—how we turned away from those streets in West Baltimore, the poor, the sick, the swollen underclass of our city trapped in the wreckage of neighborhoods which were once so prized, communities which we've failed to defend, which we have surrendered to the horrors of the drug trade, and if this disaster demands anything of us as a city, it demands that we say "enough."

Enough to the despair which makes policemen even think about surrender. Enough to the fact that these neighborhoods are not saved or are beyond the saving. Enough to this administration's indecisiveness and lethargy, to the garbage which goes uncollected, the lots and rowhouses which stay vacant, the addicts who go untreated, the working men and women who every day are denied a chance at economic freedom. Enough to the crime, which every day chokes more and more of the life from our city.

And the thing of it is, if we don't take responsibility and step up, not just for the mistakes and the miscues, but for whether or not we're going to win this battle for our streets, if that doesn't happen, we're going to lose these neighborhoods and ultimately this city forever if we don't have the courage and the conviction to fight this war the way it should be fought, the way it needs to be fought, using every weapon that we can possibly muster. If that doesn't happen, well, then we're staring at defeat. And that defeat should not and cannot and will not be forgiven.

Carcetti, in a deft performance by Gillen, expresses the outrage that drives *The Wire*'s response to the American city's decline. The religious language of forgiveness frames Carcetti's militaristic rhetoric about fighting the entrenched problems that consign overwhelmingly black Baltimore neighborhoods to permanent marginalization, that provoke politically unpalatable solutions to those difficulties, and that seem intractable in their scope, complexity, and power. This speech also allows Carcetti to announce unofficially his mayoral candidacy. An earlier scene finds political consultant Theresa D'Agostino (Brandy Burre) urging the ambitious Carcetti to confront the issue of Colvin's free zones, but Carcetti does not intend to grandstand quite as much as he does. Carcetti's passionate lecture, however, causes the assembled audience (apart from Burrell and Rawls) to offer a standing ovation while drawing the approval of Maryland State Assembly Delegate Odell Watkins (Frederick Strother). Watkins is a powerful African American leader whose support of the Caucasian Carcetti's campaign during *The Wire*'s fourth season helps Carcetti win the mayoralty of what he, D'Agostino, and Norman Wilson (Reg E. Cathey)—Carcetti's wry and intelligent African American campaign manager—frequently call a majority-black city.

Carcetti's address, however, reproduces the religiously combative rhetoric of George W. Bush's presidential administration (rhetoric that Carcetti, in other scenes, disdains) to underscore *The Wire's* skepticism about all politicians and to underline the program's subtle yet protracted criticisms of Bush's policies, positions, and posturing. Carcetti, by endorsing the bellicose war-on-drugs mentality that Colvin's drug-free zones reject, shows his political opinions to be as constrained, confused, and craven as the ineffective crime-control policies of Mayor Royce's (Glynn Turman) administration (policies that Carcetti relentlessly questions during Season Four). Carcetti astutely identifies as despair Colvin's response to the decades-long decline of Baltimore's Western District (Colvin legalizes drugs to pilot what he considers rational drug-enforcement policies reminiscent of Amsterdam, Holland), but misunderstands how much "Hamsterdam" (the largest free zone's nickname) liberates Colvin's officers from pursuing quick narcotics arrests that supplement his district's crime-enforcement statistics but do nothing to diminish the drug trade. The war on drugs, from Colvin's perspective, is an abject failure. In "All Due Respect" (3.2), for instance, he tells Deacon (Melvin Williams), a local religious leader, that "the city is worse than when I first came on"[32] as a cop nearly 30 years earlier because the drug war destroys a police officer's proper work: getting to know the residents of economically challenged neighborhoods rather than disrupting their lives with violent drug busts that transform law-enforcement personnel from trusted community partners into an uncaring government's enemy agents. Colvin creates Hamsterdam to push the drug trade into three deserted areas so that the rest of the Western District's residents may live in relative peace, safety, and dignity.

Carcetti, suitably impressed by the improvements to daily life while touring the Western District with Colvin in "Middle Ground" (3.11), becomes saddened, shocked, and intrigued by Hamsterdam.[33] Colvin tells Carcetti that he (Colvin) cannot claim victory with Hamsterdam but that he is glad to have pursued its unorthodox strategy due to the benefits experienced by the entire community. Colvin, just before taking Carcetti to Hamsterdam, says, "Look, I done showed you the good. Come on, let me show you the ugly" to reflect his clear-eyed view of the free zones' terrible cost. The sequence in which Carcetti mutely walks through Hamsterdam is heartbreaking due to the human misery and ruin on display, with addicts scrambling to buy drugs, fighting among themselves, and succumbing to sicknesses that not even the university health and drug-care workers on hand can heal. The Hamsterdam story line, according to Bowden, reflects *The Wire*'s narrative sophistication and political cynicism, since Mayor Royce must close the free zones when media attention makes their existence public knowledge:

> It's a tribute to the depth of Simon's imagination that this experiment isn't presented as a cure-all. He doesn't minimize the moral compromise inherent in Hamsterdam. Many addicts see their severe health problems worsen, and the drug-dealing zone becomes a haven for vice of all kinds. Decent people in the community are horrified by the officially sanctioned criminality and the tolerance of destructive addiction. The experiment ends ignobly when news of the unauthorized experiment reaches the ears of a *Sun* reporter. City Hall reacts to the story with predictable horror, scurrying and spinning to escape blame. Colvin loses his job, and the city goes back to the old war, which is useless but politically acceptable.[34]

Bowden notes that Royce closes Hamsterdam when threatened by federal officials with the loss of millions of dollars but misses important nuances of how intelligently *The Wire* handles Hamsterdam. Colvin's decision to create the free zones fictionally extrapolates former Baltimore Mayor Kurt L. Schmoke's drug-decriminalization preferences, views that garnered Schmoke (Baltimore's first elected African American mayor) praise from some quarters but heavy criticism from others. Both Simon and George Pelecanos say in third-season DVD audio commentaries that Schmoke, who plays Baltimore's public-health commissioner in "Middle Ground" and "Mission Accomplished," was "crucified" for advocating a courageous yet untenable policy that ended the man's political career.[35] Mayor Royce, however, in both "Middle Ground" and "Mission Accomplished," calls in academic, health, and political advisors (including Delegate Watkins) to consider the city's options. Royce, impressed by the crime reduction that Hamsterdam produces, seems genuinely interested in the free zones' success, both for his own political future (he will, after all, face reelection the following year) and for the prospect of ending the city's destructive, hopeless, and (in Bowden's term) useless drug war. Royce, in other words, tries to rescue Hamsterdam's benefits by taking seriously the suggestions of academic and public-health officials who tell him that, in addition to lowering crime, the free zones concentrate drug addicts in smaller areas that offer unprecedented access to at-risk populations who rarely seek medical assistance until they visit hospital emergency rooms.

Royce, for days after he learns about Hamsterdam, appears to favor allowing the free zones to remain open until he can calculate their social, fiscal, and political costs. Carcetti's lecture swiftly dismisses as indecisiveness and lethargy Royce's willingness to consider a new policy that may improve Baltimore's civic life. Ridding the city of the drug war appeals to Royce until federal officials—representatives of the Bush administration that Carcetti dislikes—pressure the mayor to renounce Colvin's radical solution to drug violence. Carcetti, who is elected governor of Maryland in *The Wire*'s series finale, "-30-" (5.10), by making crime his signature issue, begins his political ascent by rejecting Colvin's promising initiative. This development is one of *The Wire*'s most lacerating criticisms of the political hypocrisy that prevents American democracy from making social progress.

The Wire's third season, to its credit, presents this outcome as an ambivalent tragedy. Burrell and Rawls reduce Colvin's rank to lieutenant before forcing him to retire, while the neighborhood corners that came back to life while the free zones operated (with residents living in peace and security) revert to fear, suspicion, and violence as the drug trade resumes. Although addicts no longer congregate in concentrated areas, their lives do not improve, while the police return to the statistics-driven, run-and-gun enforcement strategies that *The Wire* depicts as failed crime-prevention strategies. The third season's final scene, indeed, finds Colvin standing amid the rubble of Hamsterdam—bulldozed by Rawls, who plays Richard Wagner's "Ride of the Valkyries" over a loudspeaker (in an homage to Francis Ford Coppola's *Apocalypse Now*) as the free zone's buildings are demolished—to contemplate the promise that Hamsterdam held for putting the city on a more enlightened path. The forlorn image of Colvin walking away from mountainous piles of debris authorizes Ethridge's declaration that "Colvin is a tragic reformer" because he "tries to work within the system... but his potential improvements are repeatedly destroyed because, although they might solve a problem, they become problematic for... particular institutions" by proposing radical solutions that, no matter how sensible, challenge conventional thinking.[36] The dilapidated buildings visible in the background of Hamsterdam's ruin testify to Simon's belief that "the American war on drugs has mutated into a brutal war against the underclass."[37] The camera lingers on this pessimistic image until "Mission Accomplished"—undiluted by happiness, optimism, or hope—fades to black.

The Wire's third season, particularly Carcetti's misguided yet complicated political opportunism (the man, indeed, honestly wishes to restore Baltimore's civic virtues), even more "graphically depicts," in Brian G. Rose's words, "the fury and futility of the city's drug war" than the first two seasons.[38] The series, therefore, may seem insufferably gloomy, but, in fact, it becomes riveting because its sociological dissection of urban America occurs within a compelling serialized narrative populated by vibrant, intriguing, and nuanced characters. David Simon, Ed Burns, executive producer Nina K. Noble, and producer Karen L. Thorson agree in DVD commentaries, behind-the-scenes documentaries, and press interviews that *The Wire*'s affection for all its characters—even venal authority figures like Burrell, Rawls, Carcetti, Royce, and Maryland State Senator R. Clayton "Clay" Davis (Isiah Whitlock Jr.)—makes the program far less cynical than it appears. This perspective is essentially correct, although, as Gibb and Sabin comment, *The Wire*'s "commitment to portraying individuals as compromised by the institutions they are committed to" results in a "diminishing depth of characterization which occurs whenever the action shifts upward to the higher echelons of power."[39] Gibb and Sabin believe that Commissioner Burrell, Mayor Royce, and State Senator Davis "lack 'that extra layer of complexity' that bell hooks has alluded to in her discussion of 'common representations of black people'" to become African American characters who, if they "still have the power to engage us it is because whether in the guise of politicians (Davis and Royce) or the pragmatic tactician (Burrell) they know how to hold an audience [that makes them] function in *The Wire*…purely as satire," with an "implied social critique in their ability to self consciously exploit what Charles Burnett has referred to as the perennial re-assuring stereotypical 'image that suggests that black people are first and foremost entertainers.'"[40] This heady analysis suggests that *The Wire*'s black leaders may be far more sophisticated characters than the shucking-and-jiving African Americans found in 19th- and 20th-century American minstrel shows but that Burrell, Royce, and Davis nonetheless bear faint minstrel traces. Gibb and Sabin also insinuate that each man subtly reproduces stereotypes about selfish, arrogant, and corrupt black politicians who manipulate racial tensions and fears to advance their own careers. Burrell, Royce, and Davis, therefore, may unintentionally embody the conservative bromide that, after Martin Luther King Jr.'s death, the "black community" lacks selfless leaders who put their people's interests before their own political welfare (a sentiment that not even Barack Obama's presidential ascendancy could stem).

Gibb and Sabin's charge gains credence when one notes the scant attention that *The Wire* pays to Burrell's, Royce's, and Davis's private lives during its five seasons. Photos of Burrell's family are occasionally visible in his office. Royce's wife rarely appears, although the mayor's affair with his administrative assistant (Tamieka Chavis) is revealed in "Soft Eyes" (4.2) when Sergeant Thomas "Herc" Hauk (Domenick Lombardozzi), a member of Royce's security detail, accidentally walks into the mayor's office to find the assistant fellating Royce. Davis's sole sexual dalliance comes in "Clarifications" (5.8), when Detective Lester Freamon (Clarke Peters) asks Davis's attractive female companion to leave before threatening to expose an illegal loan that the senator has received if Davis refuses to provide information about a courthouse employee who leaked grand-jury documents to Baltimore drug lawyers. Carcetti's wife, children, and home, by contrast, appear in several third- and fourth-season episodes while he mounts his improbable, yet finally successful, campaign against Royce.

Gibb and Sabin's concern about imbalances between *The Wire's* black and white leaders, however, overlooks notable exceptions. The Caucasian Rawls's home life, despite his wedding band and family photos, remains as mysterious as Burrell's, Royce's, and Davis's, while the image of Rawls patronizing a gay bar in "Reformation" (3.10) reveals a significant aspect of his character that *The Wire* fails to explore in any later episode. Cedric Daniels (Lance Reddick)—the African American lieutenant who supervises the surveillance detail formed to investigate the Barksdale drug organization in Season One and the longshoreman's union in Season Two, who rises to the rank of major in Season Three, and whom Carcetti appoints as commissioner of the Baltimore Police Department in Season Five—enjoys a rich personal life. He begins the series married to an intelligent and ambitious African American woman, Marla Daniels (Maria Broom), from whom he becomes estranged when he chooses, in Season Two, to remain with the police department rather than retiring to work as a lawyer, as he promises her in "Collateral Damage" (2.2). Daniels becomes romantically involved with Rhonda Pearlman in "All Due Respect" when she pursues him after realizing that he is living in the surveillance detail's office. Their relationship faces challenges during Seasons Three and Four when Daniels appears at several public events as Marla's happy husband to support her bid to join the Baltimore City Council. Daniels tells Pearlman in "Homecoming" (3.6) that Marla supported his police career for so many years that he will aid her political aspirations in any way possible, meaning that he and Pearlman cannot openly announce their interracial relationship for fear of harming Marla's image.

These counterexamples illustrate not only *The Wire*'s variegated approach to characterization but also the program's complex understanding of race, racism, and bigotry. Simon claims in *Truth Be Told* that "it's more about class than race" and, at a July 30, 2008, panel discussion at Manhattan's Times Center titled "Making *The Wire*," asserted that *The Wire* "really wasn't about race. It was about how money and power route themselves, or fail to properly route themselves."[41] He nonetheless includes more African American characters in his series than any previous American crime drama does, even *Homicide: Life on the Street*. This development fictionally acknowledges Baltimore's status as a majority-black city, or what Frank Pembleton, in the *Homicide* episode "Valentine's Day" (5.16), calls a "brown town,"[42] while the diverse black characters who demonstrate Simon's commitment to dramatizing the multifaceted backgrounds, experiences, and personalities of *The Wire*'s African American roles (just as he does in *The Corner*) include police officers Detective Shakima "Kima" Greggs (Sonja Sohn), Detective William "Bunk" Moreland (Wendell Pierce), Sergeant Ellis Carver (Seth Gilliam), Detective Leander Sydnor (Corey Parker Robinson), Freamon, Burrell, Daniels, and Colvin; drug dealers Barksdale, Stringer Bell, D'Angelo Barksdale, Preston "Bodie" Broadus (J. D. Williams), Roland "Wee-Bey" Brice (Hassan Johnson), Joseph "Proposition Joe" Stewart (Robert F. Chew), Marlo Stanfield (Jamie Hector), Chris Partlow (Gbenga Akinnagbe), and Snoop Pearson (Felicia Pearson); elected officials Royce, Davis, and Watkins; political operatives Norman Wilson and Royce's Chief of Staff Coleman Parker (Cleo Reginald Pizana); schoolchildren Namond Brice (Julito McCullum), Randy Wagstaff (Maestro Harrell), Michael Lee (Tristan Wilds), and Duquan "Dukie" Weems (Jermaine Crawford); drug addict Reginald "Bubbles" Cousins (Andre Royo); and master stickup artist Omar Little (Michael K. Williams).

This large, sprawling, and unprecedented black cast, however, creates strange effects. First, the nearly constant presence of African American faces, voices, and bodies disrupts the racial tokenism that haunts other television crime dramas (even those programs that feature multiracial casts) to normalize blackness. James McDaniel, the actor who played Lieutenant Arthur Fancy during *NYPD Blue*'s first eight seasons, for instance, once told S. Epatha Merkerson (the actress who played *Law & Order*'s Lieutenant Anita Van Buren) that "I'm the highest-paid extra on television"[43] to illustrate how his character remains subsidiary to the detectives he supervises, particularly Andy Sipowicz (Dennis Franz), despite Fancy's position of authority. *The Wire*, however, upends this idea not only by including numerous African American characters who populate all levels of legitimate and illegitimate Baltimorean society but also by showing their experiences to be as varied, contradictory, and fragmented as those of their white counterparts. The program, therefore, dislodges Caucasian characters as its normative focus, defining them against and alongside African American characters who exceed the limited and/or stereotypical roles to which television crime drama has traditionally assigned them.

Even so, *The Wire*'s major protagonist, particularly in its first, second, and fifth seasons, is the Caucasian McNulty, who instigates all but Season Four's protracted wiretap investigations by opposing, contravening, or defying his police department and City Hall superiors. McNulty's fight-the-system mentality marks him as a flawed hero, while English actor Dominic West receives top billing in the opening credits (even during the fourth season, when McNulty's role was reduced to accommodate West's desire to spend more time with his daughter in London). West's October 26, 2008, interview with Anthony Andrew claims that this casting was deliberate: "It was always accepted that you had to have a white lead, otherwise no one would watch it. I felt a bit uncomfortable about that, or more uncomfortable than I did being a Brit stealing an American job."[44] This revelation may demonstrate that Simon remained beholden to the same casting biases as network executives, who have historically assumed (often without evidence) that American television's predominantly white and middle-class audience prefers to see protagonists of its own racial and socioeconomic group. Simon, offering a more prosaic explanation for McNulty's race, says that because two-thirds of the detectives that he (Simon) observed during his year-long sojourn with the Baltimore Homicide Unit were white, "McNulty was written as white."[45] This statement suggests that, despite repeated reminders of Baltimore's dominant African American demographic, *The Wire* illustrates how the traditional white power system holds sway in the city's police department, if not in 2002 when *The Wire* begins, then in the late 1980s when Simon shadowed the Homicide Unit.

Lisa W. Kelly proposes that McNulty is "a sort of stand-in for the show's creator," or a dramatic device "offered to white viewers as a 'way in' to this black world" that reflects the paradoxical reality that African American characters, even in a program largely devoted to their experiences, remain marginal because a Caucasian character must provide the window into their professional and personal lives.[46] *The Wire* complicates McNulty's primary position, however, by casting him as a pariah whom Rawls, Daniels, Pearlman, Burrell, and, during the fifth season, even his partner Moreland reject. McNulty, despite narcissistic faith in his own investigative talents, is not the best detective within *The Wire*'s fictional world, an honor that belongs to the intelligent, secure, and wise Lester Freamon. McNulty's personal problems, similarly, are not unique. Shakima Greggs grows distant from her lesbian lover Cheryl (Melanie Nicholls-King) after recovering from gunshot injuries sustained in "The Cost" (1.10), reluctantly agrees to raise a child that Cheryl conceives through in-vitro fertilization in Season Two, and begins sleeping with other women after the baby is born in Season Three. Greggs's troubles mirror McNulty's personal difficulties to dramatize how committed police work disrupts a detective's emotional equilibrium and family life. Greggs's character, therefore, is as detailed as McNulty's, making *The Wire*'s portrait of black Baltimore more complex than Kelly asserts when she writes that "viewers are never provided with an insight into Freamon and Moreland's private lives, as, for the most part, their storylines are restricted to their roles within the force. With McNulty, however, we are introduced to his complicated private life from the outset.... Thus, viewers are indeed encouraged to identify with McNulty throughout the series."[47] Viewers, indeed, identify with multiple characters throughout *The Wire*'s five seasons, particularly people living on the social margins like Reginald "Bubbles" Cousins and Omar Little. McNulty may be the program's initial viewpoint character, but this status quickly changes when the first season adopts a dual perspective that parallels the entrenched bureaucracies of the police department and the Barksdale drug organization. The four remaining seasons enhance *The Wire*'s narrative sophistication by focusing on other elements of Baltimore's civic life, including the ports, City Hall, the public schools, the *Baltimore Sun,* and the competing factions within the police department and the city's drug crews.

Simon claims that this multifocal narration diverges from most television drama. *The Wire,* he says during a 2007 interview with novelist Nick Hornby (*About a Boy*), "isn't really structured as episodic television and it instead pursues the form of the modern, multi-POV novel."[48] Although other television dramas (such as *Hill Street Blues, Murder One,* and *24*) pursue similar narrative strategies, *The Wire* eschews easily classifiable protagonists and antagonists by creating characters that defy conventional expectations about how they should behave. Police detectives fake evidence (McNulty, in the fifth season, creates the illusion that a serial killer preys on homeless men) and make mistakes that imperil innocent witnesses (Hauk, in the fourth season, accidentally identifies Randy Wagstaff as a police informant, leading members of Marlo Stanfield's crew to firebomb the home of Randy's stepmother), while drug lords attempt to better themselves (Bell not only attends college courses but also unsuccessfully attempts to become a real-estate developer) and improve the community (Barksdale, in the third season, donates $15,000 for a boxing gym that will offer free training to West Baltimore boys). This novelistic approach, by dramatizing the intricate experiences of so many African American characters (even minor ones), alters the program's treatment of race, racism, and bigotry not merely by normalizing blackness but also by depicting a wider range of black lives than any previous crime drama (and, in truth, any previous American television drama).

The two characters that best exemplify this trend are Reginald "Bubbles" Cousins and Omar Little. Bubbles, as everyone calls him, is a heroin and cocaine addict who spends every day of his life inventing schemes to acquire enough money to sustain his drug habit (thereby resembling *The Corner*'s Gary McCullough). Bubbles steals scrap metal from vacant houses and active construction sites; runs counterfeit scams that pass off photocopied money as actual legal tender; sells T-shirts, detergent, batteries, and other household items from a battered shopping cart; and works as a paid police informant who helps Greggs and McNulty make cases against the Barksdale and Stanfield drug crews. These activities, in other crime dramas, would mark Bubbles as a low-life hustler whom the police use for their own purposes. *The Wire,* however, presents Bubbles as an honorable man who is deeply disturbed by the violence that he observes (or experiences) and who uses his police contacts to settle scores against drug soldiers that mistreat Bubbles and his friends. The pilot episode, "The Target," shows Bubbles tutoring a white drug addict named Johnny Weeks

(Leo Fitzpatrick) in the art of the scam, conflating Bubbles's paternal and vengeful instincts. Bubbles has Johnny photocopy a 10-dollar bill, then crumples and pours coffee onto the copies before placing a real bill over them. Bubbles, as a result, can, for 10 dollars, buy 30 dollars worth of drugs from a Barksdale runner in a scam that is not detected until Bubbles and Johnny leave. Bubbles, in a later scene, recommends that Johnny pace his drug use rather than slamming a speedball, telling the younger man, "Yo, man, I'm trying, I'm trying to give you a little game, man, but you want, you want to pretend like you know something." When Johnny says that he knows enough, Bubbles affectionately replies, "Naw, naw, you green. I'm trying to get you, I'm trying to get you brown, man, but you still green." Johnny nonetheless receives permission from Bubbles to run the scam alone, but he gets caught by Bodie Broadus the next day when Broadus notices the photocopied bills. Broadus and other members of D'Angelo Barksdale's drug crew beat Johnny so severely that he must be hospitalized and then undergo weeks of physical therapy. One of the pilot episode's final scenes finds Greggs called to the Johns Hopkins emergency room, where Bubbles— Greggs's best narcotics informant—despondently watches Johnny's unconscious form. Bubbles tells Greggs that he wants to help her arrest the men who injured Johnny, renewing a professional relationship that sees Bubbles not only secure valuable street intelligence for the surveillance detail but also earn the respect of McNulty, Carver, Freamon, and Daniels.

Bubbles assists the police for many reasons: protecting his friend, taking revenge on Johnny's attackers, and earning money. Bubbles is an effective informant due to his unassuming appearance, his intimate understanding of the drug trade's street codes, and his race. Although rarely mentioned by McNulty or Greggs, Bubbles could never succeed in collecting information about the Barksdale and Stanfield organizations if he were white. Simon's script for "The Target" indirectly alludes to this reality by noting Johnny's demeanor when he arrives to conduct the failed counterfeit scam: "White boy JOHNNY cruises up, trying to look as casual as a white boy in the projects can."[49] Greggs is no racist for employing Bubbles as her informant, but her decision acknowledges the largely African American racial composition of West Baltimore's projects (even if a few Caucasians like Johnny are visible in most project scenes). Bubbles manifests no clear racial allegiances, expressing his concern for Johnny out of friendship and his dislike of Broadus out of anger at the man's violence against Johnny. Joking that

Johnny is green, not brown, both recognizes and pokes fun at the racial realities of Baltimore's drug trade (according to Simon, statistics compiled by city, state, and federal authorities reveal that as many as 80 percent of Baltimore's drug addicts are African American).

Bubbles is also a man who, with the help of his Narcotics Anonymous sponsor Walon (Steve Earle), spends years trying to kick his drug habit. Several half-hearted efforts alienate Bubbles's sister Rae (Eisa Davis), who, in Season Five, allows Bubbles to live in her basement while he attempts recovery. This process involves Bubbles coming to terms with the deaths of Johnny, who expires of an overdose in Hamsterdam during Season Three, and of Sherrod (Rashad Orange), a homeless teenager whom Bubbles befriends in Season Four after learning that the boy's addict mother has died. Bubbles instructs Sherrod in the ways of the street, allows the boy to live in the small shack that Bubbles calls home, and enrolls Sherrod in middle school. This relationship becomes the most important in Bubbles's life but ends tragically when Sherrod, who routinely skips school to deal drugs, dies from accidentally taking a "hot shot" (a vial of heroin mixed with sodium cyanide) that Bubbles prepares for the vagrant who daily steals money from Bubbles's shopping-cart business (after beating Bubbles into submission). When Bubbles finds Sherrod's corpse in the fourth season's penultimate episode, "That's Got His Own" (4.12), inconsolable grief prompts him to turn himself in to Homicide Sergeant Jay Landsman (Delaney Williams) for murder in the fourth-season finale, "Final Grades" (4.13). Bubbles attempts to hang himself when left alone in the interrogation room, so Landsman chooses not to charge Bubbles with a crime, instead sending him to mandatory drug rehabilitation. When Walon arrives at the detox center, Bubbles cries uncontrollably. His sobriety, in one of *The Wire*'s most tragic statements about the drug trade, comes at the cost of Sherrod's life. Bubbles, despite Walon's prompting, refuses to talk about the boy at Narcotics Anonymous meetings until, one year after Sherrod's death, Bubbles speaks publicly about it in the episode "Late Editions" (5.9).

Bubbles's journey is troubling, maddening, funny, and touching. He is one of *The Wire*'s most fully realized characters, thanks to excellent writing and Andre Royo's beautifully textured performance. Royo is so authentic as Bubbles that director Clark Johnson, during his DVD commentary track for "The Detail" (1.2), states, "I could have sworn that Andre...went out and took on a heroin addiction just so he could play this role."[50] Royo, in *"The Wire": Truth Be Told,* reveals that, one day during the first season, "we were filming on the street; I was in makeup but away from the cameras. This guy comes up to me and handed me some drugs. He said, 'Here, man, you need a fix more than I do.' That was my street Oscar."[51] *The Wire*'s ability to make the viewer care for this troubled street addict—a character rarely given more than a few lines in other crime dramas—illuminates not only Simon's terrific writing and Royo's marvelous acting but also *The Wire*'s careful, precise, and compassionate representation of black characters. The villainy conventionally associated with addicts does not apply to Bubbles, who emerges as fully alive within the difficult, hopeful, challenging, and optimistic world that he inhabits. The final glimpse of Bubbles in the series finale, "-30-" (5.10), sees him walking upstairs from his sister's basement to join Rae and her daughter at the dinner table. Since Rae has never before allowed Bubbles access to the house, fearing that he will steal her belongings to sell for drug money, the stair imagery reflects the long road that Bubbles takes out of addiction. This small moment is a large victory for Bubbles, who, throughout *The Wire*'s five seasons, remains a triumph of African American characterization.

So, too, is Omar Little, the gay stickup artist who follows a strict, if unorthodox code: He robs only drug dealers (or, in his vernacular, people "in the game"), carries a shotgun that strikes terror in nearly everyone who sees him, conducts raids on stash houses that sometimes result in injury and death, detests profanity, never takes drugs, gives money to down-on-their-luck neighborhood residents, and takes his grandmother to church every Sunday morning. These apparent contradictions, however, make Omar (as everyone calls him) *The Wire*'s most fascinating, complex, and unconventional character. Although a composite of several Baltimore stickup artists that Burns knew and/or arrested while working as a cop (just as Bubbles is based on an actual informant known as Possum), Omar is wholly original in his motivations, dress, and speech.[52] His intelligence is also matched by his patience: He surreptitiously observes the drug crews he plans to rob for longer periods than even the narcotics detectives and surveillance teams assigned to follow those same crews.[53]

Omar's complex morality distinguishes him from many other characters, including McNulty. This development permits Michael K. Williams to deliver a finely wrought performance that, like Royo's, embodies Todd Fraley's judgment that, in *The Wire*, "color is no longer invisible but racial representations are presented in the context of class and culture to create parallels between worlds and identities commonly presented as dichotomous."[54] Omar, indeed, crosses all boundaries between the legitimate world of law enforcement and the illegitimate world of drug dealing to unseat the cultural codes that define the former occupation as socially acceptable and the latter as socially deviant. He becomes an unlikely symbol of (and spokesman for) personal integrity, responsibility, and honor that dislodges all stereotypes about homosexual African American criminals. *The Wire,* in short, succeeds in showing Omar's full humanity even if his characterization raises troubling questions about television drama's racial discourses. Two scenes in particular illustrate this notion. Omar, in the first, testifies against a Barksdale drug enforcer named Marquis "Bird" Hamilton (Fredro Starr) in "All Prologue" (2.6) to implicate Hamilton in the shooting death of William Gant (Larry Hull), the witness who not only identifies D'Angelo Barksdale as a murderer in "The Target" (1.1) but also dies by the end of that episode.[55] Omar claims that he saw Hamilton kill Gant even though McNulty and prosecutor Ilene Nathan (Susan Rome) cannot determine whether or not Omar actually witnessed the shooting. Omar, however, makes a compelling witness, charming the jury with honest confessions about his own life and crimes. When Nathan asks Omar—who wears an oversized white tie over his street clothes—about his occupation, he replies, "I robs drug dealers," provoking laughter, not derision, from the jurors and the judge.

Hamilton's defense lawyer, Barksdale house counsel Maurice "Maury" Levy (Michael Kostroff), attacks Omar's credibility during cross-examination, but Omar remains calm, secure, and forthright in his answers, using his testimony to reject Levy's condescending suggestions that Omar poses a threat to the larger community. Saying that he has never turned his shotgun on a "citizen" (Omar's term for people not involved in the drug trade), Omar nods when Levy says, "You walk the streets of Baltimore with a gun, taking what you want when you want it, willing to use violence when your demands aren't met." Yet Omar responds to Levy's statement, "You are feeding off the violence and the despair of the drug trade. You're stealing from those who themselves are stealing the lifeblood from our city. You are a parasite who leeches off the culture of drugs" by saying, "Just like you, man." Omar smiles when an outraged Levy asks, "Excuse me?" prompting Omar to comment, "I got the shotgun. You got the briefcase. It's all in the game, though, right?" This response silences Levy while placating the jury, Nathan, and McNulty (who observes Omar's testimony with admiration) as Omar suggests that Levy profits from the drug trade just as much (if not more) than Omar, who, in his telling, performs a twisted community service for Baltimore's tax-paying citizens. This scene not only contests a stereotypical presentation of Omar as a degenerate black criminal but also accentuates the institutional constraints that try, but fail, to define his identity. Nathan and McNulty suspect that Omar will make an excellent witness but cannot predict his intellectual, logical, and verbal besting of Levy. This victory, however, results from the likelihood that Omar lies (about seeing Hamilton murder Gant) as retribution for the part that Hamilton, in "The Pager" (1.5), plays in torturing and murdering Omar's lover, Brandon Wright (Michael Kevin Darnall). Omar, therefore, uses the court system to achieve the vigilante justice that he could not dispense on the street (commenting at another point that, had he encountered Hamilton before the man was arrested, no arrest or trial would be necessary). Omar's moral sensibility calls out for blood, but rather than disregarding the criminal-justice system's structures and strictures (as he does when assaulting his victims), he participates in legal proceedings against Hamilton to manipulate that system to his own ends. Omar's testimony is one of the few instances in *The Wire* of total victory over bureaucratic power that co-opts two institutions—the police department and the court system—to serve a personal agenda. That Omar accomplishes this goal by lying only extends *The Wire*'s subversion of conventional morality and bourgeois ethics.

Omar's testimony, therefore, is a narrative strategy that, as Herman Gray might argue, "destabilize[s] and decenter[s] simple and easy condemnations of media images and representations [of blackness] as evidence of secure and unified ideologies."[56] Gray's book *Watching Race: Television and the Struggle for Blackness*—one of the best studies ever written about how American commercial television constructs, represents, and dramatizes African American identity—suggests that "contemporary images of African Americans are anchored by three kinds of discursive practices" defined as "assimilationist (invisibility), pluralist (separate but equal), and multiculturalist (diversity)."[57] The courtroom scene in "All Prologue," in a remarkable rhetorical display, moves through all three discourses: Nathan's nonjudgmental questioning provokes pluralist responses from Omar that stress his separate-but-equal relationship to jurors who have no experience of living in the projects but who nonetheless appreciate Omar's success in surviving (and even mastering) his downscale environment.

Levy's patronizing attitude is assimilationist insofar as it attempts to "erase the histories of...power inequalities, conflicts, and struggles for justice and equality" by foregrounding "the individual ego as the site of social change and transformation"[58] to emphasize Omar's willingness to prey on parasitic drug dealers. And Omar's artful characterization of Levy as an equally opportunistic leech is perversely multiculturalist by stressing how a white Jewish lawyer and a black urban thief occupy similar social positions despite their divergent occupations.

Omar's facility with language, logic, and humor during his testimony, however, threatens to reduce him to another racial stereotype, that of the self-serving black hustler-clown who evades responsibility for his own actions by selling out a fellow African American (in this case, Hamilton). Omar's character development in *The Wire's* previous 18 episodes may seem to inoculate him from this charge, but Simon, in his DVD audio commentary for "Dead Soldiers" (3.3), says that, as early as the first season, Omar's mythic elements had transformed him into "a sort of iconoclastic hero figure" to many viewers, particularly younger audience members.[59] "We realized something ugly was happening, which was Omar was becoming utterly heroic," Simon continues, crediting Pelecanos with spotting this trend early in *The Wire's* broadcast life. Simon and the writing staff, therefore, incorporate this development into the show's third season in "Dead Soldiers," by having Omar's squad raid a Barksdale stash house, which provokes a street firefight that kills Tosha Mitchell (Edwina Findley), one of Omar's squad members. Omar and his two surviving partners leave Mitchell's corpse lying in the street while escaping the scene. Bunk Moreland arrives to investigate Mitchell's death but appears sickened when he sees five neighborhood children vying to play the role of Omar while enthusiastically reenacting the shootout.

Moreland, after finding an eyewitness who promises to implicate Omar in the firefight, locates the stickup artist in "Homecoming" (3.6) but listens in dismay as Omar explains why the witness, whom Omar has convinced to keep quiet, will provide no useful information.[60] Moreland's response is remarkable in its raw anger.

> OMAR. Y'all gonna have to call this one of them, um, cost-of-doing-business things y'all police be talking about all the time. You feel me? No taxpayers. Shoot, the way y'all look on things, ain't no victim to even speak on.

MORELAND.   Bullshit, boy. No victim? I just came from Tosha's people, remember? All this death, you don't think that ripples out? You don't even know what the fuck I'm talking about. (*Moreland stands and looms over Omar.*) I was a few years ahead of you at Edmondson, but I know you remember the neighborhood, how it was. (*Omar remains silent.*) We had some bad boys for real. Wasn't about guns so much as knowing what you do with your hands. Those boys could really rack. (*Moreland fakes punching Omar, who does not flinch.*)

My father had me on the straight, but like any young man, I wanted to be hard, too. So I'd turn up at all the house parties where the tough boys hung. Shit, they knew I wasn't one of them. Them hard cases would come up to me and say, "Go home, schoolboy, you don't belong here." Didn't realize at the time what they were doing for me.

As rough as that neighborhood could be, we had us a community. Nobody, no victim, who didn't matter. And now all we got is bodies and predatory motherfuckers like you. And out where that girl fell, I saw kids acting like Omar. Calling you by name, glorifying your ass. Makes me sick, motherfucker, how far we done fell.

Omar says nothing during the detective's rant, but he spits when Moreland walks away, as if rejecting his words. The remorse on Omar's face, however, reflects his guilt over Mitchell's death and his neighborhood's decline. This reaction acknowledges Moreland's ambivalent nostalgia for earlier days that, while imperfect, were better because they emphasized communal values in which even "bad boys" and "tough boys" looked out for soft "schoolboys" who could not handle their fists well enough to protect themselves from the neighborhood's "hard cases." Moreland does not romanticize the past so much as he mourns its passing to suggest that black Baltimore has suffered egregiously from the drug trade, becoming so atomized and balkanized that thieves like Omar prey on their own people.

This scene, unlike Omar's testimony in "All Prologue," transforms him into the silent receiver of Moreland's history lesson, not a performer who glibly employs assimilationist, pluralistic, and multicultural rhetoric to sidestep accountability for participating in his city's deterioration. Moreland's monologue, rather than embracing a false vision of Baltimore's utopian past, stresses Omar's agency to provoke the man to question his social position more deeply than he ever has. Omar, in Moreland's mind, chooses to act as a predator who destroys (or at least weakens) the community they once shared. Race may seem only a background element in Moreland's lament, since the detective never explicitly identifies his neighborhood or school as African American, but it pervades the monologue's subtext to reproduce what Phillip Brian Harper identifies as the paradoxical approach to black life that American television encounters when "the insistence that television faithfully represent a set of social conditions...composing a singular and unitary phenomenon known as '*the* Black experience' runs smack up against a simultaneous demand that it both recognize and help constitute the diversity of African American society."[61] Moreland's monologue distills and transcends this tension by recalling a past that, while flawed, was not as selfish as the present. The diversity implicit in Moreland's childhood recollection includes his youthful desire to assume a role he was ill equipped to play, his father's concern that he take a straight path, and the generosity of urban toughs who in their own way counseled Moreland to follow his father's advice. The stereotypical notion that "the black experience" comprises despair, resentment, economic disadvantage, and racial exclusion gives way to a broader image of black communities inhabited by people with different interests, dispositions, and goals.

Moreland's regret at "how far we done fell," therefore, is no conservative elegy for better days but instead acknowledges the responsibility that he and Omar bear for their community's social problems. The reasons for Baltimore's urban decline may be intricate, but this complexity does not allow residents to evade their civic duties. Moreland's monologue frontally assaults Omar's belief that robbing drug dealers is more righteous than robbing citizens, and it so upsets Omar that, in the following episode, "Back Burners" (3.7), he tells his friend and moneyman Butchie (S. Robert Morgan), "that fat man gave me a itch I can't scratch."[62] Omar decides to assist Moreland by paying $1,500 to purchase and return a police revolver stolen from Officer Kenneth Dozerman (Rick Otto) after Dozerman was shot while attempting an undercover drug buy in "All Due Respect" (3.2). This act of conscience, however, does not stop Omar from raiding Barksdale and Stanfield stash houses, an occupation he quits only after acquiring $400,000 from a large drug-supply robbery in "That's Got His Own." This windfall permits Omar to retire to San Juan, Puerto Rico, with his boyfriend, Renaldo (Ramon Rodriguez). Omar also murders

Bell at the end of "Middle Ground" (3.11) to avenge Brandon's death after learning that Bell ordered the killing. The doubt that Moreland induces in Omar may seem short lived, but the detective's monologue, skillfully performed by Pierce, deepens both his and Omar's personalities to demonstrate how nuanced *The Wire*'s African American characters are.

Elements such as Omar's testimony, Moreland's monologue, Bubbles's struggle with addiction, Baltimore's dysfunctional institutions, the program's complicated attitude toward race, and the human decency displayed by so many characters explain why Jacob Weisberg, in a now-famous column titled *"The Wire* on Fire: Analyzing the Best Show on Television," writes that

> *The Wire*... is surely the best TV show ever broadcast in America. This claim isn't based on my having seen all the possible rivals for the title, but on the premise that no other program has ever done anything remotely like what this one does, namely to portray the social, political, and economic life of an American city with the scope, observational precision, and moral vision of great literature.[63]

This compliment, out of the dozens bestowed by critics, editorialists, and commentators during the show's broadcast run, most strongly endorses *The Wire*'s literary ambitions. Rose summarizes the program's superlative standing by writing that *The Wire* attracted a "small, but intensely devoted audience, composed of critics (who, when not comparing it to the work of Charles Dickens or James Joyce, or Greek tragedy, continually cite it as the best program on TV); actively engaged viewers willing to work hard to follow its intricate plotlines; and, as Simon fondly notes, a strong following among both cops and criminals."[64] Rose also notes that Simon's series, although never as popular as *The Sopranos, Six Feet Under,* or *Sex and the City,* became a prestigious program for HBO that extended the cable channel's reputation for innovation and risk-taking (or what J. M. Tyree calls "the kind of critically acclaimed 'loss leader' that generates respect for the entire brand"[65]).

Simon certainly understands this reality, telling Bill Moyers in an April 17, 2009, interview that, no matter how much respect his program receives, "it's not like everybody's rushing to make...more *Wires.* I mean, you know... I've pretty much demonstrated how not to make a hit show, you know? I make a show that gets me on Bill Moyers. But...I don't get a show that, you know, makes a lot of money for a network."[66] This attitude criticizes television drama for overlooking the uncomfortable realities of American society that *The Wire* confronts, with Simon telling Moyers that, of the 749 different dramas and comedies "on television right now...748 of them are about the America that I inhabit, that you inhabit,...that most of the viewing public, I guess, inhabits." *The Wire'*s literary aspirations, in this context, may be laudable but do little to change what Simon regards as network television's bourgeois assumptions, attitudes, and outlooks.

Simon's opinions about network television, as previously discussed, not only stereotype other programs as less serious than *The Wire* but also reduce them to mere entertainments that avoid challenging, provoking, or upsetting their audiences. This reductionism accepts HBO's network slogan that its programming is "not TV" to imply that *The Wire* (like HBO's other series) occupies a higher, more substantive, and more sophisticated realm than network dramas. Simon's perspective is as limited as his problematic comments about cop and crime dramas for, as Gibb and Sabin argue, Simon's narrow view misrepresents the power, the value, and the effects of genre fiction (particularly network-television drama).

Ethridge highlights an additional complication of *The Wire'*s political argument against the institutional indifference and stultifying bureaucracies produced by American capitalism: "The problem with this moral appeal made in an entertainment television medium is that it lacks an articulation of an affirmative political project. Viewers are then just as likely to be inoculated from working to change the circumstances of the tragic characters of *The Wire.*"[67] Ethridge feels that Simon's vision may convince *The Wire'*s audience that postmodern institutions so circumscribe urban American life that "there is nothing to be done. This form of political and cultural agitation can lead to the support of established institutions just as much as traditional police procedurals."[68] Bowden similarly argues that, "like Dickens's London, Simon's Baltimore is a richly imagined caricature of its real-life counterpart, not a carbon copy."[69] *The Wire'*s coherence—no matter how astonishingly it creates a living simulacrum of Baltimore—avoids "the infuriating unfinishedness of the real world," which remains "infinitely complex and ever changing."[70] *The Wire,* for Bowden, is a marvelous work of art that, despite its authenticity, should not be mistaken for reality. This truth may apply to all artistic pieces (whether literature, television, film, painting, or music), but it points the viewer's attention to *The Wire*'s status as fiction, not documentary journalism. The program, indeed, employs realistic and naturalistic narrative strategies to argue passionately for its personal, probing, and pessimistic view of 21st-century America.

Such a view is substantially correct in its perspective, passion, and scope whether or not it moves *The Wire*'s viewers to political action. Ethridge recognizes that such criticism "places too much responsibility on Simon, and the creative staff of *The Wire*, to both agitate for change as well as to also direct that agitation" because the show's belief that America should end the war on drugs must "be joined by thoughtful arguments, articulated by others, about what that would look like and how the epidemic of drugs would be dealt with."[71] *The Wire*, however, provides a compelling fictional portrait of the drug war's conclusion in the third season's plotline about Hamsterdam, making Weisberg's lavish praise—written in response to the fourth season's vivid depiction of inner-city Baltimore's public schools—less melodramatic than it might seem. No single American television show may deserve the title of best program, but *The Wire* is one of the finest dramas ever conceived, created, and broadcast in the United States. Its carefully drawn characters, shrewd political analysis, complex unfolding story lines, insistent social realism, handsome production values, and gallows humor—out of many other attributes—qualify *The Wire* as a work of genius.

This statement does not ignore *The Wire*'s flaws or Simon's overheated declarations about the program's singular achievements. *The Wire*, indeed, charmingly incorporates cheerful profanity; abiding faith in individual action and personal redemption despite the institutional, social, and racial restrictions placed on its characters; and gentle satire of its own critical praise (especially comparisons to the novels of Charles Dickens). In the fifth season, for instance, *Baltimore Sun* Executive Editor James C. Whiting III (Sam Freed) repeatedly recommends that the newspaper's stories include "the Dickensian aspect" in coverage that addresses difficult social issues, but then resists recommendations that the *Sun* investigate racism at the University of Maryland's campus in order to protect the reputation of the university's dean of journalism (an old friend of Whiting's), thereby making a mockery of Dickens's concern with the uncomfortable (and even ugly) aspects of urban life. This season's sixth episode bears the title "The Dickensian Aspect" (5.6) to drive home how citing Dickens quickly becomes an impoverished method of convincing readers (and viewers) that aspirations toward social realism and social conscience equal careful, contextual, and scrupulous understanding of social problems.

Bodie Broadus transforms Dickens into a sexual euphemism in the episode "Home Rooms" (4.3) by lamenting, "I'm standing here like a asshole holding my Charles Dickens."[72] This memorable line both punctures and authorizes *The Wire's* similarities to Dickens's 19th-century fiction by engaging the bawdy humor, bleak attitude, and understated anger found throughout Dickens's novels. Broadus's immediate problem is maintaining a drug corner after Bell's death and Barksdale's imprisonment, but his sense of impotence speaks to *The Wire's* larger themes about an America left behind by the 21st-century's postindustrial economy, about the difficulties of surviving this harsh reality, and about comedy's redemptive capacities. *The Wire* is rife with ironic humor that saves it from becoming a callous, bitter, and unwatchable program. The series instead emerges as a remarkable, if improbable, testament to the American spirit.

Simon, during his interview with Moyers, says, "*The Wire* was actually a love letter to Baltimore." This formulation is accurate no matter how pessimistic the program appears. *The Wire* reveals not only Simon's cynicism about America's socioeconomic, political, and racial hypocrisies but also his tremendous compassion for individual Americans who struggle against the daily inequities of 21st-century life. The series finale ends with McNulty leaning against his car to observe Baltimore as a breathtaking montage of *The Wire's* many characters and the city's polyglot residents, accompanied by the Blind Boys of Alabama's version of Tom Waits's song "Way Down in the Hole," accelerates in pace until the camera returns to McNulty, who gets into his car and drives away. The camera, however, holds on Baltimore for 20 seconds before cutting to the end credits. This poetic conclusion demonstrates in one 4-minute sequence Simon's considerable talents as a writer, producer, and social realist. *The Wire,* thanks to his care, becomes an extraordinary valentine to urban America, a signature contribution to television drama, and a staggering achievement for American popular art.

Conclusion: The Two Davids: Television Auteurs

Wyatt Mason's March 15, 2010, article in the *New York Times Magazine* (devoted to David Simon's newest television series, *Treme*) bears the suggestive title "The HBO Auteur."[1] Mason recounts the development and production of Simon's return to weekly television drama after *The Wire*'s March 10, 2008, conclusion and after adapting (with Ed Burns) Evan Wright's book *Generation Kill* into an Emmy Award–winning, seven-hour HBO miniseries broadcast during July and August 2008. *Treme*—set in New Orleans, Louisiana, three months after Hurricane Katrina's August 2005 landfall—explores the music, pageantry, and culture of a city rebuilding itself in the wake of widespread devastation. Simon receives credit as *Treme*'s driving creative force even though he cocreated *Treme* with Eric Overmyer, the writer-producer who worked with him on *Homicide: Life on the Street,* joined *The Wire*'s writing staff during that program's fourth season, and has written scripts for *Close to Home* (2005–2007), *Gideon's Crossing* (2000–2001), *Law & Order* (1990–2010) *Law & Order: Criminal Intent* (2001–present), and *New Amsterdam* (2008). This development, beyond downplaying Overmyer's importance to the program's narrative life, signals an improved stature for television authors of Simon's caliber.

Some television writers and producers do not deserve the title auteur, but this study argues that David Milch and David Simon do. Each man's body of work constitutes the distinctly personal style that French New Wave film critics (particularly François Truffaut) lauded when employing auteur to describe moviemakers such as Jean Cocteau, Jean Renoir, and Alfred Hitchcock. James M. Vest, in his definitive study *Hitchcock and France: The Forging of an Auteur,* defines the title *auteur de films* as "a director who, by virtue of a uniquely personal artistic style and the will to impose it creatively, could be viewed as the unifying force behind a body of cinematic work, an *oeuvre,* and hence the fabricator of a coherent imaginary world."[2] The "notion of... film direction as a form of authorship,"[3] Vest explains, revolutionized film criticism (first in France and, later, across the world) to award primacy to the individual whose vision, style, and effort dominate the industrial and collaborative process of moviemaking. If film, as cinephiles commonly remark, is a director's medium, then television is a writer-producer's medium. The title *auteur,* if it applies to any member of a weekly television program's staff, best describes the writer-producer (and, commonly, the creator), who authors many scripts, supervises the writing staff, revises the contributions of those staff writers, and brings coherence to an otherwise-diffuse production. Milch and Simon, by this reckoning, both qualify as auteurs, especially with respect to *NYPD Blue, Deadwood, The Corner,* and *The Wire* (the programs that Milch and Simon created, supervised, and produced for the majority or the entirety of each series's broadcast life).

Milch and Simon are not the only important contributors to these programs, but their artistic control is pervasive enough to make them the most significant voice in their respective series' weekly creation. Milch, as *True Blue, Deadwood: Stories of the Black Hills,* and press interviews indicate, talks about teleplays for which he received no on-screen credit as if they are his scripts, indicating that Milch heavily revised, restructured, and/or rewrote most of *NYPD Blue*'s and *Deadwood*'s episodes even if he rarely claimed credit. George P. Pelecanos and Richard Price, in Mason's "The HBO Auteur," reveal that Simon pursues a similar strategy by working "on every script by every writer of every show he produces"[4] to ensure that his creative vision makes it onto the small screen:

"He would take a script into his room when the deadline was that night," Pelecanos told me, "and he'd go in there and lock the door, and he'd redo the whole script." The novelist Richard Price, who also wrote for *The Wire,* told me there's nothing capricious about such thorough revision: "You really need a single sensibility at the top, a writer-producer who's a ruthless rewriter. It's like an assembly line; Episode 3 has perfectly got to follow from Episode 2 and also perfectly set up Episode 4."[5]

Price's explanation, indeed, is a fact of life for each weekly television drama's staff authors, who can expect the chief writing producer (or producers) to revise every script during an episode's creation. Price, during his DVD commentary for *The Wire*'s "All Due Respect" (3.2), says that no guarantees exist that all material in any writer's teleplay will make it into the finished episode, meaning that all *Wire* writers are fortunate if 80 percent of their script appears on screen because "no one can predict how the pace of character will unfold."[6] Simon's thorough revision process (like Milch's) indicates that he was the primary creator of his television worlds no matter how much assistance other production personnel provided.

This reality should not imply that Milch and Simon arrogate all creative control to themselves. Their DVD commentary tracks, behind-the-scenes documentary observations, and press interviews generously (even fulsomely) praise their collaborators. Milch repeatedly thanks the actors, directors, producers, cinematographers, set designers, and costume designers of *NYPD Blue* and *Deadwood*, while Simon credits so many people who worked on *Homicide: Life on the Street, The Corner,* and *The Wire* that the critical viewer cannot mistake these series for one-man productions. Milch's and Simon's primacy, however, becomes apparent not only through the comments of the people who worked for them but also through each man's passion for the television dramas that he supervised. Milch's *True Blue* and *Deadwood: Stories of the Black Hills,* along with Simon's introduction to *"The Wire": Truth Be Told,* allow each man to impress his creative stamp on his respective programs by writing about each series's genesis, development, and growth.

Milch and Simon, therefore, are talented writers, producers, and artists who engage in social realism to tell labyrinthine narratives about the vagaries, inequities, and perils of America's economic, political, and cultural life. Their successes, particularly with *Deadwood* and *The Wire,* make Milch and Simon social critics and cultural observers of the first order. Their pronounced personal vision and unique style make them auteurs who, by choosing television as their medium and their métier, help transform American prime-time drama into a sophisticated narrative mode that is as entertaining, as serious, and as thoughtful as the literature, cinema, and theater available to discerning audiences. This statement might shock critics such as Theodor Adorno, Max Horkheimer, and Todd Gitlin, but such surprise does not reduce the intelligence, insight, and artistry of Milch's and Simon's television work.

This judgment implies that Milch's and Simon's future contributions to television drama will be equally mature. Milch followed *Deadwood* with *John from Cincinnati* (2007), a bizarre spiritual drama (cocreated by novelist Kem Nunn) set among the surfing culture of Imperial Beach, California, that, despite premiering after *The Sopranos*'s controversial series finale, lasted only 10 episodes. *John from Cincinnati* portrays 21st-century America as a confused culture that experiences mystical revelations when Imperial Beach's residents—the Yost family of champion surfers chief among them—meet a strange man named John Monad (Austin Nichols), who, the program implies, may be an extraterrestrial visitor or a divine presence come to earth. *John from Cincinnati,* by extending Milch's fascination with human venality and personal redemption into a fascinating-yet-kooky venue, is better than its initial reviews suggest, but the series becomes so abstract and diffuse that it counts as a minor, if noble, effort. Nancy Franklin's *New Yorker* review of *John from Cincinnati,* titled "Dead in the Water," recognizes that Milch's reach, by exceeding his grasp, signals his auteur status: "It's maddening to see a show this bad from someone so talented, but that's how it works when you're a real artist, and that's how it should work. The person who creates a *Deadwood* is also probably going to make a *John from Cincinnati* one day. If you let him."[7] *John from Cincinnati* is not as bad as Franklin claims, but the program, untethered from the generic conventions of crime drama or Western fiction, flounders even while demonstrating Milch's desire to infuse American life with more meaning than surface appearances suggest.

Milch next produced and cowrote (with friend and *NYPD Blue* executive producer Bill Clark) the pilot episode for a proposed HBO crime drama titled *Last of the Ninth.* HBO, however, refused to fund this series, which, based on Clark's early days as a New York City police officer, would have chronicled the partnership between veteran detective John Giglio (Ray Winstone) and rookie cop Timmy Adams (Brian Geraghty). The scant media reports about this series suggest that it would have examined the difficulties involved in becoming a detective, as well as corruption and graft within the New York City Police Department. The pilot episode, directed by Carl Franklin, has never been broadcast by HBO, so determining its quality is difficult.

Milch, as of this writing, is developing another series for HBO, set at a horse-racing track and titled *Luck.* Milch will produce this series with Michael Mann, who will direct the pilot episode. Dustin Hoffman, Nick Nolte, and Dennis Farina have been cast in lead roles for this program, which will explore a world with which Milch, the owner of several racehorses, is intimately familiar. The possibilities for this series suggest that it will include themes that characterize Milch's best television work, such as addiction, crime, despair, and redemption.

David Simon, as previously noted, produced *Generation Kill* for HBO while completing *The Wire*'s fifth and final season. Simon wrote (or cowrote) the teleplay for three of this miniseries's seven episodes while collaborating with Ed Burns on each installment's story. *Generation Kill* superbly adapts Evan Wright's book (expanded from Wright's three *Rolling Stone* articles) about the U.S. Marines First Reconnaissance Battalion's experiences in the 2003 American invasion of Iraq. The miniseries, however, lacks the sociological precision of *The Corner* and *The Wire* as it confines itself to the perspective of First Recon's fighting men, thereby steadfastly refusing to address the political, economic, and cultural reasons that the war is fought. *Generation Kill* offers an energetic, detailed, and fascinating portrait of how America's fighting men endure the boredom, pressure, and insanity of desert combat, but a larger sense of the war's contested origins, effects, and aftermath rarely emerges. As good as *Generation Kill* is, *The Wire*'s third season offers a better perspective about the Iraq War by making Avon Barksdale's losing battle with rival drug dealer Marlo Stanfield's combative insurgency an extended metaphor for America's disastrous Iraqi military campaign. *Generation Kill*, as is typical of Simon's television work, features dense writing, evocative dialogue, and excellent performances from a talented cast (which includes James Ransone, who played the role of Ziggy Sobotka in *The Wire*'s second season), but it does not affect its audience's intellect or emotions as deeply as *The Corner* or *The Wire*. Simon's second HBO miniseries, far from failing to capture the lives of its subjects, maintains such a rigorous focus on America's ground-level troops that the viewer learns little about life higher up the chain of command or about the perspective of Iraq's troops and civilians. *Generation Kill* not only deserves the three 2009 Emmy Awards that it won (Outstanding Special Visual Effects, Outstanding Sound Editing, and Outstanding Sound Mixing for a Miniseries, Movie, or Special) but also showcases Simon's talent for tackling different subject matter. This miniseries, however, is not as comprehensive an entertainment as Simon's previous forays into narrative television.

Simon's newest drama, *Treme*, explores the polyglot musical culture of New Orleans, Louisiana, with the same detail that *Homicide*, *The Corner*, and *The Wire* bring to Baltimore, Maryland. *Treme* casts

Wire veterans Wendell Pierce (as trombone player Antoine Batiste) and Clarke Peters (as independent contractor and Mardi Gras Indian chief Albert Lambreaux), among many others, including Khandi Alexander (*The Corner*'s Fran Boyd) and Melissa Leo (*Homicide*'s Kay Howard), to examine how the city recovers after Hurricane Katrina's destruction. The program, named after the Cajun neighborhood popularly known as the birthplace of American jazz music, weaves 10 first-season episodes into a narrative that, Mason writes, "though no less focused on the workings and failings of 21st-century American urban existence [than *The Wire*], tells its story not through a city's institutions but through its individuals."[8] This dramatic structure is not as large a departure from Simon's usual method as it seems, since *Homicide, The Corner,* and *The Wire* all feature vivid, distinct, and memorable characters. *Treme*'s success, like *Luck*'s, depends on the support that Simon and Milch receive from HBO, the pay-cable network that has become home to them both (although *Treme* fans need not worry: HBO renewed the program for a full second season after the pilot episode's initial broadcast on April 11, 2010). Neither man seems likely to return to network television unless he receives full creative freedom for the dramas he wishes to write, so, for the moment, Milch and Simon seem secure at HBO. Mason, in "The HBO Auteur," includes a comment about Chris Albrecht and Carolyn Strauss's patronage of Simon that summarizes Simon's contribution to the network's approach to television drama: "Under the pair's tenure but owing to Simon's industry, the culture at HBO had come to see itself in Simon."[9] This assessment, in one of the happiest artistic convergences in television history, also describes Milch.

Milch and Simon, indeed, are two of the most accomplished fiction writers, small-screen dramatists, and social realists working in the 21st-century American arts. Their television work, in Mark Bowden's words, so effectively "takes up as a subject the colossal, astonishing, and terrible pageant of contemporary America"[10] that no conversation about major contributions to American realism is complete without considering *Hill Street Blues, NYPD Blue, Homicide: Life on the Street, The Corner, Deadwood,* and *The Wire.* These programs (particularly *Deadwood* and *The Wire*) provoke, challenge, and confront their audiences with America's imperfect democratic institutions to unseat easy faith in the nation's history, politics, and social norms. Milch's and Simon's television dramas, in short, may not always be comfortable to watch, but they are always fascinating to encounter.

Milch and Simon, for this and many other reasons, are significant American authors. They are not novelists in the traditional sense of this term, but their novelistic television drama expands the medium's potential as a site for innovative, important, and inventive storytelling. This statement, rather than indulging the breathless sentimentalism that Gitlin's *Inside Prime Time* disparages, is an appropriate reaction to the excellence that *Hill Street Blues, NYPD Blue, Homicide: Life on the Street, The Corner, Deadwood,* and *The Wire* embody. These programs are not perfect, but neither are they shallow entertainments that soothe their viewers' unexamined beliefs about America's political, economic, civic, and cultural life. Milch and Simon instead offer darker, disturbing, and despairing fictional portraits of the American experience. These achievements place Milch and Simon not merely among the best television writers of their generation but among the finest artists of their era. Their vivid, exemplary, and memorable contributions to American popular art will linger in their nation's cultural consciousness for decades to come. David Milch and David Simon, therefore, are television auteurs of exceptional magnitude.

Notes

Introduction: Prime-Time Realism

1. Todd Gitlin, *Inside Prime Time* (1983; Berkeley and Los Angeles: University of California Press, 2000), vii.

2. Ibid.

3. Ibid.

4. Ibid., 273.

5. Newton N. Minow, "Television and the Public Interest" (keynote address, National Association of Broadcasters, Washington, D.C., May 9, 1961). Minow has published many books and articles about television's influence in the years since his "Vast Wasteland" address (as it is now commonly known). Minow's 1995 book *Abandoned in the Wasteland: Children, Television, and the First Amendment,* cowritten with Craig L. LaMay, revisits his famous speech to note that the term *vast wasteland* has become so clichéd that it obscures the address's larger themes and concerns.

6. Theodor W. Adorno and Max Horkheimer, "The Culture Industry: Enlightenment as Mass Deception," in *Dialectic of Enlightenment,* trans. Edmund Jephcott (1944; Stanford, CA: Stanford University Press, 2002), 127. "The Culture Industry" is widely available online, with an HTML version at www.marxists.org/reference/archive/adorno/1944/culture-industry.htm and a PDF version at uwf.edu/dearle/modernism/hork.pdf.

See Walter Benjamin's essay "The Work of Art in the Age of Mechanical Reproduction" (found in the book *Illuminations,* ed. Hannah Arendt) and John Berger's book *Ways of Seeing* (based on Berger's BBC series) for other well-known Marxist approaches to visual culture, mass media, and popular culture. Publication information for both texts is available in the bibliography.

7. Vincent Canby, "From the Humble Mini-Series Comes the Magnificent Megamovie," *New York Times,* October 31, 1999, http://www.nytimes.com/1999/10/31/arts/from-the-humble-mini-series-comes-the-magnificent-megamovie.html?pagewanted=all.

8. Ibid.

9. Ibid.

10. Ibid.

11. Charles McGrath, "The Triumph of the Prime-Time Novel," *New York Times Magazine*, October 22, 1995, 52, http://www.nytimes.com/1995/10/22/magazine/the-prime-time-novel-the-triumph-of-the-prime-time-novel.html?pagewanted=all.

12. Ibid., 53.

13. David Milch, *Deadwood: Stories of the Black Hills* (New York: Melcher Media, 2006), 12.

14. David Simon, introduction to *"The Wire": Truth Be Told*, by Rafael Alvarez (New York: Pocket Books, 2004), 25.

15. Mark Singer, "The Misfit," *New Yorker*, February 14 and 21, 2005, 196, http://www.newyorker.com/archive/2005/02/14/050214fa_fact_singer.

16. David Milch and Bill Clark, *True Blue* (1995; New York: Avon Books, 1997), 143.

17. Ibid., 144.

18. Singer, "Misfit," 196.

19. Ibid., 197.

20. Ibid., 196.

21. Ibid., 199.

22. Ibid., 200.

23. Ibid., 201.

24. Ibid., 194.

25. Margaret Talbot, "Stealing Life," *New Yorker*, October 22, 2007, http://www.newyorker.com/reporting/2007/10/22/071022fa_fact_talbot.

26. Cynthia Rose, "The Originator of TV's *Homicide* Remains Close to His Police-Reporter Roots," *Seattle Times*, February 18, 1999, http://web.archive.org/web/19990428142656/http://www.seattletimes.com/news/entertainment/html98/dave_021899.html.

27. Talbot, "Stealing Life."

28. Ibid.

29. David Simon, "Homicide: Life in Season 4," Volume (Disc) 6, *Homicide: Life on the Street: The Complete Season 4* DVD collection, A&E Home Video, 2006.

30. Rose, "Originator of TV's *Homicide*."

31. Simon, introduction to *Truth Be Told*, 14.

32. Ibid., 15.

33. "David Simon," *Bill Moyers Journal*, April 17, 2009, http://www.pbs.org/moyers/journal/04172009/watch.html. Visitors to the *Bill Moyers Journal* Web site may not only view the entire interview via streaming video but also access a complete transcript.

34. Tom Wolfe, "Stalking the Billion-Footed Beast: A Literary Manifesto for the New Social Novel," *Harper's Magazine*, November 1989, 46. The emphasis is Wolfe's. An online version of this article (including a PDF for download) is available for *Harper's* subscribers at http://www.harpers.org/archive/1989/11/0059090. A PDF version is available for all other readers at http://www.lukeford.net/Images/photos3/tomwolfe.pdf.

Wolfe's essay provoked passionate reactions, endorsements, and disagreements from many literary practitioners after its initial publication. *Harper's Magazine* invited several novelists to respond to Wolfe's manifesto, causing writers as diverse as Philip Roth, Walker Percy, Mary Gordon, T. Coraghessan Boyle, Scott Spencer, Madison Smartt Bell, Alison Lurie, Jim Harrison, and John Hawkes to submit letters that were printed in the magazine's February 1990 edition (available online for *Harper's* subscribers, including a PDF for download, at http://www.harpers.org/archive/1990/02/page/0006). Harrison and Hawkes are particularly vehement in their responses, with Harrison calling Wolfe's essay "a relentlessly silly and self-indulgent apologia for *The Bonfire of the Vanities*" (10) and Hawkes announcing, "I deplore Wolfe's self-serving attacks on other writers" (12).

Novelist Robert Towers published a sustained analysis (and occasional refutation) of Wolfe's claims in an essay in the *New York Times*: "The Flap over Tom Wolfe: How Real Is the Retreat from Realism?" (January 28, 1990; available at http://www.nytimes.com/1990/01/28/books/the-flap-over-tom-wolfe-how-real-is-the-retreat-from-realism.html?pagewanted=1). Towers at one point writes, "The truth is, of course, that there never was the mass defection from realism among serious young writers that he [Wolfe] alleges, creating thereby a convenient myth—or straw man—for his own purposes."

Wolfe's assertions are debatable, and his judgments of post-1960s American literature are problematic, but "Stalking the Billion-Footed Beast" remains a benchmark essay about American social realism more than 20 years after its initial release.

35. Amanda Ann Klein, "'The Dickensian Aspect': Melodrama, Viewer Engagement, and the Socially Conscious Text," in *"The Wire": Urban Decay and American Television,* ed. Tiffany Potter and C. W. Marshall (New York: Continuum, 2009), 178.

36. Jason Mittell, *Genre and Television: From Cop Shows to Cartoons in American Culture* (New York: Routlege, 2004), 7.

37. Mark Steyn, "The Maestro of Jiggle TV," *Atlantic Monthly,* September 2006, 146, http://www.theatlantic.com/magazine/archive/2006/09/the-maestro-of-jiggle-tv/5101.

38. Terry Teachout, "The Myth of 'Classic' TV," in *A Terry Teachout Reader* (New Haven, CT: Yale University Press, 2004), 174–77.

39. Steyn, "Maestro of Jiggle TV," 146.

40. Terry Teachout, "Still Repenting," *About Last Night: Terry Teachout on the Arts in New York City,* December 19, 2007, http://www.artsjournal.com/aboutlastnight/2007/12/tt_still_repenting.html. Teachout also discusses these issues in his September 12, 2006, blog posting "Repent at Leisure," available at http://www.artsjournal.com/aboutlastnight/2006/09/tt_repent_at_leisure.html.

Chapter 1: Peaks and Valleys

1. Milch was also nominated for the 1983 Emmy Award for Outstanding Writing in a Drama Series as coauthor of two other third-season *Hill Street*

episodes: "No Body's Perfect" (3.11)—Steven Bochco, Jeffrey Lewis, Michael Wagner, and Anthony Yerkovich shared this nomination with Milch—and "Eugene's Comedy Empire Strikes Back" (3.19)—Bochco, Karen Hall, Lewis, and Yerkovich shared this nomination with Milch. Hall was also nominated for her script "Officer of the Year" (3.5), while Bochco, Lewis, and Yerkovich shared a nomination for their script "A Hair of the Dog" (3.9).

Milch's award for "Trial by Fury" was *Hill Street Blues*'s third consecutive Emmy for writing. Bochco, Michael Kozoll, Lewis, Wagner, and Yerkovich had won the 1982 writing Emmy for "Freedom's Last Stand" (2.11), a season in which three other *Hill Street* scripts—"The Second Oldest Profession" (2.4), "The World according to Freedom" (2.8), and "Personal Foul" (2.16)—were nominated (the *Lou Grant* episode "Blacklist" [5.17] was the only other hour-long drama episode nominated for the 1982 award). Bochco and Kozoll won the 1981 writing Emmy for their pilot script "Hill Street Station" (1.1), a season in which one other *Hill Street* script, the two-part episode "Jungle Madness" (1.16 and 1.17), was nominated.

Milch's 1983 Emmy was the final time *Hill Street Blues* would win the Academy of Television Arts and Sciences' award for writing a one-hour drama. Although *Hill Street* received at least one writing nomination during each of its final four seasons, it never again took home the trophy. Milch's award is also the only instance of a single *Hill Street* writer winning an Emmy Award for writing.

2. David Milch and Bill Clark, *True Blue* (1995; New York: Avon Books, 1997), 19. Milch reveals that he purchased his first racehorse with the Humanitas Prize money. "Over the next ten years," Milch writes, "I bought and campaigned more horses, a few of which won big races, although on balance they'd cost me a lot more than I'd made" (19).

Milch's statement that the Catholic Church bestows the Humanitas Prize is slightly inaccurate. Father Ellwood "Bud" Kieser, a Roman Catholic priest, established the prize in 1974 to honor stories that "affirm the human person, probe the meaning of life, enlighten the use of human freedom, and reveal to each person our common humanity," but the Catholic Church provides no funding for the Humanitas Prize. A nonprofit organization named the Human Family Educational and Cultural Institute, rather, raises money for the prize's nine different writing awards. The prize does not, at least according to its official Web site (http://humanitasprize.org), target overtly religious programming for celebration.

The story in "Trial by Fury" of the Catholic Furillo's pursuit of justice for the murder of a Roman Catholic nun may be coincidental in Milch's receipt of the 1983 Humanitas Prize, even if this story line seems tailor-made for the prize's emphasis on justice and freedom. The critical reader suspects that Father Kieser might have deplored Milch's use of the award money, as well as Milch's now well-known and well-publicized addictions to gambling, alcohol, and heroin during his tenure at Yale and at *Hill Street Blues*. Milch, however, in an interview with James L. Longworth Jr. published in *TV Creators: Conversations with America's Top Producers of Television Drama* (Syracuse, NY: Syracuse University Press, 2000), reveals that, when he first met Kieser, "there was a look in his eyes...which said he knew something about me that I didn't know yet about myself" (94). Milch then says that he has "come to understand the thing that Father Kieser knew about me all those years ago, which was that the shadow I felt, I and my characters had to live in, was cast by God's loving hand" (94).

Mark Singer's profile of Milch, "The Misfit" (published in the *New Yorker*, February 14 and 21, 2005), identifies Milch's Humanitas prize money as "fifteen thousand dollars" (204). The Humanitas Prize's Web site, as of 2010, lists the prize money for all nine screenwriting categories as $10,000. Singer's information seems accurate, particularly since the *New Yorker*'s online version of "The Misfit" (http://www.newyorker.com/archive/2005/02/14/050214fa_fact_singer) offers no correction to this figure, even though it notes that Jody Worth, one of Milch's writing protégés, as well as a producer for *NYPD Blue* and *Deadwood*, was misidentified as Jody Welch in Singer's original print article. Whether Milch made $10,000 or $15,000 from his Humanitas Prize award, this amount was a significant windfall.

3. "Trial by Fury," *Hill Street Blues*, written by David Milch, directed by Gregory Hoblit, original broadcast September 30, 1982, NBC Television and MTM Enterprises, 49 min. This episode is available for viewing at www.hulu.com.

4. Furillo's faith has never before been an issue on *Hill Street Blues*. Although Furillo's Catholicism may not be surprising given his Italian heritage (Public Defender Joyce Davenport, Furillo's girlfriend and eventual wife, affectionately refers to the captain as "Pizza Man" throughout the series), Furillo never discusses his religious background or upbringing during *Hill Street's* first two seasons, while demonstrating laudable respect for all religious faiths in those rare instances when he encounters people who make an issue of their religion. "Trial by Fury" is the first episode of *Hill Street* to depict what seems to be a religiously motivated crime, although suspects Gerald Chapman and Celestine Grey say nothing about religion during their interrogations or court appearances. Furillo's episode-ending confession, therefore, is even more significant because, no matter how depressed previous cases have made him, he has never sought the Catholic confessional's solace until "Trial by Fury."

5. "Presidential Fever," *Hill Street Blues*, written by Michael Kozoll and Steven Bochco, directed by Robert Butler, original broadcast January 17, 1981, NBC Television and MTM Enterprises, 49 min. This episode is available for viewing on Disc 1 of the *Hill Street Blues: The Complete First Season* DVD collection (released by 20th Century Fox) and at www.hulu.com.

6. Furillo's concern about ethical police behavior distinguishes him from other officers, as well as from fellow command personnel and his superiors, even Chief of Police Fletcher Daniels (Jon Cypher). In "Can World War III Be an Attitude?" (1.4), Furillo tells Detective Neal Washington to refrain from helping his partner J. D. LaRue while LaRue is under investigation by Internal Affairs for a bogus bribery charge because Furillo does not want Washington to be dirtied by an unsavory association with LaRue. In "Double Jeopardy" (1.5), however, Furillo and Washington determine that LaRue's accuser, narcotics detective Ralph Macafee (Dan Hedaya), has framed LaRue to divert suspicion

from his own ethical quandary: shaking down drug dealers for money so that Macafee can support his bigamous second family (including two children by his second wife). Although Macafee implores Furillo to overlook these crimes, Furillo insists that Macafee explain himself to Internal Affairs.

In a three-episode, first-season story arc that appears in "Gatorbait" (1.10), "Life, Death, Eternity, Etc." (1.11), and "I Never Promised You a Rose, Marvin" (1.12), Furillo clashes with noted homicide detective Emil Schneider (Dolph Sweet), Division Commander Dave Swanson (George Dickerson), and Chief Daniels over the investigation of the murder of a 14-year-old girl named Rosario Rivas. Furillo eventually discovers that Rivas was accidentally killed by her shady boyfriend, Nemo Rodriguez (Don Cervantes), in an effort to protect her from the physical abuse of City Councilman Tom McAurley (Dennis Holahan), who not only patronized a sex club that illegally employed Rivas and other underage girls but also engaged in multiple acts of statutory rape by sleeping with Rivas. Detective Schneider admits that unnamed public officials pressured him to cover up McAurley's actions in return for keeping Schneider on the police force after he had committed unspecified errors in previous cases. When Furillo threatens to go public about McAurley's involvement in the Rivas case, Swanson tells Furillo that his (Furillo's) seemingly secure promotion to division commander will disappear and that Furillo will spend the rest of his career on the Hill (Scheider also calls Furillo's plan "career suicide"). Furillo follows his conscience, ending McAurley's political career and his own advancement.

In the first part of Season One's finale, "Jungle Madness, Part 1" (1.16), Chief Daniels tells Furillo that narcotics detective Charlie Weeks (Charles Hallahan)—who, in "Rites of Spring, Part 1" (1.14), shoots and kills an African American man that Weeks claims was participating in a robbery in the Hill Street precinct—will become a departmental sacrifice to placate the public anger swirling around Weeks's actions. Furillo, although he dislikes Weeks's methods, feels that the detective may be innocent. When Daniels says that he will make an example of Weeks, Furillo replies that, while he (Furillo) has bent a few rules, he will not place the department's image over morality. Weeks is eventually exonerated, proving Furillo correct but angering Daniels.

Furillo, therefore, makes ethical police conduct a crusade in *Hill Street Blues*'s first two seasons. His willingness to use public anger to force confessions out of Chapman and Grey in "Trial by Fury" marks a new development in his behavior, even if Furillo's reference to bending a few rules indicates that he is not purely noble in his work.

7. Singer, "Misfit," 204.

8. Robert J. Thompson, *Television's Second Golden Age: From "Hill Street Blues" to "ER"* (Syracuse, NY: Syracuse University Press, 1996), 59.

9. Richard Zoglin, "Hill Street, Hail and Farewell," *Time*, April 27, 1987, http://www.time.com/time/printout/0,8816,964186,00.html.

10. Tom Shales, "'Hill Street,' Hail and Farewell," *Washington Post*, May 12, 1987, final edition, D1.

11. Zoglin, "Hill Street, Hail and Farewell."

12. Larry Landrum, "Instrumental Texts and Stereotyping in *Hill Street Blues:* The Police Procedural on Television," *MELUS* 11, no. 3 (1984): 93.

13. Ibid.

14. Ibid., 97.

15. Ibid.

16. "Trial by Fury."

17. Landrum, "Stereotyping in *Hill Street Blues*," 98.

18. Ibid., 97.

19. David Milch, DVD commentary, "True Confessions," *NYPD Blue*, teleplay by David Milch and Art Monterastelli; story by Art Monterastelli, David Milch, and Steven Bochco; directed by Charles Haid; original broadcast October 12, 1993; ABC Television and Steven Bochco Productions; 48 min. This episode and Milch's commentary are available on Disc 1 of the *NYPD Blue: Season 01* DVD collection, released by 20th Century Fox.

Milch reports that he flew the unnamed writer, who based this letter on his doctoral dissertation, to *NYPD Blue*'s set as a gesture of thanks.

20. "Hill Street Station," *Hill Street Blues*, written by Michael Kozoll and Steven Bochco, directed by Robert Butler, original broadcast January 15, 1981, NBC Television and MTM Enterprises, 49 min. This episode is available for viewing on Disc 1 of the *Hill Street Blues: The First Complete Season* DVD collection and at www.hulu.com.

21. Landrum, "Stereotyping in *Hill Street Blues*," 99.

22. Ibid.

23. Ibid.

24. Crais has become a well-known crime, mystery, and thriller novelist. His Elvis Cole and Joe Pike book series are best sellers, while his 2002 novel *Hostage* became a 2005 film starring Bruce Willis, adapted by Doug Richardson and directed by Florent Emilio Siri. Crais worked as a member of *Hill Street Blues*'s writing staff only during its second season. He went on to write episodes of *Cagney & Lacey* (1981–1988), *The Equalizer* (1985–1989), CBS's 1980s revival of Rod Serling's *The Twilight Zone* (1985–1989), *Miami Vice* (1984–1989), *L.A. Law* (1986–1994), and *JAG* (1995–2005).

25. Robert Crais, DVD commentary, "Freedom's Last Stand," *Hill Street Blues*, teleplay by Steven Bochco, Anthony Yerkovich, Jeffrey Lewis, and Michael Wagner; story by Michael Kozoll and Steven Bochco; directed by Gregory Hoblit; original broadcast January 18, 1982; NBC Television and MTM Enterprises; 48 min. This episode and Crais's commentary are available on Disc 2 of the *Hill Street Blues: Season Two* DVD collection, released by 20th Century Fox. The episode itself is available for viewing at www.hulu.com.

26. Singer, "Misfit," 199.

27. Ibid., 196.

28. Ibid., 199.

29. Ibid., 196.

30. Ibid., 197.

31. Christopher P. Wilson, "True and True(r) Crime: Cop Shops and Crime Scenes in the 1980s," *American Literary History* 9, no. 4 (1997): 721.

32. Ibid.

33. Ibid., 720–21. Wilson refers to Bourdieu's 1992 book *An Invitation to Reflexive Sociology* (coauthored by Loïc J. D. Wacquant), first published by the University of Chicago Press, as the source of the terms *field of power, authoritarian populism,* and *popular conservatism* despite the fact that they appear in the writing of many Marxist theorists, particularly Antonio Gramsci.

34. Ibid., 721.

35. Bochco and Kozoll had worked as writers and/or producers on many cop, crime, and private-eye dramas before creating *Hill Street Blues*. Bochco was a writer-producer for *Banacek* (1972–1974), *Griff* (1973–1974), and *Delvecchio* (1976–1977), while he also wrote episodes of *Columbo* (1971–1990), including that show's first episode, "Murder by the Book" (1.1), directed by Steven Spielberg; *McMillan & Wife* (1971–1977); and *Paris* (1979–1980). Kozoll had written episodes of *McCloud* (1970–1977), *Switch* (1975–1978), *Quincy M.E.* (1976–1983), *Delvecchio, Kojak* (1973–1978), and *Paris.*

Grant Tinker induced Bochco and Kozoll to create *Hill Street Blues* for MTM Enterprises by promising them full creative control of the series, as well as the freedom to reinvent the cop drama however they saw fit. Bochco, in numerous interviews, DVD documentaries, and television appearances, has credited Tinker's trust with making *Hill Street* the innovative program that it was.

36. Wilson, "True and True(r) Crime," 735–36.

37. David Milch, DVD commentary, "Simone Says," *NYPD Blue,* teleplay by David Milch and Walon Green; story by Steven Bochco, David Milch, and Walon Green; directed by Gregory Hoblit; original broadcast November 15, 1994; ABC Television and Steven Bochco Productions; 48 min. This episode and Milch's commentary are available on Disc 2 of the *NYPD Blue: Season 02* DVD collection, released by 20th Century Fox.

Chapter 2: Blue, Black, and White

1. Mark Singer, "The Misfit," *New Yorker,* February 14 and 21, 2005, 199, http://www.newyorker.com/archive/2005/02/14/050214fa_fact_singer. Singer also states that Milch, as of the article's publication, had earned "more than sixty million [dollars], with plenty more to come from future syndication rights" (199) from *NYPD Blue.*

2. Ibid., 197.

3. *Homicide: Life on the Street* premiered on all NBC affiliate stations on January 31, 1993, immediately following Super Bowl XXVII. *NYPD Blue* premiered on 168 of ABC's 225 affiliate stations (according to David Milch and Bill Clark, *True Blue* [1995; New York: Avon Books, 1997], 81) on September 21, 1993.

4. Richard Clark Sterne, "*N.Y.P.D. Blue,*" in *Prime Time Law: Fictional Television as Legal Narrative,* ed. Robert M. Jarvis and Paul R. Joseph (Durham, NC: Carolina Academic Press, 1998), 100.

5. Milch, before departing *NYPD Blue* in 2000 after completing work on its seventh season, closely supervised the program's writing staff, frequently visited the set to suggest alterations to scenes while they were being rehearsed

and/or filmed, and, when no full script was available, improvised scenes after filming had begun. *True Blue* offers numerous anecdotes of Milch's time on *NYPD Blue*'s set, particularly his efforts to deal with the disruptions caused by David Caruso's problematic work habits and abrasive personality during the program's first season.

6. Sterne, "*N.Y.P.D. Blue*," 89; Christopher P. Wilson, "True and True(r) Crime: Cop Shops and Crime Scenes in the 1980s," *American Literary History 9*, no. 4 (1997): 719.

7. Sterne, "*N.Y.P.D. Blue*," 88.

8. Milch and Clark, *True Blue*, 1–13.

9. Ibid., 5.

10. Ibid.

11. Ibid., 40.

12. Ibid., 168.

13. Ibid., 144.

14. Exceptions to this rule exist, particularly in the case of Aaron Sorkin's *The West Wing* (1999–2006). During its first four seasons (when Sorkin was *The West Wing*'s executive producer), scripts were shot as written, meaning that Sorkin allowed only on-set changes that he personally approved. Actor improvisation, therefore, rarely—if ever—occurred. As novelist, memoirist, and former *Law & Order* producer Lorenzo Carcaterra says in an interview with this author (*Belles Lettres*, September–December 2005), "No one—not the actors, the directors, or the crew—could change a comma without Aaron Sorkin's approval" (Vest 9). See Peter C. Rollins and John E. O'Connor's *The West Wing: The American Presidency as Television Drama* (Syracuse, NY: Syracuse University Press, 2003), for further information.

Similar stories about the four later *Star Trek* series (*The Next Generation, Deep Space Nine, Voyager,* and *Enterprise*) have circulated for years, promulgated by these programs' actors, producers, and writers, many of whom report that, due to the technical vocabulary that characterizes *Star Trek* stories, on-set dialogue changes required approval by the executive producers.

15. Milch and Clark, *True Blue*, 112.

16. David Milch, DVD commentary, "True Confessions," *NYPD Blue*, teleplay by David Milch and Art Monterastelli; story by Art Monterastelli, David Milch, and Steven Bochco; directed by Charles Haid; original broadcast October 12, 1993; ABC Television and Steven Bochco Productions; 48 min. This episode and Milch's commentary are available on Disc 1 of the *NYPD Blue: Season 01* DVD collection, released by 20th Century Fox.

17. Sterne, "*N.Y.P.D. Blue*," 94.

18. Ibid., 95.

19. Ibid., 93.

20. Larry Landrum, "Instrumental Texts and Stereotyping in *Hill Street Blues:* The Police Procedural on Television," *MELUS* 11, no. 3 (1984): 93–100.

21. George C. Thomas III and Richard A. Leo, "Interrogating Guilty Suspects: Why Sipowicz Never Has to Admit He Is Wrong," in *What Would Sipowicz Do? Race, Rights and Redemption in "NYPD Blue,"* ed. Glenn Yeffeth (Dallas, TX: BenBella Books, 2004), 35.

22. "Girl Talk," *NYPD Blue,* teleplay by Theresa Rebeck, story by Theresa Rebeck and Bill Clark, directed by Perry Lang, original broadcast March 19, 1996, ABC Television and Steven Bochco Productions, 47 min. This episode is available on Disc 3 of the *NYPD Blue: Season 03* DVD collection, released by 20th Century Fox.

23. Sterne, "*N.Y.P.D. Blue,*" 94.

24. "Pilot," *NYPD Blue,* teleplay by David Milch, story by David Milch and Steven Bochco, directed by Gregory Hoblit, original broadcast September 21, 1993, ABC Television and Steven Bochco Productions, 49 min. This episode is available on Disc 1 of the *NYPD Blue: Season 01* DVD collection, released by 20th Century Fox.

25. "Brown Appetit," *NYPD Blue,* teleplay by David Milch, story by David Milch and Steven Bochco, directed by Gregory Hoblit, original broadcast October 5, 1993, ABC Television and Steven Bochco Productions, 49 min. This episode is available on Disc 1 of the *NYPD Blue: Season 01* DVD collection, released by 20th Century Fox.

26. Kenneth Meeks, "Racism and Reality in *NYPD Blue,*" in *What Would Sipowicz Do? Race, Rights and Redemption in "NYPD Blue,"* ed. Glenn Yeffeth (Dallas, TX: BenBella Books, 2004), 49.

27. Singer, "Misfit," 197.

28. Meeks, "Racism and Reality in *NYPD Blue,*" 49.

29. "Oscar, Meyer, Weiner," *NYPD Blue,* written by Ted Mann and Gardner Stern, directed by Bradley Silberling, original broadcast December 7, 1993, ABC Television and Steven Bochco Productions, 49 min. This episode is available on Disc 3 of the *NYPD Blue: Season 01* DVD collection, released by 20th Century Fox.

30. Bradley Silberling, DVD commentary, "Oscar, Meyer, Weiner," available on Disc 3 of the *NYPD Blue: Season 01* DVD collection, released by 20th Century Fox.

31. Milch and Clark, *True Blue,* 168.

32. Ibid., 169–70.

33. Ibid., 170.

34. Ibid., 172. Although Ted Mann and Gardner Stern are the credited writers of "Oscar, Meyer, Weiner," Milch never mentions them in *True Blue*'s account, speaking as if he wrote the Futrel scenes himself. This intriguing development suggests that Milch either wrote these scenes or so heavily supervised their writing that he is their real author. This possibility, if true, illustrates that Milch followed the same writing process for *NYPD Blue* that Singer, in "The Misfit," describes for *Deadwood:* "While the others sat on a sofa or chairs, Milch reclined on the floor in the center of the room, a few feet from a microphone and a twenty-inch computer monitor, on the other side of which was a desk where an amanuensis, seated in front of a computer and another monitor, was poised to type whatever he dictated" (194).

35. Milch and Clark, *True Blue,* 177.

36. Silberling, DVD commentary, "Oscar, Meyer, Weiner."

37. Martin Luther King Jr., "Letter from Birmingham Jail," in *A Testament of Hope: The Essential Writings and Speeches of Martin Luther King Jr.,* ed. James Melvin Washington (San Francisco: HarperSanFrancisco, 1991), 293.

38. Milch and Clark, *True Blue,* 179. The emphasis is Milch's.
39. Ibid., 181.
40. Ibid.
41. Ibid., 180–81.
42. Ibid., 181.
43. Sterne, *"N.Y.P.D. Blue,"* 98.
44. "The Backboard Jungle," *NYPD Blue,* written by David Mills, story by William L. Morris, directed by Mark Tinker, original broadcast January 16, 1996, ABC Television and Steven Bochco Productions, 45 min. This episode is available on Disc 2 of the *NYPD Blue: Season 03* DVD collection, released by 20th Century Fox.

45. Numerous reports published by the United Nations, Amnesty International, Human Rights Watch, the American Civil Liberties Union, and the New York City Police Department (NYPD) itself reveal the department's problems with corruption, racial profiling, racially motivated brutality, and racial bias in its hiring and disciplinary practices. Amnesty International's June 1996 report *Police Brutality and Excessive Force in the New York City Police Department* (http://asiapacific.amnesty.org/library/Index/ENGAMR510361996?open&of=ENG-USA), published between *NYPD Blue*'s third and fourth seasons, documents persistent police misconduct, particularly NYPD officers and detectives employing excessive and illegal force against suspects, who, if they are poor, minority, and/or ex-convicts, receive a disproportionate amount of the brutality meted out by NYPD cops.

Human Rights Watch's June 1998 report *Shielded from Justice: Police Brutality and Accountability in the United States* (http://www.hrw.org/legacy/reports98/police/index.htm), published between *NYPD Blue*'s fifth and sixth seasons, provides a detailed overview of police misconduct across the nation, although one section addresses the NYPD's problems with brutality, racial profiling, and internal racism.

The United Nations Committee on Human Rights published *In the Shadows of the War on Terror: Persistent Police Brutality and Abuse of People of Color in the United States* in December 2007 (www.ushrnetwork.org/files/ushrn/images/linkfiles/CERD/9_Police Brutality.pdf). This report reviews widespread problems with excessive force in large and small American police departments (with New York and Los Angeles receiving special mentions). Although *NYPD Blue* concluded more than one year before this document was published, the problems it diagnoses, as the report itself says, were well known and, in some instances, widely reported.

Marilynn S. Johnson's 2003 scholarly study *Street Justice: A History of Police Violence in New York City* (Boston: Beacon Press) and Jack R. Greene's 2007 *The Encyclopedia of Police Science,* 3rd ed. (New York: Taylor & Francis) both report numerous instances of inappropriate and illegal NYPD brutality, including the famous Amadou Diallo and Abner Louima cases.

These external reports, however, are not the only sources that document the NYPD's checkered history of abuse, racism, and corruption. By the time that David Milch completed his December 1, 1992, draft of *NYPD Blue*'s pilot script, six different commissions had examined corruption inside New York City's police force: the Lexow Commission (1895), the Curran Committee

(1912), the Seabury Investigation (1932), the Helfand Investigation (1949–1950), the Knapp Commission (1970–1973), and the Mollen Commission (1992). Amnesty International's *Police Brutality and Excessive Force*, indeed, "acknowledges that a number of reforms have taken place within the NYPD during the past three years, partly in response to a commission of inquiry into police corruption which was appointed in 1992 [the Mollen Commission]" (quoted in Sterne, *"N.Y.P.D. Blue,"* 89).

Reform, therefore, is possible. Greene writes that each commission's report "resulted in organizational changes and policy reforms designed to curtail or eliminate the prevailing corrupt practices of the day. While these reforms were moderately successful, in each instance new patterns of corrupt activity ultimately evolved within a period of about twenty years" (803). *NYPD Blue,* however, deals with corruption only in terms of individual officers, often accompanied by a visit from the hated "Rat Squad" (Sipowicz's lingo for the Internal Affairs Division), and, in 12 seasons, never directly addresses the institutional problems of corruption, excessive force, and racism.

46. "Where's 'Swaldo?" *NYPD Blue,* written by Stephen Gaghan, Michael R. Perry, and David Milch; directed by Mark Tinker; original broadcast November 12, 1996; ABC Television and Steven Bochco Productions; 46 min. This episode is available on Disc 1 of the *NYPD Blue: Season 04* DVD collection, released by 20th Century Fox.

47. Meeks, "Racism and Reality in *NYPD Blue,*" 51.

48. Sterne, *"NYPD Blue,"* 103.

49. Ibid., 91.

50. Milch and Clarke, *True Blue,* 172–73. The emphasis is Milch's.

51. W.E.B. Du Bois, *The Souls of Black Folk,* ed. Henry Louis Gates Jr. and Terri Hume Oliver (New York: W. W. Norton, 1999), 11. See Gerald Early's scholarly anthology *Lure and Loathing: Essays on Race, Identity, and the Ambivalence of Assimilation* (New York: Allen Lane, 1993) for several fascinating analyses of Du Bois's concept of double consciousness. Stanley Crouch's "Who Are We? Where Did We Come From? Where Are We Going?" in that book criticizes Du Bois's use of this term, while Alton B. Pollard III's "The Last Great Battle of the West: W.E.B. Du Bois and the Struggle for African America's Soul" traces its importance in Du Bois's political activism.

Dickson D. Bruce Jr.'s "W.E.B. Du Bois and the Idea of Double Consciousness," found on pages 236–44 of Gates and Oliver's 1999 Norton critical edition of *The Souls of Black Folk,* offers a useful, lucid, and significant analysis of the sources on which Du Bois drew to fashion his now-famous elaboration of double consciousness.

52. Du Bois, *Souls of Black Folk,* 11.

53. Milch and Clark, *True Blue,* 173.

54. Ibid., 174.

55. Ibid., 176.

56. Ibid., 177.

57. Ibid., 176.

58. Tom Shales, "Hill and Renko Being Careful Out There," *Washington Post,* April 28, 1983, D1+.

59. "Taillight's Last Gleaming," *NYPD Blue*, written by David Mills, directed by Randall Zisk, original broadcast February 18, 1997, ABC Television and Steven Bochco Productions, 45 min. This episode is available on Disc 3 of the *NYPD Blue: Season 04* DVD collection, released by 20th Century Fox.

60. "Raging Bulls," *NYPD Blue*, written by Leonard Gardner; story by Steven Bochco, David Milch, and Bill Clark; directed by Steven DePaul; original broadcast December 18, 1998; ABC Television and Steven Bochco Productions; 45 min.

61. Meeks, "Racism and Reality in *NYPD Blue*," 49.

62. Ibid.

63. Ibid., 54.

64. Ibid., 55.

65. For further information about America's and Hollywood's marginalization of minority citizens and artists, please consult the following sources (publication information for each source is available in the bibliography): James Baldwin's "The Fire Next Time" and other writings in *Collected Essays;* Daniel Bernardi's *The Persistence of Whiteness: Race and Contemporary Hollywood Cinema;* Taylor Branch's *Parting the Waters: America in the King Years 1954–63, Pillar of Fire: America in the King Years 1963–65,* and *At Canaan's Edge: America in the King Years 1965–68;* Larry Ceplair and Steven Englund's *The Inquisition in Hollywood: Politics and the Film Community, 1930–1960;* Ashley W. Doane and Eduardo Bonilla-Silva's *White Out: The Continuing Significance of Racism;* W.E.B. Du Bois's *The Souls of Black Folk* and *Black Reconstruction in America 1860–1880;* Gerald Early's *Tuxedo Junction: Essays on American Culture* and *Lure and Loathing;* Ralph Ellison's *Shadow and Act* and *The Collected Essays of Ralph Ellison;* Adam Fairclough's *Better Day Coming: Blacks and Equality, 1890–2000;* John Hope Franklin's *From Slavery to Freedom: A History of African Americans* and *Reconstruction after the Civil War;* Henry Louis Gates Jr.'s *The Signifying Monkey: A Theory of African-American Literary Criticism* and *The Trials of Phillis Wheatley: America's First Black Poet and Encounters with the Founding Fathers;* Allison Graham's *Framing the South: Hollywood, Television, and Race during the Civil Rights Struggle;* Henry Hampton and Steve Fayer's *Voices of Freedom: An Oral History of the Civil Rights Movement from the 1950s through the 1980s;* Nathan Hare's *The Black Anglo-Saxons;* bell hooks's *Killing Rage: Ending Racism* and *Ain't I a Woman: Black Women and Feminism;* Zora Neale Hurston's *Mules and Men* and *Every Tongue Got to Confess: Negro Folk-Tales from the Gulf States;* Vincent F. Rocchio's *Reel Racism: Confronting Hollywood's Construction of Afro-American Culture;* Sasha Torres's *Living Color: Race and Television in the United States;* and Cornel West's *Race Matters* and *Keeping Faith: Philosophy and Race in America.*

66. James L. Longworth Jr., *TV Creators: Conversations with America's Top Producers of Television Drama* (Syracuse, NY: Syracuse University Press, 2000), 100.

67. Ibid.

68. Sterne, "*N.Y.P.D. Blue*," 103.

69. Ibid., 103, 104.

70. Milch and Clark, *True Blue*, 195.

71. Andy Meisler, "Out of N.Y.P.D., into 'N.Y.P.D. Blue,'" *New York Times,* November 7, 1995, http://www.nytimes.com/1995/11/07/arts/out-of-nypd-into-nypd-blue.html.

72. Milch and Clark, *True Blue,* 198.

73. Ibid., 201.

74. Milch, in *True Blue*'s 13th chapter, discusses his father, Elmer Milch, at length, confessing at one point that "I think it's closer to the truth to say Sipowicz's personality is more like my dad's" (136). Singer, in "The Misfit," agrees with this perspective (see page 200 for Singer's comments about this issue).

Chapter 3: Red Balls

1. Barry Levinson, DVD commentary, "Gone for Goode," *Homicide: Life on the Street,* written by Paul Attanasio, directed by Barry Levinson, original broadcast January 31, 1993, NBC Television and Baltimore Pictures, 48 min. This episode and Levinson's commentary are available on Volume (Disc) 1 of the *Homicide: Life on the Street: The Complete Seasons 1&2* DVD collection, released by A&E Home Video.

2. Ibid.

3. James Yoshimura and Eric Overmyer, DVD commentary, "The Documentary," *Homicide: Life on the Street,* teleplay by Eric Overmyer; story by Tom Fontana, James Yoshimura, and Eric Overmyer; directed by Barbara Kopple; original broadcast January 3, 1997; NBC Television and Baltimore Pictures; 45 min. This episode, along with Yoshimura and Overmyer's commentary, is available on Volume (Disc) 3 of the *Homicide: Life on the Street: The Complete Season 5* DVD collection, released by A&E Home Video.

Overmyer says that, when "created by Paul Attanasio" appears at the end of *Homicide*'s opening titles, this credit is "not true. Tom Fontana created *Homicide* with a lot of help from Jim Yoshimura."

4. Tom Fontana, DVD commentary, "Gone for Goode."

5. ABC Television originally intended *NYPD Blue* to premiere in September 1992, but concerns about the program's nudity, profanity, and violence caused a year-long delay in broadcasting the first season. Steven Bochco entered protracted negotiations with the network to determine exactly how much violence and nudity were permissible, to develop a glossary of acceptable profane words, and to determine how many such utterances could be heard in every episode. This postponement gave Milch time to research New York City detective work, leading him to meet Bill Clark. See Bochco's and Milch's comments about this period in "The Making of Season One," a behind-the-scenes documentary included on Disc 6 of the *NYPD Blue: Season 01* DVD collection, and Milch's analysis of the delay in *NYPD Blue*'s production in the first three chapters of Milch and Clark's *True Blue* (1995; New York: Avon Books, 1997).

6. David Simon, "Homicide: Life in Season 4," Volume (Disc) 6, *Homicide: Life on the Street: The Complete Season 4* DVD collection, A&E Home Video.

7. Ibid.

8. David Simon, *Homicide: A Year on the Killing Streets* (1991; New York: Ivy Books-Ballantine, 1993), 197.

9. Ibid., 198.

10. Ibid.

11. "The Documentary."

12. Richard Clark Sterne, "*N.Y.P.D. Blue*," in *Prime Time Law: Fictional Television as Legal Narrative,* ed. Robert M. Jarvis and Paul R. Joseph (Durham, NC: Carolina Academic Press, 1998), 87–104.

13. James L. Longworth Jr., *TV Creators: Conversations with America's Top Producers of Television Drama* (Syracuse, NY: Syracuse University Press, 2000), 41.

14. Ibid.

15. Ibid., 47.

16. Ibid.

17. Ibid.

18. Simon, "Homicide: Life in Season 4." Simon, ever cynical about Hollywood, then cheerfully says, "Little did I know the phrase 'get somebody who knows what they're doing' is never uttered by anyone in Hollywood."

19. David Simon, "Inside Homicide: An Interview with David Simon and James Yoshimura," Volume (Disc) 6, *Homicide: Life on the Street: The Complete Season 5* DVD collection, A&E Home Video.

20. Ibid.

21. Ibid.

22. Christopher P. Wilson, "True and True(r) Crime: Cop Shops and Crime Scenes in the 1980s," *American Literary History* 9, no. 4 (1997): 720–21.

23. Ibid., 721.

24. Ibid.

25. Ibid., 719, 722.

26. Simon, *Year on the Killing Streets,* 59–60.

27. Wilson, "True and True(r) Crime," 721.

28. Ibid.

29. Simon, *Year on the Killing Streets,* 20.

30. Ibid., 23.

31. "Three Men and Adena," *Homicide: Life on the Street,* written by Tom Fontana, directed by Martin Campbell, original broadcast March 3, 1993, NBC Television and Baltimore Pictures, 48 min. This episode is available on Volume (Disc) 2 of the *Homicide: Life on the Street: The Complete Seasons 1&2* DVD collection, released by A&E Home Video.

32. *Anatomy of a "Homicide: Life on the Street,"* written and directed by Theodore Bogosian, original broadcast November 4, 1998, PBS Television, 120 min. This documentary is available on Volume (Disc) 6 of the *Homicide: Life on the Street: The Complete Season 6* DVD collection, released by A&E Home Video.

33. Simon, *Year on the Killing Streets,* 69.

34. Sterne, "*N.Y.P.D. Blue,*" 101.

35. Simon, *Year on the Killing Streets,* 42.

36. Ibid., 73.

37. Ibid., 74.

38. Ibid.

39. "Bop Gun," *Homicide: Life on the Street,* written by David Simon and David Mills, story by Tom Fontana, directed by Stephen Gyllenhaal, original broadcast January 6, 1994, NBC Television and Baltimore Pictures, 47 min. This episode is available on Volume (Disc) 4 of the *Homicide: Life on the Street: The Complete Seasons 1&2* DVD collection, released by A&E Home Video.

40. "Bad Medicine," *Homicide: Life on the Street,* teleplay by David Simon, story by Tom Fontana and Julie Martin, directed by Kenneth Fink, original broadcast October 25, 1996, NBC Television and Baltimore Pictures, 46 min. This episode is available on Volume (Disc) 1 of the *Homicide: Life on the Street: The Complete Season 5* DVD collection, released by A&E Home Video.

41. David P. Kalat, *"Homicide: Life on the Street": The Unofficial Companion* (Los Angeles: Renaissance Books, 1998), 232.

42. Ibid., 270.

43. "Blood Ties (Part 2)," *Homicide: Life on the Street,* teleplay by David Simon, story by Tom Fontana and James Yoshimura, directed by Nick Gomez, original broadcast October 24, 1997, NBC Television and Baltimore Pictures, 46 min. This episode is available on Volume (Disc) 1 of the *Homicide: Life on the Street: The Complete Season 6* DVD collection, released by A&E Home Video.

44. Thomas A. Mascaro, "Shades of Black on *Homicide: Life on the Street:* Progress in Portrayals of African American Men," *Journal of Popular Film and Television* 32, no. 1 (2004): 12. Mascaro's article, along with its companion piece "Shades of Black on *Homicide: Life on the Street:* Advances and Retreats in Portrayals of African American Women" (*Journal of Popular Film and Television* 33, no. 2 [2005]), is the best analysis of *Homicide's* depiction of African American characters yet written.

45. "Blood Ties (Part 3)," *Homicide: Life on the Street,* teleplay by David Simon and Anya Epstein; story by Tom Fontana, Julie Martin, and James Yoshimura; directed by Mark Pellington; original broadcast October 31, 1997; NBC Television and Baltimore Pictures; 47 min. This episode is available on Volume (Disc) 1 of the *Homicide: Life on the Street: The Complete Season 6* DVD collection, released by A&E Home Video.

46. Kalat, *Unofficial Companion,* 275.

47. Ibid.

48. "Sideshow (Part 2)," *Homicide: Life on the Street,* written by David Simon, directed by Ed Sherin, original broadcast February 19, 1999, NBC Television and Baltimore Pictures, 44 min. This episode is available on Volume (Disc) 4 of the *Homicide: Life on the Street: The Complete Season 7* DVD collection, released by A&E Home Video.

Chapter 4: Street Talk

1. Jacob Weisberg, "*The Wire* on Fire: Analyzing the Best Show on Television," *Slate,* September 13, 2006, http://www.slate.com/id/2149566.

2. David Simon and Edward Burns, *The Corner: A Year in the Life of an Inner-City Neighborhood* (New York: Broadway Books, 1997), n.p.

3. "Gary's Blues," *The Corner,* written by David Mills and David Simon, directed by Charles S. Dutton, original broadcast April 16, 2000, HBO Television and Blown Deadline Productions, 64 min. This episode is available on Disc 1 of *The Corner* DVD collection, released by HBO Video.

4. Simon and Burns, *Year in the Life,* 538.

5. Ibid., 539.

6. Ibid., 537.

7. David Simon, introduction to *"The Wire": Truth Be Told,* by Rafael Alvarez (New York: Pocket Books, 2004), 15.

8. Ibid.

9. Ibid.

10. Simon and Burns, *Year in the Life,* 540.

11. Ibid.

12. Ibid., 540–41.

13. Simon, introduction to *Truth Be Told,* 14.

14. Jonathan Boudreaux, "*The Corner* DVD Review," *TVDVDReviews,* August 24, 2003, http://www.tvdvdreviews.com/corner.html.

15. "Fran's Blues," *The Corner,* written by David Mills, directed by Charles S. Dutton, original broadcast April 30, 2000, HBO Television and Blown Deadline Productions, 60 min. This episode is available on Disc 1 of *The Corner* DVD collection, released by HBO Video.

16. Simon and Burns, *Year in the Life,* 16.

17. Ibid., 160.

18. Ibid., 161.

19. Hugh K. David, "*The Corner,*" *DVD Times,* July 23, 2005, http://dvd times.co.uk/content.php?contentid=57882.

20. "Everyman's Blues," *The Corner,* written by David Mills and David Simon, directed by Charles S. Dutton, original broadcast May 21, 2000, HBO Television and Blown Deadline Productions, 74 min. This episode is available on Disc 2 of *The Corner* DVD collection, released by HBO Video.

21. Simon and Burns, *Year in the Life,* 93.

22. Ibid., 91.

23. Ibid., 12.

24. Ibid., 187.

25. Ibid., 188.

26. Ibid.

27. Ibid., 58.

28. Ibid., 15.

29. "Everyman's Blues." *A Year in the Life of an Inner-City Neighborhood* also quotes these words on page 532.

30. Simon and Burns, in a significant detail, reveal on page 540 of the book's epilogue that they followed the Corner's residents for four years even though *A Year in the Life of an Inner-City Neighborhood* only chronicles a single year.

31. Simon and Burns, *Year in the Life,* 531.

32. Ibid.

33. Ibid., 541.

34. Cynthia Rose, "The Originator of TV's *Homicide* Remains Close to His Police-Reporter Roots," *Seattle Times,* February 18, 1999, http://web.archive. org/web/19990428142656/http://www.seattletimes.com/news/entertain ment/html98/dave_021899.html.

Chapter 5: American Savagery

1. Mark Singer, "The Misfit," *New Yorker,* February 14 and 21, 2005, 201, http://www.newyorker.com/archive/2005/02/14/050214fa_fact_singer.

2. Ibid.

3. Ibid.

4. Ibid., 192.

5. "The New Language of the Old West" and "An Imaginative Reality" are both available on Disc 6 of Season One of the *Deadwood: The Complete Series* DVD collection released by HBO Video. They are also available on Disc 6 of the *Deadwood: Season One* DVD collection released by HBO Video.

6. In "The New Language of the Old West," Milch says that the Hays Code's first principle stated that obscenity is an offense against God and natural law. The actual Hays Code, still available in print and electronic form, begins with three general principles:

1. No picture shall be produced that will lower the moral standards of those who see it. Hence the sympathy of the audience should never be thrown to the side of crime, wrongdoing, evil, or sin.

2. Correct standards of life, subject only to the requirements of drama and entertainment, shall be presented.

3. Law, natural or human, shall not be ridiculed, nor shall sympathy be created for its violation.

Milch conflates the first and third principle in his "New Language of the Old West" chat with Keith Carradine and in his interview with *Salon.com's* Heather Havrilesky, although his summary is essentially accurate. The Hays Code's three principles do not directly mention God, but the reader, like Milch, can easily infer God's centrality to the code from its moralizing diction.

For full-text versions of the Hays Code, see "The Motion Picture Production Code of 1930 (Hays Code)" at http://www.artsreformation.com/a001/ hays-code.html and "The Production Code of the Motion Picture Industry (1930–1967)" at http://productioncode.dhwritings.com/multipleframes_ productioncode.php.

7. In "The New Language of the Old West," Milch says, in typically colorful fashion, that the studio chiefs did not want to "queer their hustle" by permitting the release of too many objectionable films. They assented to the Hays Code's control to increase their own profits and to prevent government censorship of their films' content.

8. Heather Havrilesky, "The Man behind *Deadwood,"* *Salon.com,* March 5, 2005, http://dir.salon.com/story/ent/feature/2005/03/05/milch/index. html.

9. Ibid.

10. Ibid.

11. David Milch, *Deadwood: Stories of the Black Hills* (New York: Melcher Media, 2006), 12. Milch refers to Hawthorne's 1850 short story "Ethan Brand," in which the titular protagonist searches for the unpardonable sin, only to discover that violating the sanctity of another person's heart is unforgivable.

12. Lee Siegel, *Not Remotely Controlled: Notes on Television* (New York: Basic Books, 2007), 131.

13. Ibid.

14. Ibid.

15. Ibid., 132.

16. Ibid., 135.

17. Jason Jacobs, "Al Swearengen, Philosopher King," in *Reading Deadwood: A Western to Swear By*, ed. David Lavery, Reading Contemporary Television Series (London: I. B. Tauris, 2006), 11.

18. Havrilesky, "Man behind *Deadwood*."

19. Several Web sites and books archive the Western films produced since Edwin S. Porter's 1903 *The Great Train Robbery* inaugurated the genre. Both FilmandTV.com's and Wikipedia's entries exhaustively chronicle the Western movies produced in America since 1903. See http://www.filmsandtv.com/genre.php?gs=1950Western and http://en.wikipedia.org/wiki/List_of_Western_films, respectively, for thorough lists of Western films produced during the 20th and 21st centuries. For further information and scholarship about the Western genre, consult the following sources (publication details are in the bibliography): Angela Aleiss's *Making the White Man's Indian: Native Americans and Hollywood Movies*, John G. Cawelti's *The Six-Gun Mystique* and *The Six-Gun Mystique Sequel*, David Lusted's *The Western*, Patrick McGee's *From "Shane" to "Kill Bill": Rethinking the Western*, Jim Kitses and Gregg Rickman's *A Western Reader*, Scott Simmon's *The Invention of the Western Film: A Cultural History of the Genre's First Half Century*, Richard Slotkin's *Gunfighter Nation: The Myth of the Frontier in Twentieth-Century America*, and Jane Tompkins's *West of Everything: The Inner Life of Westerns*.

20. Havrilesky, "Man behind *Deadwood*."

21. Ibid.

22. John Leonard, "True West," *New York Magazine*, n.d., http://nymag.com/nymetro/arts/tv/reviews/n_10058/.

23. Horace Newcomb, *"Deadwood,"* in *The Essential HBO Reader*, ed. Gary R. Edgerton and Jeffrey P. Jones, Essential Readers in Contemporary Media and Culture Series (Lexington: University Press of Kentucky, 2008), 98.

24. Ibid., 99.

25. Ibid. Milch's comments about minimizing revenge can be found in Singer, "Misfit," 201.

26. Pete Dexter, *Deadwood* (1986; New York: Vintage Contemporaries, 2005).

27. Frederick Jackson Turner, "The Significance of the Frontier in American History," in *The Frontier in American History* (1920; Mineola, NY: Dover, 1996), 3–4.

28. Ibid., 4.

29. Ibid., 37.

30. "Deadwood," *Deadwood*, written by David Milch, directed by Walter Hill, original broadcast March 21, 2004, HBO Television and Red Board Productions, 62 min. This episode is available on Disc 1 of Season One of *Deadwood: The Complete Series*, the DVD collection released by HBO Home Video. It is also available on Disc 1 of the *Deadwood: Season One* DVD collection released by HBO Video.

31. Turner, "Significance of the Frontier in American History," 3.

32. David Milch, "Deadwood," teleplay dated August 20, 2002, http:// www.weeklyscript.com/Deadwood-Pilot.txt.

33. Singer, "Misfit," 201–2.

34. Scott Eric Kaufman, "*Deadwood* and To Whom Its Dialogue Is Beholden," *Acephalous*, August 22, 2006, http://acephalous.typepad.com/ acephalous/2006/08/deadwood_and_to.html.

35. Milch, *Stories of the Black Hills*, 19.

36. Newcomb, "*Deadwood*," 96.

37. Geoffrey Nunberg, "Obscenity Rap," Geoffrey Nunberg University of California-Berkeley Home Page, June 20, 2004, http://people.ischool.berkeley. edu/~nunberg/deadwood.html.

38. Singer, "Misfit," 194.

39. Milch, *Stories of the Black Hills*, 19.

40. Ibid., 121.

41. Ibid.

42. Ibid.

43. Ibid., 121, 126.

44. Ibid., 126.

45. David Scott Diffrient, "Deadwood Dick: The Western (Phallus) Reinvented," in Lavery, *Reading* Deadwood, 191.

46. "A Lie Agreed Upon, Part I," *Deadwood*, written by David Milch, directed by Ed Bianchi, original broadcast March 6, 2005, HBO Television and Red Board Productions, 50 min. This episode is available on Disc 1 of Season Two of the *Deadwood: The Complete Series* DVD collection and on Disc 1 of the *Deadwood: Season Two* DVD collection, both released by HBO Video.

47. Erin Hill, "'What's Afflictin' You?': Corporeality, Body Crises, and the Body Politic in *Deadwood*," in Lavery, *Reading* Deadwood, 173.

48. "Deep Water," *Deadwood*, written by Malcolm MacRury, directed by Davis Guggenheim, original broadcast March 24, 2004, HBO Television and Red Board Productions, 56 min. This episode is available on Disc 1 of Season One of the *Deadwood: The Complete Series* DVD collection and on Disc 1 of the *Deadwood: Season One* DVD collection, both released by HBO Video.

49. "Complications," *Deadwood*, written by Victoria Morrow, directed by Gregg Fienberg, original broadcast April 3, 2005, HBO Television and Red Board Productions, 57 min. This episode is available on Disc 3 of Season Two of the *Deadwood: The Complete Series* DVD collection and on Disc 3 of the *Deadwood: Season Two* DVD collection, both released by HBO Video.

50. "Reconnoitering the Rim," *Deadwood*, written by Jody Worth, directed by Davis Guggenheim, original broadcast April 4, 2004, HBO Television, Red Board Productions, 52 min. This episode is available on Disc 2 of Season One of the *Deadwood: The Complete Series* DVD collection and on Disc 2 of the *Deadwood: Season One* DVD collection, both released by HBO Video.

51. Singer, "Misfit," 194.

52. Milch, *Stories of the Black Hills*, 35.

53. Ibid., 12. Sean O'Sullivan's excellent essay "Old, New, Borrowed, Blue: *Deadwood* and Serial Fiction," found on pages 115–29 of David Lavery's *Reading* Deadwood, precisely analyzes Milch's debt to Charles Dickens. O'Sullivan argues that serial narratives create tension between the old and the new that readers/viewers must constantly negotiate. O'Sullivan's signature insight explains how tradition influences serial narrative: "Such a dynamic speaks not only to the way that some embryonic communities create identities for themselves by favoring tradition (however new that tradition might be) over innovation, but the way Milch uses labyrinthine plots and dialogue as hazing rituals for viewers, forcing us to become locals very quickly or get the hell out of town" (122).

54. Joseph Millichap, "Robert Penn Warren, David Milch, and the Literary Contexts of *Deadwood*," in Lavery, *Reading* Deadwood, 105.

55. Newcomb, "*Deadwood*," 100.

56. Leslie Fielder, *Love and Death in the American Novel* (1966; rev. ed., New York: Scarbarough-Stein and Day, 1982), 409.

57. David Simon, introduction to *"The Wire": Truth Be Told*, by Rafael Alvarez (New York: Pocket Books, 2004), 2.

58. Ned Martel, "Resurrecting the Western to Save the Crime Drama," *New York Times*, March 21, 2004, http://www.nytimes.com/2004/03/21/arts/television-resurrecting-the-western-to-save-the-crime-drama.html?pagewanted=1.

59. Hill, "'What's Afflictin' You?'" 181.

60. "No Other Sons or Daughters," *Deadwood*, written by George Putnam, directed by Ed Bianchi, original broadcast May 16, 2004, HBO Television and Red Board Productions, 58 min. This episode is available on Disc 4 of Season One of the *Deadwood: The Complete Series* DVD collection and on Disc 4 of the *Deadwood: Season One* DVD collection, both released by HBO Video.

61. Singer, "Misfit," 195.

62. "Boy-the-Earth-Talks-To," written by Ted Mann, directed by Ed Bianchi, original broadcast May 22, 2005, HBO Television and Red Board Productions, 55 min. This episode is available on Disc 5 of Season Two of the *Deadwood: The Complete Series* DVD collection and on Disc 5 of the *Deadwood: Season Two* DVD collection, both released by HBO Video.

63. Milch, *Stories of the Black Hills*, 153.

64. "I Am Not the Fine Man You Take Me For," *Deadwood*, written by David Milch and Regina Corrado, directed by Dan Attias, original broadcast June 18, 2006, HBO Television and Red Board Productions, 53 min. This episode is available on Disc 1 of Season Three of the *Deadwood: The Complete Series* DVD

collection and on Disc 1 of the *Deadwood: Season Three* DVD collection, both released by HBO Video.

65. "The Catbird Seat," *Deadwood*, written by Bernadette McNamara, directed by Gregg Fienberg, original broadcast August 20, 2006, HBO Television and Red Board Productions, 50 min. This episode is available on Disc 5 of Season Three of the *Deadwood: The Complete Series* DVD collection and on Disc 5 of the *Deadwood: Season Three* DVD collection, both released by HBO Video.

66. "Tell Him Something Pretty," *Deadwood*, written by Ted Mann, directed by Mark Tinker, original broadcast August 27, 2006, HBO Television and Red Board Productions, 50 min. This episode is available on Disc 5 of Season Three of the *Deadwood: The Complete Series* DVD collection and on Disc 5 of the *Deadwood: Season Three* DVD collection, both released by HBO Video.

67. "Unauthorized Cinnamon," *Deadwood*, written by Regina Corrado, directed by Mark Tinker, original broadcast July 23, 2006, HBO Television, Red Board Productions, 50 min. This episode is available on Disc 3 of Season Three of the *Deadwood: The Complete Series* DVD collection and on Disc 3 of the *Deadwood: Season Three* DVD collection, both released by HBO Video.

68. "True Colors," *Deadwood*, written by Regina Corrado and Ted Mann, directed by Gregg Fienberg, original broadcast June 25, 2006, HBO Television and Red Board Productions, 52 min. This episode is available on Disc 2 of Season Three of the *Deadwood: The Complete Series* DVD collection and on Disc 2 of the *Deadwood: Season Three* DVD collection, both released by HBO Video.

69. Milch, *Stories of the Black Hills*, 55.

70. "Leviathan Smiles," written by Kem Nunn, directed by Ed Bianchi, original broadcast July 30, 2006, HBO Television and Red Board Productions, 54 min. This episode is available on Disc 4 of Season Three of the *Deadwood: The Complete Series* DVD collection and on Disc 4 of the *Deadwood: Season Three* DVD collection, both released by HBO Video.

71. "A Two-Headed Beast," written by David Milch, directed by Daniel Minahan, original broadcast July 9, 2006, HBO Television and Red Board Productions, 54 min. This episode is available on Disc 3 of Season Three of the *Deadwood: The Complete Series* DVD collection and on Disc 3 of the *Deadwood: Season Three* DVD collection, both released by HBO Video.

72. Paul Wright and Hailin Zhou, "Divining the 'Celestials': The Chinese Subculture of *Deadwood*," in Lavery, *Reading* Deadwood, 160.

73. Milch, *Stories of the Black Hills*, 213.

74. "Mr. Wu," written by Bryan McDonald, directed by Daniel Minahan, original broadcast May 23, 2004, HBO Television and Red Board Productions, 53 min. This episode is available on Disc 4 of Season One of the *Deadwood: The Complete Series* DVD collection and on Disc 4 of the *Deadwood: Season One* DVD collection, both released by HBO Video.

75. Milch, *Stories of the Black Hills*, 207.

76. "Requiem for a Gleet," written by Ted Mann, directed by Alan Taylor, original broadcast March 27, 2005, HBO Television and Red Board Productions, 53 min. This episode is available on Disc 2 of Season Two of the *Deadwood: The Complete Series* DVD collection and on Disc 2 of the *Deadwood: Season Two* DVD collection, both released by HBO Video.

77. Milch, *Stories of the Black Hills*, 207.
78. Ibid., 213.
79. Ibid.

Chapter 6: All the Pieces Matter

1. David Simon, introduction to *"The Wire": Truth Be Told*, by Rafael Alvarez (New York: Pocket Books, 2004), 2, 4.
2. Ibid., 4.
3. Ibid., 8.
4. Ibid.
5. Both of the preceding quotations are from ibid., 10.
6. Margaret Talbot, "Stealing Life," *New Yorker*, October 22, 2007, http://www.newyorker.com/reporting/2007/10/22/071022fa_fact_talbot.
7. Ibid.
8. Simon, introduction to *Truth Be Told*, 4, 2.
9. Jane Gibb and Roger Sabin, "Who Loves Ya, David Simon? Notes toward Placing *The Wire*'s Depiction of African-Americans in the Context of American TV Crime Drama," *Darkmatter: In the Ruins of Imperial Culture*, May 29, 2009, http://www.darkmatter101.org/site/2009/05/29/who-loves-ya-david-simon/.
10. Ibid.
11. Elayne Rapping, *Law and Justice as Seen on TV* (New York: New York University Press, 2003), 255.
12. David Simon, "Letter to HBO," in Alvarez, *Truth Be Told*, 37.
13. Gibb and Sabin, "Who Loves Ya, David Simon?"
14. See Gibb and Sabin's article for this quotation, as well as a recording of Simon's interview with Laverne at *The Culture Show*'s Web site, http://www.bbc.co.uk/cultureshow/videos/2008/07/s5_e7_wire/index.shtml.
15. Alberto Toscano and Jeff Kinkle, "Baltimore as World and Representation: Cognitive Mapping and Capitalism in *The Wire*," *Dossier*, http://dossierjournal.com/read/theory/baltimore-as-world-and-representation-cognitive-mapping-and-capitalism-in-the-wire/.
16. This and the following quotations in this paragraph are from Simon, introduction to *Truth Be Told*, 5, 6.
17. Ibid., 7.
18. Ibid., 25.
19. Tom Wolfe, "Stalking the Billion-Footed Beast: A Literary Manifesto for the New Social Novel," *Harper's Magazine*, November 1989, 46. The emphasis is Wolfe's. An online version of this article is available for *Harper's* subscribers at http://www.harpers.org/archive/1989/11/0059090. A PDF version is available at http://www.lukeford.net/Images/photos3/tomwolfe.pdf.
20. Ibid., 50.
21. Mark Bowden, "The Angriest Man in Television," *Atlantic Monthly*, January–February 2008, 51, http://www.theatlantic.com/doc/200801/bowden-wire.

22. "The Target," *The Wire,* written by David Simon, story by David Simon and Ed Burns, directed by Clark Johnson, original broadcast June 2, 2002, HBO Television and Blown Deadline Productions, 63 min. This episode is available on Disc 1 of Season One of *The Wire: The Complete Series* DVD collection and on Disc 1 of *The Wire: Season One* DVD collection, both released by HBO Video.

23. David Simon, *Homicide: A Year on the Killing Streets* (1991; New York: Ivy Books-Ballantine, 1993), 570.

24. Talbot, "Stealing Life."

25. Ibid.

26. Blake D. Ethridge, "Baltimore on *The Wire:* The Tragic Moralism of David Simon," in *It's Not TV: Watching HBO in the Post-Television Era,* ed. Marc Leverette, Brian L. Ott, and Cara Louise Buckley (New York: Routledge, 2008), 153.

27. Sophie Fuggle, "Short Circuiting the Power Grid: *The Wire* as Critique of Institutional Power," *Darkmatter: In the Ruins of Imperial Culture,* May 29, 2009, http://www.darkmatter101.org/site/2009/05/29/short-circuiting-the-power-grid-the-wire-as-critique-of-institutional-power/.

28. Ethridge, "Baltimore on *The Wire,*" 153.

29. David Simon, DVD commentary, "The Target." This episode and Simon's commentary track are available on Disc 1 of Season One of *The Wire: The Complete Series* DVD collection and on Disc 1 of *The Wire: Season One* DVD collection, both released by HBO Video.

30. Amanda Ann Klein, "'The Dickensian Aspect': Melodrama, Viewer Engagement, and the Socially Conscious Text," in The Wire: *Urban Decay and American Television,* ed. Tiffany Potter and C. W. Marshall (New York: Continuum, 2009), 178.

31. "Mission Accomplished," *The Wire,* teleplay by David Simon, story by David Simon and Ed Burns, directed by Ernest Dickerson, original broadcast December 19, 2004, HBO Television and Blown Deadline Productions, 64 min. This episode and its audio commentary track (by Simon and producer Karen L. Thorson) are available on Disc 5 of Season Three of *The Wire: The Complete Series* DVD collection and on Disc 5 of *The Wire: Season Three* DVD collection, both released by HBO Video.

32. "All Due Respect," *The Wire,* teleplay by Richard Price, story by David Simon and Richard Price, directed by Steve Shill, original broadcast September 27, 2004, HBO Television and Blown Deadline Productions, 59 min. This episode and its audio commentary track (by Price) are available on Disc 1 of Season Three of *The Wire: The Complete Series* DVD collection and on Disc 1 of *The Wire: Season Three* DVD collection, both released by HBO Video.

33. "Middle Ground," *The Wire,* teleplay by George Pelecanos, story by David Simon and George Pelecanos, directed by Joe Chappelle, original broadcast December 12, 2004, HBO Television and Blown Deadline Productions, 59 min. This episode and its audio commentary track (by Pelecanos and Chappelle) are available on Disc 5 of Season Three of *The Wire: The Complete Series* DVD collection and on Disc 5 of *The Wire: Season Three* DVD collection, both released by HBO Video.

34. Bowden, "Angriest Man in Television," 52, 54.

35. George Pelecanos's audio commentary for "Middle Ground" and David Simon's audio commentary for "Mission Accomplished" include their thoughts about Schmoke's drug-decriminalization stance.

36. Ethridge, "Baltimore on *The Wire*," 159.

37. Simon, introduction to *Truth Be Told*, 12.

38. Brian G. Rose, "*The Wire*," in *The Essential HBO Reader*, ed. Gary R. Edgerton and Jeffrey P. Jones, Essential Readers in Contemporary Media and Culture Series (Lexington: The University Press of Kentucky, 2008), 85.

39. Gibb and Sabin, "Who Loves Ya, David Simon?"

40. Ibid.

41. Rafael Alvarez, The Wire: *Truth Be Told* (New York: Pocket Books, 2004), 42; "Making *The Wire*" Panel Discussion, Pinewood Dialogues, Museum of the Moving Image, July 30, 2008, transcript at www.movingimage source.us/dialogues/view/309. Simon's comment is available on page 16 of the transcript.

42. "Valentine's Day," *Homicide: Life on the Street*, written by Tom Fontana, directed by Clark Johnson, original broadcast February 14, 1997, NBC Television and Baltimore Pictures, 46 min. This episode is available on Volume (Disc) 5 of the *Homicide: Life on the Street: The Complete Season 5* DVD collection released by A&E Home Video.

43. Sandra P. Angulo, "Cop to It," *Entertainment Weekly*, June 3, 1999, http://www.ew.com/ew/article/0,,84423,00.html.

44. Andrew Anthony, "Way out West," *Guardian*, October 26, 2008, http://www.guardian.co.uk/culture/2008/oct/26/dominic-west-the-wire-television.

45. Simon made this comment at a 2008 event titled *Q&A at the Glasgow Film Theatre* held in Glasgow, Scotland. Lisa W. Kelly's "Casting *The Wire*: Complicating Notions of Performance, Authenticity, and 'Otherness'" (*Darkmatter: In the Ruins of Imperial Culture*, May 29, 2009, http://www.darkmatter101.org/ site/2009/05/29/casting-the-wire-complicating-notions-of-performance-authenticity-and-otherness/#foot_src_21) also mentions it.

46. Kelly, "Casting *The Wire*."

47. Ibid.

48. Nick Hornby, "David Simon: Creator-Writer-Producer of HBO's *The Wire*," *The Believer*, August 2007, http://www.believermag.com/ issues/200708/?read=interview_simon.

49. Final shooting draft of "The Target," October 21, 2001, 50.

50. Clark Johnson, DVD audio commentary, "The Detail," *The Wire*, teleplay by David Simon, story by David Simon and Ed Burns, directed by Clark Johnson, original broadcast June 9, 2002, HBO Television and Blown Deadline Productions, 58 min. This episode and Johnson's commentary track are available on Disc 1 of Season One of *The Wire: The Complete Series* DVD collection and on Disc 1 of *The Wire: Season One* DVD collection, both released by HBO Video.

51. Alvarez, *Truth Be Told*, 98. Talbot also mentions this incident in "Stealing Life."

52. See pages 85–89 of Alvarez's *Truth Be Told* for background information about Omar Little and pages 97–102 for background information about Bubbles.

53. David Simon, in his DVD audio commentary for "Dead Soldiers" (3.3), says that Omar's absolute patience distinguishes him as a character because "he'll endure longer surveillance than even the police." This episode and its commentary track are available on Disc 2 of Season Three of *The Wire: The Complete Series* DVD collection and on Disc 2 of *The Wire: Season Three* DVD collection, both released by HBO Video.

54. Todd Fraley, "A Man's Gotta Have a Code: Identity, Racial Codes, and HBO's *The Wire*," *Darkmatter: In the Ruins of Imperial Culture*, May 29, 2009, http://www.darkmatter101.org/site/2009/05/29/a-mans-gotta-have-a-code-identity-racial-codes-and-hbos-the-wire/.

55. "All Prologue," *The Wire*, teleplay by David Simon, story by David Simon and Ed Burns, directed by Steve Shill, original broadcast July 6, 2003, HBO Television and Blown Deadline Productions, 59 min. This episode, along with a commentary track by Dominic West and Michael K. Williams, is available on Disc 3 of Season Two of *The Wire: The Complete Series* DVD collection and on Disc 3 of *The Wire: Season Two* DVD collection, both released by HBO Video.

56. Herman Gray, *Watching Race: Television and the Struggle for Blackness* (1995; Minneapolis: University of Minnesota Press, 2004), 4.

57. Ibid., 84.

58. Ibid., 85.

59. David Simon, DVD audio commentary, "Dead Soldiers," *The Wire*, teleplay by Dennis Lehane, story by David Simon and Dennis Lehane, directed by Rob Bailey, original broadcast October 3, 2004, HBO Television and Blown Deadline Productions, 59 min. This episode and Simon's commentary track are available on Disc 2 of Season Three of *The Wire: The Complete Series* DVD collection and on Disc 2 of *The Wire: Season Three* DVD collection, both released by HBO Video.

60. "Homecoming," *The Wire*, teleplay by Rafael Alvarez, story by David Simon and Rafael Alvarez, directed by Leslie Libman, original broadcast October 31, 2004, HBO Television and Blown Deadline Productions, 58 min. This episode is available on Disc 3 of Season Three of *The Wire: The Complete Series* DVD collection and on Disc 3 of *The Wire: Season Three* DVD collection, both released by HBO Video.

61. Phillip Brian Harper, "Extra-Special Effects: Televisual Representation and the Claims of 'the Black Experience,'" in *Living Color: Race and Television in the United States*, ed. Sasha Torres (Durham, NC: Duke University Press, 1998), 71. The emphasis is Harper's.

62. "Back Burners," *The Wire*, teleplay by Joy Lusco Kecken, story by David Simon and Joy Lusco Kecken, directed by Tim Van Patten, original broadcast November 7, 2004, HBO Television and Blown Deadline Productions, 56 min. This episode is available on Disc 3 of Season Three of *The Wire: The Complete Series* DVD collection and on Disc 3 of *The Wire: Season Three* DVD collection, both released by HBO Video.

63. Jacob Weisberg, "*The Wire* on Fire: Analyzing the Best Show on Television," *Slate,* September 13, 2006, http://www.slate.com/id/2149566.

64. Rose, "*The Wire,*" 89–90.

65. J. M. Tyree, "*The Wire:* The Complete Fourth Season," DVD review, *Film Quarterly* 61, no. 3 (Spring 2008): 32.

66. "David Simon," *Bill Moyers Journal,* April 17, 2009, http://www.pbs.org/moyers/journal/04172009/watch.html. Visitors to the *Bill Moyers Journal* Web site may not only view the entire interview via streaming video but also access a complete transcript.

67. Ethridge, "Baltimore on *The Wire,*" 163.

68. Ibid.

69. Bowden, "Angriest Man in Television," 54.

70. Ibid., 55.

71. Ethridge, "Baltimore on *The Wire,*" 163.

72. "Home Rooms," *The Wire,* teleplay by Richard Price, story by Ed Burns and Richard Price, directed by Seith Mann, original broadcast September 17, 2006, HBO Television and Blown Deadline Productions, 59 min. This episode is available on Disc 1 of Season Four of *The Wire: The Complete Series* DVD collection and on Disc 1 of *The Wire: Season Four* DVD collection, both released by HBO Video.

Conclusion: The Two Davids

1. Wyatt Mason, "The HBO Auteur," *New York Times Magazine,* March 15, 2010, http://www.nytimes.com/2010/03/21/magazine/21simon-t.html?ref=magazine&pagewanted=all.

2. James M. Vest, *Hitchcock and France: The Forging of an Auteur* (Westport, CT: Praeger, 2003), 51.

3. Ibid., x.

4. Mason, "The HBO Auteur."

5. Ibid.

6. Richard Price, DVD commentary, "All Due Respect," *The Wire,* teleplay by Richard Price, story by David Simon and Richard Price, directed by Steve Shill, original broadcast September 27, 2004, HBO Television and Blown Deadline Productions, 59 min. This episode and Price's audio commentary track are available on Disc 1 of Season Three of *The Wire: The Complete Series* DVD collection and on Disc 1 of *The Wire: Season Three* DVD collection, both released by HBO Video.

7. Nancy Franklin, "Dead in the Water," *New Yorker,* June 25, 2007, http://www.newyorker.com/arts/critics/television/2007/06/25/070625crte_television_franklin.

8. Mason, "The HBO Auteur."

9. Ibid.

10. Mark Bowden, "The Angriest Man in Television," *Atlantic Monthly,* January–February 2008, 51, http://www.theatlantic.com/doc/200801/bowden-wire.

Bibliography

Adorno, Theodor W., and Max Horkheimer. "The Culture Industry: Enlightenment as Mass Deception." In *Dialectic of Enlightenment*, translated by Edmund Jephcott, 120–67. 1944. Stanford, CA: Stanford University Press, 2002.

Aleiss, Angela. *Making the White Man's Indian: Native Americans and Hollywood Movies*. Westport, CT: Praeger, 2005.

Alvarez, Rafael. *"The Wire": Truth Be Told*. New York: Pocket Books, 2004.

Amnesty International. *Police Brutality and Excessive Force in the New York City Police Department*. June 1996. http://asiapacific.amnesty.org/library/Index/ENGAMR510361996?open&of=ENG-USA.

Angulo, Sandra P. "Cop to It." *Entertainment Weekly*, June 3, 1999. http://www.ew.com/ew/article/0,,84423,00.html.

Anthony, Andrew. "Way out West." *Guardian*, October 26, 2008. http://www.guardian.co.uk/culture/2008/oct/26/dominic-west-the-wire-television.

Baldwin, James. *Collected Essays: Notes of a Native Son, Nobody Knows My Name, The Fire Next Time, No Name in the Street, The Devil Finds Work, Other Essays*. New York: Library of America, 1998.

Benjamin, Walter. "The Work of Art in the Age of Mechanical Reproduction." In *Illuminations*, edited by Hannah Arendt, 217–51. New York: Schocken Books, 1968.

Berger, John. *Ways of Seeing*. 1972. London: British Broadcasting Corporation and Penguin Books, 2003.

Bernardi, Daniel, ed. *The Persistence of Whiteness: Race and Contemporary Hollywood Cinema*. New York: Routledge, 2007.

Blau, Robert. *The Cop Shop: True Crime on the Streets of Chicago*. Upper Saddle River, NJ: Addison-Wesley, 1993.

Boudreaux, Jonathan. *"The Corner* DVD Review." *TVDVDReviews*, August 24, 2003. http://www.tvdvdreviews.com/corner.html.

Bourdieu, Pierre, and Loïc J. D. Wacquant. *An Invitation to Reflexive Sociology*. Chicago: University of Chicago Press, 1992.

Bowden, Mark. "The Angriest Man in Television." *Atlantic Monthly,* January–February 2008, 50–57. http://www.theatlantic.com/doc/200801/bowden-wire.

Boyd-Bowman, Susan. "The MTM Phenomenon: The Company, The Book, The Programmes." *Screen* 26, no. 6 (1985): 75–87.

Branch, Taylor. *At Canaan's Edge: America in the King Years, 1965–68.* New York: Simon and Schuster Paperbacks, 2006.

Branch, Taylor. *Parting the Waters: America in the King Years, 1954–63.* 1988. New York: Touchstone, 1989.

Branch, Taylor. *Pillar of Fire: America in the King Years, 1963–65.* New York: Simon and Schuster Paperbacks, 1998.

Bruce, Dickson D., Jr. "W.E.B. Du Bois and the Idea of Double Consciousness." In Du Bois, *Souls of Black Folk,* 236–44.

Buckley, Tom. "TV: *Hill Street Blues,* New NBC Police Series." *New York Times,* January 17, 1981. http://www.nytimes.com/1981/01/17/arts/tv-hill-street-blues-new-nbc-police series.html.

Canby, Vincent. "From the Humble Mini-Series Comes the Magnificent Megamovie." *New York Times,* October 31, 1999. http://www.nytimes.com/1999/10/31/arts/from-the-humble-mini-series-comes-the-magnificent-megamovie.html?pagewanted=all.

Cawelti, John G. *The Six-Gun Mystique.* 2nd ed. Bowling Green, KY: Bowling Green State University Press, 1984.

Cawelti, John G. *The Six-Gun Mystique Sequel.* Madison, WI: Popular Press, 1999.

Ceplair, Larry, and Steven Englund. *The Inquisition in Hollywood: Politics and the Film Community, 1930–1960.* 1979. Berkeley and Los Angeles: University of California Press, 1983.

Corliss, Richard. "Midwinter Night's Dreams: *Hill Street Blues.*" *Time,* January 26, 1991, 72.

Corliss, Richard. "Video: Too Good for Television?" *Time,* September 14, 1981, 88.

Crais, Robert. *Hostage.* New York: Doubleday, 2001.

Crichton, Michael. *Disclosure.* New York: Alfred A. Knopf, 1994.

Crouch, Stanley. "Who Are We? Where Did We Come From? Where Are We Going?" In Early, *Lure and Loathing,* 67–78.

David, Hugh K. "*The Corner.*" *DVD Times,* July 23, 2005. http://dvdtimes.co.uk/content.php?contentid=57882.

Dexter, Pete. *Deadwood.* 1986. New York: Vintage Contemporaries, 2005.

Diffrient, David Scott. "Deadwood Dick: The Western (Phallus) Reinvented." In Lavery, *Reading "Deadwood,"* 185–99.

Doane, Ashley W., and Eduardo Bonilla-Silva, eds. *White Out: The Continuing Significance of Racism.* New York: Routledge, 2003.

Du Bois, W.E.B. *Black Reconstruction in America 1860–1880.* 1935. New York: Free Press, 1998.

Du Bois, W.E.B. *The Souls of Black Folk.* Edited by Henry Louis Gates Jr. and Terri Hume Oliver. Centenary Edition. New York: W. W. Norton, 1999.

Early, Gerald, ed. *Lure and Loathing: Essays on Race, Identity, and the Ambivalence of Assimilation.* New York: Allen Lane, 1993.

Early, Gerald. *Tuxedo Junction: Essays on American Culture*. New York: Ecco Press, 1989.

Edgerton, Gary R., and Jeffrey P. Jones, eds. *The Essential HBO Reader*. Lexington: University Press of Kentucky, 2008.

Ellison, Ralph. *The Collected Essays of Ralph Ellison*. Edited by John F. Callhan. New York: Modern Library, 2003.

Ellison, Ralph. *Shadow and Act*. New York: Vintage, 1995.

Ethridge, Blake D. "Baltimore on *The Wire:* The Tragic Moralism of David Simon." In *It's Not TV: Watching HBO in the Post-Television Era*, edited by Marc Leverette, Brian L. Ott, and Cara Louise Buckley, 152–64. New York: Routledge, 2008.

Euripides. *Medea and Other Plays*. Translated by Philip Vellacott. 1963. New York: Penguin Books, 1982.

Fairclough, Adam. *Better Day Coming: Blacks and Equality, 1890–2000*. New York: Viking, 2001.

Fielder, Leslie. *Love and Death in the American Novel*. 1966. Rev ed., New York: Scarbarough-Stein and Day, 1982.

Fiske, John. *Television Culture*. 1987. London: Routledge, 2006.

Fraley, Todd. "A Man's Gotta Have a Code: Identity, Racial Codes, and HBO's *The Wire*." *Darkmatter: In the Ruins of Imperial Culture*, May 29, 2009. http://www.darkmatter101.org/site/2009/05/29/a-mans-gotta-have-a-code-identity-racial-codes-and-hbos-the-wire/.

Francis, Susan Beth. "*Hill Street Blues*." In Jarvis and Joseph, *Prime Time Law*, 17–20.

Franklin, John Hope. *From Slavery to Freedom: A History of African Americans*. New York: Alfred A. Knopf, 2000.

Franklin, John Hope. *Reconstruction after the Civil War*. Chicago: University of Chicago Press, 1994.

Franklin, Nancy. "Dead in the Water." *New Yorker*, June 25, 2007. http://www.newyorker.com/arts/critics/television/2007/06/25/070625crte_television_franklin.

Fuggle, Sophie. "Short Circuiting the Power Grid: *The Wire* as Critique of Institutional Power." *Darkmatter: In the Ruins of Imperial Culture*, May 29, 2009. http://www.darkmatter101.org/site/2009/05/29/short-circuiting-the-power-grid-the-wire-as-critique-of-institutional-power/.

Gates, Henry Louis, Jr. *The Signifying Monkey: A Theory of African-American Literary Criticism*. Oxford, UK: Oxford University Press, 1989.

Gates, Henry Louis, Jr. *The Trials of Phillis Wheatley: America's First Black Poet and Encounters with the Founding Fathers*. New York: Basic Civitas Books, 2003.

Gelman, Mitch. *Crime Scene: On the Streets with a Rookie Police Reporter*. New York: Crown, 1992.

Gibb, Jane, and Roger Sabin. "Who Loves Ya, David Simon? Notes toward Placing *The Wire*'s Depiction of African-Americans in the Context of American TV Crime Drama." *Darkmatter: In the Ruins of Imperial Culture*, May 29, 2009. http://www.darkmatter101.org/site/2009/05/29/who-loves-ya-david-simon/.

Gitlin, Todd. *Inside Prime Time*. 1983. Berkeley and Los Angeles: University of California Press, 2000.

Graham, Allison. *Framing the South: Hollywood, Television, and Race during the Civil Rights Struggle*. Baltimore, MD: Johns Hopkins University Press, 2003.

Gray, Herman. *Watching Race: Television and the Struggle for Blackness*. 1995. Minneapolis: University of Minnesota Press, 2004.

Greene, Jack R., ed. *The Encyclopedia of Police Science*. 3rd ed. New York: Taylor & Francis, 2007.

Grey, Zane. *Riders of the Purple Sage*. 1912. New York: Penguin Books, 1990.

Hampton, Henry, and Steve Fayer. *Voices of Freedom: An Oral History of the Civil Rights Movement from the 1950s through the 1980s*. 1990. New York: Bantam Books, 1991.

Hare, Nathan. *The Black Anglo-Saxons*. 1965. Chicago: Third World Press, 2001.

Harper, Phillip Brian. "Extra-Special Effects: Televisual Representation and the Claims of 'the Black Experience.'" In *Living Color: Race and Television in the United States*, edited by Sasha Torres, 62–81. Durham, NC: Duke University Press, 1998.

Havrilesky, Heather. "The Man behind *Deadwood*." *Salon.com*. March 5, 2005. http://dir.salon.com/story/ent/feature/2005/03/05/milch/index.html.

Hendershot, Heather. "My So-Called Independents." *Nation*, June 16, 2008, 44–47.

Hill, Erin. "'What's Afflictin' You?' Corporeality, Body Crises, and the Body Politic in *Deadwood*." In Lavery, *Reading "Deadwood,"* 171–83.

hooks, bell. *Ain't I a Woman: Black Women and Feminism*. Cambridge, MA: South End Press, 1981.

hooks, bell. *Killing Rage: Ending Racism*. New York: Henry Holt, 1995.

Hornby, Nick. "David Simon: Creator-Writer-Producer of HBO's *The Wire*." *The Believer*, August 2007. http://www.believermag.com/issues/200708/?read=interview_simon.

Human Rights Watch. *Shielded from Justice: Police Brutality and Accountability in the United States*. June 1998. http://www.hrw.org/legacy/reports98/police/index.htm.

Hurston, Zora Neale. *Every Tongue Got to Confess: Negro Folk-Tales from the Gulf States*. Edited by Carla Kaplan. New York: HarperCollins, 2001.

Hurston, Zora Neale. *Mules and Men*. 1935. New York: Perennial, 1990.

Jacobs, Jason. "Al Swearengen, Philosopher King." In Lavery, *Reading "Deadwood,"* 11–21.

Jameson, Fredric. *Postmodernism, or, The Cultural Logic of Late Capitalism*. Durham, NC: Duke University Press, 1991.

Jarvis, Robert M., and Paul R. Joseph, eds. *Prime Time Law: Fictional Television as Legal Narrative*. Durham, NC: Carolina Academic Press, 1998.

Johnson, Marilynn S. *Street Justice: A History of Police Violence in New York City*. Boston: Beacon Press, 2003.

Kalat, David P. *"Homicide: Life on the Street": The Unofficial Companion*. Los Angeles: Renaissance Books, 1998.

Kaufman, Scott Eric. "*Deadwood* and To Whom Its Dialogue Is Beholden." *Acephalous,* August 22, 2006. http://acephalous.typepad.com/acepha lous/2006/08/deadwood_and_to.html.

Kelly, Lisa W. "Casting *The Wire:* Complicating Notions of Performance, Authenticity, and 'Otherness.'" *Darkmatter: In the Ruins of Imperial Culture,* May 29, 2009. http://www.darkmatter101.org/site/2009/05/29/cast ing-the-wire-complicating-notions-of-performance-authenticity-and-otherness/#foot_src_21.

King, Martin Luther, Jr. "Letter from Birmingham Jail." In *A Testament of Hope: The Essential Writings and Speeches of Martin Luther King Jr.,* edited by James Melvin Washington, 289–302. San Francisco: HarperSanFrancisco, 1991.

Kitses, Jim, and Gregg Rickman, eds. *A Western Reader.* Limelight Edition. New York: Proscenium, 1998.

Klein, Amanda Ann. "'The Dickensian Aspect': Melodrama, Viewer Engagement, and the Socially Conscious Text." In *"The Wire": Urban Decay and American Television,* edited by Tiffany C. Potter and C. W. Marshall, 177–89. New York: Continuum, 2009.

L'Amour, Louis. *Guns of the Timberlands.* 1955. New York: Bantam Books, 1984.

Landrum, Larry. "Instrumental Texts and Stereotyping in *Hill Street Blues*: The Police Procedural on Television." *MELUS* 11, no. 3 (1984): 93–100.

Lane, Philip J. "The Existential Condition of Television Crime Drama." *Journal of Popular Culture* 34, no. 4 (2001): 137–51.

Lavery, David, ed. *Reading "Deadwood": A Western to Swear By.* Reading Contemporary Television Series. London: I. B. Tauris, 2006.

Lehane, Dennis. *Mystic River.* 2001. New York: HarperTorch, 2002.

Leonard, John. "True West." *New York Magazine,* n.d. http://nymag.com/ nymetro/arts/tv/reviews/n_10058/.

Lewis, R.W.B. *The Jameses: A Family Narrative.* 1991. New York: Anchor, 1993.

Longworth, James L., Jr. *TV Creators: Conversations with America's Top Producers of Television Drama.* Syracuse, NY: Syracuse University Press, 2000.

Lotz, Amanda D. *The Television Will Be Revolutionized.* New York: New York University Press, 2007.

Lusted, David. *The Western.* Inside Film Series. Upper Saddle River, NJ: Longman, 2003.

Making "The Wire." Transcript of panel discussion. Pinewood Dialogues. Museum of the Moving Image. July 30, 2008. www.movingimagesource.us/ dialogues/view/309.

Mander, Jerry. *Four Arguments for the Elimination of Television.* 1978. New York: Perennial, 2002.

Martel, Ned. "Resurrecting the Western to Save the Crime Drama." *New York Times,* March 21, 2004. http://www.nytimes.com/2004/03/21/ arts/television-resurrecting-the-western-to-save-the-crime-drama. html?pagewanted=1.

Mascaro, Thomas A. "Shades of Black on *Homicide: Life on the Street*: Advances and Retreats in Portrayals of African American Women." *Journal of Popular Film and Television* 33, no. 2 (2005): 56–67.

Mascaro, Thomas A. "Shades of Black on *Homicide: Life on the Street*: Progress in Portrayals of African American Men." *Journal of Popular Film and Television* 32, no. 1 (2004): 10–19.

Mason, Wyatt. "The HBO Auteur." *New York Times Magazine*, March 15, 2010. http://www.nytimes.com/2010/03/21/magazine/21simon-t.html.

McCabe, Janet, and Kim Akass, eds. *Quality TV: Contemporary American Television and Beyond*. London: I. B. Tauris, 2007.

McGee, Patrick. *From "Shane" to "Kill Bill": Rethinking the Western*. New Approaches to Film Genre Series. Malden, MA: Blackwell, 2007.

McGrath, Charles. "The Triumph of the Prime-Time Novel." *New York Times Magazine*, October 22, 1995, 52+. http://www.nytimes.com/1995/10/22/magazine/the-prime-time-novel-the-triumph-of-the-prime-time-novel.html?pagewanted=all.

McMurtry, Larry. *Lonesome Dove*. 1985. New York: Pocket Books, 1986.

Meeks, Kenneth. "Racism and Reality in *NYPD Blue*." In Yeffeth, *What Would Sipowicz Do?*, 49–55.

Meisler, Andy. "Out of N.Y.P.D., into 'N.Y.P.D. Blue.'" *New York Times*, November 7, 1995. http://www.nytimes.com/1995/11/07/arts/out-of-nypd-into-nypd-blue.html.

Milch, David. *Deadwood: Stories of the Black Hills*. New York: Melcher Media, 2006.

Milch, David. "Deadwood." Teleplay dated August 20, 2002. *Weekly Script*, September 25, 2008. http://www.weeklyscript.com/Deadwood - Pilot.txt.

Milch, David, and Bill Clark. *True Blue*. 1995. New York: Avon Books, 1997.

Millichap, Joseph. "Robert Penn Warren, David Milch, and the Literary Contexts of *Deadwood*." In Lavery, *Reading "Deadwood,"* 101–13.

Minow, Newton M. "Television and the Public Interest." Keynote address, National Association of Broadcasters, Washington, D.C., May 9, 1961. http://www.americanrhetoric.com/speeches/newtonminow.htm.

Minow, Newton M., and Craig L. LaMay. *Abandoned in the Wasteland: Children, Television, and the First Amendment*. 1995. New York: Hill and Wang, 1996.

Mittell, Jason. *Genre and Television: From Cop Shows to Cartoons in American Culture*. New York: Routledge, 2004.

"The Motion Picture Production Code of 1930 (Hays Code)." ArtsReformation.com. http://www.artsreformation.com/a001/hays-code.html.

Newcomb, Horace. "*Deadwood*." In Edgerton and Jones, *The Essential HBO Reader*, 92–102.

Nunberg, Geoffrey. "Obscenity Rap." Geoffrey Nunberg University of California-Berkeley Home Page. June 20, 2004. http://people.ischool.berkeley.edu/~nunberg/deadwood.html.

O'Sullivan, Sean. "Old, New, Borrowed, Blue: *Deadwood* and Serial Fiction." In Lavery, *Reading "Deadwood,"* 115–29.

Pelecanos, George P. *The Sweet Forever*. 1988. New York: Dell, 1989.

Pollard, Alton B., III. "The Last Great Battle of the West: W.E.B. Du Bois and the Struggle for African America's Soul." In Early, *Lure and Loathing*, 104–15.

Price, Richard. *Clockers*. Boston: Houghton Mifflin, 1992.

"The Production Code of the Motion Picture Industry (1930–1967)." Production Code Writings. http://productioncode.dhwritings.com/multiple-frames_productioncode.php.

Rapping, Elayne. *Law and Justice as Seen on TV*. New York: New York University Press, 2003.

Robert, Henry M. *Robert's Rules of Order*. 1876. Cambridge, MA: Perseus Books, 2000.

Rocchio, Vincent F. *Reel Racism: Confronting Hollywood's Construction of Afro-American Culture*. Boulder, CO: Westview Press, 2000.

Rollins, Peter C., and John E. O'Connor, eds. *The West Wing: The American Presidency as Television Drama*. Syracuse, NY: Syracuse University Press, 2003.

Rose, Brian G. "*The Wire*." In Edgerton and Jones, *The Essential HBO Reader*, 82–91.

Rose, Cynthia. "The Originator of TV's *Homicide* Remains Close to His Police-Reporter Roots." *Seattle Times*, February 18, 1999. http://web.archive.org/web/19990428142656/http://www.seattletimes.com/news/entertainment/html98/dave_021899.html.

Selby, Hubert, Jr. *Last Exit to Brooklyn*. 1964. New York: Grove Press, 1965.

Selby, Hubert, Jr. *Requiem for a Dream*. 1978. New York: Thunder's Mouth Press, 2000.

Shales, Tom. "Hill and Renko Being Careful Out There." *Washington Post*, April 28, 1983, D1.

Shales, Tom. "'Hill Street,' Hail and Farewell." *Washington Post*, May 12, 1987, final edition, D1.

Siegel, Lee. *Not Remotely Controlled: Notes on Television*. New York: Basic Books, 2007.

Simmon, Scott. *The Invention of the Western Film: A Cultural History of the Genre's First Half Century*. Genres in American Cinema Series. Cambridge: Cambridge University Press, 2003.

Simon, David. *Homicide: A Year on the Killing Streets*. 1991. New York: Ivy Books, 1993.

Simon, David. Introduction to "*The Wire*": *Truth Be Told*, by Rafael Alvarez, 2–34. New York: Pocket Books, 2004.

Simon, David. "Letter to HBO." In "*The Wire*": *Truth Be Told*, by Rafael Alvarez, 35–39. New York: Pocket Books, 2004.

Simon, David, and Edward Burns. *The Corner: A Year in the Life of an Inner-City Neighborhood*. New York: Broadway Books, 1997.

Singer, Mark. "The Misfit." *New Yorker*, February 14 and 21, 2005, 192–205. http://www.newyorker.com/archive/2005/02/14/050214fa_fact_singer.

Slotkin, Richard. *Gunfighter Nation: The Myth of the Frontier in Twentieth-Century America*. 1992. Norman: University of Oklahoma Press, 1998.

Smith, Adam. *The Wealth of Nations: Books I–III*. Edited by Andrew Skinner. 1776. New York: Penguin Books, 1999.

Sophocles. *Oedipus Rex (Oedipus the King)*. *The Three Theban Plays*. Translated by Robert Fagles. 1982. New York: Penguin Books, 1984.

Spiegel, Lynn, and Jan Olsson. *Television after TV: Essays on a Medium in Transition.* Durham, NC: Duke University Press, 2004.

Sterne, Richard Clark. *"N.Y.P.D. Blue."* In Jarvis and Joseph, *Prime Time Law,* 87–104.

Steyn, Mark. "The Maestro of Jiggle TV." *Atlantic Monthly,* September 2006, 146–47.

Talbot, Margaret. "Stealing Life." *New Yorker,* October 22, 2007. http://www. newyorker.com/reporting/2007/10/22/071022fa_fact_talbot.

Teachout, Terry. "The Myth of 'Classic' TV." In *A Terry Teachout Reader,* 174–77.

Teachout, Terry. "Repent at Leisure." *About Last Night: Terry Teachout on the Arts in New York,* September 12, 2006. http://www.artsjournal.com/aboutlastnight/archives20040905.shtml.

Teachout, Terry. "Still Repenting." *About Last Night: Terry Teachout on the Arts in New York,* December 19, 2007. http://www.artsjournal.com/aboutlastnight/2007/12/tt_still_repenting.html.

Teachout, Terry. *A Terry Teachout Reader.* New Haven, CT: Yale University Press, 2004.

Thomas, George C. III, and Richard A. Leo. "Interrogating Guilty Suspects: Why Sipowicz Never Has to Admit He Is Wrong." In Yeffeth, *What Would Sipowicz Do?,* 35–46.

Thomas, Jeffrey E. *"Murder One."* In Jarvis and Joseph, *Prime Time Law,* 65–85.

Thompson, Robert J. *Television's Second Golden Age: From "Hill Street Blues" to "ER."* Syracuse, NY: Syracuse University Press, 1996.

Tompkins, Jane. *West of Everything: The Inner Life of Westerns.* Oxford, UK: Oxford University Press, 1992.

Torres, Sasha, ed. *Living Color: Race and Television in the United States.* Durham, NC: Duke University Press, 1998.

Toscano, Alberto, and Jeff Kinkle. "Baltimore as World and Representation: Cognitive Mapping and Capitalism in *The Wire.*" *Dossier.* http://dossierjournal.com/read/theory/baltimore-as-world-and-representation-cognitive-mapping-and-capitalism-in-the-wire/.

Towers, Robert. "The Flap over Tom Wolfe: How Real Is the Retreat from Realism?" *New York Times,* January 28, 1990.

Turner, Frederick Jackson. *The Frontier in American History.* 1920. Mineola, NY: Dover, 1996.

Tyree, J. M. *"The Wire:* The Complete Fourth Season." *Film Quarterly* 61, no. 3 (Spring 2008): 32–38.

United Nations Committee on Human Rights. *In the Shadows of the War on Terror: Persistent Police Brutality and Abuse of People of Color in the United States.* December 2007. www.ushrnetwork.org/files/ushrn/images/linkfiles/CERD/9_Police Brutality.pdf.

Vande Berg, Leah, Lawrence A. Wenner, and Bruce E. Gronbeck. *Critical Approaches to Television.* Boston: Houghton Mifflin, 2004.

Vest, James M. *Hitchcock and France: The Forging of an Auteur.* Westport, CT: Praeger, 2003.

Vest, Jason. "Interview with Lorenzo Carcaterra." *Belles Lettres*, September–December 2005, 8–10.

Warren, Robert Penn. *All the King's Men*. 1936. New York: Harcourt Brace and Company, 1974.

Warren, Robert Penn, R.W.B. Lewis, and Cleanth Brooks, eds. *American Literature: The Makers and the Making*. New York: St. Martin's Press, 1973.

Weisberg, Jacob. "*The Wire* on Fire: Analyzing the Best Show on Television." *Slate*, September 13, 2006. http://www.slate.com/id/2149566.

West, Cornel. *Keeping Faith: Philosophy and Race in America*. New York: Routledge, 1993.

West, Cornel. *Race Matters*. 1993. Boston: Beacon Press, 2001.

Williams, Raymond. *Television: Technology and Cultural Form*. 1974. London: Routledge, 2003.

Wilson, Christopher P. "True and True(r) Crime: Cop Shops and Crime Scenes in the 1980s." *American Literary History* 9, no. 4 (1997): 718–43.

Wister, Owen. *The Virginian: A Horseman of the Plains*. 1902. Oxford, UK: Oxford University Press, 2009.

Wolfe, Tom. "Stalking the Billion-Footed Beast: A Literary Manifesto for the New Social Novel." *Harper's Magazine*, November 1989, 45–56.

Wright, Evan. *Generation Kill: Devil Dogs, Iceman, Captain America, and the New Face of American War*. 2004. New York: Berkley Caliber, 2008.

Wright, Paul, and Hailin Zhou. "Divining the 'Celestials': The Chinese Subculture of *Deadwood*." In Lavery, *Reading "Deadwood,"* 157–68.

Yeffeth, Glenn, ed. *What Would Sipowicz Do? Race, Rights and Redemption in NYPD Blue*. Dallas, TX: BenBella Books, 2004.

Zoglin, Richard. "Hill Street, Hail and Farewell." *Time*, April 27, 1987. http://www.time.com/time/printout/0,8816,964186,00.html.

Films, Television Programs, and Songs Cited

Films

Apocalypse Now. Directed by Francis Ford Coppola. Screenplay by John Milius and Francis Ford Coppola, from the novel *Heart of Darkness* by Joseph Conrad. Narration by Michael Herr. 153 min. American Zoetrope Studios, 1979.

Diner. Directed by Barry Levinson. Screenplay by Barry Levinson. 110 min. Metro-Goldwyn- Mayer and SLM Production Group, 1982.

Disclosure. Directed by Barry Levinson. Screenplay by Paul Attanasio, from the novel *Disclosure* by Michael Crichton. 128 min. Warner Bros. Pictures, Baltimore Pictures, and Constant c Productions, 1994.

Good Morning, Vietnam. Directed by Barry Levinson. Screenplay by Mitch Markowitz. 121 min. Touchstone Pictures and Silver Screen Partners III, 1987.

La Haine. Directed by Mathieu Kassovitz. Screenplay by Mathieu Kassovitz. 96 min. Canal+, Cofinergie 6, Egg Pictures, and Polygram Filmed Entertainment, 1995.

High Plains Drifter. Directed by Clint Eastwood. Screenplay by Ernest Tidyman. 105 min. The Malpaso Company, 1973.

Hostage. Directed by Florent Emilio Siri. Screenplay by Doug Richardson, from the novel *Hostage* by Robert Crais. 113 min. Miramax Films, Stratus Film Co., and Cheyenne Enterprises, 2005.

Last Exit to Brooklyn. Directed by Uli Edel. Screenplay by Desmond Nakano, from the novel *Last Exit to Brooklyn* by Hubert Selby Jr. 102 min. Allied Filmmakers, Bavaria Film, and Neue Constantin Film, 1989.

Little Big Man. Directed by Arthur Penn. Screenplay by Calder Willingham, from the novel *Little Big Man* by Thomas Berger. 147 min. Cinema Center Films and Stockbridge-Hiller Productions, 1970.

Natural, The. Directed by Barry Levinson. Screenplay by Roger Towne and Phil Dusenberry, from the novel *The Natural* by Bernard Malamud. 134 min. Delphi II Productions and TriStar Pictures, 1984.

Open Range. Directed by Kevin Costner. Screenplay by Craig Storper, based on the novel *The Open Range Men* by Lauran Paine. 139 min. Touchstone Pictures, Cobalt Media Group, Beacon Pictures, and Tig Productions, 2003.

Quiz Show. Directed by Robert Redford. Screenplay by Paul Attanasio, based on the book *Remembering America: A Voice from the Sixties* by Richard N. Goodwin. 133 min. Baltimore Pictures, Hollywood Pictures, and Wildwood Enterprise, 1994.

Rain Man. Directed by Barry Levinson. Screenplay by Ronald Bass and Barry Morrow. Story by Barry Morrow. 133 min. United Artists and the Guber-Peters Company, 1988.

Requiem for a Dream. Directed by Darren Aronofsky. Screenplay by Hubert Selby Jr. and Darren Aronofsky, based on the novel *Requiem for a Dream* by Hubert Selby Jr. 102 min. Truth and Soul Pictures, 2000.

Super Fly. Directed by Gordon Parks Jr. Screenplay by Phillip Fenty. 93 min. Sig Shore Productions and Warner Bros. Pictures, 1972.

Unforgiven. Directed by Clint Eastwood. Screenplay by David Webb Peoples. 131 min. Malpaso Productions and Warner Bros. Pictures, 1992.

Television

Episodes are listed alphabetically underneath their parent series.

24. Created by Robert Cochran and Joel Surnow. Imagine Entertainment, Real Time Productions, Teakwood Lane Productions, and Fox Network Television, 2001–2010.

Adventures of Brisco County, Jr., The. Created by Jeffrey Boam and Carlton Cuse. Boam/Cuse Productions, Warner Bros. Television, and Fox Network Television, 1993–1994.

Anatomy of a "Homicide: Life on the Street." Written and directed by Theodore Bogosian. PBS Television, November 4, 1998. 120 min.

Banacek. Created by Anthony Wilson. Universal TV Studios and NBC Television, 1972–1974.

Beverly Hills Buntz. Created by David Milch and Jeffrey Lewis. MTM Enterprises and NBC Television, 1987–1988.

Big Valley, The. Created by A. I. Bezzerides and Louis F. Edelman. Levee-Gardner-Laven Productions, Four Star Productions, and ABC Television, 1965–1969.

Bill Moyers Journal. Created by Bill Moyers. WNET Channel 13 New York and PBS Television, 1972–2010.

- "David Simon." April 17, 2009. http://www.pbs.org/moyers/journal/04172009/watch.html.

Bonanza. Created by David Dortort and Fred Hamilton. NBC Television, 1959–1973.

Brooklyn South. Created by Steven Bochco, Michael Duggan, and David Milch. Steven Bochco Productions and CBS Television, 1997–1998.

Cagney & Lacey. Created by Barbara Avedon and Barbara Corday. Filmways Pictures, Orion Television, and CBS Television, 1981–1988.

Capital News. Created by David Milch and Christian Williams. MTM Enterprises and ABC Television, 1990.

CBS Reports. CBS Television, 1959–1971 and 2009–present.

Chicago Hope. Created by David E. Kelley. 20th Century Fox Television, David E. Kelley Productions, and CBS Television, 1994–2000.

Close to Home. Created by Jim Leonard. Jerry Bruckheimer Television, Warner Bros. Television, and CBS Television, 2005–2007.

Columbo. Created by Richard Levinson and William Link. NBC Television, 1971–1990.

- "Murder by the Book." Written by Steven Bochco. Directed by Steven Spielberg. Original broadcast September 15, 1971. 76 min.

Corner, The. Created by David Simon, based on the book *The Corner: A Year in the Life of an Inner-City Neighborhood* by David Simon and Edward Burns. Blown Deadline Productions and HBO Television, 2000.

- "Corner Boy Blues." Written by David Mills and David Simon. Directed by Charles S. Dutton. Original broadcast May 14, 2000. 61 min.
- "Dope Fiend Blues." Written by David Simon. Directed by Charles S. Dutton. Original broadcast May 7, 2000. 59 min.
- "Everyman's Blues." Written by David Mills and David Simon. Directed by Charles S. Dutton. Original broadcast May 21, 2000. 74 min.
- "Fran's Blues." Written by David Mills. Directed by Charles S. Dutton. Original broadcast April 30, 2000. 60 min.
- "Gary's Blues." Written by David Mills and David Simon. Directed by Charles S. Dutton. Original broadcast April 16, 2000. 64 min.

CSI: Crime Scene Investigation. Created by Anthony E. Zuiker. Jerry Bruckheimer Television and CBS Television, 2000–present.

Deadwood. Created by David Milch. Red Board Productions and HBO Television, 2004–2006.

- "Amalgamation and Capital." Written by Elizabeth Sarnoff. Directed by Ed Bianchi. Original broadcast May 1, 2005. 48 min.
- "Amateur Night." Written by Nick Towne and Zack Whedon. Directed by Adam Davidson. Original broadcast August 6, 2006. 49 min.
- "Boy-the-Earth-Talks-To." Written by Ted Mann. Directed by Ed Bianchi. Original broadcast May 22, 2005. 55 min.
- "Catbird Seat, The." Written by Bernadette McNamara. Directed by Gregg Fienberg. Original broadcast August 20, 2006. 50 min.
- "Complications." Written by Victoria Morrow. Directed by Gregg Fienberg. Original broadcast April 3, 2005. 57 min.

- "Constant Throb, A." Written by W. Earl Brown. Directed by Mark Tinker. Original broadcast August 13, 2006. 49 min.
- "Deadwood." Written by David Milch. Directed by Walter Hill. Original broadcast March 21, 2004. 62 min.
- "Deep Water." Written by Malcolm MacRury. Directed by Davis Guggenheim. Original broadcast March 24, 2004. 56 min.
- "Full Faith and Credit." Written by Ted Mann. Directed by Ed Bianchi. Original broadcast July 2, 2006. 52 min.
- "Here Was a Man." Written by Elizabeth Sarnoff. Directed by Alan Taylor. Original broadcast April 11, 2004. 59 min.
- "I Am Not the Fine Man You Take Me For." Written by David Milch and Regina Corrado. Directed by Dan Attias. Original broadcast June 18, 2006. 53 min.
- "Imaginative Reality, An." DVD documentary. Season One, Disc 6. *Deadwood: The Complete Series* DVD collection. HBO Video. 28 min.
- "Leviathan Smiles." Written by Kem Nunn. Directed by Ed Bianchi. Original broadcast July 30, 2006. 54 min.
- "Lie Agreed Upon, Part I, A." Written by David Milch. Directed by Ed Bianchi. Original broadcast March 6, 2005. 50 min.
- "Mr. Wu." Written by Bryan McDonald. Directed by Daniel Minahan. Original broadcast May 23, 2004. 53 min.
- "New Language of the Old West, The." DVD documentary. Season One, Disc 6. *Deadwood: The Complete Series* DVD collection. HBO Video. 30 min.
- "No Other Sons or Daughters." Written by George Putnam. Directed by Ed Bianchi. Original broadcast May 16, 2004. 58 min.
- "Plague." Written by Malcolm MacRury. Directed by Davis Guggenheim. Original broadcast April 25, 2004. 52 min.
- "Reconnoitering the Rim." Written by Jody Worth. Directed by Davis Guggenheim. Original broadcast April 4, 2004. 52 min.
- "Requiem for a Gleet." Written by Ted Mann. Directed by Alan Taylor. Original broadcast March 27, 2005. 53 min.
- "Rich Find, A." Written by Alix Lambert. Directed by Tim Hunter. Original broadcast July 9, 2006. 53 min.
- "Sold Under Sin." Written by Ted Mann. Directed by Davis Guggenheim. Original broadcast June 13, 2004. 60 min.
- "Suffer the Little Children." Written by Elizabeth Sarnoff. Directed by Daniel Minahan. Original broadcast May 9, 2004. 56 min.
- "Tell Him Something Pretty." Written by Ted Mann. Directed by Mark Tinker. Original broadcast August 27, 2006. 50 minutes.
- "Trial of Jack McCall, The." Written by John Beluso. Directed by Ed Bianchi. Original broadcast April 18, 2004. 56 min.
- "True Colors." Written by Regina Corrado and Ted Mann. Directed by Gregg Fienberg. Original broadcast June 25, 2006. 52 min.
- "Two-Headed Beast, A." Written by David Milch. Directed by Daniel Minahan. Original broadcast July 9, 2006. 54 min.
- "Unauthorized Cinnamon." Written by Regina Corrado. Directed by Mark Tinker. Original broadcast July 23, 2006. 50 min.

Delvecchio. Created by Joseph Polizzi and Sam Rolfe. Crescendo Productions, Universal TV, and CBS Television, 1976–1977.

Dragnet. Created by Jack Webb. Mark VII Ltd and NBC Television, 1951–1959.

East Side/West Side. Created by Robert Alan Aurthur and David Susskind. United Artists Television and CBS Television, 1963–1964.

Equalizer, The. Created by Richard Lindheim and Michael Sloan. Universal TV and CBS Television, 1985–1989.

ER. Created by Michael Crichton. Amblin Television, John Wells Productions, Warner Bros. Television, and NBC Television, 1994–2009.

Generation Kill. Created by David Simon and Ed Burns, based on the book *Generation Kill: Devil Dogs, Iceman, Captain America, and the New Face of American War* by Evan Wright. Blown Deadline Productions, Company Pictures, and HBO Television, 2008.

Gideon's Crossing. Created by Paul Attanasio. Heel and Toe Films, Touchstone Television, and ABC Television, 2000–2001.

Griff. Created by Larry Cohen. Groverton Production, Universal TV, and ABC Television, 1973–1974.

Gunsmoke. Created by Norman MacDonnell and John Meston. Filmstar Productions, Arness Production Company, and CBS Television, 1955–1975.

Hawaii Five-O. Created by Leonard Freeman. Leonard Freeman Productions and CBS Television, 1968–1980.

Hill Street Blues. Created by Michael Kozoll and Steven Bochco. MTM Enterprises and NBC Television, 1981–1987.

- "Can World War III Be an Attitude?" Written by Michael Kozoll and Steven Bochco. Directed by Robert Butler. Original broadcast January 24, 1981. 49 min.
- "Double Jeopardy." Written by Michael Kozoll and Steven Bochco. Directed by Robert Butler. Original broadcast January 31, 1981. 50 min.
- "Eugene's Comedy Empire Strikes Back." Teleplay by Michael Wagner, David Milch, and Karen Hall. Story by Steven Bochco, Jeffrey Lewis, and Anthony Yerkovich. Directed by David Anspaugh. Original broadcast February 24, 1983. 50 min.
- "Freedom's Last Stand." Teleplay by Steven Bochco, Anthony Yerkovich, Jeffrey Lewis, and Michael Wagner. Story by Michael Kozoll and Steven Bochco. Directed by Gregory Hoblit. Original broadcast January 18, 1982. 49 min.
- "Gatorbait." Written by E. Jack Kaplan. Directed by Georg Stanford Brown. Original broadcast March 7, 1981. 49 min.
- "Hair of the Dog, A." Written by Steven Bochco, Anthony Yerkovich, and Jeffrey Lewis. Directed by Gregory Hoblit. Original broadcast November 25, 1982. 50 min.
- "Hill Street Station." Written by Michael Kozoll and Steven Bochco. Directed by Robert Butler. Original broadcast January 15, 1981. 50 min.
- "I Never Promised You a Rose, Marvin." Written by Anthony Yerkovich. Directed by Robert C. Thompson. Original broadcast March 21, 1981. 49 min.

- "It Ain't Over Till It's Over." Written by Jeffrey Lewis, David Milch, and John Romano. Directed by Stan Lathan. Original broadcast May 12, 1987. 47 min.
- "Jungle Madness, Parts 1 and 2." Written by Michael Kozoll, Steven Bochco, and Anthony Yerkovich. Directed by Corey Allen. Original broadcast May 26, 1981. 95 min.
- "Life, Death, Eternity, Etc." Written by Gregory Hoblit and David Zlotoff. Directed by Jack Starrett. Original broadcast March 14, 1981. 49 min.
- "Little Boil Blue." Written by Robert Earll. Directed by David Anspaugh. Original broadcast November 11, 1982. 50 min.
- "No Body's Perfect." Teleplay by Michael Wagner and David Milch. Story by Steven Bochco, Anthony Yerkovich, and Jeffrey Lewis. Directed by Randa Haines. Original broadcast December 9, 1982. 50 min.
- "Officer of the Year." Written by Karen Hall. Directed by David Anspaugh. Original broadcast October 28, 1982. 49 min.
- "Personal Foul." Written by Steven Bochco, Anthony Yerkovich, Jeffrey Lewis, and Michael Wagner. Directed by David Anspaugh. Original broadcast April 25, 1982. 48 min.
- "Presidential Fever." Written by Michael Kozoll and Steven Bochco. Directed by Robert Butler. Original broadcast January 17, 1981. 50 min.
- "Requiem for a Hairbag." Written by Mark Frost. Directed by Bob Kelljan. Original broadcast November 18, 1982. 49 min.
- "Rites of Spring, Parts 1 and 2." Written by Michael Kozoll and Steven Bochco. Directed by Gregory Hoblit. Original broadcast May 19, 1981. 95 min.
- "Second Oldest Profession, The." Teleplay by Steven Bochco, Anthony Yerkovich, and Robert Crais. Story by Michael Kozoll, Steven Bochco, and Anthony Yerkovich. Directed by Robert Butler. Original broadcast November 19, 1981. 48 min.
- "Stan the Man." Written by David Milch. Directed by Thomas Carter. Original broadcast November 4, 1982. 50 min.
- "Trial by Fury." Written by David Milch. Directed by Gregory Hoblit. Original broadcast September 30, 1982. 50 min.
- "World according to Freedom, The." Written by Michael Wagner. Directed by Jeff Bleckner. Original broadcast January 7, 1982. 48 min.

Homicide: Life on the Street. Created by Paul Attanasio, based on the book *Homicide: A Year on the Killing Streets* by David Simon. Baltimore Pictures and NBC Television, 1993–1999.

- "Bad Medicine." Teleplay by David Simon. Story by Tom Fontana and Julie Martin. Directed by Kenneth Fink. Original broadcast October 25, 1996. 46 min.
- "Blood Ties (Part 2)." Teleplay by David Simon. Story by Tom Fontana and James Yoshimura. Directed by Nick Gomez. Original broadcast October 24, 1997. 46 min.

- "Blood Ties (Part 3)." Teleplay by David Simon and Anya Epstein. Story by Tom Fontana, Julie Martin, and James Yoshimura. Directed by Mark Pellington. Original broadcast October 31, 1997. 47 min.
- "Bop Gun." Written by David Simon and David Mills. Story by Tom Fontana. Directed by Stephen Gyllenhaal. Original broadcast January 6, 1994. 47 min.
- "Crosetti." Teleplay by James Yoshimura. Story by Tom Fontana and James Yoshimura. Directed by Whitney Ransick. Original broadcast December 2, 1994. 50 min.
- "Damage Done, The." Teleplay by Jorge Zamacona. Story by Henry Bromell and Tom Fontana. Directed by Jace Alexander. Original broadcast May 3, 1996. 48 min.
- "Documentary, The." Teleplay by Eric Overmyer. Story by Tom Fontana, James Yoshimura, and Eric Overmyer. Directed by Barbara Kopple. Original broadcast January 3, 1997. 45 min.
- "Gone for Goode." Written by Paul Attanasio. Directed by Barry Levinson. Original broadcast January 31, 1993. 48 minutes.
- "Have a Conscience." Written by James Yoshimura. Directed by Uli Edel. Original broadcast January 17, 1997. 46 min.
- "Homicide: Life in Season 4." DVD documentary. Volume (Disc) 6. *Homicide: Life on the Street: The Complete Season 4* DVD collection. A&E Home Video. 18 min.
- "Inside Homicide: An Interview with David Simon and James Yoshimura." Volume (Disc) 6. *Homicide: Life on the Street: The Complete Season 5* DVD collection. A&E Home Video. 13 min.
- "See No Evil." Written by Paul Attanasio. Directed by Chris Menaul. Original broadcast January 13, 1994. 48 min.
- "Shades of Gray." Teleplay by T. J. English. Story by Julie Martin and David Simon. Directed by Adam Bernstein. Original broadcast January 8, 1999. 45 min.
- "Sideshow (Part 2)." Written by David Simon. Directed by Ed Sherin. Original broadcast February 19, 1999. 44 min.
- "Three Men and Adena." Written by Tom Fontana. Directed by Martin Campbell. Original broadcast March 3, 1993. 48 min.
- "Valentine's Day." Written by Tom Fontana. Directed by Clark Johnson. Original broadcast February 14, 1997. 46 min.

JAG. Created by Donald P. Bellisario. Belisarius Productions, Paramount Television, and NBC Television, 1995–1996. CBS Television, 1996–2005.
John from Cincinnati. Created by David Milch and Kem Nunn. Red Board Productions, Satiocy Productions, and HBO Television, 2007.
Kojak. Created by Abby Mann. Universal TV and CBS Television, 1973–1978.
L.A. Law. Created by Steven Bochco and Terry Louise Fisher. 20th Century Fox Television and NBC Television, 1986–1994.
Law & Order. Created by Dick Wolf. Wolf Productions and NBC Television, 1990–2010.

- "Sideshow." Written by René Balcer. Directed by Ed Sherin. Original broadcast February 17, 1999. 46 min.

Law & Order: Criminal Intent. Created by Dick Wolf. Developed by René Balcer. Wolf Productions, NBC Television, and USA Television, 2001–2011.

Lonesome Dove. Based on the novel *Lonesome Dove,* by Larry McMurtry. Directed by Simon Wincer. Motown Productions, Pangaea, Qintex Entertainment, and CBS Television, 1989.

Lou Grant. Created by James L. Brooks, Allan Burns, and Gene Reynolds. Developed by Leon Tokatyan. MTM Enterprises and CBS Television, 1977–1982.

- "Blacklist." Written by Seth Freeman. Directed by Burt Brinckerhoff. Original broadcast April 5, 1982. 47 min.

Luck. Created by David Milch. Red Board Productions and HBO Television, 2011–present.

McCloud. Created by Herman Miller. Universal TV and NBC Television, 1970–1977.

McMillan & Wife. Created by Leonard Stern. Universal TV and NBC Television, 1971–1977.

Miami Vice. Created by Anthony Yerkovich. Michael Mann Productions, Universal TV, and NBC Television, 1984–1989.

Murder One. Created by Steven Bochco, Charles H. Eglee, and Channing Gibson. Steven Bochco Productions and ABC Television, 1995–1997.

Naked City. Based on the motion picture *The Naked City.* Screen Gems Television, Shelle Productions, and ABC Television, 1958–1963.

New Amsterdam. Created by Allan Loeb and Christian Taylor. LaHa Films, Regency Television, Sarabande Productions, Scarlet Fire Entertainment, and Fox Television, 2008.

Northern Exposure. Created by Joshua Brand and John Falsey. Cine-Nevada Productions, Universal TV, and CBS Television, 1990–1995.

NYPD Blue. Created by David Milch and Steven Bochco. Steven Bochco Productions and ABC Television, 1993–2005.

- "Backboard Jungle, The." Written by David Mills. Story by William L. Morris. Directed by Mark Tinker. Original broadcast January 16, 1996. 45 min.
- "Bad Rap." Written by Thad Mumford. Directed by Matthew Penn. Original broadcast March 29, 1997. 46 min.
- "Brown Appetit." Teleplay by David Milch. Story by David Milch and Steven Bochco. Directed by Gregory Hoblit. Original broadcast October 5, 1993. 49 min.
- "Girl Talk." Teleplay by Theresa Rebeck. Story by Theresa Rebeck and Bill Clark. Directed by Perry Lang. Original broadcast March 19, 1996. 47 min.

- "Hollie and the Blowfish." Teleplay by David Simon. Story by Bill Clark and David Simon. Directed by Davis Guggenheim. Original broadcast March 26, 1996. 47 min.
- "My Wild Irish Nose." Written by Hugh Levick. Directed by Robert J. Doherty. Original broadcast January 7, 1997. 46 min.
- "Oscar, Meyer, Weiner." Written by Ted Mann and Gardner Stern. Directed by Bradley Silberling. Original broadcast December 7, 1993. 49 min.
- "Pilot." Teleplay by David Milch. Story by David Milch and Steven Bochco. Directed by Gregory Hoblit. Original broadcast September 21, 1993. 49 min.
- "Raging Bulls." Written by Leonard Gardner. Story by Steven Bochco, David Milch, and Bill Clark. Directed by Steven DePaul. Original broadcast December 18, 1998. 45 min.
- "Simone Says." Teleplay by David Milch and Walon Green. Story by Steven Bochco, David Milch, and Walon Green. Directed by Gregory Hoblit. Original broadcast November 15, 1994. 48 min.
- "Taillight's Last Gleaming." Written by David Mills. Directed by Randall Zisk. Original broadcast February 18, 1997. 45 min.
- "True Confessions." Teleplay by David Milch and Art Monterastelli. Story by Art Monterastelli, David Milch, and Steven Bochco. Directed by Charles Haid. Original broadcast October 12, 1993. 48 min.
- "Where's 'Swaldo?" Written by Stephen Gaghan, Michael R. Perry, and David Milch. Directed by Mark Tinker. Original broadcast November 12, 1996. 46 min.

Oz. Created by Tom Fontana. The Levinson-Fontana Company, Rysher Entertainment, and HBO Television, 1997–2003.

Paris. Created by Steven Bochco. MTM Enterprises and CBS Television, 1979–1980.

Picket Fences. Created by David E. Kelley. 20th Century Fox Television, Nina Saxon Film Design, David E. Kelley Productions, and CBS Television, 1992–1996.

Police Story. Created by Joseph Wambaugh. Columbia Pictures Television, David Gerber Productions, Screen Gems Television, and NBC Television, 1973–1977.

Quincy, M.E. Created by Glen A. Larson and Lou Shaw. Glen A. Larson Productions, Universal TV, and NBC Television, 1976–1983.

Raising the Bar. Created by Steven Bochco and David Feige. Steven Bochco Productions and TNT Television, 2008–2009.

Rifleman, The. Created by Sam Peckinpah. Four Star Productions, Sussex Productions, and ABC Television, 1958–1963.

Rome. Created by Bruno Heller, William J. MacDonald, and John Milius. HD Vision Studios, British Broadcasting Corporation, and HBO Television, 2005–2007.

Shield, The. Created by Shawn Ryan. MiddKid Productions, Sony Pictures Television, 20th Century Fox Television, and FX Television, 2002–2008.

Sopranos, The. Created by David Chase. HBO Television, 1999–2007.

Starsky and Hutch. Created by William Blinn. Spelling-Goldberg Productions and ABC Television, 1975–1979.

St. Elsewhere. Created by Joshua Brand and John Falsey. Developed by Mark Tinker and John Masius. MTM Enterprises and NBC Television, 1982–1988.

Streets of San Francisco, The. Created by Dennis Donnelly and Theodore J. Flicker. Quinn Martin Productions, Warner Bros. Television, and ABC Television, 1972–1977.

Switch. Created by Glen A. Larson. Glen A. Larson Productions, Universal TV, and CBS Television, 1975–1978.

Treme. Created by David Simon and Eric Overmyer. Blown Deadline Productions and HBO Television, 2010–present.

Twilight Zone, The. Created by Rod Serling. Cayuga Productions and CBS Television, 1959–1964. Atlantis Films, MGM Television, and CBS Television, 1985–1989.

Wagon Train. Created by Howard E. Johnson and Leo Sherman. Revue Studios, NBC Television, and ABC Television, 1957–1965.

West Wing, The. Created by Aaron Sorkin. John Wells Productions, Warner Bros. Television, and NBC Television, 1999–2006.

Wild Wild West, The. Created by Michael Garrison. Bruce Lansbury Productions, Michael Garrison Productions, and CBS Television, 1965–1969.

Wire, The. Created by David Simon. Blown Deadline Productions and HBO Television, 2002–2008.

- "-30-." Teleplay by David Simon. Story by David Simon and Ed Burns. Directed by Clark Johnson. Original broadcast March 10, 2008. 94 min.
- "All Due Respect." Teleplay by Richard Price. Story by David Simon and Richard Price. Directed by Steve Shill. Original broadcast September 27, 2004. 59 min.
- "All Prologue." Teleplay by David Simon. Story by David Simon and Ed Burns. Directed by Steve Shill. Original broadcast July 6, 2003. 59 min.
- "Back Burners." Teleplay by Joy Lusco Kecken. Story by David Simon and Joy Lusco Kecken. Directed by Tim Van Patten. Original broadcast November 7, 2004. 56 min.
- "Clarifications." Teleplay by Dennis Lehane. Story by David Simon and Dennis Lehane. Directed by Anthony Hemingway. Original broadcast February 24, 2008. 59 min.
- "Collateral Damage." Teleplay by David Simon. Story by David Simon and Ed Burns. Directed by Clark Johnson. Original broadcast June 8, 2003. 59 min.
- "Cost, The." Teleplay by David Simon. Story by David Simon and Ed Burns. Directed by Brad Anderson. Original broadcast August 11, 2002. 56 min.
- "Dead Soldiers." Teleplay by Dennis Lehane. Story by David Simon and Dennis Lehane. Directed by Rob Bailey. Original broadcast October 3, 2004. 59 min.

- "Detail, The." Teleplay by David Simon. Story by David Simon and Ed Burns. Directed by Clark Johnson. Original broadcast June 9, 2002. 58 min.
- "Final Grades." Teleplay by David Simon. Story by David Simon and Ed Burns. Directed by Ernest Dickerson. Original broadcast December 10, 2006. 79 min.
- "Homecoming." Teleplay by Rafael Alvarez. Story by David Simon and Rafael Alvarez. Directed by Leslie Libman. Original broadcast October 31, 2004. 58 min.
- "Home Rooms." Teleplay by Richard Price. Story by Ed Burns and Richard Price. Directed by Seith Mann. Original broadcast September 17, 2006. 59 min.
- "Late Editions." Teleplay by George Pelecanos. Story by David Simon and George Pelecanos. Directed by Joe Chappelle. Original broadcast March 3, 2008. 60 min.
- "Middle Ground." Teleplay by George Pelecanos. Story by David Simon and George Pelecanos. Directed by Joe Chappelle. Original broadcast December 12, 2004. 59 min.
- "Mission Accomplished." Teleplay by David Simon. Story by David Simon and Ed Burns. Directed by Ernest Dickerson. Original broadcast December 19, 2004. 64 min.
- "Pager, The." Teleplay by David Simon. Story by David Simon and Ed Burns. Directed by Clark Johnson. Original broadcast June 30, 2002. 61 min.
- "Reformation." Teleplay by Ed Burns. Story by David Simon and Ed Burns. Directed by Christine Moore. Original broadcast November 28, 2004. 59 min.
- "Soft Eyes." Teleplay by David Mills. Story by Ed Burns and David Mills. Directed by Christine Moore. Original broadcast September 17, 2006. 59 min.
- "Target, The." Teleplay by David Simon. Story by David Simon and Ed Burns. Directed by Clark Johnson. Original broadcast June 2, 2002. 63 min.

Songs and Music

"Get Off My Back." Written by James Henry Boxley, Keith Boxley, Jerome Brailey, George Clinton Jr., William Earl Collins, William Jonathan Drayton, Gary Rinaldo, Garry M. Shider, David L. Spradley, and Phillipe E. Wynn. Performed by Public Enemy. *Greatest Misses.* Compact disc. Def Jam Records, 1992.

"Killer." Written by Adam Tinley and Seal (Henry Olusegun Olumide Adeola Samuel). Performed by Adamski and Seal. *Seal.* Compact disc. Sire Records and London/Rhino Records, 1991.

Lucia di Lammermoor. First performed September 26, 1835. Written by Gaetano Donizetti. 3 compact discs. Performed by the Royal Opera House Covent Garden. ADRM Records, 1985.

"My Funny Valentine." *Babes in Arms.* First performed April 14, 1937. Written by Richard Rodgers and Lorenz Hart. Compact disc. Performed by the New Jersey Symphony Orchestra. New World Records, 1992.

"Ride of the Valkyries, The." *Die Walküre (The Valkyrie). Der Ring des Niebulungen.* First performed June 26, 1870. Written by Richard Wagner. 14 compact discs. Performed by the Wiener Philharmoniker. Conducted by Sir Georg Solti. Decca Records, 1997.

"Way Down in the Hole." Written by Tom Waits. Performed by the Blind Boys of Alabama. *"The Wire": ". . . and All the Pieces Matter": Five Years of Music from "The Wire."* Compact disc. Nonesuch Records and Home Box Office, 2008.

Index

About the Author

JASON P. VEST is Associate Professor of English and Applied Linguistics at the University of Guam. Vest is the author of two previous books: *Future Imperfect: Philip K. Dick at the Movies* (Praeger, 2007) and *The Postmodern Humanism of Philip K. Dick* (2009).